More jumping
JavaScript

THE SUN MICROSYSTEMS PRESS
JAVA SERIES

▼ **Core Java 1.2, Volume 1 - Fundamentals**
Cay S. Horstmann & Gary Cornell

▼ **Core Java 1.2, Volume 2 - Advanced Features**
Cay S. Horstmann & Gary Cornell

▼ **Graphic Java 1.2, Volume I: AWT**
David M. Geary

▼ **Graphic Java 1.2, Volume II: Swing**
David M. Geary

▼ **Graphic Java 1.2, Volume III: Advanced Swing**
David M. Geary

▼ **Graphic Java 1.2, Volume IV: 2D API**
David M. Geary

▼ **Inside Java Workshop 2.0**
Lynn Weaver

▼ **Instant Java, Third Edition**
John A. Pew & Stephen G. Pew

▼ **Java by Example 1.2**
Jerry R. Jackson & Alan L. McClellan

▼ **Java Studio by Example**
Lynn Weaver & Leslie Robertson

▼ **Jumping JavaScript**
Janice Winsor & Brian Freeman

▼ **Just Java 1.2**
Peter van der Linden

▼ **More Jumping JavaScript**
Janice Winsor, Brian Freeman, & Bill Anderson

▼ **Not Just Java, Second Edition**
Peter van der Linden

More jumping JavaScript

JANICE WINSOR•BRIAN FREEMAN•BILL ANDERSON

Sun Microsystems Press
A Prentice Hall Title

The publisher offers discounts on this book when ordered in bulk quantities. For more information, contact Corporate Sales Department, Prentice Hall PTR , One Lake Street, Upper Saddle River, NJ 07458. Phone: 800-382-3419; FAX: 201- 236-7141. E-mail: corpsales@prenhall.com.

Editorial/production supervision: *Joanne Anzalone and Craig Little*
Cover design director: *Jerry Votta*
Cover designer: *Anthony Gemmellaro*
Cover illustration: *Karen Strelecki*
Manufacturing manager: *Alexis R. Heydt*
Marketing manager: *Kaylie Smith*
Acquisitions editor: *Gregory G. Doench*
Sun Microsystems Press publisher: *Rachel Borden*

10 9 8 7 6 5 4 3 2 1

ISBN 0-13-922832-2

Sun Microsystems Press
A Prentice Hall Title

Contents

Chapter 4
Positioning HTML Content, 131

Appendix A
What's New in JavaScript 1.3, 399

Preface

This book is your comprehensive guide to new functionality that was added to client-side JavaScript™ 1.2 as implemented in the Netscape® Navigator™ 4.0 release and to client-side JavaScript 1.3 as implemented in the Navigator 4.06-4.5 release. It contains hundreds of complete script examples along with screen shots that illustrate the results of loading each script. The scripts are included on the CD-ROM.

Audience

This book is for Web authors who are interested in using the client-side JavaScript language in their HTML pages and who are familiar with the basics of the JavaScript 1.0 and 1.1 releases.

JavaScript Version

This book describes new features that are available in the Navigator 4.0 and 4.5 versions of the JavaScript language. Although we make occasional references to JScript, Microsoft's implementation of the JavaScript language in Internet Explorer 4.0, none of the scripts in this book were tested on the Internet Explorer browser.

Because Netscape first implemented the JavaScript language in its Navigator 2.01 release, it's common to refer to the JavaScript version by Navigator release number. The JavaScript language does, however, have its own version numbering system, which is shown in Table P-1.

Table P-1 JavaScript Version Numbers

Browser	JavaScript Version Number
Navigator 2.x	1.0
Navigator 3.x	1.1
Internet Explorer 3.x	1.0
Navigator/Communicator 4.0	1.2
Navigator/Communicator 4.06 and 4.5	1.3

Internet Sources of Information

You can find lots of information about the JavaScript language on the Web. This section provides a list of URLs to some sites that we have found to contain useful reference information about the JavaScript language.

ECMA References

ECMA-262 Language Specification:

```
http://www.ecma.ch/stand/ecma-262.htm
```

ECMA Web site:

```
http://www.ecma.ch/news.htm
```

ECMA Standardizing Information and Communication Systems Standards (Blue Cover):

```
http://www.ecma.ch/
```

ECMA Technical Committees and Working Groups:

```
http://www.ecma.ch/teccom.htm
```

WC3 References

Web style sheets:

```
http://www.w3.org/Style
```

CSS1:

```
http://www.w3.org/TR/REC-CSS1
```

CSS2:

    http://www.w3.org/TR/PR-CSS2

The W3C's draft on client-side scripting:

    http://www.w3.org/pub/WWW/TR/WD-script

The W3C's draft on Positioning HTML Elements with Cascading Style Sheets:

    http://www.w3.org/pub/WWW/TR/WD-script

HTML References

Rob Schluter's HTML tag list:

    http://www.spacerock.com/htmlref/

HTML 3.2 Specification:

    http://www.w3.org/TR/REC-html32

HTML 4.0 Specification

    http://www.w3.org/TR/REC-html40/

Extensions to HTML 2.0:

    http://home.netscape.com/assist/net_sites/html_extensions.html

Extensions to HTML 3.0:

    http://home.netscape.com/assist/net_sites/html_extensions_3.html

Background and foreground color specifications:

    http://home.netscape.com/assist/net_sites/bg/index.html

Microsoft Information

Microsoft JScript product information:

    http://microsoft.com/devonly/prodinfo/jscript/

Netscape Resources

Netscape release notes:

    http://home.netscape.com/eng/mozilla/3.0/relnotes

JavaScript documentation:

    http://developer.netscape.com/docs/manuals/
    javascript.html

Netscape 4.0 release notes:

    http://home.netscape.com/eng/mozilla/4.0/relnotes/

What's new in JavaScript 1.2:

    http://developer.netscape.com/docs/manuals/communicator/
    jsguide/js1_2.htm

What's new in JavaScript 1.3:

```
http://developer.netscape.com/docs/manuals/communicator/
jsref/js13.html
```

Netscape JavaScript Debugger:

```
http://developer.netscape.com/docs/manuals/jsdebug/index.htm
```

Reporting new Netscape bugs:

```
http://cgi.netscape.com/cgi-bin/auto-bug.cgi
```

Netscape product information:

```
http://www.netscape.com/comprod/products/navigator/
version_2.0/script/
```

Visual JavaScript:

```
http://developer.netscape.com/software/tools/
index.html?content=/software/visualjs.html
```

Netscape Beta Central:

```
http://home.netscape.com/eng/beta_central/
```

JavaScript FAQ:

```
http://www.freqgrafx.com/411/jsfaq.html
```

Introduction to JavaScript 1.2:

```
http://developer.netscape.com/library/documentation/
communicator/js1_2.htm
```

JavaScript 1.2 enhancement CodeStock notes:

```
http://developer.netscape.com/library/javascript/codesto1.html
```

Dynamic fonts font enhancements in Communicator:

```
http://developer.netscape.com/library/documentation/
communicator/dynhtml/webfont4.htm
```

Other JavaScript resources:

```
http://developer.netscape.com/library/documentation/jsresource.html
```

Dynamic style sheets:

```
http://developer.netscape.com/library/documentation/
communicator/stylesheets/jssindex.htm
```

JavaScript and User Interface Design from the View Source article by Danny Goodman:

```
http://developer.netscape.com/news/viewsource/goodman_ui.html
```

The JavaScript Apostle: Getting Ready for JavaScript 1.2 Events by Danny Goodman:

http://developer.netscape.com/news/viewsource/goodman_events.html

JavaScript Date Object Techniques by Danny Goodman:

http://developer.netscape.com/news/viewsource/
goodman_dateobject.html

Glossary for Layers and JavaScript Extensions for Layers:

http://home.netscape.com/comprod/products/communicator/
layers/layers_glossary.html

Positioning HTML elements using style sheets or layers:

http://developer.netscape.com/library/documentation/
communicator/software/layering.html

New Java security model with object signing:

http://developer.netscape.com/library/documentation/
signedobj/overview.html

Communicator Documentation

Communicator preview documentation:

http://developer.netscape.com/library/documentation/communicator/

Dynamic HTML resources:

http://developer.netscape.com/library/documentation/
htmlguid/dynamic_resources.html

Table improvements in Netscape Communicator:

http://developer.netscape.com/library/documentation/
communicator/software/tables.htm

Netscape Communicator Reviewers Guide:

http://home.netscape.com/comprod/products/
communicator/guide_intro.html

JAR Installation Manager Developer's Guide:

http://developer.netscape.com/library/documentation/
communicator/software/jarman/index.htm

Composer Plug-in Guide:

http://developer.netscape.com/library/documentation/
communicator/software/composer/plugin/index.htm

Plug-in Guide:

http://developer.netscape.com/library/documentation/
communicator/software/plugin/index.htm

Netscape DevEdge Communicator newsgroup:

```
http://developer.netscape.com/members/doc/community/doc/
newsgroups/ newsgrp.html#communicator
```

Netscape's bug reporting form:

```
http://developer.netscape.com/support/bugs/bugform.html
```

Conventions Used in This Book

Table P-2 shows the typographic conventions used in this book.

Table P-2 Typographic Conventions

Typeface or Symbol	Description
courier	Indicates a command, file name, object name, method, argument, JavaScript keyword, HTML tag, file content, or code excerpt.
courier italics	Indicates a variable that you should replace with a valid value.
italics	Indicates definitions, emphasis, or a book title.

How This Book Is Organized

This book is divided into 12 chapters and 2 appendixes.

Chapter 1, "Introduction," introduces features that are new with the JavaScript 1.2 and 1.3 releases and introduces Netscape's JavaScript debugging tool.

Chapter 2, "Core Language Changes," describes changes to JavaScript 1.2 operators, statements, functions and literal notation for creating objects.

Chapter 3, "Style Sheets," describes how to create style sheets with both CSS and JavaScript syntax.

Chapter 4, "Positioning HTML Content," describes how to position HTML content with both CSS and <LAYER> tag syntax.

Chapter 5, "Dynamic and Downloadable Fonts," describes how to create PFR files and incorporate them in your Web pages so that the fonts are automatically included when users download your pages.

Chapter 6, "Dynamic HTML," explains the different elements that collectively are called dynamic HTML, introduces the JavaScript layer object, and shows a complex example.

Chapter 7, "Regular Expressions," describes the properties, methods, and event handlers of the new RegExp object.

Chapter 8, "Object Signing," describes Netscape's new security model for creating signed scripts that enable users to grant or deny access to information that might be considered a security risk.

Chapter 9, "New Event Model," describes the new event handlers that enable Web programmers to intercept, route, and handle events that are initiated by a mouse click or a key press.

Chapter 10, "Global Methods and Objects," describes changes to existing `Object`, `Number`, `String`, and `navigator` objects, and introduces the new `screen` object.

Chapter 11, "What's New in Windows ," describes the extensive new properties, methods, and event handlers that have been added to the `window` object.

Chapter 12, "What's New in Documents," describes changes to existing objects that operate within a document.

Appendix A, "New Features in JavaScript 1.3," describes what's new in the JavaScript 1.3 release.

Appendix B, "JavaScript Quick Reference," provides a comprehensive reference to JavaScript.

A glossary contains a list of terms.

CD Contents

The CD-ROM accompanying this book includes all of the JavaScript examples referred to in this book formatted for X11, Macintosh®, and Microsoft® Windows™ 95 platforms. To run files off the CD-ROM, mount the CD-ROM in the way specified by your platform and double-click on the `index.html` file at the top level. This `index.html` file is then loaded into your Web browser and provides links to the entire script hierarchy on the CD-ROM.

The script examples for this book are also available from the following URL: http://www.bill-anderson.com/jjs

The CD-ROM was created with Creative Digital Research's CDR Publisher® HyCD™, which integrates PC, Macintosh, and UNIX® formats onto a single CD-ROM. HyCD is compliant with all of the existing CD-ROM standards:

- PC CD-ROM Format: ISO 9660
- Macintosh CD-ROM Format: HFS

- UNIX CD-ROM Format: ISO 9660 with Rock Ridge Extension
- PC Windows 95 / NT 4.0 Format: Joliet File System

For more information about HyCD and the CDR Publisher, visit Creative Digital Research's Web site at `http://www.hycd.com`.

Note – If you are using a Macintosh computer, the first time you load the CD-ROM, you may be asked to rebuild the CD desktop. After that, you can simply double-click on any file with an `.html` extension to run it in the browser.

Acknowledgements

The authors would like to thank the following people for their contributions to this book:

Greg Doench of Prentice Hall for his infinite patience, help, and support on this project.

Joanne Anzalone and Craig Little of Prentice Hall for production help.

Rachel Borden and John Bortner of SunSoft Press for their patience and unfailing diligence in helping with this project.

Mary Lou Nohr for editing this manuscript with her usual skill and tact.

Janice would like to thank the following people for their contributions to this book:

Brian Freeman for his script examples and explanations of some of the thornier conceptual issues of JavaScript.

Bill Anderson for stepping in at the end of the project and helping with scripting examples.

My husband Maris for his love and support and for his willingness to include his sculptures as part of our Two Loons Gallery example in the Dynamic HTML chapter.

Brian would like to thank the following people for their contributions to this book:

Joe Ushana, Engineering Manager, Silicon Surf Team of Silicon Graphics, Inc., for his support and understanding.

Judy, Loren, Mom, and Dad, for their support and listening.

Bill would like to thank the following people for their contributions to this book:

My wife Kay for putting up with my working all hours of the day and night.

Introduction

This chapter introduces JavaScript 1.2 and 1.3 new functionality, describes the ECMAScript standard, and introduces Netscape's JavaScript Debugging tool.

What's New in JavaScript 1.2

JavaScript 1.2 introduces several new key features and changes some of the ways in which core JavaScript functionality works.

The changes fall into the following major categories:

*   Core language changes
*   JavaScript style sheets
*   Layers
*   Regular expressions

- Object signing
- New event model
- New objects
- New properties/methods/event handlers for the `window` object
- New properties/methods/event handlers for other objects

The following sections summarize the major changes. The rest of this book provides detailed information and examples about how you can use the advanced features of JavaScript 1.2 to create lively and interesting Web pages.

Core Language Changes

Equality Operators

JavaScript 1.2 interprets the following equality operators differently than in previous releases:

- `==`
- `!=`

The behavior of these operators changes yet again in the JavaScript 1.3 release. See Appendix A, "What's New in JavaScript 1.3," for more information.

delete Operator

You can use the `delete` operator to delete the property of any object or any element at a specified index in an array. If the operation is successful, the `delete` operator sets the property or element to `undefined` and returns a value of `true`; otherwise, it returns a value of `false`.

Statements

The JavaScript 1.2 release provides the following new statements that you can use to control or break out of loops:

- `labeled`
- `break`
- `continue`
- `switch`
- `do ... while`
- `import`
- `export`

Functions

JavaScript 1.2 provides the following new function behavior and new functions:

JavaScript 1.2 now supports nested functions. The nested functions can also use the arguments and variables of the outer function. The outer function cannot use the arguments and variables of the functions nested within it. In other words, JavaScript now supports lambda expressions and lexical closures.

- You can use the `arguments` function to create an array that corresponds to the arguments that are passed to a function

- You can use the new `arity` property to indicate the number of arguments expected by a function.

You can use the `Number` function to convert a specified object to a number.

You can use the `String` function to convert a specified object to a string.

JavaScript Style Sheets

Style sheets enable you to control the presentation and fonts that are displayed in your Web pages. Using style sheets, you can control attributes such as text color, margins, font sizes, font styles, font weights, and alignment of elements. The Navigator 4.x release supports two syntaxes for designing style sheets:

- Cascading Style Sheets (CSS)

- JavaScript style sheets

CSS is the static approach to specifying style, and JavaScript is the programmatic approach.

Layers

Layers enable you to define overlapping layers of transparent or solid content in a Web page. Each HTML layer has a corresponding `layer` object that enables you to use JavaScript to manipulate the layer.

Regular Expressions

Regular expressions provide you with a powerful way to search for and manipulate text. You first create patterns to match character combinations. Then, you can use these patterns to find, copy, and replace pieces of text.

You create a regular expression as a `RegExp` object which has methods that are used to execute a match against a string. You can also pass the regular expression as arguments to the new `String` object methods `match()`, `replace()`, `search()`, and `split()`. The `RegExp` construction object has properties most of which are set when a match is successful. To complete the regular expression implementation, the `Array` object has new properties that provide information about a successful match.

Object Signing

Scripts can now gain access to information that is normally restricted. You gain access to restricted information by writing signed scripts that request expanded privileges. This new functionality provides greater security than data tainting, which has been removed from the JavaScript 1.2 release.

New Event Model

The JavaScript event model has been expanded to include a new `event` object, new events, and event capturing.

- The `event` object contains properties, such as the event type and the pointer location at the time of the event, that describe a JavaScript event. The object is passed as an argument to an event handler when an event occurs.

- A window or document can now intercept an event before the target object such as a link or a button receives it. The window and document object have the following new methods that support event capturing:

  - `captureEvents()` — Sets the window, document, or layer to capture the specified events.

  - `enableExternalCapture()` — Enables a window with frames to capture events in pages loaded from different locations (servers).

  - `disableExternalCapture()` — Disables external event capturing set by the `enableExternalCapture()` method.

  - `releaseEvents()` — Releases the specified events.

Objects that receive events have these new methods for routing and handling events:

- `routeEvent()` — Routes the event from its capturer through its normal event hierarchy.

- `handleEvent()` — Triggers the event handler for the specified event.

The following events have been revised (as shown by the asterisk) or added:

- `Click*` — When a user clicks a link or form element.

- `DblClick` — When a user double-clicks a mouse key over a link or form element.

- `DragDrop` — When a user drops an object onto a Navigator window.

- `KeyDown` — When a user presses a key on the keyboard.

- `KeyPress` — When a user presses or holds down a key on the keyboard.

- `KeyUp` — When a user releases a key on the keyboard.

- `MouseDown` — When a user presses a mouse button.

- `MouseMove` — When a user moves the cursor.

- `MouseOut*` — When a user moves the cursor out of an object.

- `MouseOver*` — When a user moves the cursor over an object.

- `MouseUp` — When a user releases a mouse button.

- `Move` — When a user or script moves a window.

- `Resize` — When a user or script resizes a window.

New Objects

The JavaScript 1.2 release provides the following new objects:

- `event` object — Contains properties that describe a JavaScript event. This object is passed as an argument to an event handler when the event occurs.

- `Event` object — Different from the `event` object, contains a set of constants that you use to reference specific events.

- `Layer` object — Corresponds to an HTML layer in a page and provides properties and methods that enable you to manipulate each layer.

- `RegExp` object — Contains properties and methods that you can use to perform pattern matching in strings.

- `screen` object — Contains properties that describe the display screen and its colors.

Figure 1–1 shows the JavaScript object hierarchy. The boxes with the dashed lines show the objects that were added with the JavaScript 1.1 release (Navigator 3). The box with the double-dashed line around the `layer` object represents the object added with the JavaScript 1.2 release (Navigator 4).

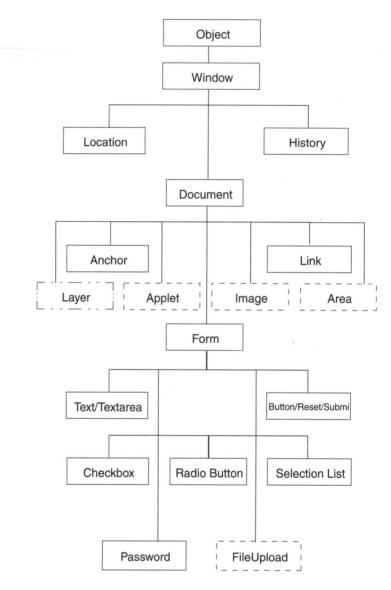

Figure 1–1 Object hierarchy for the JavaScript 1.2 release

The JavaScript 1.2 release also has added several new objects to the set of system objects, shown in Figure 1–2, which are not a part of the object hierarchy. The dashed lines indicate objects that were added with the JavaScript 1.1 release and the double-dashed lines indicate objects that were added with the JavaScript 1.2 release.

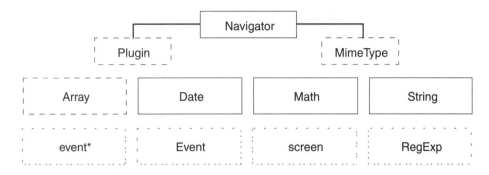

Figure 1-2 System objects

New Properties, Methods, and Event Handlers for the window Object

In the JavaScript 1.2 release you can add a button to the Personal Toolbar that activates a JavaScript command.

The following properties have been added to the `window` object in support of style sheets and layers:

- `innerHeight` — Specifies the vertical dimension of the content area of the window, in pixels; replaces `height`, which remains available for backward compatibility. In previous releases the `height` property rounded numbers smaller than 100 pixels up to 100. In the JavaScript 1.2 release, both the `innerHeight` and `height` properties do a security check to see if the script has permission to set the property to a number smaller than 100 pixels.

- `innerWidth` — Specifies the horizontal dimension of the content area of the window, in pixels; replaces `width`, which remains for backward compatibility. In previous releases the `width` property rounded numbers smaller than 100 pixels up to 100. In the JavaScript 1.2 release, both the `innerWidth` and `width` properties do a security check to see if the script has permission to set the property to a number smaller than 100 pixels.

- `locationbar` — Enables you to show or hide the location bar of the targeted window.

- `menubar` — Enables you to show or hide the menu bar of the targeted window.

- `outerHeight` — Specifies the vertical dimension of the outside boundary of the window, in pixels.

- `outerWidth` — Specifies the horizontal dimension of the outside boundary of the window, in pixels.

- `pageXOffset` — Specifies the x-position of the viewed document in the window, in pixels. When the window has only a single document, then the offset is always 0. If the document is in a frame, the document is treated as being in a separate window, because each frame has its own `window` object. Because of this behavior, this property is only useful with DHTML documents, where each layer represents a separate document.

- `pageYOffset` — Specifies the y-position of the viewed document in the window, in pixels. When the window has only a single document, then the offset is always 0. If the document is in a frame, the document is treated as being in a separate window because each frame has its own `window` object. Because of this behavior, this property is only useful with DHTML documents, where each layer represents a separate document.

- `personalbar` — Enables you to show or hide the personal (or directories) bar of the targeted window.

- `scrollbars` — Enables you to show or hide the scrollbars of the targeted window.

- `statusbar` — Enables you to show or hide the status bar of the targeted window.

- `toolbar` — Enables you to show or hide the toolbar of the targeted window.

The following `window` methods have been added or revised.

- `back()` — Revised to undo the last history step in any frame within the top-level window, not just to back up a step in the frame in which the call to `back()` occurs.

- `clearInterval()` — Cancels `setInterval()`.

- `disableExternalCapture()` — Disables external capturing of events.

- `enableExternalCapture()` — Enables a window with frames to capture events in pages loaded from different locations.

- `find()` — Finds the specified text string in the contents of the window.

- `forward()` — Goes to the next URL in the current history list.

- `home()` — Goes to the URL specified as the user's home page in the preferences.

- `moveBy()` — Moves the window by the specified number of pixels.

- `moveTo()` — Moves the window to the specified pixel coordinates.

- `open()` — Revised to include a number of new window features.

- `print()` — Prints the contents of the window.

- `resizeBy()` — Resizes the window by the specified amount.

- `resizeTo()` — Resizes the window to the specified size in pixels.

- `scrollBy()` — Scrolls the contents of the window by the specified amount.

- `scrollTo()` — Scrolls the contents of the window to the specified x-y coordinates. `scrollTo()` replaces `scroll()`, which remains for backward compatibility.

- `setInterval()` — Repeatedly evaluates an expression after a specified number of milliseconds has elapsed. The expression is evaluated until you call `cancelInterval()`. This method was also designed to support function arguments, although Netscape no longer supports this syntax.

- `setTimeout()` — Revised so that it can either evaluate an expression or call a function. However, calling a function from this method is no longer supported by Netscape.

- `stop()` — Stops the current download.

New Properties, Methods, and Event Handlers for Other Objects

You can create objects using literal notation.

- `arguments` — Includes new properties that provide information about the invoked function.

Anchor and Link Property

- `text` — Contains the content of the corresponding <A> tag.

Function Property

- `arity` — Indicates the number of arguments expected by a function.

Navigator Properties

- `language` — Indicates what translation of the Navigator is being used. This property is particularly useful for JAR management.

- `platform` — Indicates the machine type for which the Navigator was compiled. This property is particularly useful for JAR management.

Array Object

The `Array` object includes the following new features and changes:

- Literal notation — You can now create arrays by using literal notation.

- Under JavaScript 1.2, when the `<SCRIPT>` tag includes `LANGUAGE="JavaScript1.2"`, then `array(1)` creates a new array with `a[0]=1`.

- With regular expressions, when created as the result of a match between a regular expression and a string, arrays have new properties that provide information about the match.

The `Array` object also includes the following new and changed methods:

- `concat()` — Joins two arrays and returns a new array.

- `pop()` — Removes the last element from an array and returns that element.

- `push()` — Adds one or more elements to the end of an array and returns the last element added.

- `shift()` — Removes the first element from an array and returns that element.

- `unshift()` — Adds one or more elements to the front of an array and returns the new length of the array.

- `slice()` — Extracts a section from an array and returns a new array.

- `splice()` — Adds and/or removes elements from an array and returns the removed elements.

- `sort()`* — Now works on all platforms. It no longer converts undefined elements to `null`; instead, it sorts them to the high end of the array.

Document Method
- `getSelection()` — Returns a string containing the text of the current selection.

Navigator Method
- `preference()` — Enables a script to get and set certain Navigator preferences such as enabling or disabling Java.

String Methods
- `charCodeAt()` — Returns a number specifying the ISO-Latin-1 codeset value of the character at the specified index in a string object.

- `concat()` — Combines the text of two strings and returns a new string.

- `fromCharCode()` — Constructs a string from a specified sequence of numbers that are ISO-Latin-1 codeset values.

- `match()` — Executes a search for a match between a string and a regular expression.

- `replace()` — Executes a search for a match between a string and a regular expression and replaces the matched substring with a new substring.

- `search()` — Tests for a match between a string and a regular expression.

- `slice()` — Extracts a section of a string and returns a new string.

- `split()`* — Includes the following new features and changes. It can take a regular expression argument, as well as a fixed string, which is used to split the object string. It can take a limit count so that it won't include trailing empty elements in the resulting array. If you specify `LANGUAGE="JavaScript1.2"` in the `<SCRIPT>` tag, then `string.split(" ")` splits on any run of one or more whitespace characters including spaces, tabs, line feeds, and carriage returns.

- `substr()` — Returns the characters in a string, collecting the specified number of characters beginning with a specified location in the string.

- `substring()`* — If you specify `LANGUAGE="JavaScript1.2"` in the `<SCRIPT>` tag, this method no longer swaps index numbers when the first index is greater than the second.

Shared Methods

- `eval()` — No longer a method of individual objects; only available as a global function.

- `watch()` — New method of all objects. Watches for a property to be assigned a value and runs a function when that occurs.

- `unwatch()` — New method of all objects. Removes a watchpoint set with the `watch()` method.

- `captureEvents()` — `window`, `document`, and `layer` object method. Sets the window, document, or layer to capture the specified events.

- `handleEvent()` — Method of all objects with event handlers. Invokes the handler for the specified event.

- `releaseEvents()` — `window`, `document`, and `layer` object method. Sets the window, document, or layer to release the specified events.

- `routeEvent()` — `window`, `document`, and `layer` object method. Sets the window, document, or layer to pass a captured event along the normal event hierarchy.

- `toString()`* — Converts the object or array to a literal. For this behavior, you must specify `LANGUAGE="JavaScript1.2"` in the `<SCRIPT>` tag.

- `Number()`* — Now returns `NaN` rather than an error if *x* is a string that does not contain a well-formed numeric literal.

What's New in JavaScript 1.3

In the JavaScript 1.3 release, the most significant change is that it now complies with the following two specifications:

- The European Computer Manufacturers Association (ECMA) ECMA-262 specification
- The International Organization for Standards specification, ISO-16262

The JavaScript 1.3 release also includes the following new features and changes. See Appendix A, "What's New in JavaScript 1.3," for more information.

New Features

The JavaScript 1.3 release offers the following new features:

- Unicode compliance
- New top-level properties: `NaN`, `Infinity`, and `undefined`
- Global function `isFinite()`
- `toSource()` method
- New and changed features of the `Date` object
- New `call()` and `apply()` methods of the `Function` object
- Strict equality operators
- JavaScript console that records JavaScript error messages

Changes

The JavaScript 1.3 release made changes to the following areas:

- Specifying the version of JavaScript
- Equality operator
- `Array` object
- `replace()` method of `String` object
- `Boolean` object
- `toString()` function

ECMAScript Standard

JavaScript is Netscape's cross-platform, object-based scripting language for client and server applications. It contains the elements common to both client- and server-side JavaScript. The ECMA specification, second edition, says that the ECMA standard is based on several originating technologies, the most well know being JavaScript (Netscape Communications) and JScript (Microsoft Corporation). ECMAScript is a general purpose, cross-platform programming language based on the core language subset of client-side JavaScript 1.1 and JScript 1.0.

ECMA is an acronym for the European Computer Manufacturers Association. It is an international standards association for information and communication systems. Standardization means that when you write JavaScript code, it should behave the same way in all applications that support the standard.

ECMA completed the first version of the ECMAScript specification, ECMA-262, in June 1997. ECMAScript, as defined by the ECMA, is an object-oriented programming language for performing computations and manipulating objects within a host environment. More recently, the ECMA-262 standard was also approved by ISO. Note that ECMA does not specify the Document Object Model (DOM), being standardized by W3C, which defines the way in which the HTML document objects are exposed to scripts.

Debugging Tools

Netscape provides a JavaScript debugger that enables you to debug client-side JavaScript code. You cannot use the debugger to debug server-side JavaScript, Java™, or HTML.

The Netscape JavaScript Debugger, written in Java, is available for the Microsoft® Windows™ 95/Windows NT™, Macintosh PowerPC™, and UNIX platforms. Capabilities include such features as a watch mechanism, conditional breakpoints, enhanced error reporter, signed script support, and stepping through code.

You must be running Netscape Communicator 4.02 or later to be able to use the Netscape JavaScript debugger. You cannot use the debugger with other browsers.

You can download the Netscape JavaScript Debugger from:

    http://developer.netscape.com/software/jsdebug.html#download

Documentation for the debugger is available from:

    http://developer.netscape.com/docs/manuals/jsdebug/index.htm

Chapter 2

Core Language Changes

▼OPERATORS

▼STATEMENTS

▼FUNCTIONS

▼LITERAL NOTATION FOR CREATING OBJECTS

This chapter describes changes made to the the following elements of the JavaScript core language in the JavaScript 1.2 release:

- `==` and `!=` comparison operators
- `delete` operator
- Statements
  - labeled
  - `break`
  - `continue`
  - `switch`
  - `do...while` loops
  - `import`

- `export`
- Functions
  - Nested
  - Arguments
  - `arity` property
- Objects can now be created with literal notation

Operators

The following sections describe changes to comparison operators == and != and introduce the new `delete` operator that enables you to delete items from an array.

Comparison Operators (==. !=)

If the <SCRIPT> tag uses LANGAGE="JavaScript1.2", then the equals (==) and not equal to (!=) comparison operators work differently than in the 1.0 and 1.1 releases. In JavaScript 1.2, these comparison operators behave in the following ways:

- The == and != operators never attempt to convert operands from one type to another. To convert operands, follow the data conversion guidelines in Table 2-1.

- The == and != operators always compare identity of like-typed operands. If the operands do not have like type, they are not equal.

These core language changes were made to avoid errors, maintain transitivity, and simplify the language.

To convert data from one type to another, follow the guidelines in Table 2-1.

Table 2-1 Guidelines for Converting Data Types

Conversion	Syntax
Convert x to a string	`" " + x`
Convert x to a number	`x - 0`
Nav 4.0 only: convert x to a string	`String(x)`
Nav 4.0 only: convert x to a number	`Number(x)`

In the JavaScript 1.0 and 1.1 releases, the comparison operators behave in the following ways:

- If both operands are objects, compare object references.

- If either operand is null, convert the other operand to an object and compare references.

- If one operand is a string and the other is an object, convert the object to a string and compare string characters.

- Otherwise, convert both operands to numbers and compare numeric identity.

Examples of Comparison Operators

The `equal.html` script creates a set of tables that demonstrate the changes in the `==` comparison operator in all releases. The script itself is shown after the figures. Figure 2–1 shows the result of loading the `equal.html` script. The first part of the script shows the behavior of the `==` comparison operator in JavaScript 1.0 and 1.1 releases.

```
┌─────────────────────────────────────────────────────────────────────┐
│ ▭        Netscape: Comparison Operator ==                      ▭ ▤ │
├─────────────────────────────────────────────────────────────────────┤
│  Back  Forward  Reload  Home  Search  Guide  Images  Print  Security  Stop   N  │
├─────────────────────────────────────────────────────────────────────┤
│ Location : file:///Macintosh%20HD/Desktop%20Folder/JSBook-1.2/core/equal.html │
└─────────────────────────────────────────────────────────────────────┘
```

Before the JavaScript 1.2 release, the comparison operators behaved in the following way:

- If both operands are objects, their object references are compared.
- If either operand is null, the other operand is converted to an object and object references are compared.
- If one operand is a string and the other is an object, the object is converted to a string and the string characters are compared.
- Otherwise, both operands are converted to numbers and their numeric identities are compared.

Below is a series of scripts that show the behavior before the JavaScript 1.2 release.

No language attribute set

Script	Result

`<script>`
`document.write( "7" == 7 )`
`</script>`
	true

`<script>`
`document.write( ("7"-0) == 7 )`
`</script>`
	true

Note: subtracting zero from a string converts the string's value to numeric.

LANGUAGE="JavaScript"

Script	Result

`<script language="JavaScript">`
`document.write( "7" == 7 )`
`</script>`
	true

`<script language="JavaScript">`
`document.write( ("7"-0) == 7 )`
`</script>`
	true

LANGUAGE="JavaScript1.1"

Script	Result

`<script language="JavaScript1.1">`
`document.write( "7" == 7 )`
`</script>`
	true

`<script language="JavaScript1.1">`
`document.write( ("7"-0) == 7 )`
`</script>`
	true

Figure 2–1 Behavior of the == comparison operator in JavaScript 1.0 and 1.1 releases

Figure 2–2 shows the behavior of the == comparison operator in JavaScript 1.2.

With JavaScript 1.2, setting the SCRIPT tag's LANGUAGE attribute to "JavaScript1.2" simplifies how the comparison operators work. In JavaScript 1.2:

- The comparison operators always compare the identity of like-typed operands. If the operands do not have like type, they are not equal.

In the example below, the left operand is a string and the right operand is a numeric. The operands don't have the same type, so they are not equal. In the second example, the string "7" is converted to a numeric value by subtraction of 0 from it. Thus, you have two numerics with values equal to 7.

LANGUAGE="JavaScript1.2"

Script	Result
`<script language="JavaScript1.2"> document.write( "7" == 7 ) </script>`	false
`<script language="JavaScript1.2"> document.write( ("7"-0) == 7 ) </script>`	true

Figure 2-2 Behavior of the == comparison operator in JavaScript 1.2

The following `equal.html` script creates a set of tables that compare the behavior of the == comparison operator for all releases.

```
<!--
                equal.html

    This example demonstrates the change in the JavaScript 1.2
    comparison operator ==.

-->
<HTML>
  <HEAD>
    <TITLE>Comparison Operator == </TITLE>
  </HEAD>
  <BODY>

    <P>Before the JavaScript 1.2 release, the comparison
       operators behaved in the following way:</P>
    <UL>
      <LI>If both operands are objects, their object references
    are compared.
      <LI>If either operand is null, the other operand is
    converted to an object and object references are
    compared.
      <LI>If one operand is a string and the other is an object,
    the object is converted to a string and the string
    characters are compared.
      <LI>Otherwise, both operands are converted to numbers and
    their numeric identities are compared.
    </UL>

    <P>Below is a series of scripts that show the behavior
```

```
      before the JavaScript 1.2 release.</P>

<CENTER>
    <table border="1">
<TC>No language attribute set</TC>
<TH>Script</TH>
<TH>Result</TH>
<TR>
  <TD>
    &lt;script&gt;<BR>
    document.write( "7" == 7 )<BR>
    &lt;/script&gt;
  </TD>
  <TD>
    <SCRIPT>
      document.write( "7" == 7 )
    </SCRIPT>
  </TD>
</TR>
<TR>
  <TD>
    &lt;script&gt;<BR>
    document.write( ("7"-0) == 7 )<BR>
    &lt;/script&gt;
  </TD>
  <TD>
    <SCRIPT>
      document.write( ("7"-0) == 7 )
    </SCRIPT>
  </TD>
</TR>
    </TABLE>
</CENTER>

<P>Note: subtracting zero from a string converts the
   string's value to numeric.</P>

<CENTER>
    <table border="1">
<TC>LANGUAGE="JavaScript"</TC>
<TH>Script</TH>
<TH>Result</TH>
<TR>
  <TD>
    &lt;script language="JavaScript"&gt;<BR>
    document.write( "7" == 7 )<BR>
    &lt;/script&gt;
  </TD>
```

```
   <TD>
     <SCRIPT LANGUAGE="JavaScript">
       document.write( "7" == 7 )
     </SCRIPT>
   </TD>
 </TR>
 <TR>
   <TD>
     &lt;script language="JavaScript"&gt;<BR>
     document.write( ("7"-0) == 7 )<BR>
     &lt;/script&gt;
   </TD>
   <TD>
     <SCRIPT LANGUAGE="JavaScript">
       document.write( ("7"-0) == 7 )
     </SCRIPT>
   </TD>
 </TR>
   </TABLE>
 </CENTER>

 <P></P>
 <CENTER>
   <table border="1">
 <TC>LANGUAGE="JavaScript1.1"</TC>
 <th
>Script</TH>
   <TH>Result</TH>
   <TR>
     <TD>
       &lt;script language="JavaScript1.1"&gt;<BR>
       document.write( "7" == 7 )<BR>
       &lt;/script&gt;
     </TD>
     <TD>
       <SCRIPT LANGUAGE="JavaScript1.1">
         document.write( "7" == 7 )
       </SCRIPT>
     </TD>
   </TR>
   <TR>
     <TD>
       &lt;script language="JavaScript1.1"&gt;<BR>
       document.write( ("7"-0) == 7 )<BR>
       &lt;/script&gt;
     </TD>
     <TD>
       <SCRIPT LANGUAGE="JavaScript1.1">
```

```
        document.write( ("7"-0) == 7 )
      </SCRIPT>
    </TD>
  </TR>
    </TABLE>
  </CENTER>
```

<P>With JavaScript 1.2, setting the SCRIPT tag's LANGUAGE
   attribute to "JavaScript1.2" simplifies how the
   comparison operators work. In JavaScript 1.2:</P>

<UL>
   <LI>The comparison operators always compare the
identity of like-typed operands. If the operands do
not have like type, they are not equal.
   </UL>

<P>In the example below, the left operand is a string and
   the right operand is a numeric. The operands don't have
   the same type, so they are not equal. In the second
   example, the string "7" is converted to a numeric value
   by subtraction of 0 from it. Thus, you have two numerics
   with values equal to 7.</P>

```
<P></P>
<CENTER>
  <table border="1">
<TC>LANGUAGE="JavaScript1.2"</TC>
<TH>Script</TH>
<TH>Result</TH>
<TR>
  <TD>
    &lt;script language="JavaScript1.2"&gt;<BR>
    document.write( "7" == 7 )<BR>
    &lt;/script&gt;
  </TD>
  <TD>
    <SCRIPT LANGUAGE="JavaScript1.2">
      document.write( "7" == 7 )
    </SCRIPT>
  </TD>
</TR>
<TR>
  <TD>
    &lt;script language="JavaScript1.2"&gt;<BR>
    document.write( ("7"-0) == 7 )<BR>
    &lt;/script&gt;
  </TD>
```

```
        <TD>
          <SCRIPT LANGUAGE="JavaScript1.2">
            document.write( ("7"-0) == 7 )
          </SCRIPT>
        </TD>
      </TR>
        </TABLE>
      </CENTER>
      <P></P>
    </BODY>
  </HTML>
```

The following notEqual.html script creates a set of tables that demonstrate the changes in the JavaScript 1.2 ! = comparison operator.

```
<!--

              notEqual.html

    This example demonstrates the change in the
    JavaScript 1.2 comparison operator !=.

-->

<HTML>
  <HEAD>
    <TITLE>Comparison Operator !=</TITLE>
  </HEAD>
  <BODY>

    <CENTER>
      <table border="1">
    <TC>No language attribute set</TC>
    <TH>Script</TH>
    <TH>Result</TH>
    <TR>
      <TD>
        &lt;script&gt;<BR>
        document.write( "7" != 7 )<BR>
        &lt;/script&gt;
      </TD>
      <TD>
        <SCRIPT>
          document.write( "7" != 7 )
        </SCRIPT>
      </TD>
    </TR>
    <TR>
      <TD>
        &lt;script&gt;<BR>
```

```
      document.write( ("7"-0) != 7 )<BR>
      &lt;/script&gt;
    </TD>
    <TD>
      <SCRIPT>
        document.write( ("7"-0) != 7 )
      </SCRIPT>
    </TD>
  </TR>
    </TABLE>
  </CENTER>

<P></P>
<CENTER>
   <table border="1">
<TC>LANGUAGE="JavaScript"</TC>
<TH>Script</TH>
<TH>Result</TH>
<TR>
  <TD>
    &lt;script language="JavaScript"&gt;<BR>
    document.write( "7" != 7 )<BR>
    &lt;/script&gt;
  </TD>
  <TD>
    <SCRIPT LANGUAGE="JavaScript">
      document.write( "7" != 7 )
    </SCRIPT>
  </TD>
</TR>
<TR>
  <TD>
    &lt;script language="JavaScript"&gt;<BR>
    document.write( ("7"-0) != 7 )<BR>
    &lt;/script&gt;
  </TD>
  <TD>
    <SCRIPT LANGUAGE="JavaScript">
      document.write( ("7"-0) != 7 )
    </SCRIPT>
  </TD>
</TR>
    </TABLE>
  </CENTER>

<P></P>
<CENTER>
   <table border="1">
```

```
<TC>LANGUAGE="JavaScript1.1"</TC>
<TH>Script</TH>
<TH>Result</TH>
<TR>
  <TD>
    &lt;script language="JavaScript1.1"&gt;<BR>
    document.write( "7" != 7 )<BR>
    &lt;/script&gt;
  </TD>
  <TD>
    <SCRIPT LANGUAGE="JavaScript1.1">
      document.write( "7" != 7 )
    </SCRIPT>
  </TD>
</TR>
<TR>
  <TD>
    &lt;script language="JavaScript1.1"&gt;<BR>
    document.write( ("7"-0) != 7 )<BR>
    &lt;/script&gt;
  </TD>
  <TD>
    <SCRIPT LANGUAGE="JavaScript1.1">
      document.write( ("7"-0) != 7 )
    </SCRIPT>
  </TD>
</TR>
  </TABLE>
</CENTER>

<P></P>
<CENTER>
  <table border="1">
<TC>LANGUAGE="JavaScript1.2"</TC>
<TH>Script</TH>
<TH>Result</TH>
<TR>
  <TD>
    &lt;script language="JavaScript1.2"&gt;<BR>
    document.write( "7" != 7 )<BR>
    &lt;/script&gt;
  </TD>
  <TD>
    <SCRIPT LANGUAGE="JavaScript1.2">
      document.write( "7" != 7 )
    </SCRIPT>
  </TD>
</TR>
```

```
<TR>
  <TD>
    &lt;script language="JavaScript1.2"&gt;<BR>
    document.write( ("7"-0) != 7 )<BR>
    &lt;/script&gt;
  </TD>
  <TD>
    <SCRIPT LANGUAGE="JavaScript1.2">
      document.write( ("7"-0) != 7 )
    </SCRIPT>
  </TD>
</TR>
  </TABLE>
  </CENTER>

  </BODY>
</HTML>
```

Figure 2–3 shows the result of loading the notEqual.html script.

Netscape: Comparison Operator !=	

Back Forward Reload Home Search Guide Images Print Security Stop

Location: `file:///Macintosh%20HD/Desktop%20Folder/JSBook-1.2/core/notEqual.html`

No language attribute set

Script	Result

`<script>`
`document.write( "7" != 7 )`
`</script>`
	false

`<script>`
`document.write( ("7"-0) != 7 )`
`</script>`
	false

LANGUAGE="JavaScript"

Script	Result

`<script language="JavaScript">`
`document.write( "7" != 7 )`
`</script>`
	false

`<script language="JavaScript">`
`document.write( ("7"-0) != 7 )`
`</script>`
	false

LANGUAGE="JavaScript1.1"

Script	Result

`<script language="JavaScript1.1">`
`document.write( "7" != 7 )`
`</script>`
	false

`<script language="JavaScript1.1">`
`document.write( ("7"-0) != 7 )`
`</script>`
	false

LANGUAGE="JavaScript1.2"

Script	Result

`<script language="JavaScript1.2">`
`document.write( "7" != 7 )`
`</script>`
	true

`<script language="JavaScript1.2">`
`document.write( ("7"-0) != 7 )`
`</script>`
	false

Figure 2–3 Result of loading the `notEqual.html` script

delete Operator

The `delete` operator removes the property or element for an object at a specified index in an array. If successful, the `delete` operator sets the property or element to `undefined` and returns a value of `true`; otherwise, it returns `false`.

You reference the `delete` operator in one of the following ways:

```
delete objectName.property
delete objectname[index]
delete property (only valid within a with statement)
```

Example of Using the delete Operator

The following `delete.html` script creates an array with ten elements and prints the array. It then deletes two of the elements in the array and prints the array again.

```
<!--
                    delete.html

        This example deletes elements out of an array by using the
        delete operator.
-->
<HTML>
  <HEAD>
    <TITLE>Delete</TITLE>

    <SCRIPT LANGUAGE="JavaScript">
      <!-- HIDE
      // Create an array of ten elements.
      var strArray = new Array(10)

      // Pre-load the array strings.
      for (var i=0; i < 10; i++) {
      strArray[i] = new String(i)
      }
      // STOP HIDE -->
    </SCRIPT>
  </HEAD>
<BODY>

    <P><CODE>delete</CODE> is a new core language operator.
      If successful, it operates on the property or element
      and  sets it to <CODE>undefined</CODE>.</P>

    <P>Suppose we create an array of 10 strings, assigning the
      index value to each string as we create the array. The code
      looks like this:</P>

    <P>
      <CODE>var strArray = new Array(10)<BR>
      <BR>
      for (var i=0; i < 10; i++) {<BR>
        strArray[i] = new String(i)<BR>
      }</CODE>
    </P>

    <P>Now let's print out <CODE>strArray</CODE>.</P>
```

```
<SCRIPT LANGUAGE="JavaScript">
  <!-- HIDE
  for (var i=0; i < strArray.length; i++) {
document.write(strArray[i] + " ")
  }
  // STOP HIDE -->
</SCRIPT>

<P>Now let's delete the third and fifth elements and print
  the array again. The code looks like this:</P>
<P>
  <CODE>delete strArray[3]<BR>
  delete strArray[5]</CODE>
</P>

<SCRIPT LANGUAGE="JavaScript">
  <!-- HIDE
  delete strArray[3]
  delete strArray[5]

  for (var i=0; i < strArray.length; i++) {
document.write(strArray[i] + " ")
  }
  // STOP HIDE -->
</SCRIPT>

<P>As you can see, the strings in the third and fifth positions
  are replaced with <CODE>undefined</CODE>.

  </BODY>
</HTML>
```

Figure 2–4 shows the result of loading the delete.html script.

Netscape: Delete

Back Forward Reload Home Search Guide Images Print Security Stop

Location: file:///Macintosh%20HD/Desktop%20Folder/JSBook-1.2/core/delete.html

delete is a new core language operator. If successful, it operates on the property or element and sets it to undefined.

Suppose we create an array of 10 strings, assigning the index value to each string as we create the array. The code looks like this:

```
var strArray = new Array(10)

for (var i=0; i < 10; i++) {
  strArray[i] = new String(i)
}
```

Now let's print out strArray.

Now let's delete the third and fifth elements and print the array again. The code looks like this:

```
delete strArray[3]
delete strArray[5]
```

As you can see, the strings in the third and fifth positions are replaced with undefined.

Figure 2–4 Result of loading the `delete.html` script

Statements

The following sections describe changes to existing statements or new statements available in the JavaScript 1.2 release:

- Labeled statements
- `break`
- `continue`
- `switch`
- `do...while` loops
- `import`
- `export`

Labeled Statements

You can use labeled statements to break out of nested loops or to continue a loop outside the current one.

A labeled statement provides an identifier that can be used as the destination of a `break` or `continue` statement. You can think of it as setting a bookmark in your script. If you find a labeled statement, you should expect a `break` or `continue` statement in the code nearby. Because it's standard programming practice to use labeled statements in conjunction with `break` or `continue` statements, be judicious in their use. To help others interpret your code, we recommend that you restrict your use of labels to their recommended purpose.

Syntax
You create a label statement by using the following syntax:

```
label : statement
```

where `label` is an identifier and `statement` is a block of one or more statements.

You can use `break` with any labeled statement and `continue` with any looping labeled statements.

Example of a Labeled Statement
The following `labeled.html` script shows how to define a label. In direct violation of our recommendation, this example does not use the labeled statement in conjunction with a `break` or `continue` statement.

```
<!--
                labeled.html
-->
<HTML>
  <HEAD>
    <TITLE>Labeled Statement</TITLE>
    <SCRIPT LANGUAGE="JavaScript">
      <!-- HIDE FROM OLD BROWSERS

      label:
        document.write("Hi<BR>")


      // STOP HIDING -->
    </SCRIPT>
  </HEAD>
<BODY>

  <P>The word and break on the previous line are created
    as a labeled statement. Labeled statements provide an
    identifier that can be used as a destination of a <CODE>
    break</CODE> or <CODE>continue</CODE> statement.</P>

  <P>See the examples for <CODE>break</CODE> and <CODE>
  continue</CODE> for a more complete picture.</P>

  </BODY>
</HTML>
```

Figure 2–5 shows the result of loading the `labeled.html` script.

```
┌─────────────────────────────────────────────────────────────────┐
│ □              Netscape: Labeled Statement                ▣▤ │
├─────────────────────────────────────────────────────────────────┤
│  ◄    ◊    ◙    ⌂    ✎    ⬆    ▣    ▣    ❄    N │
│ Back Forward Reload Home Search Guide Images Print Security Stop  │
├─────────────────────────────────────────────────────────────────┤
│ Location: 🔖 file:///Macintosh%20HD/Desktop%20Folder/JSBook-1.2/core/labeled.html │
├─────────────────────────────────────────────────────────────────┤
│ Hi                                                                │
│                                                                   │
│ The word and break on the previous line are created as a labeled statement. Labeled statements provide │
│ an identifier that can be used as a destination of a break or continue statement. │
│                                                                   │
│ See the examples for break and continue for a more complete picture. │
└─────────────────────────────────────────────────────────────────┘
```

Figure 2–5 Result of loading the `labeled.html` script

break Statement

The `break` statement now supports an optional label that enables you to break out of a labeled statement.

In previous releases, a `break` statement terminated the current `while` or `for` loop and transferred program control to the statement that followed the terminated loop.

With JavaScript 1.2, you can add an identifying label statement as an argument to the `break` statement. When you use a label with a `break` statement, the break must be within the statement identified by the label. Control is transferred to the statement immediately after the label statement. You can use the label and `break` statements together to break out of an arbitrarily deep nesting of labeled statements.

Syntax
Use the following syntax to use the optional label with `break`:

```
break
break label
```

where `label` is the identifier associated with a labeled statement.

Example of Using a Labeled Statement with the break Statement
The following `break.html` script starts by showing a simple `break` statement, then adds labeled statements so you can see how the script executes under different conditions.

```
<!--
          break.html

     Several examples of the break statement.
-->
```

```
<HTML>
  <HEAD>
    <TITLE>break statement</TITLE>
  </HEAD>
  <BODY>

    <P>With JavaScript 1.2, you can add an optional labeled
      statement identifier as an argument to the <CODE>break
      </CODE> statement.</P>

    <P>The following result breaks out of a <CODE>while</CODE>
      loop without using a labeled statement.</P>
    <SCRIPT LANGUAGE="JavaScript">
      <!-- HIDE FROM OLD BROWSERS

      var x = 0
      while ( true ) {
        document.write(x)
        if ( x >= 10) {
          break
        }
        x += 1;
      }
      document.write("-done-<BR>")

      // STOP HIDING -->
    </SCRIPT>

    <P>This result breaks out of one labeled statement. Note that
      the only real change here is the addition of the
      label. </P>
    <SCRIPT LANGUAGE="JavaScript">
      <!-- HIDE FROM OLD BROWSERS
      var x = 0

      alabel:
    while ( true ) {
      document.write(x)
      if ( x >= 10) {
        break
      }
      x += 1;
    }
      document.write("-done-<BR>")

      // STOP HIDING -->
    </SCRIPT>
```

```
<P>Now we play around and show the result of breaking
 out of one labeled statement with each <CODE>break
 </CODE> statement.</P>

<SCRIPT LANGUAGE="JavaScript">
  <!-- HIDE FROM OLD BROWSERS
  var x = 0

  alabel:
while ( true ) {
  document.write(" " + x + "-")
      anotherlabel:
        for (var j=0; j < 10; j++) {
          document.write(" " + j + " ")
          if (j >= 5 ) {
            break anotherlabel
          }
        }
  document.write("<BR>")
  if ( x >= 10) {
    break alabel
  }
  x += 1;
}
  document.write("-done-<BR>")

  // STOP HIDING -->
</SCRIPT>

<P>Now, by just changing the label on the innermost <CODE>
 break</CODE> statement, we show the result of breaking
 out of multiple levels at once. </P>

<SCRIPT LANGUAGE="JavaScript">
  <!-- HIDE FROM OLD BROWSERS
  var x = 0

  alabel:
while ( true ) {
  document.write(" " + x + "-")
      anotherlabel:
        for (var j=0; j < 10; j++) {
          document.write(" " + j + " ")
          if (j >= 5 ) {
            break alabel
          }
        }
  document.write("<BR>")
```

```
      if ( x >= 10) {
        break alabel
      }
      x += 1;
    }
      document.write("-done-<BR>")

      // STOP HIDING -->
    </SCRIPT>

  </BODY>
</HTML>
```

Figure 2–6 shows the result of loading the break.html script.

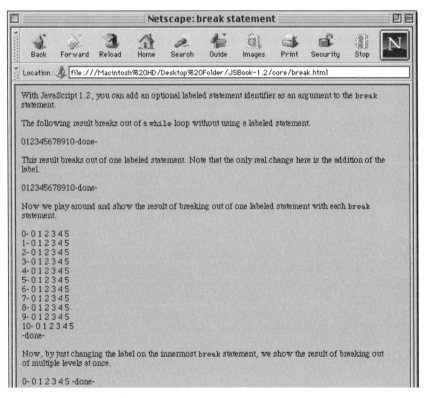

Figure 2–6 Result of loading the break.html script

continue Statement

The continue statement can now include an optional label that enables the script to end execution of a labeled statement and continue to the specified label statement.

In previous releases, `continue` terminated execution of a `for` or `while` loop, and transfered execution of the loop to its next iteration.

With JavaScript 1.2, `continue` supports an optional identifier of a labeled statement as an argument. `continue` must be in a looping statement identified by the label used as the argument to `continue`.

Syntax

Use the following syntax to use the optional label with `continue`:

```
continue
continue label
```

where `label` is the identifier of a labeled statement.

Example of Using Labeled Statements with continue

The following `continue.html` script creates a `while` loop that puts parentheses around negative numbers when it prints the output. The example then adds a label and then changes the format to output positive numbers twice.

```
<!--

                 continue.html


     Several examples of the continue statement.
-->
<HTML>
  <HEAD>
    <TITLE>continue statement</TITLE>
  </HEAD>
  <BODY>

    <P>The <CODE>continue</CODE> statement terminates
       execution of the block of statements in a <CODE>while
       </CODE>or <CODE>for</CODE> loop and continues
       execution of the loop with the next iteration.</P>

    <P>For example, while <CODE>i</CODE> is negative in the
       following script, a different output format is used:</P>
    <PRE>
      <CODE>var i = -10

      while ( i < 10 ) {
        i += 1
        if ( i < 0 ) {
          document.write("(" + i + ") ")
          continue
        }
        document.write(i + " ")
      }
```

```
     document.write("-done-&lt;br&gt;")</CODE>
</PRE>

<P>which outputs:</P>
<SCRIPT LANGUAGE="JavaScript">
  <!-- HIDE FROM OLD BROWSERS
  var i = -10

  while ( i < 10 ) {
    i += 1
    if ( i < 0 ) {
      document.write("(" + i + ") ")
      continue
    }
    document.write(i + " ")
  }
  document.write("-done-<BR>")

  // STOP HIDING -->
</SCRIPT>

<P>Starting with JavaScript 1.2, <CODE>continue</CODE>
  supports an optional argument of a labeled statement
  identifier, thus enabling a program to continue to a
  specified labeled statement.</P>

<P>The following example rewrites the previous example to
use a label:</P>
<PRE>
  <CODE>var i = -10

  alabel:
while ( i < 10 ) {
  i += 1;
  if ( i < 0 ) {
    document.write("(" + i + ") ")
    continue alabel
  }
  document.write(i + " ")
}
  document.write("-done-&lt;br&gt;")</CODE>
</PRE>

<P>The output is the same:</P>
<SCRIPT LANGUAGE="JavaScript">
  <!-- HIDE FROM OLD BROWSERS
  var i = -10
```

```
    alabel:
while ( i < 10 ) {
  i += 1;
  if ( i < 0 ) {
    document.write("(" + i + ") ")
    continue alabel
  }
  document.write(i + " ")
}
    document.write("-done-<BR>")
    // STOP HIDING -->
</SCRIPT>
```

<P>In the following example, positive numbers are output twice:</P>
<PRE>
```
  <CODE>var i = -10

  outer:
while ( i < 10 ) {
  i += 1;
      inner:
    for (var j=10; j > 0; j--) {
          if (i != j) {
            continue inner
          }
          document.write( i + " ")
    }
  document.write(i + " &lt;br&gt;")
}
    document.write("-done-&lt;br&gt;")</CODE>
</PRE>
```

<P>The output is:</P>
<SCRIPT LANGUAGE="JavaScript">
```
  <!-- HIDE FROM OLD BROWSERS
  var i = -10

  outer:
while ( i < 10 ) {
  i += 1;
      inner:
    for (var j=10; j > 0; j--) {
          if (i != j) {
            continue inner
          }
          document.write( i + " ")
    }
```

```
        document.write(i + " <BR>")
    }
        document.write("-done-<BR>")
        // STOP HIDING -->
    </SCRIPT>

    </BODY>
  </HTML>
```

Figure 2–7 shows the first two examples that are the result of loading the `continue.html` script.

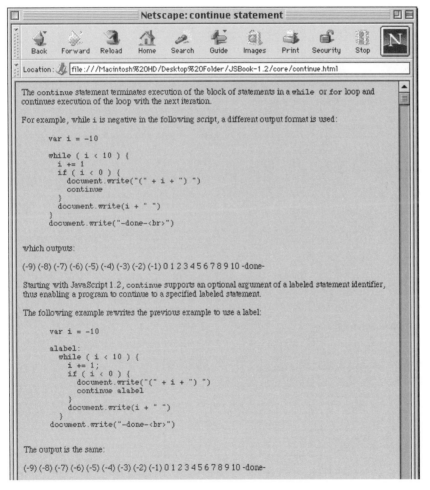

Figure 2–7 Result of first two examples from loading the `continue.html` script

Figure 2–8 shows the result of the final example from loading the
`continue.html` script.

```
In the following example, positive numbers are output twice:

    var i = -10

    outer:
        while ( i < 10 ) {
            i += 1;
            inner:
                for (var j=10; j > 0; j--) {
                    if (i != j) {
                        continue inner
                    }
                    document.write( i + " ")
                }
                document.write(i + " <br>")
        }
        document.write("-done-<br>")

The output is:

-9
-8
-7
-6
-5
-4
-3
-2
-1
0
1 1
2 2
3 3
4 4
5 5
6 6
7 7
8 8
9 9
10 10
-done-
```

Figure 2–8 Result of the final example from loading the `continue.html`
script

switch Statement

The `switch` statement is new in JavaScript 1.2. It enables you to evaluate an
expression and attempt to match the value to supplied cases. If a match is found,
the associated statement is executed.

Syntax

The syntax for the `switch` statement is:

```
switch(expression) {
  case label :
    statement
    break
  case label :
    statement
```

```
      break
    ...
   default :
     statement
 }
```

where *expression* is the value matched against the label , *label* is an identifier used to match against expression, and *statement* is any statement or block of statements.

Description of switch Statement

The `switch` statement is evaluated by a search for a label that matches the value of *expression*. If one is found, the associated statement is executed. If no label matches *expression* and the optional `default` statement is present, the statement following the `default` statement is executed. If the `default` statement is not present, program execution continues with the statement following the `switch`.

You can associate optional `break` statements with each label's case. Doing so ensures that execution breaks to the statement following the switch. Omitting the `break` statement enables execution to continue with the next statement contained within the `switch` statement, which is sometimes the desired behavior.

Example of switch Statements

The folllowing `switch.html` script includes a `switch` statement as part of the `onClick` event handler for the Test button. The `switch` statement displays text in an alert dialog that is based on the case. It also contains a default statement to display an error message if neither case is met, although with this script, the case should always be met.

```
<!--
             switch.html

     Example of the JavaScript switch statement.

-->
<HTML>
  <HEAD>
    <TITLE>switch Statement</TITLE>
    <SCRIPT LANGUAGE="JavaScript">
      <!-- HIDE FROM OLD BROWSERS

      function test() {
     switch(document.example.answer[0].checked) {
       case true :
         alert("True")
         break
```

```
      case false :
        alert("False")
        break
    default :
      alert("Error")
    }
      }


    // STOP HIDING -->
   </SCRIPT>
</HEAD>
<BODY>

  <P>Behind the Test button is a basic <CODE>switch</CODE>
     statement. It tests if the first radio button is checked
   and pops up an alert dialog based on the case.</P>

  <FORM NAME="example">
    The sun is shining.<BR><BR>
    <INPUT TYPE="radio" NAME="answer" checked> True<BR>
    <INPUT TYPE="radio" NAME="answer"> False<BR><BR>?
    <INPUT TYPE="button" NAME="btn" VALUE="Test"
  onClick="test()">
   </FORM>


   <P>Click on a radio button, then on Test.</P>

  </BODY>
 </HTML>
```

Figure 2–9 shows the result of loading the switch.html script and clicking on
the Test button with True checked. An alert is displayed showing that the value
for the switch case is true.

```
                      Netscape: switch Statement

  Back   Forward  Reload   Home   Search   Guide   Images   Print  Security  Stop    N

  Location:  file:///Macintosh%20HD/Desktop%20Folder/JSBook-1.2/core/switch.html

  Behind the Test button is a basic switch statement. It tests if the first radio button is checked and
  pops up an alert dialog based on the case.

  The sun is shining.

  ⦿ True
  ○ False

  [ Test ]

  Click on a radio button, then on Test.

  ┌────────────────────[JavaScript Application]────────────────────┐
  │                                                                │
  │    ⚠    True                                                   │
  │   /!\                                                          │
  │                                                                │
  │                                                                │
  │                                                                │
  │                                                                │
  │                                               [    OK    ]     │
  │                                                                │
  └────────────────────────────────────────────────────────────────┘
```

Figure 2–9 Result of loading `switch.html` and clicking on the Test button with True checked

Figure 2–10 shows the result of loading the `switch.html` script and clicking on the Test button with False checked. An alert is displayed showing that the value for the switch case is `false`.

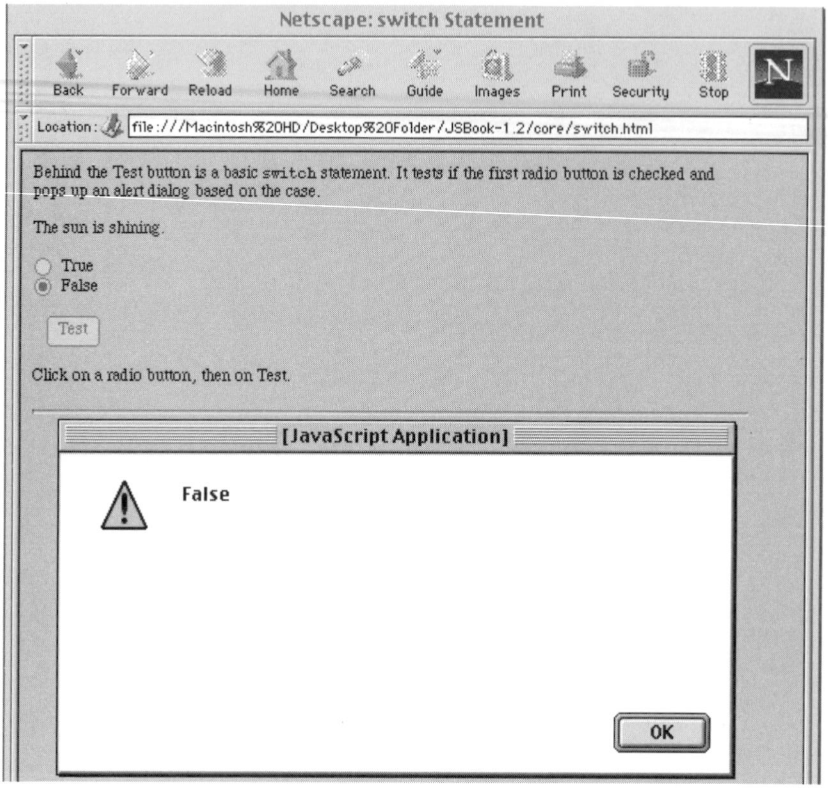

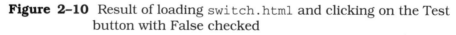

Figure 2–10 Result of loading `switch.html` and clicking on the Test button with False checked

The following `switchFallThrough.html` script does not contain any `break` statements. As a result, once you click on one of the radio buttons and then click on the Test button, a series of alerts is displayed starting with the case you checked and falling all the way through to the final `default` Error alert. When you click on the OK button in the alert, the next alert in the sequence is displayed.

```
<!--

            switchFallThrough.html

    Examples of a switch statement with cases that fall into the
    next case.

-->
<HTML>
  <HEAD>
    <TITLE>switch Statement with No breaks</TITLE>
    <SCRIPT LANGUAGE="JavaScript">
```

```
    <!-- HIDE FROM OLD BROWSERS

    function test() {
  switch(document.ex.answer.value) {
    case "premier" :
      alert("You have Premier service")
    case "gold" :
      alert("You have Gold service")
    case "certified" :
      alert("You have Certified service")
  default :
    alert("Error")
  }
    }

    // STOP HIDING -->
  </SCRIPT>
</HEAD>
<BODY>

  <P>Leaving the breaks out of a <CODE>switch</CODE>
    statement can be useful. In this case, people with
    premier service get all of the benefits of the lower
    service levels.</P>

  <FORM NAME="ex">
    What level of service do you have?<BR><BR>
    <INPUT TYPE="hidden" NAME="answer" VALUE="premier">
    <INPUT TYPE="radio" NAME="question" VALUE="premier" checked
  onClick="document.ex.answer.VALUE='premier'"> Premier<BR>
    <INPUT TYPE="radio" NAME="question" VALUE="gold"
      onClick="document.ex.answer.VALUE='gold'"> Gold<BR>
    <INPUT TYPE="radio" NAME="question" VALUE="certified"
      onClick="document.ex.answer.VALUE='certified'">
Certified<BR><BR>
    <INPUT TYPE="button" NAME="btn" VALUE="Test"
  onClick="test()">
  </FORM>

  <P>Click on a radio button, then on Test.</P>

  </BODY>
</HTML>
```

Figure 2–11 shows the result of loading the switchFallThrough.html script and clicking on the Test button. Note that although the figure shows all of the alerts on the screen at the same time, when you load the script, the alerts are actually displayed in series.

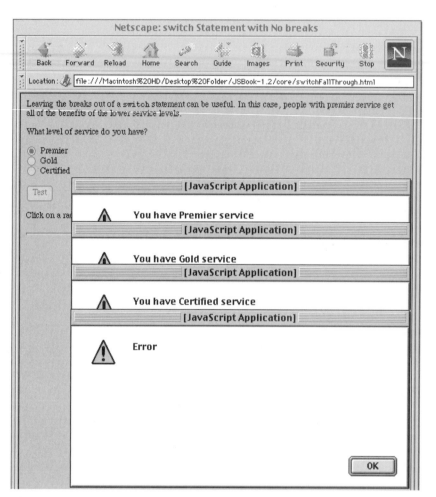

Figure 2–11 Result of loading the `switchFallThrough.html` script and clicking on the Test button

The following `switchNoDefault.html` script contains a `switch` statement with no default clause. Any case that does not match the `switch` statement is ignored.

```
<!--

            switchNoDefault.html

    Example of a switch statement that has no default clause.

-->
<HTML>
  <HEAD>
```

```
<TITLE>switch Statement with No default</TITLE>
<SCRIPT LANGUAGE="JavaScript">
  <!-- HIDE FROM OLD BROWSERS

  function test() {
    switch (document.ex.inField.value) {
      case "hiking" :
        alert("I like hiking.")
        break
      case "walking" :
        alert("I like walking.")
        break
    }
  }

  // STOP HIDING -->
  </SCRIPT>
</HEAD>
<BODY>


  <P>If a <CODE>switch</CODE> statement doesn't have
    a default clause, all nonmatching cases are ignored.</P>

  <FORM NAME="ex">
    What activities do you like?<BR>
    <INPUT TYPE="text" NAME="inField" VALUE="walking">
  </FORM>

  <P>Try entering "hiking" as an activity.</P>
  <P>Then try entering "swimming" as an activity.</P>

  <FORM NAME="exBtns">
    <INPUT TYPE="button" NAME="testBtn" VALUE="Test"
  onClick="test()">
  </FORM>

</BODY>
</HTML>
```

Figure 2–12 shows the result of loading the switchNoDefault.html script, typing hiking, and clicking on the Test button. Because hiking is one of the defined cases, an alert is displayed. If you type swimming and click on the Test button, nothing happens because swimming is not one of the cases defined in the switch statement.

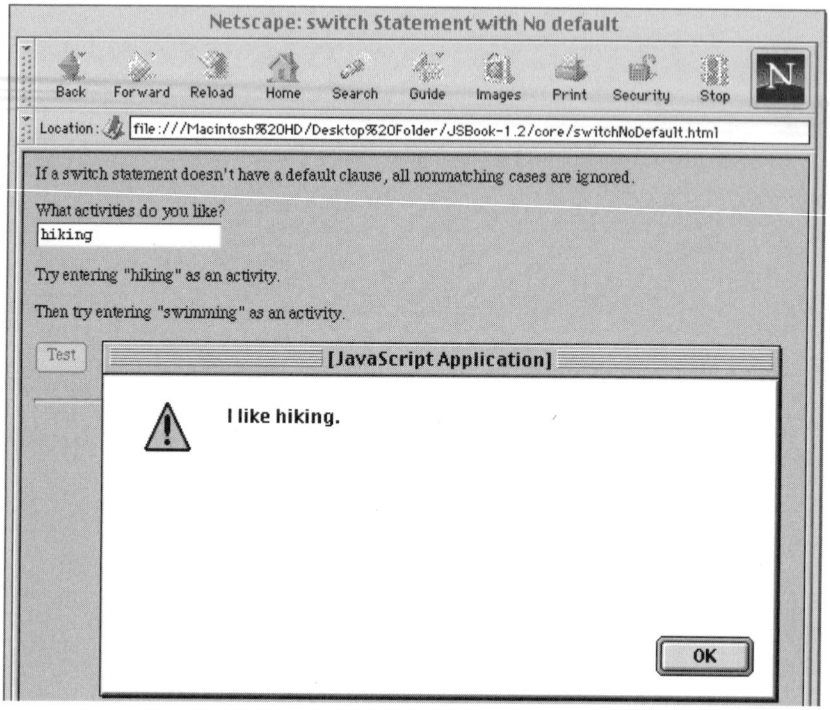

Figure 2–12 Example of loading the `switchNoDefault.html` script

do...while Loops

The JavaScript release enables you to create `do...while` loops, which repeat a loop until the conditions evaluate to `false`. The statement is evaluated at least once.

Syntax

`do...while` loops have the following syntax:

```
do
  statement
while ( condition )
```

where *statement* is a block of statements that is executed for each iteration of the loop. The block of statements is executed at least once. *condition* is evaluated after each iteration of the loop. If *condition* evaluates to `false`, then execution continues with the statement following the `do while` statement. If *condition* evaluates to `true`, then the statement block is executed again.

Example of a do ... while Loop

The following `dowhile.html` script contains a `do...while` statement that continues to loop until i is less than or equal to zero.

```
<!--
                    dowhile.html

       An example of the do while statement.

-->
<HTML>
  <HEAD>
    <TITLE>do...while Statement</TITLE>
  </HEAD>
  <BODY>

    <P>The <CODE>do...while</CODE> statement repeats a
      block of statements until the condition returns
      <CODE>false</CODE>.</P>

    <P>For example, the following code continues to execute until
    <CODE>i</CODE> &lt;= 0.</P>
    <PRE>
      <CODE>var i = 10

      do {
        document.write( i + "... ")
        i -= 1
      } while ( i > 0 )

      document.write("done.&lt;br&gt;")</CODE>
    </PRE>

    <P>which produces:</P>

    <SCRIPT LANGUAGE="JavaScript">
      <!-- HIDE FROM OLD BROWSERS

      var i = 10

      do {
        document.write( i + "... ")
        i -= 1
      } while ( i > 0 )

      document.write("done.<BR>")

      // STOP HIDING -->
```

```
    </SCRIPT>

  </BODY>
</HTML>
```

Figure 2–13 shows the result of loading the `dowhile.html` script.

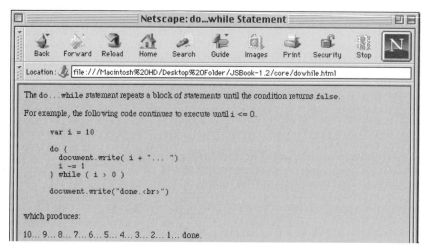

Figure 2–13 Result of loading the `dowhile.html` script

import Statement

The `import` statement enables a script to import functions from a signed script that has exported the information. Typically, information in a signed script is available only to scripts that are signed by the same principals. When you export properties, functions, or objects by using the `export` statement in a signed script, this information is available to any script whether signed or unsigned. The receiving script can access this information by using the `import` statement.

The receiving script must load the export script into a window or layer before it can import and use any of the exported functions.

Syntax

You create an import statement by using the following syntax:

```
import objectName.name1, objectName.name2, ...,
objectName.nameN
import objectName.*
```

where *nameN* is a list of functions to import from the export file and *objectName* is the name of the object that receives the imported names. * imports all functions from the export script.

For more information about signed scripts, see Chapter 8, "Object Signing."

export Statement

The `export` statement enables a script to export functions or objects to other signed or unsigned scripts. Typically, information in a signed script is available only to scripts that are signed by the same principals. When you export properties, functions, or objects by using the `export` statement in a signed script, this information is available to any script whether signed or unsigned. The receiving script can access this information by using the `import` statement.

The receiving script must load the export script into a window or layer before it can import and use any of the exported functions.

Syntax

You create an `export` statement by using the following syntax:

```
export name1, name2, ..., nameN
export *
```

where *nameN* is a list of functions to be exported. `*` exports all functions from the script.

For more information about signed scripts, see Chapter 8, "Object Signing."

Functions

The following sections describe nested functions and the new `arguments` and `arity` properties of the `function` object.

Nested Functions

You can now nest a function within another function. To create one, you simply define it inside the body of another functions.

Syntax

The syntax for creating nested functions is no different than normal function syntax. You simply include a nested function within the curly braces of the outer function:

```
function functionA(arguments) {
...
    function functionB(arguments) {
    ...
    }
}
```

Example of a Nested Function

The following `nestedFunction.html` script defines two functions, A and B, and nests function B inside of function A. Each function returns a string when it is called.

```
<!--

                    nestedFunction.html

        This example shows how you can nest a function inside
        another one.

-->
<HTML>
  <HEAD>
    <TITLE>Nested Function</TITLE>
  </HEAD>
  <BODY>

    <SCRIPT LANGUAGE="JavaScript">
      <!-- HIDE FROM OLD BROWSERS

      //
      // function A
      //
      //    Contains one function, B. B() is called in the return
      //    statement.
      //
      function A() {

        //
        // function B
        //
        //    A function nested inside of function A. It returns
        //    a string when called.
        //
        function B() {
          return "<DD>So was B."
        }

        return "A was here<BR>" + B()
      }

      document.write(A())

      // STOP HIDING -->
    </SCRIPT>

  </BODY>
</HTML>
```

Figure 2–14 shows the result of loading the `nestedFunction.html` script.

Figure 2–14 Result of loading the `nestedFunction.html` script

Scope

When you start nesting functions, keep the scope in mind. *Scope*, in a programming language, refers to the section of program or script where a particular item such as a variable or function can be accessed. A variable or function declared inside a block of code can be used only within that block of code and within any other blocks enclosed by it after it was declared.

The scope of a nested function determines how you can reference other variables or functions. It's like being behind a one-way mirror. You can see out, but nobody can see in. For example, a nested function can see and use the arguments and variables of the outer function. Yet, the outer function cannot see or use the arguments and variables of the nested function.

Using a model of an egg and a bowl, let's look at how scoping works.

Example of Nested Functions Calling Other Functions at the Same Level

The following `nestedFcnScope.html` script shows how scoping works by setting up the functions to mimic real life. It uses the model of a bowl and an egg. In general, a bowl has no more subparts. Kind of boring. An egg, on the other hand, has a shell, yoke, and a white.

When you look at the functions, notice that `egg()` contains just a `shell()`. Inside `shell()` is a `white()` and a `yoke()`. `white()` and `yoke()` are at the same level because I couldn't remember my biology well enough to tell if a yoke is really, completely inside a white.

Functions can't see inside of their siblings. For example, `yoke()` can't see inside of `white()` and vice versa. In the same way, `bowl()` cannot see inside of `egg()`.

```
<!--

        nestedFcnScope.html


    This example shows how the nested functions white and yoke
    may be called in shell() because they are within the scope
    of shell().

-->
```

```
<HTML>
  <HEAD>
    <TITLE>Nested Function Scope</TITLE>
  </HEAD>
  <BODY>

    <SCRIPT LANGUAGE="JavaScript">
      <!-- HIDE FROM OLD BROWSERS

      function bowl() {
        return "bowl<BR>"
      }

      function egg() {

        function shell() {
            function white() {
              return "white<BR>"
        }

            function yoke() {
              return "yoke<BR>"
        }
          return "shell<BR>" + white() + yoke()
      }

        return shell()
      }

      document.write(bowl() + egg())

      // STOP HIDING -->
    </SCRIPT>

  </BODY>
</HTML>
```

Figure 2–15 shows the result of running the `nestedFcnScope.html` script.

```
┌─────────────────────────────────────────────────────────────────┐
│ ▣          Netscape: Nested Function Scope                  ▣▣   │
├─────────────────────────────────────────────────────────────────┤
│   👆     ✏️      3       🏠      🖊️     📣      📰     🖨️    🔒    🛑    │  N  │
│  Back  Forward  Reload  Home  Search  Guide  Images  Print Security Stop │
├─────────────────────────────────────────────────────────────────┤
│ Location : 📄 file:///Macintosh%20HD/Desktop%20Folder/JSBook-1.2/core/nestedFcnScope.html │
├─────────────────────────────────────────────────────────────────┤
│ bowl                                                              │
│ shell                                                             │
│ white                                                             │
│ yoke                                                              │
└─────────────────────────────────────────────────────────────────┘
```

Figure 2–15 Result of running the `nestedFcnScope.html` script

Example of a Nested Function Calling an Outer Function

The following `nestedFcnScope2.html` script continues with the bowl and egg model. It shows that if you are in an interior function you can reference a function or variable declared before it in an outer block of code. Put your frame of reference inside the function `white()`. From that vantage point, you can see the function `bowl()`, so you can call it.

```
<!--
                nestedFcnScope2.html

    This example shows how an interior function, white(), can
    use functions or variables defined in an outer scope.
    In this case, white() calls the function bowl.

-->
<HTML>
  <HEAD>
    <TITLE>Nested Function Scope</TITLE>
  </HEAD>
  <BODY>

    <SCRIPT LANGUAGE="JavaScript">
      <!-- HIDE FROM OLD BROWSERS

      function bowl() {
        return "bowl<BR>"
      }

      function egg() {
    function shell() {
      function white() {
        return "white " + bowl()
      }

      function yoke() {
```

```
      return "yoke<BR>"
    }
        return "shell<BR>" + white() + yoke()
  }
      return shell()
    }

    document.write(bowl() + egg())


    // STOP HIDING -->
  </SCRIPT>

  </BODY>
</HTML>
```

Figure 2–16 shows the result of loading the `nestedFcnScope2.html` script.

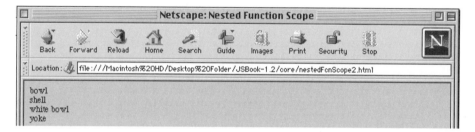

Figure 2–16 Result of loading the `nestedFcnScope2.html` script

Example of a Nested Function Calling a Function at the Wrong Level

The following `nestedFcnScopeError.html` script violates the scoping rules. The `document.write()` method calls `yoke()`. According to the scoping rules, the `document.write()` method cannot access the `yoke()` function. As a result, an error is generated when you run the script.

```
<!--

          nestedFcnScopeError.html

    A function cannot use functions or variables that are nested
    inside another function. In this example, the
    document.write() method tries to call yoke() which is nested
    deep within egg().

-->
<HTML>
  <HEAD>
    <TITLE>Nested Function Scope Error</TITLE>
  </HEAD>
```

```
<BODY>

  <SCRIPT LANGUAGE="JavaScript">
    <!-- HIDE FROM OLD BROWSERS


    function bowl() {
      return "bowl<BR>"
    }

    function egg() {
    function shell() {
    function white() {
      return "white<BR>"
    }

    function yoke() {
      return "yoke<BR>"
    }

        return "shell<BR>" + white() + yoke()
  }

      return shell()
    }

    document.write(bowl() + yoke())


    // STOP HIDING -->
  </SCRIPT>

  <P>An alert window is displayed with an error message
   stating "yoke is not defined."</P>

</BODY>
</HTML>
```

Figure 2–17 shows the result of loading the nestedFcnScopeError.html
script. Because the function is not available, an alert window is displayed with an
error message stating yoke is not defined.

Netscape: Nested Function Scope Error

Back Forward Reload Home Search Guide Images Print Security Stop

Location: file:///Macintosh%20HD/Desktop%20Folder/JSBook-1.2/core/nestedFcnScopeError.html

An alert window is displayed with an error message stating "yoke is not defined."

Jumping JavaScript
by Janice Winsor and Brian Freeman
core/nestedFcnScopeError.html

Netscape: Alert

JavaScript Error:
file:/Macintosh%20HD/Desktop%20Folder/JSBook-1.2/core/nestedFcnScopeError.html, **line 38:**

yoke is not defined.

OK

Figure 2–17 Result of loading the `nestedFcnScopeError.html` script

arguments Property

The `arguments` property of the `function` object enables you to call a function with more arguments than the function is formally declared to accept. This property can be useful when a function can be passed a variable number of arguments. You can use the `arguments.length` property to determine the number of arguments passed to the function and then deal with each argument by using the `arguments` array.

You can only access the `arguments` array from within a function declaration. An error is generated if you try to access the `arguments` array from outside of the function declaration.

`arguments` is an array that provides information about a function at the time it was invoked. In previous releases, the `arguments` array provided a list of indexed elements and a `length` property. In the JavaScript 1.2 release, it includes the following additional properties:

- Formal arguments — Each argument passed to the function at invocation.

- Local variables — Each local variable within the function.

- `caller` — Who invoked the function. If there is not a caller, the value is `undefined`.

- `callee` — A property whose value is the function reference. This property is a pointer to the function itself.

Example of Printing the Contents of the Arguments Array

The following `fcnArgs.html` script prints out the contents of the `arguments` array.

```
<!--
                fcnArgs.html

    Print the argument array the function printArguments is
    called with.

-->
<HTML>
  <HEAD>
    <TITLE>Function Arguments</TITLE>
    <SCRIPT LANGUAGE="JavaScript">
      <!-- HIDE FROM OLD BROWSERS

      //
      // Print the arguments array.
      //
      function printArguments(x) {
        for ( i=0; i < arguments.length; i++) {
          document.write(arguments[i] + " ")
        }
        document.write("<BR>")
      }

      // STOP HIDING -->
    </SCRIPT>
  </HEAD>
  <BODY>

    <P><CODE>printArguments()</CODE> expects one
      argument, <CODE>x</CODE>. If called with
      the value of <CODE>1</CODE>, the <CODE>arguments
      </CODE> array contains:</P>

    <SCRIPT LANGUAGE="JavaScript">
      <!-- HIDE FROM OLD BROWSERS

      printArguments(1)
```

```
      // STOP HIDING -->
    </SCRIPT>

    <P>Invoking <CODE>printArguments()</CODE> with:
    1, 2, 3 you get:</P>
    <SCRIPT LANGUAGE="JavaScript">
      <!-- HIDE FROM OLD BROWSERS

      printArguments(1, 2, 3)

      // STOP HIDING -->
    </SCRIPT>

  </BODY>
</HTML>
```

Figure 2–18 shows the result of loading the `fcnArgs.html` script.

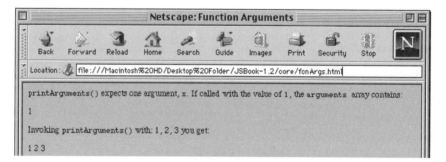

Figure 2–18 Result of loading the `fcnArgs.html` script

Example Showing the Old and New Ways to Index into the arguments Array
The following `fcnArgsFormal.html` script shows both the old and new ways to access the formal arguments of a function.

```
<!--
                fcnArgsFormal.html

    This example shows how the formal arguments of a function
    may be accessed either by indexing into the arguments
    array or, starting with JavaScript 1.2, by using
    properties of the arguments array.

-->
<HTML>
  <HEAD>
    <TITLE>Formal Function Arguments</TITLE>
    <SCRIPT LANGUAGE="JavaScript">
```

```
    <!-- HIDE FROM OLD BROWSERS

    //
    // Print the formal arguments by using indexes into the
    // arguments array.
    //
    function formalIndex(x, y) {
      document.write("x = " + arguments[0] + "<BR>")
      document.write("y = " + arguments[1] + "<BR>")
    }


    //
    // Print the formal arguments by using their properties in
    // of the arguments array. This feature became available in
    // JavaScript 1.2.
    //
    function formalProperties(x, y) {
      document.write("x = " + arguments.x + "<BR>")
      document.write("y = " + arguments.y + "<BR>")
    }

    // STOP HIDING -->
  </SCRIPT>
</HEAD>
<BODY>

  <P>Starting in JavaScript 1.2, a function's formal arguments
    are added to the <CODE>arguments</CODE> array. <BR>

    The function <CODE>formalIndex</CODE> takes two arguments,
    <CODE>x</CODE> and <CODE>y</CODE>; and prints their
    value by indexing into the <CODE>arguments</CODE> array:</P>

  <SCRIPT LANGUAGE="JavaScript">
    <!-- HIDE FROM OLD BROWSERS

    formalIndex(1, 2)

    // STOP HIDING -->
  </SCRIPT>

  <P>The function <CODE>formalProperties</CODE>, on the
    other hand, accesses its two arguments <CODE>x</CODE>
    and <CODE>y</CODE> through their properties in the
    <CODE>arguments</CODE> array:</P>

  <SCRIPT LANGUAGE="JavaScript">
```

```
<!-- HIDE FROM OLD BROWSERS

formalProperties(1, 2)

// STOP HIDING -->
</SCRIPT>

</BODY>
</HTML>
```

Figure 2–19 shows the result of loading the `fcnArgsFormal.html` script.

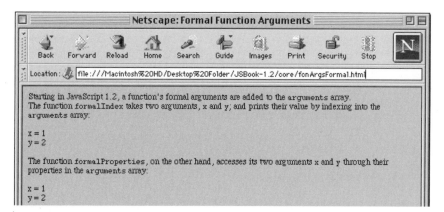

Figure 2–19 Result of loading the `fcnArgsFormal.html` script

Example of Referencing Local Variables as Properties of the arguments Array
The following `fcnArgsLocalVars.html` shows how variables local to a
function have been added as properties of the `arguments` array.

```
<!--
              fcnArgsLocalVars.html

    This example shows how, starting with JavaScript 1.2, local
    variables are accessible through properties of the arguments
    array.

-->
<HTML>
  <HEAD>
    <TITLE>Function Argument Local Variables</TITLE>
    <SCRIPT LANGUAGE="JavaScript">
      <!-- HIDE FROM OLD BROWSERS

      function localVars() {
        var x = 100
        var y = 200
```

```
        document.write("x = " + arguments.x + "<BR>")
        document.write("y = " + arguments.y + "<BR>")
    }

    // STOP HIDING -->
  </SCRIPT>
</HEAD>
<BODY>

  <P>The function <CODE>localVars</CODE> contains two
    local variables, <CODE>x</CODE> and <CODE>y</CODE>:</P>

  <SCRIPT LANGUAGE="JavaScript">
    <!-- HIDE FROM OLD BROWSERS

    localVars()

    // STOP HIDING -->
  </SCRIPT>

</BODY>
</HTML>
```

Figure 2–20 shows the result of loading the `fcnArgsLocalVars.html` script.

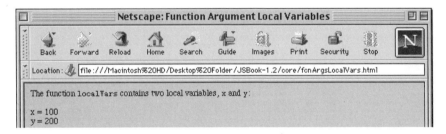

Figure 2–20 Result of loading the `fcnArgsLocalVars.html` script

Example of Using the caller Property

The following `fcnArgsCaller.html` script shows the use of the
`arguments.caller` property, which stores the value of the calling functions
arguments array. If there is no calling function, the value is `undefined`. Note that
once the function that yields `undefined` is called indirectly, calling it directly
again it does not yield `undefined`. It looks as though `arguments.caller` is
not being initialized properly.

```
<!--
                    fcnArgsCaller.html

        Show the function object's arguments array's caller
        property.

-->
<HTML>
  <HEAD>
    <TITLE>Function Arguments Caller</TITLE>
    <SCRIPT LANGUAGE="JavaScript">
      <!-- HIDE FROM OLD BROWSERS

      function a() {
        document.write("a()'s arguments array = <BR>")

        for ( i=0; i < arguments.length; i++) {
          document.write(arguments[i] + " ")
        }
        document.write("<BR>")
        b()
      }

      function b() {
        document.write("b()'s arguments.caller = <BR>")

        if (arguments.caller == null) {
          document.write("undefined")
        } else {
      for ( i=0; i < arguments.caller.length; i++) {
        document.write(arguments.caller[i] + " ")
      }
        }
        document.write("<BR>")
      }

      // STOP HIDING -->
    </SCRIPT>
  </HEAD>
<BODY>

  <P>The value of the calling functions <CODE>arguments</CODE>
    array is stored in the <CODE>caller</CODE> property of
    the <CODE>arguments</CODE> array. If there is no calling
    function, the value is <CODE>undefined</CODE>.</P>

  <P>Calling <CODE>b()</CODE> directly should yield an
   <CODE>undefined</CODE> value for <CODE>caller</CODE>.</P>
```

```
<SCRIPT LANGUAGE="JavaScript">
  <!-- HIDE FROM OLD BROWSERS

  b()

  // STOP HIDING -->
</SCRIPT>
```

<P>For example, a() calls b(). So, b()'s arguments.caller should equal a()'s arguments array.</P>

```
<SCRIPT LANGUAGE="JavaScript">
  <!-- HIDE FROM OLD BROWSERS

  a(1, 2, 3)

  // STOP HIDING -->
</SCRIPT>
```

<P>Now, an interesting thing is that if you call <CODE>b()</CODE> directly again, it doesn't yield <CODE>undefined</CODE> as before. Looks like <CODE>arguments.caller</CODE> isn't being properly initialized.</P>

```
<SCRIPT LANGUAGE="JavaScript">
  <!-- HIDE FROM OLD BROWSERS

  b()

  // STOP HIDING -->
</SCRIPT>

  </BODY>
</HTML>
```

Figure 2–21 shows the result of loading the `fcnArgsCaller.html` script.

```
┌─────────────────────────────────────────────────────────────────┐
│  □ ═══════════════ Netscape: Function Arguments Caller ════ ▣ ▣  │
│  ┌──────────────────────────────────────────────────────────┐    │
│   ◀      ▲      ▤      ⌂      ✐      ⬆      ⬛     ⬛      ⬛   │ N │
│  Back  Forward Reload  Home  Search  Guide  Images  Print Security Stop │
│  ────────────────────────────────────────────────────────────── │
│  Location: 📍 file:///Macintosh%20HD/Desktop%20Folder/JSBook-1.2/core/fcnArgsCaller.html │
│  ──────────────────────────────────────────────────────────     │
│  The value of the calling functions arguments array is stored in the caller property of the arguments │
│  array. If there is no calling function, the value is undefined.  │
│                                                                   │
│  Calling b() directly should yield an undefined value for caller. │
│                                                                   │
│  b()'s arguments.caller =                                         │
│  undefined                                                        │
│                                                                   │
│  For example, a() calls b(). So, b()'s arguments.caller should equal a()'s arguments array. │
│                                                                   │
│  a()'s arguments array =                                          │
│  1 2 3                                                            │
│  b()'s arguments.caller =                                         │
│  1 2 3                                                            │
│                                                                   │
│  Now, an interesting thing is that if you call b() directly again, it doesn't yield undefined as before. │
│  Looks like arguments.caller isn't being properly initialized.    │
│                                                                   │
│  b()'s arguments.caller =                                         │
│  1 2 3                                                            │
└─────────────────────────────────────────────────────────────────┘
```

Figure 2–21 Result of loading the `fcnArgsCaller.html` script

Example of Using the callee Property

The following `fcnArgsCallee.html` script shows an example of using the `argument.callee` property, which is simply another way of referencing the function itself.

```
<!--

              fcnArgsCallee.html

    Show the function object's arguments array's callee
    property.

-->
<HTML>
  <HEAD>
    <TITLE>Function Arguments Callee</TITLE>
    <SCRIPT LANGUAGE="JavaScript">
      <!-- HIDE FROM OLD BROWSERS

      function a() {
        document.write("a()'s callee = " + arguments.callee)
      }

      // STOP HIDING -->
    </SCRIPT>
  </HEAD>
  <BODY>
```

```
<P>The <CODE>callee</CODE> property of the
 <CODE>function</CODE> object's <CODE>arguments</CODE>
  array is simply a self-reference to the function. </P>

<SCRIPT LANGUAGE="JavaScript">
  <!-- HIDE FROM OLD BROWSERS

  a()

  // STOP HIDING -->
</SCRIPT>

</BODY>
</HTML>
```

Figure 2–22 shows the result of loading the `fcnArgsCallee.html` script.

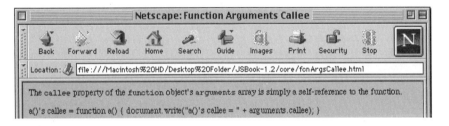

Figure 2–22 Result of loading the `fcnArgsCallee.html` script

arity Property

When the SCRIPT tag contains `"LANGUAGE = JavaScript1.2"`, the `arity` property of the `function` object indicates the number of arguments expected by a function.

Syntax

You reference the `arity` property by using the following syntax:

> `functionName.arity`

where `functionName` is the name of a function.

Example of Using the arity Property

The following `fcnArity.html` script shows how to use the `arity` property of the `function` object.

```
<!--

                    fcnArity.html

        This example shows how to use the arity property
        of the function object.

-->
<HTML>
  <HEAD>
    <TITLE>Function Arity Property</TITLE>
    <SCRIPT LANGUAGE="JavaScript1.2">
      <!-- HIDE FROM OLD BROWSERS

      function one(x) {
        document.write("one():<BR>")
        document.write("x = " + x + "<BR>")
        document.write("arity = " + arity + "<BR>")
      }

      function two(x, y) {
        document.write("two():<BR>")
        document.write("x = " + x + "<BR>")
        document.write("y = " + y + "<BR>")
        document.write("arity = " + arity + "<BR>")
      }

      // STOP HIDING -->
    </SCRIPT>
  </HEAD>
<BODY>


    <P>When the LANGUAGE attribute of the SCRIPT tag is
      "JavaScript 1.2", this property indicates the number of
      arguments expected by a function.</P>

  <P>From a function, you can directly reference the
      property as you would any local variable.</P>

    <SCRIPT LANGUAGE="JavaScript1.2">
      <!-- HIDE FROM OLD BROWSERS

  one(1)
      document.write("<BR>")
  two(1, 2)

      // STOP HIDING -->
    </SCRIPT>
```

```
<P>You can also inspect a function by referencing the
   property via <CODE>functionName.property</CODE>.</P>

<SCRIPT LANGUAGE="JavaScript1.2">
  <!-- HIDE FROM OLD BROWSERS

document.write("one()'s arity = " + one.arity + "<BR>")
document.write("two()'s arity = " + two.arity + "<BR>")

  // STOP HIDING -->
  </SCRIPT>

  </BODY>
</HTML>
```

Figure 2–23 shows the result of loading the `fcnArity.html` script.

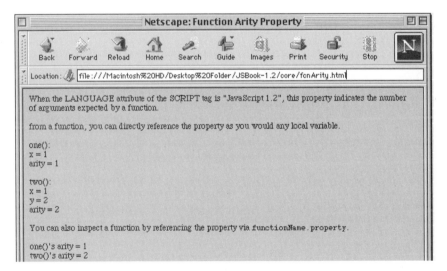

Figure 2–23 Result of loading the `fcnArity.html` script

Global Functions

Table 2-2 lists all of the JavaScript client-side global functions. Global functions that are new in the JavaScript 1.2 release are marked with an asterisk and explained in further detail in this chapter.

Table 2-2 JavaScript Client-side Global Functions

Function	Description
escape("*string*")	Encodes special characters in the specified string and returns a new string. It encodes spaces, punctuation, and any other character that is not an ASCII alphanumeric character, except for * @ - _ + . /
eval(*string*)	Evaluates a string of JavaScript code without referencing a specific object.
isNaN(*value*)	Evaluates an argument to determine if it is not a number.
Number(*object*)*	Converts the specified object to a number.
parseFloat(*string*)	Parses a string argument and returns a floating point number.
parseInt(*string*,*radix*)	Parses a string argument and returns an integer of the specified radix.
String(*object*)*	Converts the specified object to a string.
taint(*dataElement*)	Removed from Navigator 4.0. The taint() function was part of the Navigator 3.0 security model.
unescape("*string*")	Returns the ASCII string for the specified value.
untaint(*dataElement*)	Removed from Navigator 4.0. the untaint() function was part of the Navigator 3.0 security model.

Number() Function

The Number() function converts the specified object to a number.

Function

Number(*object*)

Returns

The specified object as a number. If the specified object cannot be converted to a number, returns NaN.

When *object* is a Date object, Number() returns a value in milliseconds measured from 01 January, 1970 UTC (GMT). If the date is after this date, the number is positive. If the date is before this date, the number is negative.

If *object* is a string that the Number() function cannot parse, it returns NaN.

The following number-1.html script illustrates the use of the String() and Number() functions.

```
<!--

                    number-1.html

The scripts in this document illustrate the use of the String and
Number functions.

-->

<HTML>

  <HEAD>
    <TITLE>Using String and Number Functions</TITLE>

<SCRIPT LANGUAGE="JavaScript1.2">
<!--
var strObj = new String("0.032e-2")
var errStrObj = new String("0xFF")
var numObj = new Number(12.5)
var bolObj = new Boolean(true)
var dateObj = new Date()
var strArray = new Array("12", "13", "14")
var funObj = new Function("x", "return x * x")
//-->

</SCRIPT>
  </HEAD>

  <BODY>

    <P>The following checks object conversion by String() and
Number():</P>

<SCRIPT LANGUAGE="JavaScript1.2">
<!--

document.write("String to Number = "+Number(strObj)+"<BR>")
document.write("String with Error = "+Number(errStrObj)+"<BR>")
document.write("Number to String = "+String(numObj)+"<BR>")
```

```
document.write("Boolean to Number = "+Number(bolObj)+"<BR>")
document.write("Boolean to String = "+String(bolObj)+"<BR>")
document.write("Date to Number = "+Number(dateObj)+"<BR>")
document.write("Date to String = "+String(dateObj)+"<BR>")
document.write("Array to Number = "+Number(strArray)+"<BR>")
document.write("Array to String = "+String(strArray)+"<BR>")
document.write("Function to Number = "+Number(funObj)+"<BR>")
document.write("Function to Number = "+String(funObj)+"<BR>")
//-->

</SCRIPT>
  </BODY>
</HTML>
```

Figure 2–24 shows the result of loading the `number-1.html` script.

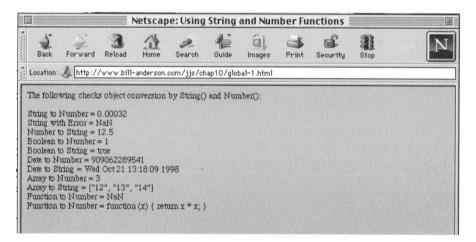

Figure 2–24 Result of loading the `number-1.html` script

String() Function

The `String()` function converts the specified object to a string.

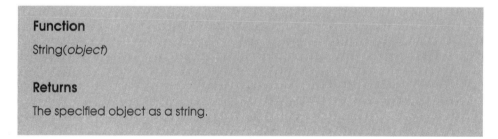

When `object` is a `Date` object, `String()` returns a string representation of the date in the format:

```
Day Month Date hh:mm:ss Timezone Year
```

For example:

```
Wed Oct 21 13:40:07 1998
```

The `number-1.html` script in the previous section also shows how to use the `String()` function to convert the `Date` object.

Literal Notation for Creating Objects

With the JavaScript 1.2 release, in addition to creating an object by using its constructor function, you can also create an object by using literal notation. When you create an object by using literal notation in a top-level script, the object is interpreted each time the script evaluates the expression containing the object literal. In addition, when you use an object literal in a function, the object is created each time the function is called.

Syntax

You use the following syntax to create an object by using literal notation:

```
objectName = { property1:value1, property2:value2, ...,
propertyN:valueN }
```

where *objectName* is the name of the new object, *propertyN* is an identifier that can be a name, a number, or a string literal. *valueN* is an expression whose value is assigned to *propertyN*.

Examples of Creating an Object by Using Literal Notation

The following `literalAssignment.html` script shows constructing an object by using the constructor function and creating the same object by using literal notation.

```
<!--

          literalAssignment.html

    This example shows how to create an object using literal
    notation.

-->
<HTML>
  <HEAD>
    <TITLE>Object Literal Notation - Assignment</TITLE>
    <SCRIPT LANGUAGE="JavaScript">
      <!-- HIDE FROM OLD BROWSERS
```

```
    // Display method for the Name object.
    //
    function displayName() {
      alert(this.firstName + " " +
      this.middleInitial + " " +
      this.lastName)
    }

    // Name Object
    //
    function Name(first, mi, last) {
      // properties
      this.firstName     = first
      this.lastName      = last
      this.middleInitial = mi
    }

    // STOP HIDING -->
  </SCRIPT>
</HEAD>
<BODY>

  <P>Before the JavaScript 1.2 release, the only way to
    create an instance of an object was to call its
    constructor. In the case of the Name object,
    defined in the HEAD of this page, you would create
    a new instance as follows:</P>

  <DL>
    <DT><CODE>var aName = new Name("Brian", "K.",
    "Freeman")</CODE>
  </DL>

  <SCRIPT LANGUAGE="JavaScript">
    <!-- HIDE FROM OLD BROWSERS

    // global variable that stores name input from the form
    var aName = new Name("Brian", "K.", "Freeman")


    // STOP HIDING -->
  </SCRIPT>

  <P>With JavaScript 1.2, you can create an object using
    literal notation. So the above becomes:

  <DL>
    <DT><CODE>var theName = { firstN:"Brian", mi:"K.",
```

```
    lastN:"Freeman" }</CODE>
  </DL>

  <SCRIPT LANGUAGE="JavaScript1.2">
    <!-- HIDE FROM OLD BROWSERS

  var theName = { firstN:"Brian", mi:"K.", lastN:"Freeman" }

    // STOP HIDING -->
  </SCRIPT>

  </BODY>
</HTML>
```

Figure 2–25 shows the result of loading the `literalAssignment.html` script.

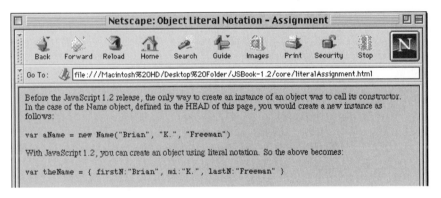

Figure 2–25 Result of loading the `literalAssignment.html` script

Example of Creating an Object with a Property

The following `literalProperty.html` script shows how to embed another object as a property of an object created with literal notation.

```
<!--
              literalProperty.html

    This example shows how an object defined with literal
    notation can have another object embedded as a property.

-->
<HTML>
  <HEAD>
    <TITLE>Object Literal Notation - Property</TITLE>
  </HEAD>
  <BODY>

    <P>Using literal notation, you can define an object that
```

embeds another object as a property. You simply repeat the
parentheses when assigning the value to the property. As
so:

```
<DL>
  <DT><CODE>var myCar = { make:"aMake", model:"aModel", engine:{
cyl:"8", hpr:"200" }, color:"red" }</CODE>
</DL>

<SCRIPT LANGUAGE="JavaScript">
  <!-- HIDE FROM OLD BROWSERS

  var myCar = { make:"aMake",
                model:"aModel",
                engine:{ cyl:"8", hpr:"200" },
                color:"red"
              }

  // STOP HIDING -->
</SCRIPT>

    </BODY>
  </HTML>
```

Figure 2–26 shows the result of loading the `literalProperty.html` script.

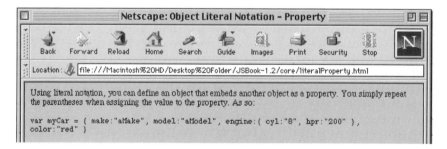

Figure 2-26 Result of loading the `literalProperty.html` script

Example of an Object Based on a Conditional

The following `literalConditional.html` script creates an object that is based
on the value of the conditional statement, `aCondition`. The object is created with
a different value. The object is interpreted each time the conditional statement is
evaluated.

```
<!--
              literalConditional.html

    Based on a condition, the value of an object is defined
```

```
    differently by using literal notation.

-->
<HTML>
  <HEAD>
    <TITLE>Object Literal Notation - Conditional</TITLE>
  </HEAD>
  <BODY>


    <P>Using literal notation, you can easily define the
      value of an object based on a condition.</P>

    <P><CODE>aCondition</CODE>'s value = </P>
    <SCRIPT LANGUAGE="JavaScript">
      <!-- HIDE FROM OLD BROWSERS
      var aCondition = true

      if (aCondition == true) {
        anObject = { aProp:"aValue" }
      } else {
        anObject = { aProp:"anotherValue" }
      }

      document.write(anObject.aProp)

      // STOP HIDING -->
    </SCRIPT>

  </BODY>
</HTML>
```

Figure 2–27 shows the result of loading the `literalConditional.html` script.

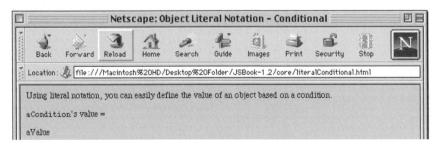

Figure 2–27 Result of loading the `literalConditional.html` script

Style Sheets

Style sheets enable you, as creator of Web pages, to control fonts, colors, and layouts. Before style sheets were introduced, the user's browser determined what fonts were available and how the text was displayed and positioned on the page.

With style sheets, you have greater control over the presentation of your Web documents. Style sheets enable you to specify stylistic attributes, such as text color, margins, alignment of elements, of your Web page as well as to specify font styles, font sizes, and font weights for specific HTML tags, such as paragraphs and headings. In addition, multiple Web pages can use a single existing style sheet as a template or master page. You can think of style sheets as being like templates for word processing applications.

Style sheets are a part of the functionality provided by dynamic HTML. The other components of dynamic HTML are content positioning (layers) and downloadable fonts, which are described in subsequent chapters. You can use any of the dynamic HTML elements independently. For example, you can create a document with a style sheet without using layers or downloadable fonts. For information about content positioning, see Chapter 4, "Positioning HTML Content." For information about downloadable fonts, see Chapter 5, "Dynamic and Downloadable Fonts."

Netscape Communicator 4.x supports two types of syntax for designing style sheets:

- Cascading Style Sheets (CSS)

- JavaScript style sheets

CSS is the static approach to specifying style, and JavaScript is the programmatic approach. When you define a CSS style sheet, you specify its type as `"text/CSS"`. A JavaScript style sheet has a type of `"text/JavaScript"`. Although you can define style sheets by using JavaScript syntax, the CSS standard is much more widely used; we recommend that you follow the trend. The primary emphasis in this chapter is on how to create CSS style sheets. We do include brief examples of JavaScript syntax at the end of the chapter.

Cascading style sheets are collections of rules formed into style sheets. Cascading style sheets are called cascading because more than one style sheet can influence the presentation of a document. Different style sheets are thought of as coming in a series or cascade.

Style sheets can come from multiple sources:

- The browser

- The Web page designer

- The user (possibly)

Each browser has a default style sheet that describes how it displays a document that does not have its own style sheet. The default style sheet contains all the presentation style rules that Web designers have come to expect; for example, to italicize text inside the <EM> element. This default style sheet is merged with any other style sheets the author or user has associated with the document. Because the default style sheet always includes the common presentation rules, Web page authors and users do not need to put them into their style sheets.

Any conflicts between style sheets are resolved by the browser. Usually, the designer's style sheet has the highest priority claim on the document, followed by the user's and then the browser's default style sheet.

CSS1 became a W3C recommendation in December 1996. CSS2 became a W3C recommendation in May 1998. Currently, no browsers support CSS2, but they're on the way. CSS are supported by both Netscape Communicator 4.x and Internet

Explorer 4.x. This chapter describes the Netscape Communicator 4.x implementation of CSS. If you are interested in reviewing the original specifications, refer to: http://www.w3.org/TR/REC-CSS1 and http://www.w3.org/TR/REC-CSS2.

HTML Brushup — <STYLE></STYLE> Tags

HTML 4.0 provides <STYLE></STYLE> tags to enable you to specify styles for a set of attributes. You can define styles by using either CSS or JavaScript syntax. You specify the style as part of the opening <STYLE> tag, list the attributes and values for each HTML tag-identifier, and close with the </STYLE> tag.

CSS Syntax:

```
<STYLE TYPE="text/css">
    tag-identifier (attribute:value;}
</STYLE>
```

The following example changes the font family of <P> tags to Helvetica:

```
<STYLE TYPE="text.css">
    p (font-family:Helvetica;}
</STYLE>
```

JavaScript Syntax:

```
<STYLE TYPE="text/JavaScript">
    document.tags.tag-identifier.attribute="value"
</STYLE>
```

The following example change the font family of <P> tags to Helvetica:

```
<STYLE TYPE="text/JavaScript">
    document.tags.p.fontFamily="Helvetica"
</STYLE>
```

Style Sheet Properties

Regardless of whether you use CSS or JavaScript syntax, a style sheet is nothing more than a collection of stylistic properties or attributes and the values that you specify. You specify these values either as part of the <STYLE></STYLE> HTML

tags, or by using the STYLE attribute within a specific HTML tag. You first
identify whether you are specifying a CSS or JavaScript style, list the properties
you want to use, assign values to them, and then apply the style to text.

Table 3-1 lists the complete set of properties you can use for both CSS and
JavaScript style sheets. Note that the syntax is different for each type of style
sheet. JavaScript properties are case sensitive. CSS properties are case insensitive.

Table 3-1 Style Sheet Properties

CSS Property	JavaScript Property	Possible Values
background-color	backgroundColor	A named color, such as blue; a 6-digit hexadecimal value, such as #0000FF; or an rgb color value, such as rgb(0%, 0%, 100%).
background-image	backgroundImage	URL.
border-color	borderColor	none, a named color, such as blue; a 6-digit hexadecimal value, such as #0000FF; or an rgb color value, such as rgb(0%, 0%, 100%).
border-style	borderStyle	none, solid, double, inset, outset, groove, or ridge. You must also set a border width for these settings to be visible.
border-top-width, border-bottom-width, border-left-width, border-right-width	borderTopWidth, borderBottomWidth, borderLeftWidth, borderRightWidth	Length as a numerical measurement with a value, such as 0.4in, 18pt.
border-width	borderWidths()	Length as a numerical measurement with a value, such as 0.4in, 18pt. Set all border widths with one property. Arguments are top, right, bottom, and left, in that order.
color	color	A named color, such as blue; a 6-digit hexadecimal value, such as #0000FF; or an rgb color value, such as rgb(0%, 0%, 100%).
display	display	block, inline, list-item, none.

Table 3-1 Style Sheet Properties (Continued)

CSS Property	JavaScript Property	Possible Values
float	align (float is a reserved word in JavaScript)	Align an element within its parent. left, right, none.
font-family	fontFamily	serif, sans-serif, cursive, monospace, fantasy, or the name of a specific font family such as Helvetica or Arial.
font-size	fontSize	larger, smaller, xx-small, x-small, small, medium, large, x-large, xx-large, a length such as 24pt, or a percentage, such as 120%.
font-style	fontStyle	normal or italic.
font-weight	fontWeight	normal, bold, bolder, lighter, or a value from 100 to 900, with 400 as normal and 700 as bold.
line-height	lineHeight	normal; a number without a unit of measurement to multiply the font size of the current element by the numerical value; length, as a numerical measurement with a value, such as 0.4in, 18pt; or percentage of the element's font size, such as 120%.
list-style-type	listStyleType	disc, circle, square, decimal, lower-roman, upper-roman, lower-alpha, upper-alpha, none.
margin-left, margin-right, margin-top, margin-bottom	marginLeft, marginRight, marginTop, marginBottom	auto; length as a numerical measurement with a value, such as 0.4in, 18pt; or percentage of the element's font size, such as 120%.
margin	margins()	Set all margins at once. Arguments are top, right, bottom, and left margin values, in that order.

Table 3-1 Style Sheet Properties (Continued)

CSS Property	JavaScript Property	Possible Values
`padding-top`, `padding-right`, `padding-bottom`, `padding-left`	`paddingTop`, `paddingRight`, `paddingBottom`, `paddingLeft`	Length as a numerical measurement with a value, such as `0.4in`, `18pt`; or percentage of the element's font size, such as `120%`.
`paddings`	`paddings()`	Set all paddings at once. Arguments are top, right, bottom, and left padding values, in that order.
`text-align`	`textAlign`	`left`, `right`, `center`, `justify`.
`text-decoration`	`textDecoration`	`none`, `underline`, `line-through`, `blink`.
`text-indent`	`textIndent`	Length as a numerical value with units, such as `3em`; or percentage of the parent element's width, such as `25%`.
`text-transform`	`textTransform`	`capitalize`, `uppercase`, `lowercase`, `none`.
`white-space`	`whiteSpace`	`normal`, `pre`.
`width`	`width`	`auto`; length as a numerical measurement with a value, such as `0.4in`, `18pt`; or percentage of the element's font size, such as `120%`.

The border, margin, and padding properties enable you to control the space around each element. The background color and image properties enable you to specify a color or an image to use as the background

You can think of the elements as a set of nested boxes. The following `spaces.html` script illustrates the nested structure and shows the `border`, `margin`, and `padding` properties for a `<P>` element. On the outside it has a transparent margin of 10 pixels that lets the background color show through, then a blue border of 10 pixels, followed by padding of 20 more pixels, then the text content.

```
<!--

                        spaces.html

    This example shows the various spaces: margin, border and
    padding of a block level element. It accomplishes this by
```

```
     setting values for each attribute.

  -->
  <HTML>
    <HEAD>
      <TITLE>Element Spaces</TITLE>
      <STYLE TYPE="text/css">
        <!-- /* Hide from browsers that don't support */

        #aLayer {
                   position:           absolute;
                   left:                50px;
                   top:               100px;
                   border:            1px;
                   background-color:  orange;
                 }


            p {
                   margin:            10px;
                   border:            10px ridge blue;
                   padding:           20px;
                   background-color:  yellow;
                 }
         -->
      </STYLE>
    </HEAD>
    <BODY>

      <DIV ID="aLayer"><P>This space is the content of a P
      element. A transparent margin of 10 pixels is outside,
      enclosing a blue border of 10 pixels, followed by padding
      of 20 more pixels before this text.</P></DIV>

    </BODY>
  </HTML>
```

Figure 3–1 marks the `spaces.html` script with the location of the margin, border, padding, and content.

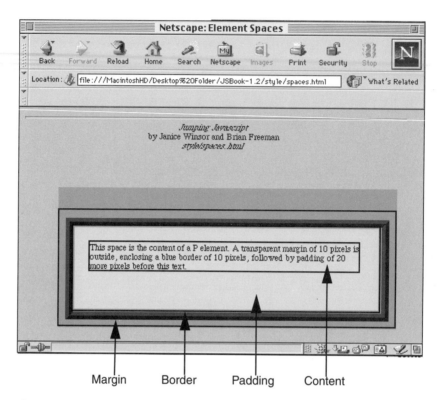

Margin   Border   Padding   Content

Figure 3–1 Location of margin, border, padding, and content

Comments in CSS

CSS support comments in standard C style to enable you to put comments in your style sheets. Each comment begins with a slash and an asterisk (/*) and ends with an asterisk and a slash (*/):

```
/* This comment is used with CSS syntax */
```

CSS Syntax

A *rule* is a statement about one stylistic aspect of one or more elements in a style sheet. A *style sheet* contains one or more rules. You can specify a style for each HTML tag such as H1 or P by identifying a style property such as font-size and then by assigning a value to it. The HTML tag is called the *selector*. The curly braces containing the property, the colon, and the value make a *declaration*, as illustrated below.

Note – You do not use the angle braces (<>) when you specify the name of an HTML tag for which you want to define a style.

The syntax for a CSS rule is shown below:

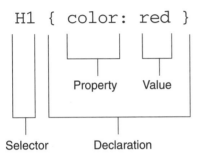

A rule has two parts:

- Selector — The part before the left curly brace
- Declaration — The part within the curly braces

A declaration has two parts separated by a colon:

- Property — The part before the colon
- Value — The part after the colon

To apply CSS styles throughout a document, you define the style type as text/css by including the following statement in the head of the document:

```
<STYLE TYPE="text/css">
```

You then include rules for the HTML tags you want to define, concluding the definitions with a </STYLE> tag. Refer to the HTML Brushup box for details about <STYLE> tag syntax.

Note – If you miss a semicolon when combining rules, the style definitions are ignored.

The following cssStyle.html script shows a basic example of the <STYLE> tag. It includes comments to hide from other browsers and basic font and margin definitions for the <H1> and <P> tags. To keep the example short, some of the text has been omitted from the example. The complete script is available on the CD-ROM.

```
<!--

              cssStyle.html

    An example of a CSS style sheet.

-->
<HTML>
  <HEAD>
    <TITLE>CSS STYLE Tag</TITLE>

    <STYLE TYPE="text/css">
      <!-- /* Hide from browsers that don't support */

      h1 { font-size:14pt; }
      p { font-size:12pt; margin-left:10%; margin-right:10%;}

      -->
    </STYLE>
  </HEAD>
<BODY>

    <H1>Janice Winsor</H1>
    <H2>ARTIST'S STATEMENT</H2>

    <P>I have developed my own techniques to paint dream images,
      which are the inspiration for many of my paintings.  I
      design stencils from the human form, experimenting with the
      minimum abstract form required to suggest a human figure.
      There is a constant shifting dialogue between figure and
      ground.  In addition to stencils being used as an integral
      part of painting compositions, they become art objects in
      themselves.</P>

  ...

    </BODY>
</HTML>
```

Figure 3–2 shows the result of loading the `cssStyle.html` script.

Netscape: CSS STYLE Tag

Back Forward Reload Home Search Guide Images Print Security Stop   N

Location: file:///MacintoshHD/Desktop%20Folder/JSBook-1.2/style/cssStyle.html

Janice Winsor

ARTIST'S STATEMENT

I have developed my own techniques to paint dream images, which are the inspiration for many of my paintings. I design stencils from the human form, experimenting with the minimum abstract form required to suggest a human figure. There is a constant shifting dialogue between figure and ground. In addition to stencils being using as an integral part of painting compositions, they become art objects in themselves.

I use a variety of techniques to translate the designs into a finished piece. Sometimes I transfer the images onto canvas with spray paint. At other times I cut the stencils into paper or into photographs I have taken. Additional images sprayed onto the glass frequently complete the composition.

Experimentation with different photographic techniques such as overlapping images, double exposures, multiple refractive lenses, and closeups of other paintings provide warped images that are less representational than traditional photography.

I am also exploring the potentials of alternate photographic processes for creating "sun prints" that include cyanotype, Van Dyke, and salt printing. I paint photosensitive chemicals on paper and develop the prints by putting stencil drawings or objects on the paper and exposing them to the sun. On some of these sun prints, I combine different chemical processes, multiple exposures, and overlapping images.

These techniques provide me with an expressive mixture of realism and surrealism. I shift perspectives and scale, overlapping images to give the paintings a dreamlike quality.

To my photography, I bring my artistic sense of form and composition to show the beauty of wildlife and nature. I particularly enjoy taking closeup photographs of objects to emphasize the beauty of the small.

ONE-ARTIST SHOWS-Paintings

- June 1-30, 1991, San Carlos Library, San Carlos, CA
- August 1-September 30, 1990, Terman Park Library, Palo Alto, CA

You are offline. Choose "Go Online..." to connect.

Figure 3–2 Result of loading the `cssStyle.html` script

You can specify more than one property per declaration as a comma-separated list. For example, you can combine the following three rules:

```
H1 { font-weight: bold }
H2 { font-weight: bold }
H3 { font-weight: bold }
```

into a single rule:

```
H1, H2, H3 { font-weight: bold }
```

This rule produces the same result as the first three individual rules.

You can combine more than one declaration within a selector by specifying them as a semicolon-separated list.

For example, you could write a style sheet with the following two rules:

```
H1 { color: red }
H1 { text-align: center }
```

Alternatively, you can group the declarations that relate to the same sector into a semicolon-separated list:

```
H1 {
  color: red;
  text-align: center;
}
```

The following `grouping.html` script specifies the same left margin for the `<H2>` and `<H3>` tags.

```
<!--

                 grouping.html


     This example shows how to group CSS styles in the same rule.

-->
<HTML>
  <HEAD>
    <TITLE>Grouping of Styles</TITLE>

    <STYLE TYPE="text/css">
      <!-- /* Hide from browsers that don't support */

      h1        { text-transform:uppercase; }
      h2,h3     { margin-left:5%; }
      p         { font-size:12pt;
                  margin-left:10%;
                  margin-right:10%;
                }
      -->
    </STYLE>
  </HEAD>
<BODY>

    <H1>This is a heading 1</H1>
    <P>This paragraph has a 12 point font. The right and left
      margins are set at 10 percent.</P>

    <H2>This is a heading 2</H2>
    <P>This paragraph has a 12 point font. The right and left
      margins are set at 10 percent.</P>
```

```
<H3>This is a heading 3</H3>
<P>This paragraph has a 12 point font. The right and left
   margins are set at 10 percent.</P>

</BODY>
</HTML>
```

Figure 3–3 shows the result of loading the `grouping.html` script.

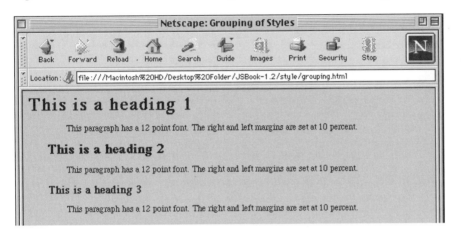

Figure 3–3 Result of loading the `grouping.html` script

For any style sheet to affect the HTML document, you must incorporate it into that file. In other words, the style sheet and the HTML document must be combined so that they can work together to produce the whole document.

You can incorporate style sheets in an HTML document in any of the following ways:

- Use the <STYLE> tag to apply the basic style sheet document wide.

- Use the STYLE attribute to apply a style sheet to an individual tag.

- Use the <LINK> tag to link an external style sheet to the document. Use this method to reference alternative style sheets that the browser can use if a previous one cannot be displayed.

- Use the SRC attribute to the <STYLE> tag to link an external style sheet to the document.

- Use the CSS @import notation to import a style sheet. Use this method to automatically import and merge an external style sheet with the current style sheet.

You can incorporate multiple style sheets by using any combination of these ways. When you combine style sheets, STYLE attributes take precedence over style sheets defined in a <STYLE> tag, which take precedence over those imported by using the SRC attribute of the <STYLE> tag, the <LINK> tag, or the @import notation. If all style sheets are imported, styles are applied sequentially in the order in which the style sheets are listed in the Web page. The style defined in the last style sheet is applied last.

Specifying a Style for an Individual HTML Tag

You can specify different styles for individual HTML tags by including the STYLE attribute as part of the tag definition. The following styleAttribute.html script contains two separate definitions for the <P> tag, with different colors and font sizes for each.

```
<!--

             styleAttribute.html


             This example shows how to specify CSS style
             attributes in the body of a document.
-->
<HTML>
  <HEAD>
    <TITLE>CSS Style Attribute in Body Elements</TITLE>
  </HEAD>
  <BODY>

    <P STYLE="color:red;fontSize:18pt">"You can't have
      everything. Where would you put it?"</P>
    <P STYLE="fontSize:12pt">-Steven Wright-</P>

  </BODY>
</HTML>
```

Figure 3–4 shows the result of loading the styleAttribute.html script. Although you can't tell from the screen print, the first line is red and the second is black.

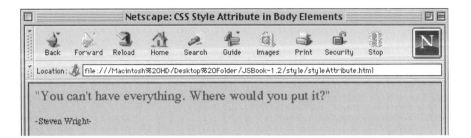

Figure 3–4 Result of loading the `styleAttribute.html` script

Importing an External Style Sheet with the <LINK> Tag

You can store your styles in a separate document and import external style sheets into the page by using the `<LINK>` tag.

HTML Brushup — <LINK> Tag

Use the <LINK> tag to import an external document into a Web page.

<LINK>	Import an external document
REL	Define the relationship of the document. For style sheets, you specify the value REL="stylesheet". Other possible values are Alternate, Start, Next, Prev, Contents, Index, Glossary, Copyright, Section, Subsection, Appendix, Help, and Bookmark.
TYPE	The type of style sheet, either "text/css" or "text/JavaScript"
HREF	The URL for the style sheet you are importing
TITLE	The name of the style sheet

The following example uses the <LINK> tag to import first a CSS and then a JavaScript style sheet:

<LINK REL="stylesheet" TYPE="text/css" HREF="style.css">

<LINK REL="stylesheet" TYPE="text/javascript" HREF="style2.jss">

The following `style.css` style sheet specifies body color and font family, alignment for `<H1>` tags, font size and margins for `<P>` tags, background margins and padding for `<UL>` tags, and color, background, margin, and padding for `<LI>` tags.

```
/* style.css */
body
  {
  color:black;
  font-family:courier;
  }

h1
  {
  text-align:center;
  }

p
  {
  font-size:12pt;
  margin-left:10%;
  margin-right:10%;
  }

ul
  {
  background: white;
  margin: 16pt 4pt 4pt 16pt;
  padding: 8pt 2pt 2pt 8pt;
  }

li
  {
  color: red;
  background: blue;
  margin: 8pt 2pt 2pt 8pt;
  padding: 4pt 2pt 2pt 4pt;

  }
```

The following `cssLink.html` script imports `style.css` to the document.

```
<!--

                cssLink.html

    The example shows the style contained in style.css being
    imported with the LINK element.

-->
<HTML>
  <HEAD>
    <TITLE>CSS Link Element</TITLE>
    <LINK REL="stylesheet" TYPE="text/css" HREF="style.css"
TITLE="myStyle">
```

```
</HEAD>
<BODY>

   <H1>Sculpture Curriculum Vitae of:</H1>
   <H1>Maris Raudzins</H1>

   <P>D.O.B. 27/03/46</P>

   <P>Arrived in Australia 1949</P>

   <P>Studied Architecture</P>

   <P>Studied Graphics at Claremont Technical College</P>

...
   </BODY>
</HTML>
```

Figure 3–5 shows the result of loading the `cssLink.html` script.

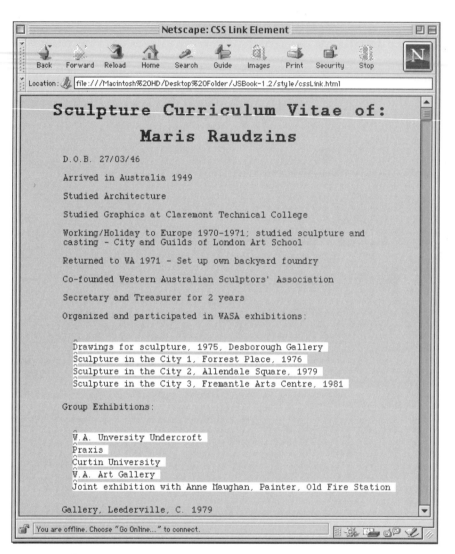

Figure 3–5 Result of loading the `cssLink.html` script

Importing an External Style Sheet by Using the SRC Attribute of the <STYLE> Tag

The <STYLE> tag has an SRC attribute that you can use to import style sheets defined in external files. If you specify multiple style sheets by using the SRC attribute, the styles are applied in the order the style sheets are listed. Styles defined by the STYLE attribute for a specific HTML tag have precedence over styles defined in the <STYLE> tag as well as those defined in external files.

The following `cssSrc.html` script uses the SRC attribute of the `<STYLE>` tag to import the external `style.css` style sheet. Note that the SRC attribute does not currently work in Communicator 4.0.3 on the Mac, PC, or UNIX platforms. To keep the example short, some of the text has been omitted from the example. The complete script is available on the CD-ROM.

```
<!--
                cssSrc.html

     The example shows the SRC attribute of the STYLE tag.

-->
<HTML>
  <HEAD>
    <TITLE>CSS Style SRC Attribute </TITLE>
    <STYLE TYPE="text/css" SRC="style.css"></STYLE>
  </HEAD>
  <BODY>

    <H1>Sculpture Curriculum Vitae of:</H1>
    <H1>Maris Raudzins</H1>

    <P>D.O.B. 27/03/46</P>

    <P>Arrived in Australia 1949</P>

    <P>Studied Architecture</P>

    <P>Studied Graphics at Claremont Technical College</P>

 ...
  </BODY>
</HTML>
```

Figure 3–6 shows the result of loading the `cssSrc.html` script.

```
╔══════════ Netscape: CSS Style SRC Attribute ══════════╗
║  Back  Forward  Reload  Home  Search  Guide  Images  Print  Security  Stop    N  ║
║  Location: file:///MacintoshHD/Desktop%20Folder/JSBook-1.2/style/cssSrc.html    ║
╠════════════════════════════════════════════════════════╣
```

Sculpture Curriculum Vitae of:

Maris Raudzins

D.O.B. 27/03/46

Arrived in Australia 1949

Studied Architecture

Studied Graphics at Claremont Technical College

Working/Holiday to Europe 1970-1971; studied sculpture and casting - City and Guilds of London Art School

Returned to WA 1971 - Set up own backyard foundry

Co-founded Western Australian Sculptors' Association

Secretary and Treasurer for 2 years

Organized and participated in WASA exhibitions:

- Drawings for sculpture, 1975, Desborough Gallery
- Sculpture in the City 1, Forrest Place, 1976
- Sculpture in the City 2, Allendale Square, 1979
- Sculpture in the City 3, Fremantle Arts Centre, 1981

Group Exhibitions:

- W.A. Unversity Undercroft
- Praxis
- Curtin University
- W.A. Art Gallery
- Joint exhibition with Anne Maughan, Painter, Old Fire Station

Gallery, Leederville, C. 1979

Figure 3–6 Result of loading the `cssSrc.html` script on the Mac

Importing a Style Sheet by Using the CSS @import Notation

Although you should be able to use the @import notation as another way to import an external style sheet, this notation does not work in Communicator 4.0.3 on the Mac, PC, or UNIX platforms. This notation may not be supported by Netscape. The following `cssImport.html` script shows the syntax for importing a file using @import.

```
<!--
```

```
                    cssImport.html
```

```
        The example shows the style contained in style.css being
        imported with the CSS @import notation.
```

```
-->
<HTML>
  <HEAD>
    <TITLE>CSS Import Notation</TITLE>
    <STYLE TYPE="text/css">
      <!-- /* Hide from browsers that don't support */
      @import url(style.css);
      -->
    </STYLE>
  </HEAD>
  <BODY>

    <H1>Sculpture Curriculum Vitae of:</H1>
    <H1>Maris Raudzins</H1>

    <P>D.O.B. 27/03/46</P>

    <P>Arrived in Australia 1949</P>

    <P>Studied Architecture</P>

    <P>Studied Graphics at Claremont Technical College</P>

  . . .

  </BODY>
</HTML>
```

Figure 3–7 shows the result of loading the `cssImport.html` script in a Mac Navigator browser. As you can see by comparing this figure with Figure 3–5, the `style.css` style sheet has not been applied to the document and it displays with the default specifications.

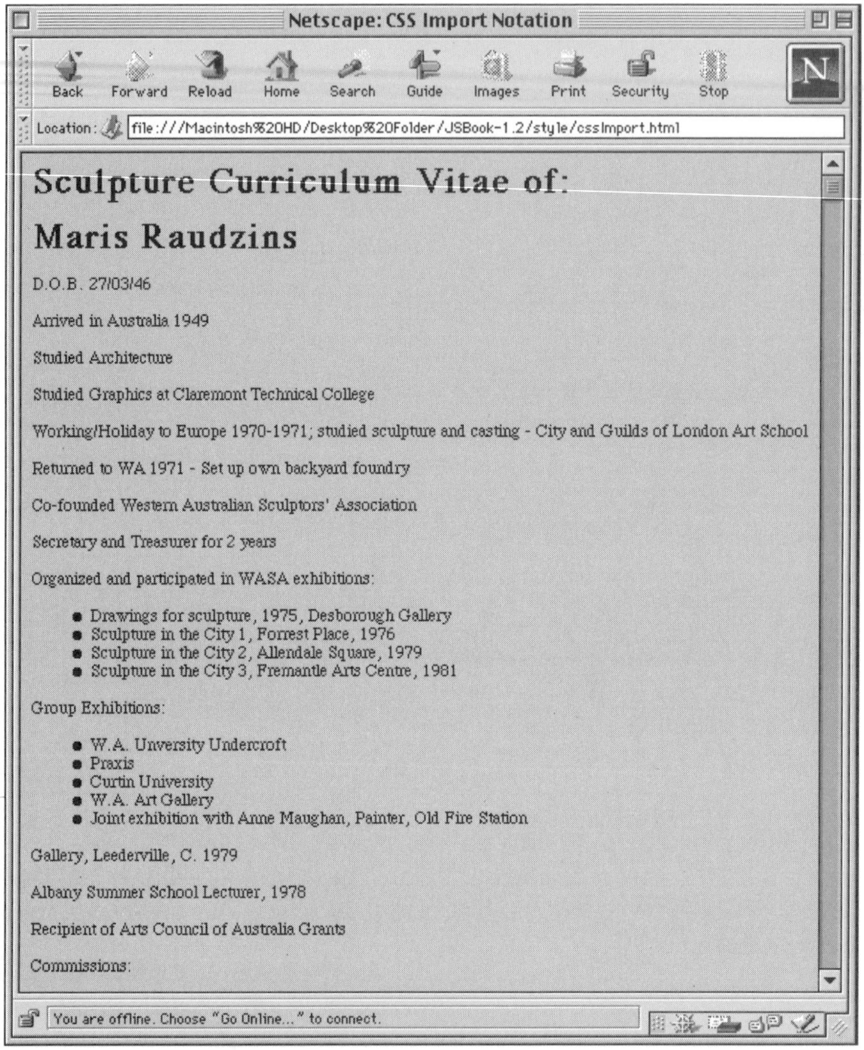

Figure 3–7 Result of loading the `cssImport.html` script

Inheriting Styles

Styles for individual HTML tags are hierarchical. An HTML tag that contains
another element is considered to be the *parent* element. The element contained by
the parent element is considered to be its *child* element.

In many cases, child elements inherit or acquire the styles of their parent elements. For example, if you specify a body color of red and a font of courier, then all of the child elements inherit the same style attributes.

Parent-Child Inheritance

If you change the font of a child element such as <B> or <EM>, the text uses the specified emphasis but still maintains the style elements specified for the body of the document.

The following inheritance.html script defines a body color of red and a font family of courier. The text also contains a phrase that has bold emphasis. Note that when you load the script, the bold text is bold red courier.

```
<!--
                inheritance.html

                This example shows how style is inherited from the
                BODY tag. P and B descend from the BODY tag, and
                thus they inherit its style.

-->
<HTML>
  <HEAD>
    <TITLE>Inheritance</TITLE>
  </HEAD>
  <BODY STYLE="color:red; font-family:courier;">

    <H1>A Header</H1>

    <P>This is text in a &lt;p&gt; tag. If we <B>bold
    something</B>, note the text change.</P>

  </BODY>
</HTML>
```

Figure 3–8 shows the result of loading the inheritance.html script.

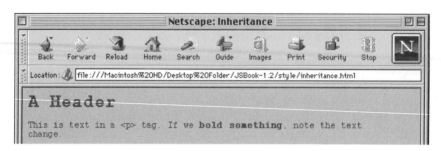

Figure 3-8 Result of loading the `inheritance.html` script

Controlling the Style of Child Elements

Even though the child elements inherit the style of the parent, you can control the style of child elements independently of the body attributes by specifying the style as part of the individual HTML tag itself.

The following `inheritance2.html` script assigns a color of blue and a font family of Times to the HTML `<B>` tag.

```
<!--

              inheritance2.html

              This example shows that the child can modify
              the parent's style.

-->
<HTML>
  <HEAD>
    <TITLE>Inheritance</TITLE>
  </HEAD>
  <BODY STYLE="color:red; font-family:courier">

    <H1>A Header</H1>

    <P>This is text in a &lt;p&gt; tag. If we <b style="color:
    blue;font-family:times">bold something</B>, note the
    text change.</P>

  </BODY>
</HTML>
```

Figure 3–9 shows the result of loading the `inheritance2.html` script.

```
┌─────────────────────────────────────────────────────────────┐
│░░░░░░░░░░░░░░░░░░░░ Netscape: Inheritance ░░░░░░░░░░░░░░ 凹 目 │
├─────────────────────────────────────────────────────────────┤
│  ↰      ◇      ⭲     🏠     🔍     👆     🞄     🞄     🞄    [N] │
│ Back  Forward Reload  Home  Search  Guide Images Print Security Stop│
├─────────────────────────────────────────────────────────────┤
│ Location: 🔖 file:///Macintosh%20HD/Desktop%20Folder/JSBook-1.2/style/inheritance2.html│
├─────────────────────────────────────────────────────────────┤
│ A Header                                                      │
│ This is text in a <p> tag. If we bold something, note the text change.│
└─────────────────────────────────────────────────────────────┘
```

Figure 3–9 Result of loading the `inheritance2.html` script

Marking a Section of Text for a Style

You can mark a section of text to use a particular style by using the
`<SPAN></SPAN>` tags. The following `span.html` script changes the color and
font family for the phrase enclosed within the `<SPAN></SPAN>` tags.

HTML Brushup — <SPAN></SPAN> Tag

Use the <SPAN></SPAN> tags to mark a section of text to use a particular style.
page.

<SPAN>	Mark the beginning of the section of text to use the specified style
STYLE	Specify the style
CLASS	Specify a style by using the name of a class
</SPAN>	Mark the end of the text

The following example changes the color and font family of the marked text:

<P>This text uses the default style. <SPAN STYLE="color: green; font-family:
courier">This text is green courier.</SPAN></P>

```
<!--

                span.html

         This example shows how to use the SPAN tag
         to mark a section of text for a style.

-->
<HTML>
  <HEAD>
    <TITLE>SPAN Tag</TITLE>
```

```
    </HEAD>
    <BODY>
      <H1>A Header</H1>

      <P>This is text in a
        <SPAN STYLE="color: blue;font-family:courier"> &lt;p&gt;
            </SPAN> tag. If we <B>bold something</B>,
        <SPAN STYLE="color: green; font-family:courier"> note
            the text change.</SPAN></P>

    </BODY>
</HTML>
```

Figure 3–10 shows the result of loading the span.html script. The color and font of <P> and note the text change are changed.

Figure 3–10 Result of loading the span.html script

Defining Classes of Styles

When a document includes a style sheet or imports one, all of the styles defined in the style sheet can be used in the document.

At times, however, you may want to selectively apply a style to HTML tags. For example, you might want some of the paragraphs in a document to be red and others to be blue.

To define a class, first you specify the style class in the style sheet, then you use the CLASS attribute to apply that style to the individual HTML tags.

You can either specify, by name, which HTML tags can use a style. Alternatively, you can use the keyword all to enable all elements to use the style class.

The following cssClass.html script uses the all keyword to define two classes—ared and ablue—and then applies them to different <P> tags.

```
<!--
               cssClass.html
-->
<HTML>
  <HEAD>
    <TITLE>Classes of Styles - CSS Syntax</TITLE>
    <STYLE TYPE="text/css">
      <!--

      all.ablue { color: blue; font-Size: 18pt; }
      all.ared { color: red;  font-Size:  12pt; }

      -->
    </STYLE>
  </HEAD>
  <BODY>

    <P>This paragraph uses the default style. </P>
    <P CLASS = ablue>This paragraph uses the style class
      ablue.</P>
    <P CLASS = ared>This paragraph uses the style class
      ared.</P>

  </BODY>
</HTML>
```

Figure 3–11 shows the result of loading the `cssClass.html` script.

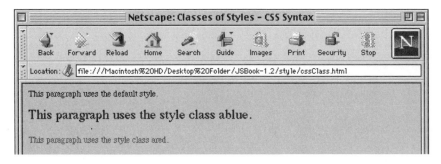

Figure 3–11 Result of loading the `cssClass.html` script

You can also define classes that can be used only for specific HTML tags. You identify the specific tag by name before the class name instead of using the `all` keyword:

```
tagname.classname {style specifications}
```

The following `cssClassElement.html` script defines classes for individual HTML tags. It defines one class that can be applied to the `<H1>` tag and another that can be applied to the `<P>` tag.

```
<!--
                cssClassElement.html
-->
<HTML>
  <HEAD>
    <TITLE>Classes of Styles - CSS Syntax</TITLE>
    <STYLE TYPE="text/css">
      <!--

      h1.ablue { color: blue; }
      p.ared   { color: red;  font-Size: 10pt; }

      -->
    </STYLE>
  </HEAD>
  <BODY>

    <h1 class = ablue>This is a blue heading 1</H1>

    <P>This is a default paragraph.</P>
    <P CLASS = ared>This is a red paragraph with a 10 point font
size.</P>

  </BODY>
</HTML>
```

Figure 3–12 shows the result of loading the `cssClassElement.html` script.

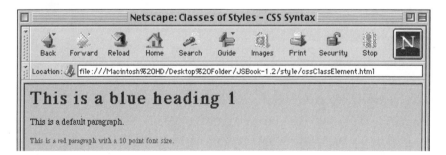

Figure 3–12 Result of loading the `cssClassElement.html` script

Defining Named Individual Styles

To provide further flexibility, you can alter the stylistic elements of a class by creating individual styles and naming them. You can then apply the named individual styles to an individual HTML tag by using the ID= attribute within the HTML tag. Named individual styles thus enable you to create stylistic exceptions to a class of style.

You can also use named individual styles to define layers of precisely positioned HTML content. For more details about layers, see Chapter 4, "Positioning HTML Content."

You create named individual styles by defining an ID selector. An ID selector is a string preceded by a hash mark (#). Once you define the ID selector, you call it by using the ID= attribute. The hash mark is not part of the value of ID.

The following cssId.html script defines the named individual styles—left, center, and right—that are used to modify the stmnt class.

```
<!--

               cssId.html


    An HTML element can use both a class of style with the class
    attribute and a named individual style with the ID attribute.
    Individual named styles allow stylistic exceptions to a style
    class.

    In this example, the named individual styles -- left, center,
    and right -- are used to modify the stmnt class.

-->
<HTML>
  <HEAD>
    <TITLE>Named Individual Styles - CSS Syntax</TITLE>
    <STYLE TYPE="text/css">
      <!--

      all.stmnt {
                  line-height: 16pt;
                  font-size:   12pt;
                  text-align:  justify;
                }
      #left      { text-align:  left; }
      #center    { text-align:  center; }
      #right     { text-align:  right; }

      -->
    </STYLE>
```

```
</HEAD>
<BODY>

  <H1>Janice Winsor</H1>
  <H2>ARTIST'S STATEMENT</H2>

  <P CLASS=stmnt>I have developed my own techniques to paint
    dream images, which are the inspiration for many of my
    paintings. I design stencils from the human form,
    experimenting with the minimum abstract form required to
    suggest a human figure. There is a constant shifting dialogue
    between figure and ground.  In addition to stencils being used
    as an integral part of painting compositions, they become art
    objects in themselves.</P>

  <P CLASS=stmnt ID=left>I use a variety of techniques to
    translate the designs into a finished piece.  Sometimes
    I transfer the images onto canvas with spray paint. At other
    times I cut the stencils into paper or into photographs I
    have taken. Additional images sprayed onto the glass
    frequently complete the composition.</P>

  <P CLASS=stmnt ID=center>Experimentation with different
    photographic techniques such as overlapping images, double
    exposures, multiple refractive lenses, and closeups of other
    paintings of mine provide warped images that are less
    representational than those of traditional photography.</P>

  <P CLASS=stmnt ID=center>I am also exploring the potentials of
    alternate photographic processes for creating "sun prints"
    that include cyanotype, Van Dyke, and salt printing. I paint
    photosensitive chemicals on paper and develop the prints
    by putting stencil drawings or objects on the paper and
    exposing them to the sun.  On some of these sun prints, I
    combine different chemical processes, multiple exposures,
    and overlapping images.</P>

  <P CLASS=stmnt ID=center>These techniques provide me with an
    expressive mixture of realism and surrealism. I shift
    perspectives and scale, overlapping images to give the
    paintings a dreamlike quality.</P>

  <P CLASS=stmnt ID=right>To my photography, I bring my artistic
    sense of form and composition to show the beauty of wildlife
    and nature. I particularly enjoy taking closeup photographs
    of objects to emphasize the beauty of the small.</P>
  </BODY>
</HTML>
```

Figure 3–13 shows the result of loading the `cssId.html` script.

Netscape: Named Individual Styles – CSS Syntax

Back   Forward   Reload   Home   Search   Guide   Images   Print   Security   Stop

Location: file:///MacintoshHD/Desktop%20Folder/JSBook-1.2/style/cssId.html

Janice Winsor

ARTIST'S STATEMENT

I have developed my own techniques to paint dream images, which are the inspiration for many of my paintings. I design stencils from the human form, experimenting with the minimum abstract form required to suggest a human figure. There is a constant shifting dialogue between figure and ground. In addition to stencils being used as an integral part of painting compositions, they become art objects in themselves.

I use a variety of techniques to translate the designs into a finished piece. Sometimes I transfer the images onto canvas with spray paint. At other times I cut the stencils into paper or into photographs I have taken. Additional images sprayed onto the glass frequently complete the composition.

Experimentation with different photographic techniques such as overlapping images, double exposures, multiple refractive lenses, and closeups of other paintings of mine provide warped images that are less representational than those of traditional photography.

I am also exploring the potentials of alternate photographic processes for creating "sun prints" that include cyanotype, Van Dyke, and salt printing. I paint photosensitive chemicals on paper and develop the prints by putting stencil drawings or objects on the paper and exposing them to the sun. On some of these sun prints, I combine different chemical processes, multiple exposures, and overlapping images.

These techniques provide me with an expressive mixture of realism and surrealism. I shift perspectives and scale, overlapping images to give the paintings a dreamlike quality.

To my photography, I bring my artistic sense of form and composition to show the beauty of wildlife and nature. I particularly enjoy taking closeup photographs of objects to emphasize the beauty of the small.

You are offline. Choose "Go Online..." to connect.

Figure 3–13 Result of loading the `cssId.html` script

Defining Contextual Selection Criteria

Because style sheets inherit styles from one another, you can specify an overall style and then use *contextual selection criteria* to list any exceptions to the default style. The selection criteria are contextual because you define the exceptions only for HTML tags that are nested within another specific HTML tag. For example, you could specify contextual selection criteria if you want bold text to have a different font size and color only when it is displayed inside a <P> tag. Any other bold text on the page would use the default style.

You specify CSS contextual selection criteria by a space-separated list of the HTML tags in their hierarchical order before the opening curly brace of the properties list.

```
parent-tag contextual-tag {attribute:value; attribute:value; ...
}
```

Nesting the `contextual-tag`(s) inside the `parent-tag` creates a search pattern. The browser applies the `contextual-tag` values to the HTML tag only when it appears in the context you specify.

Contextual selectors can search for tag names, CLASS attributes, ID attributes, and combinations. You can also specify multiple parent-tag elements. The following example displays bold text as 150 percent green only when it occurs in an unnumbered list that is within a paragraph:

```
p ul b {color: green; font-size: 150%; }
```

The following `cssContextual.html` script defines a context in which any bold that is embedded in a <P> tag is displayed in green with a 150 percent font size.

```
<!--

            cssContextual.html


    If you need more control over when a style is used, you can
    use the contextual selection criteria to be specific. In this
    example, only bold elements inside paragraphs will be green
    and 150% the normal size.

-->
<HTML>
  <HEAD>
    <TITLE>Contextual Selection - CSS Syntax</TITLE>
    <STYLE TYPE="text/css">
      <!--

      p b { color: green; font-size: 150%; }

      -->
    </STYLE>
  </HEAD>
  <BODY>

    <P>This is a test of <B>contextual</B> selection</P>
    <UL>
        <LI>This is a test of <B>contextual</B> selection
    </UL>

  </BODY>
</HTML>
```

Figure 3–14 shows the result of loading the `cssContextual.html` script. Note that the style defined for the bold text in `<P>` tags is not applied to the bold text in the unnumbered list.

![Netscape browser window titled "Netscape: Contextual Selection - CSS Syntax" showing navigation buttons and location bar file:///Macintosh%20HD/Desktop%20Folder/JSBook-1.2/style/cssContextual.html with text "This is a test of **contextual** selection" followed by a bulleted item "This is a test of **contextual** selection"]

Figure 3–14 Result of loading the `cssContextual.html` script

JavaScript Style Sheets

You create JavaScript style sheets by using `<STYLE></STYLE>` tags. Because JavaScript style sheets are integrated with the rest of the JavaScript functionality, you can do some things with JavaScript style sheets that you can't do with CSS. For example, using existing JavaScript functionality, you can test values in the user's browser for screen resolution and color depth to optimize display of fonts and colors in your document.

Of course, when you use JavaScript style sheets, the user's browser must be JavaScript enabled.

Comments in JavaScript Style Sheets

JavaScript style sheets support comments in standard C++ style to enable you to put comments in your style sheets. Each line of the comment begins with two slashes (//):

```
//This comment is used with JavaScript syntax
```

JavaScript Style Sheet Syntax

You specify JavaScript style sheets in the `<STYLE>` tag by setting the `TYPE` attribute to `"text/javascript"`. You then define the style for specific tags by using the JavaScript document object model: each Web page is an object that has properties that you can set or access. Each property can be an object that has its own set of properties. For example, reading the following code example from right to left, the value `"red"` is assigned to the `color` property of the `H1` property of the `tags` property of the `document` object:

```
document.tags.H1.color = "red"
```

Omitting document Object from the Definitions

Because the `tags` property always applies to the current `document` object, you can omit `document` from the expression, as follows:

```
tags.H1.color = "red"
```

Using a with Statement to Shorten Style Definitions

In fact, you can shorten the style specifications for elements that have several style settings by using the `with (document.tags)` syntax. The following example defines a font size for the <H1> tag and a font size and left and right margins for the <P> tag.

```
<STYLE TYPE="text/javascript">

  with (document.tags) {
    h1.fontSize="14pt"
    p.fontSize="12pt"
    p.marginLeft="10%"
    p.marginRight="10%"
  }

</STYLE>
```

Using Semicolons in JavaScript Style Sheets

CSS syntax requires semicolons at the end of each style statement. The JavaScript language does not require semilcolons as statement separators, although you can include them and your scripts will work. Use semicolons consistently. Either use them or don't, but stick with the original style you choose. For example, if your programming style is to use semicolons in your script, also use them in your style sheets. The following example has semicolons at the end of each statement.

```
<STYLE TYPE="text/javascript">

  document.tags.h1.fontSize="14pt";
  document.tags.p.fontSize="12pt";
  document.tags.p.marginLeft="10%";
  document.tags.p.marginRight="10%";

</STYLE>
```

Combining Style Elements in a Group

Because of the document object-model syntax of JavaScript style sheets, you cannot group style elements in the same statement as you can with CSS.

You can, however, group element properties by using the `with` statement, for example,

```
with (tags.p) {
fontSize = "14 pt"
rightMargin+"10%"
}
```

Specifying a Style for an HTML Tag

You can specify a style for an individual HTML tag by specifying the STYLE attribute as part of the individual HTML tag itself. Before you can specify a style for an individual tag, you must have a style definition in the head of the document, as shown in the following example.

```
<HEAD>
  <STYLE TYPE="text/javascript">
    <!-- // Hide from browsers that don't support

    with (tags.body) {
      color       = "red";
      fontFamily  = "Courier";
      fontSize    = "125%";
      marginTop   = "24pt";
      marginLeft  = "10%";
      marginRight = "10%";
    }
    // -->
  </STYLE>
</HEAD>
<BODY>
```

Once you have defined a general style, you can change the specification for an individual tag by including the STYLE attribute as part of the tag, as shown in the following example.

```
<P STYLE="fontFamily = 'Helvetica';">- Caption for cartoon:
  The Dejected Rooster</P>
```

You cannot mix CSS attribute definitions and JavaScript style sheet syntax in the same document.

Importing an External Style Sheet

You can link an external style sheet to the document by creating the style sheet as a separate document and importing it into the page by using the <LINK> tag.

The following style.jss style sheet specifies body color and font family, alignment for <H1> tags, font size and margins for <P> tags, background margins and padding for <UL> tags, and color, background, margin, and padding for <LI> tags.

```
// style.jss

with (tags.body) {
  color = "black";
  fontFamily = "courier";
}

with (tags.h1) {
  textAlign = "center";
}

with (tags.p) {
  fontSize = "12pt";
  marginLeft = "10%";
  marginRight = "10%";
}

with (tags.ul) {
  background =  "white";
  margin =  "16pt 4pt 4pt 16pt";
  padding =  "8pt 2pt 2pt 8pt";
}

with (tags.li) {
  color =  "red";
  background =  "blue";
  margin =  "8pt 2pt 2pt 8pt";
  padding =  "4pt 2pt 2pt 4pt";
}
```

You import the `style.jss` to the document by using the following statement in the head of the document.

```
<LINK REL="stylesheet" TYPE="text/javascript" HREF="style.jss"
TITLE="myStyle">
```

Importing a Style Sheet by Using the SRC Attribute of the <STYLE> Tag

The `<STYLE>` tag has an SRC attribute that you can use to import style sheets defined in external files. If you specify multiple style sheets by using the SRC attribute, styles are applied in the order the style sheets are listed. If any styles conflict, the last style sheet takes precedence over previously listed style sheets. Styles defined by using the STYLE attribute have precedence over styles defined in the `<STYLE>` tag as well as those defined in external style sheets.

The following example script uses the SRC attribute of the `<STYLE>` tag to import the style sheet defined in `style.jss`.

```
<HEAD>
  <TITLE>JavaScript Style SRC Attribute </TITLE>
  <STYLE TYPE="text/javascript" SRC="style.jss"></STYLE>
</HEAD>
```

Inheriting Styles

Styles for individual HTML tags are hierarchical. An HTML tag that contains another element is considered to be the *parent* element. The element contained by the parent element is considered to be its *child* element.

In many cases, child elements inherit or acquire the styles of their parent elements. For example, if you specify a body color of red and a font of courier, then all of the child elements inherit the same style attributes.

With CSS we found that you could not add uncommented text after the opening `<!--` comment; if you did so, the style was not displayed properly in the document. JavaScript style sheets display the styles properly regardless of whether you include a comment on the opening comment line. However, as inside `<SCRIPT>` tags, you need to add an additional two-slash comment in front of the usual closing comment to hide the code from browsers that don't support it.: `// -->`.

The following example specifies a body color of blue, a font family of Helvetica,sans-serif, and a font size of 125 percent.

```
<STYLE TYPE="text/javascript">
  <!-- Hide from browsers that don't support

with (tags.body) {
  color = "blue"
  fontFamily = "Helvetica,sans-serif"
  fontSize = "125%"
}
// -->
</STYLE>
```

Parent-Child Inheritance

When you change the font of a child element such as `<B>` or `<EM>`, the text uses the specified emphasis but still maintains the style elements specified for the body of the document.

Note – In JavaScript style sheets, specifying a style as part of the `<BODY>` tag is buggy on the Mac and X11 and works only partially in the Windows 95 implementation.

The following example defines a body color of red and a font family of Courier. The text also contains a phrase that has bold emphasis. However, when you load the example, the styles are not applied.

```
<HEAD>
  <TITLE>Inheritance w/JavaScript Syntax</TITLE>
</HEAD>
<BODY STYLE="color = 'red'; fontFamily = 'courier';">

  <H1>A Header</H1>

  <P>This is text in a &lt;p&gt; tag. If we <B>bold
  something</B>, note the text change.</P>

</BODY>
```

Controlling the Style of Child Elements

Even though the child elements inherit the style of the parent, you can control the style of child elements independently by specifying the style as part of the individual HTML tag itself.

The following example assigns a color of blue and a font family of Times to the HTML <B> tag.

```
<BODY STYLE="color = 'red'; fontFamily = 'courier';">
```

Because of the bug in applying styles that are defined in the <BODY> tag, the styles are not applied when you load the example on the Mac or X11 platforms.

Marking a Section of Text for Style

You can mark a section of text for a particular style by using the <SPAN></SPAN> tags. However, as with defining attributes in JavaScript style sheets, you must first define a style before you can modify the attributes of a section of text by using the <SPAN></SPAN> tags.

The following example first defines a style and then specifies a style for a selection by using the <SPAN> tag.

```
<HTML>
  <HEAD>
    <TITLE>JavaScript Syntax in a SPAN tag</TITLE>
    <STYLE TYPE="text/javascript">
      <!-- Hide from browsers that don't support

      with (tags.body) {
        color = "blue"
        fontFamily = "Helvetica,sans-serif"
        fontSize = "125%"
      }
```

```
        // -->
      </STYLE>
    </HEAD>
    <BODY>

      <P>An ancient pond<br>
        A frog jumps in<br>
        Plop!</P>

      <SPAN STYLE="fontFamily='Courier';">
        <P>- Basho</P>
      </SPAN>

    </BODY>
  </HTML>
```

Defining Classes of Styles

When a document includes a style sheet or links to one, all of the styles defined in the style sheet can be used in the document.

At times, however, you may want to selectively apply a style to HTML tags. For example, you might want some of the paragraphs in a document to be red and others to be blue.

To define a class in a JavaScript style sheet, first you define a `classes` object and assign as its first property the name you want to use for that class. If you want the class to be available to all HTML tags, you use the `all` keyword at the end of the statement:

```
classes.classname.all
```

You then specify the style elements you want to use for that class.

When you apply the style to a specific element, you include the statement:

```
class = classname
```

as part of the HTML tag.

The following example defines two classes: `ablue` and `ared`.

```
        <STYLE TYPE="text/javascript">
          <!-- Hide from browsers that don't support

          with (classes.ablue.all) {
            color    = "blue"
            fontSize = "18pt"
          }
          with (classes.ared.all) {
            color    = "red"
            fontSize = "12pt"
```

```
        }
```

To apply those style classes to different <P> tags, include the CLASS attribute as part of the tag definition, as shown in the following example.

```
<P>This paragraph has the default style.</P>
<P CLASS = ablue>This paragraph uses the style class
    ablue.</P>
<P CLASS = ared>This paragraph uses the style class
    ared.</P>
```

You can also define classes that can be used only for specific HTML tags. You identify the specific tag by name after the class name instead of using the all keyword:

```
classes.classname.tagname
```

The following example defines classes for individual HTML tags. It defines one class that can be applied to the <H1> tag and another that can be applied to the <P> tag.

```
<STYLE TYPE="text/javascript">
  <!-- Hide from browsers that don't support

  with (classes.ablue.h1) {
    color    = "blue"
  }
  with (classes.ared.p) {
    color    = "red"
    fontSize = "10pt"
  }

  // -->
</STYLE>
```

Defining Named Individual Styles

To provide further flexibility, you can alter the stylistic elements of a class by creating individual styles and naming them. You can then apply the named individual styles to an individual HTML tag by using the ID= attribute within the HTML tag. Named individual styles thus enable you to create stylistic exceptions to a class of style.

You can also use named individual styles to define layers of precisely positioned HTML content. For more details about layers, see Chapter 4, "Positioning HTML Content."

You create named individual styles by defining an ID selector. An ID selector is a string preceded by a hash mark (#). Once you define the ID selector, you call it by using the ID= attribute. The hash mark is not part of the value of ID.

The following example defines the named individual styles —left, center, and right—that are used to modify the stmnt class.

```
<STYLE TYPE="text/javascript">
  <!--

  with (classes.stmnt.all) {
      lineHeight = "16pt";
      fontSize   = "12pt";
      textAlign  = "justify";
  }
  ids.left.textAlign   = "left";
  ids.center.textAlign = "center";
  ids.right.textAlign  = "right";


  // -->
</STYLE>
```

To apply the style, you include the class statement as part of the tag, as shown in the following example.

```
<P CLASS=stmnt ID=left>I use a variety of techniques to
  translate the designs into a finished piece.  Sometimes
  I transfer the images onto canvas with spray paint. At other
  times I cut the stencils into paper or into photographs I
  have taken. Additional images sprayed onto the glass frequently
  complete the composition.</P>

<P CLASS=stmnt ID=center>Experimentation with different
  photographic techniques such as overlapping images, double
  exposures, multiple refractive lenses, and closeups of other
  paintings of mine provide warped images that are less
  representational than those of traditional photography.</P>

<P CLASS=stmnt ID=right>To my photography, I bring my artistic
  sense of form and composition to show the beauty of wildlife
  and nature. I particularly enjoy taking closeup photographs
  of objects to emphasize the beauty of the small.</P>
```

Defining Contextual Selection Criteria

Because style sheets inherit styles from one another, you can specify an overall style and then use *contextual selection criteria* to list any exceptions to the default style. The selection criteria are contextual because you define the exceptions for HTML tags that are nested within another specific HTML tag. For example, you would specify contextual selection criteria if you want bold text to have a different font size and color only when it is displayed inside a <P> tag. Any other bold text on the page would use the default style.

You specify JavaScript contextual selection criteria by using the predefined contextual() method. Within the method, you provide a comma-separated list of the HTML tags in their hierarchical order before specifying the style you want to apply to those contextual tags:

```
contextual(tags.firstTag, tags.secondTag, ...
tags.lastTag).property    = "value";
```

The following example defines a context in which any bold text that is embedded in a <P> tag is displayed in green with a 150 percent font size.

```
<STYLE TYPE="text/javascript">
  <!-- Hide from browsers that don't support

  contextual(tags.p, tags.b).color    = "green";
  contextual(tags.p, tags.b).fontSize = "150%";

  // -->
</STYLE>
```

When you use the tag in the specified context, the style is applied. The same tag used in any other context does not apply the style.

Combining Style Sheet Syntaxes

You can combine multiple style sheets for a single page. These style sheets can define different elements or can have multiple definitions for the same element. You can mix internal and external CSS and JavaScript style sheets.

When you combine style sheets, style sheets defined with the STYLE attribute always take precedence over styles defined with the <STYLE> tag and over styles imported from external style sheet files.

After following the precedence rules specified in the previous paragraph, styles are applied in the order they are specified within the document. If there is any conflict in style specifications, the last style is applied last. For an example of combining CSS and JavaScript style sheets, see "JavaScript Style Sheets" on page 111.

The following example uses style sheets defined in two external files: style.js and style2.js, both shown below.

```
// style.js

with (tags.body) {
  color = "black";
```

```
    fontFamily = "courier";
  }

with (tags.h1) {
  textAlign = "center";
}

with (tags.p) {
  fontSize = "12pt";
  marginLeft = "10%";
  marginRight = "10%";
}

with (tags.ul) {
  background =  "white";
  margin =  "16pt 4pt 4pt 16pt";
  padding =  "8pt 2pt 2pt 8pt";
}

with (tags.li) {
  color =  "red";
  background =  "blue";
  margin =  "8pt 2pt 2pt 8pt";
  padding =  "4pt 2pt 2pt 4pt";
}


// style2.js

with (tags.h1) {
  color =  "red";
  textTransform = "Capitalize";
  marginTop = "18 pt";
}

with (tags.p) {
  color = "blue";
  fontFamily = "Courier";
}

with (tags.ul) {
  background = "none";
}

with (tags.li) {
  margin  = "10pt 4pt 4pt 10pt";
  padding = "16pt 8pt 8pt 16pt";
}
```

You combine the two style sheets by using `<LINK>` tags, as shown in the following example.

```
<HEAD>
  <TITLE>Combining Style Sheets</TITLE>
  <LINK REL="stylesheet" TYPE="text/javascript" HREF="style.js"
  <LINK REL="stylesheet" TYPE="text/javascript" HREF="style2.jss">
</HEAD>
<BODY>
```

Pseudoclasses and Pseudoelements

Usually a style is attached to an HTML tag on the basis of its position in the document structure. However, some common style effects, such as changing the style of anchors that are unvisited, visited, or active cannot be defined in this way. The CSS Level 1 Specification defines a set of pseudoclasses and pseudoelements that do not exist in the HTML source.

Table 3-2 lists the pseudoclasses and pseudoelements that are defined in the CSS Level 1 Specification. For more information, refer to:

```
http://www.w3.org/TR/REC-CSS1#pseudo-classes-and-pseudo-elements
```

Table 3-2 Pseudoclasses and Pseudoelements

Pseudoclass/ Pseudoelement	Description	Supported by Netscape
Anchor	Display newly visited anchors differently from older ones.	Yes, but buggy
first-line	Display the first line of an element differently from the rest of the line.	No
first-letter	Display the first letter of an element differently from the rest of the word.	No

According to `http://style.webreview.com`, anchor pseudoclasses are supported by Netscape. `first-line` and `first-letter` are not.

Using the Anchor Pseudoclass

Browsers typically display newly visited anchors differently from older ones. If you want further control over the style of anchors, you can use the anchor pseudoclass to differentiate between subparts of an element.

Syntax

You specify style elements for the following anchor elements by using the following syntax:

```
A:link { attribute: value } /* unvisited link */
A;visited  { attribute: value } /* visited link */
A;active  { attribute: value } /* active link */
```

The browser is not required to reformat the current document when the status of a
link changes, so the behavior of these pseudoclasses varies, depending on the
user's browser.

Example of Using the Anchor Pseudoclass

The following anchor.html script specifies a different font size for unvisited
and visited links. Because active links are buggy, this script does not define one.
An active link is one that is currently being chosen, for example, by the user
pressing a mouse button. The anchor.html script also uses the anchor
pseudoclass to specify a purple border around the image.

```
<!--

                anchor.html

    The anchor pseudoclass allows a style sheet to differentiate
    between different anchor element types.

-->
<HTML>
  <HEAD>
    <TITLE>Anchor Pseudoclasses</TITLE>
    <STYLE TYPE="text/css">
      <!--

      A:link    { font-size: 20pt; } /* unvisited links */
      A:visited { font-size: 16pt; } /* visited links */
      A:active  { font-size: 12pt; } /* active links */

      A:link IMG {   border: purple; }


      -->
    </STYLE>
  </HEAD>
  <BODY>

    <P STYLE="margin-top: 18pt;">Below are a series of links
      defined to display in a 20 point font if unvisited, 16
      point if visited, and 12 point if active. Included around
      the image is an anchor pseudoclass used in a contextual
      selector. But, as per the <a
    HREF="http://www.w3.org/TR/REC-CSS1">CSS
    Recommendation</A>:</P>
    <BLOCKQUOTE>
      A UA is not required to reformat a currently displayed
```

```
     document due to anchor pseudoclass transitions. E.g., a
     style sheet can legally specify that the 'font-size' of an
     'active' link should be larger that a 'visited' link, but
     the UA is not required to dynamically reformat the document
     when the reader selects the 'visited' link.
   </BLOCKQUOTE>

   <P>So, your mileage will vary on this example.</P>

   <UL>
     <LI>An <A HREF="non_existent.html">unvisited</A> link.
     <LI>A <A HREF="anchor.html">visited</A> link.
     <LI>An active link is one that is currently being selected
   (e.g. by a mouse button press) by the reader.
   </UL>

   <CENTER>
     <A HREF="../images/AyersRock.jpg">
   <IMG SRC="../images/AyersRock.jpg"></img>
     </A>
   </CENTER>

 </BODY>
</HTML>
```

Figure 3–15 shows the result of loading the `anchor.html` script. As you can see, the links are displayed in a different font size than the rest of the text.

Netscape: Anchor Pseudoclasses

Back | Forward | Reload | Home | Search | Guide | Images | Print | Security | Stop

Location: file:///MacintoshHD/Desktop%20Folder/JSBook-1.2/style/anchor.html

Below are a series of links defined to display in a 20 point font if unvisited, 16 point if visited, and 12 point if active. Included around the image is an anchor pseudoclass used in a contextual selector. But, as per the CSS Recommendation:

> A UA is not required to reformat a currently displayed document due to anchor pseudoclass transitions. E.g., a style sheet can legally specify that the 'font-size' of an 'active' link should be larger that a 'visited' link, but the UA is not required to dynamically reformat the document when the reader selects the 'visited' link.

So, your mileage will vary on this example.

- An unvisited link.
- A visited link.
- An active link is one that is currently being selected (e.g. by a mouse button press) by the reader.

Figure 3–15 Result of loading the `anchor.html` script

Combining Style Sheet Syntaxes

You can combine multiple style sheets for a single page. These style sheets can define different elements or can have multiple definitions for the same element. You can mix internal and external CSS and JavaScript style sheets.

When you combine style sheets, style sheets defined with the STYLE attribute always take precedence over styles defined with the <STYLE> tag and over styles imported from external style sheet files.

After following the precedence rules specified in the previous paragraph, styles are applied in the order they are specified within the document. If there is any conflict in style specifications, the last style is applied last.

For example, the following `combining.html` script contains two specifications for bold font size:

```
b-font-size = 80% (CSS)
b-fontSize = 120% (JavaScript)
```

Because of this overlap, the bold font is first reduced by 80 percent and then increased to 120 percent, which means that the browser displays the bold font size at 120 percent.

```
<!--

                combining.html


    This example combines two style sheet definitions. The first
    definition uses CSS syntax, whereas the latter one uses JavaScript
    syntax. Note that the last definition takes precedence.

-->
<HTML>
  <HEAD>
    <TITLE>Combining Style Sheets</TITLE>

    <STYLE TYPE="text/css">
      <!--

      p {
                font-family: Helvetica;
           background-color: #CCCCFF;
         }
      b {
                font-size: 80%;
           text-transform: uppercase;
         }

      -->
    </STYLE>

    <STYLE TYPE="text/javascript">
      <!-- Hide from browsers that don't support

      tags.p.marginTop    = "18 pt";
      tags.p.borderWidth = " 4 pt";
      tags.p.borderColor = "blue";
      tags.p.borderStyle = "inset";

      tags.b.fontFamily   = "Courier";
      tags.b.fontSize     = "120%";

      // -->
```

```
     </STYLE>
   </HEAD>
   <BODY>

     <P>This is a test of combining two style sheets. This is
       <B>only</B> a test. In the case of an <B>actual page</B>,
       you would be reading something else <B>;-)</B></P>

   </BODY>
 </HTML>
```

Figure 3–16 shows the result of loading the `combining.html` script.

Figure 3–16 Result of loading the `combining.html` script

The following example uses style sheets defined in two external files: `style.css` and `style2.css`, which are shown below.

```
/* style.css */
body
  {
  color:black;
  font-family:courier;
  }

h1
  {
  text-align:center;
  }

p
  {
  font-size:12pt;
  margin-left:10%;
  margin-right:10%;
  }

ul
  {
```

```
background: white;
margin: 16pt 4pt 4pt 16pt;
padding: 8pt 2pt 2pt 8pt;
}

li
{
color: red;
background: blue;
margin: 8pt 2pt 2pt 8pt;
padding: 4pt 2pt 2pt 4pt;

}



/* style2.css */
h1
{
color:red;
text-transform:Capitalize;
margin-top:18 pt;
}

p
{
color:blue;
font-family:Courier;
}

ul
{
background: none;
}

li
{
margin: 10pt 4pt 4pt 10pt;
padding:16pt 8pt 8pt 16pt;
}
```

The two style sheets are imported into the following cssCombining.html script with <LINK> tags. Note that because the style2.css style sheet is referenced last, any definitions it might redefine, such as the background for unnumbered lists, take precedence over those in style.css.

```
<!--

              cssCombining.html

     This example combines two cascading style sheet definitions:
     style.css and style2.css. Note that the last style
     encountered takes precedence over previously listed styles.

-->
<HTML>
  <HEAD>
    <TITLE>Combining Style Sheets</TITLE>
    <LINK REL="stylesheet" TYPE="text/css" HREF="style.css">
    <LINK REL="stylesheet" TYPE="text/css" HREF="style2.css">

  </HEAD>
  <BODY>

    <H1>Great truths about life that little children have learned</H1>

    <P>(From the net)</P>

    <UL>
      <LI>No matter how hard you try, you can't baptize cats.

      <LI>When your mom is mad at your dad, don't let her brush
    your hair.

      <LI>If your sister hits you, don't hit her back. They
    always catch the second person.

      <LI>Never ask your 3-year old brother to hold a tomato.

      <LI>You can't trust dogs to watch your food.

      <LI>Reading what people write on desks can teach you a
    lot.

      <LI>Don't sneeze when someone is cutting your hair.

      <LI>Puppies still have bad breath even after eating a tic
    tac.

      <LI>Never hold a dustbuster and a cat at the same time.

      <LI>School lunches stick to the wall.

      <LI>You can't hide a piece of broccoli in a glass of milk.
```

```
<LI>Don't wear polka-dot underwear under white shorts.

     <LI>The best place to be when you are sad is in Grandma's
lap.

  </UL>

 </BODY>
</HTML>
```

Figure 3–17 shows the result of loading the `cssCombining.html` script.

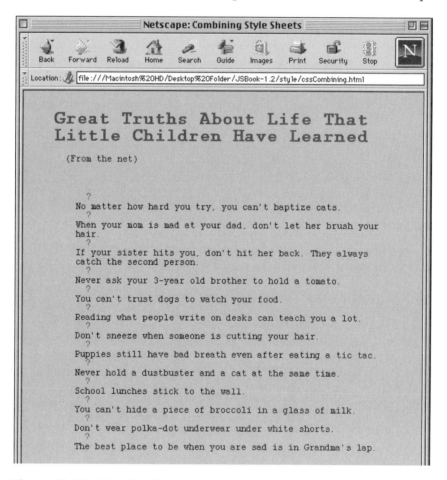

Figure 3–17 Result of loading the `cssCombining.html` script

Positioning HTML Content

▼ CHOOSING A POSITIONING FORMAT

▼ POSITIONING PROPERTIES

▼ CSS POSITIONING

▼ <LAYER> TAG POSITIONING

A positioning block of HTML content is considered to be a *layer*. There are two ways you can create a layer. For each layer that you define, JavaScript creates a corresponding `layer` object that enables you to use JavaScript to access information about the layer and to manipulate it. You can write JavaScript code to move, hide, expand, contract, and change the overlapping sequence of layers. You can also change the content of layers and create new layers on the fly. Using layers, you can create dynamic animations and self-modifying Web pages.

This chapter describes how you create the layers by using the CSS positioning syntax and the Netscape Navigator 4.0 <LAYER> tags. The descriptions in the CSS Positioning and <LAYER> Tag Positioning sections are almost identical except for the examples so that you can refer to each section independently. For information about using the Netscape `layer` object, see Chapter 6, "Dynamic HTML."

Choosing a Positioning Format

Just as with style sheets, Netscape Communicator 4.x supports two types of syntax for positioning HTML content:

- Cascading Style Sheets-Positioning (CSS-P) layers are defined by using the `position` property

- Netscape Navigator 4.0 layers are defined by using the `<LAYER>` or `<ILAYER>` tags

CSS-P functionality began as a separate working group effort but has been adopted by W3.org. CSS-P uses a syntax that extends the CSS1 vocabulary.

Because the CSS-P work was incomplete when Navigator 4 was under development, Netscape implemented its own `<LAYER>` tag and has been lobbying to have it included as part of the HTML 4.0 standard. Unfortunately for Netscape and Navigator 4, the `<LAYER>` tag was not adopted by the WC3 for HTML 4.0. If you are writing Web pages for a Navigator-only audience, the `<LAYER>` tag is handy. However, if you are writing Web pages for a wider audience, you should use the CSS-P syntax. Fortunately, Navigator also supports the CSS-P syntax, and most of its properties are available to the `layer` object.

By contrast, Internet Explorer 4.0 implements the CSS-P specification. However, it uses VBScript instead of the Netscape layer object to work with the dynamic scripting aspects of layers. Because of the different implementations, scripts written on one browser cannot be displayed on the other.

Positioning Properties

Table 4-1 describes all of the attributes that you can specify when defining layers for both CSS and `<LAYER>` tag syntax. It does not include style definitions, although a style definition for a layer can also include any style property. For a list of style sheet properties, refer to Table 3-1 on page 82.

Table 4-1 Positioning Attributes

CSS Attribute	`<LAYER>` Attribute	Possible Values
background-color	BGCOLOR	A named color, such as blue or a 6-digit hexadecimal value, such as #0000FF.
background-image	BACKGROUND	The URL of an image.
CLIP	CLIP	The boundaries of the visible area of the layer. The value is a comma-separated set of numbers specifying the left, top, right, and bottom value in pixels. You can optionally enclose the set of numbers in quotes. You can specify the value as a set of two numbers that specify the right and bottom values. If you specify two numbers, the top and left values default to 0.
HEIGHT	HEIGHT	The height of the clipping region of the layer. Values can be expressed as an integer (pixels) or as a percentage of the height of the containing layer. Note that elements, such as images, that cannot be clipped extend the height of the layer to accommodate all of the elements.
ID	ID	Previously called NAME. Use this optional attribute to specify the name of a layer. The ID value must begin with an alphabetic character.
LEFT, TOP	LEFT, TOP	In pixels, the horizontal and vertical positions of the top-left corner of the layer either within the document or within its containing layer. The value must be an integer.
No equivalent	onMouseOver, onMouseOut, onFocus, onBlur, onLoad	Event handlers. Value is either a JavaScript function or JavaScript code.

Table 4-1 Positioning Attributes (Continued)

CSS Attribute	<LAYER> Attribute	Possible Values
No equivalent	PAGEX, PAGEY	In pixels, the horizontal and vertical position of the top-left corner of the layer relative to the document rather than the enclosing layer.
POSITION	No equivalent. Instead, use <LAYER> and <ILAYER> tags.	Used only for layers that are defined as styles. absolute or relative.
source-include	SRC	The URL for an external file that contains HTML-formatted text to be displayed in this layer.
VISIBILITY	VISIBILITY	hide, show, inherit.
WIDTH	WIDTH	The width at which the contents of the layer wrap. Values can be expressed as an integer (pixels) or as a percentage of the width of the containing layer. Note that elements. such as images, that cannot be wrapped extend the width of the layer to accommodate all of the contents.
Z-INDEX	Z-INDEX, ABOVE, BELOW	The stacking order of the layers. Value must be a positive integer for the Z-INDEX attribute. Higher-numbered values are stacked above those with lower values. The ABOVE and BELOW attributes specify, by ID attribute value, the name of the layer just above or below the current layer.

CSS Positioning

Cascading style sheets provide a syntax to define styles for positioning blocks of HTML content. For the original W3C specification, see:
http://www.w3.org/pub/WWW/TR/WD-positioning.

When you define a style for positioning blocks of HTML content, the style definition always includes the position property. The position property can have the following values:

- absolute specifies a layer with an absolute position within its containing layer.

- relative specifies a layer with a position relative to the current position in the document.

- `top` and `left` specify the horizontal indent from the containing layer for an absolutely positioned layer, or the current position in the document for a relatively positioned layer.

The default value for the `position` property is `static`. Unless you specify the `position` property and specify a value of either `absolute` or `relative`, the layer cannot be positioned or repositioned.

Note – When you use the `position` property, you can also specify any of the other style elements.

The following `css.html` script positions the footer for our script examples 100 pixels from the top, 175 pixels from the left, with a width of 400 pixels, and a font family of Courier by using CSS positioning syntax.

```
<!--

                           css.html


        This example positions the document footer with CSS
        Positioning syntax.

-->
<HTML>
  <HEAD>
    <TITLE>CSS Positioning</TITLE>
    <STYLE TYPE="text/css">
      <!-- /* Hide from browsers that don't support */

      #aLayer {
                 position:    absolute;
                 top:         100px;
                 left:        175px;
                 width:       400px;
                 font-family: Courier;
               }
      -->
    </STYLE>
  </HEAD>
  <BODY>
    <SPAN ID="aLayer">
      <CENTER><hr SIZE=3 WIDTH="100%">
        <DT><I>Jumping Javascript</I></DT>
```

```
        <DT>by Janice Winsor and Brian Freeman</DT>
        <DT><I>positioning/css.html</I></DT>
      </CENTER>
    </SPAN>
  </BODY>
</HTML>
```

Figure 4–1 shows the result of loading the css.html script.

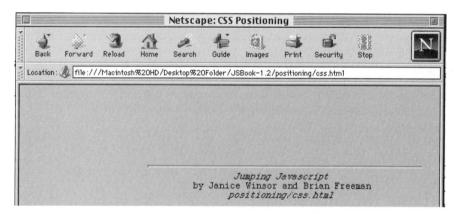

Figure 4–1 Result of loading the css.html script

Absolute Positioning

The absolute positioning property enables you to specify the location, in pixels, of the upper left corner of the HTML content for the specified layer. The following cssAbsolute.html script positions the content of the aLayer layer at 200,200 and changes the background color to yellow.

```
<!--

                    cssAbsolute.html

    This script uses CSS positioning syntax to absolutely
    position its content.

-->
<HTML>
  <HEAD>
    <TITLE>CSS Absolute Positioning</TITLE>
    <STYLE TYPE="text/css">
      <!-- /* Hide from browsers that don't support */

      #aLayer {
              position:          absolute;
              left:              200px;
```

```
                top:                200px;
                background-color:   yellow;
            }
      -->
    </STYLE>
  </HEAD>
  <BODY>

    The content begins here.
    <DIV ID="aLayer">
      aLayer's content starts and ends here.
    </DIV>
    End of the content.

    <CENTER><hr SIZE=3 WIDTH="100%">
      <DT><I>Jumping Javascript</I></DT>
      <DT>by Janice Winsor and Brian Freeman</DT>
      <DT><I>positioning/cssAbsolute.html</I></DT>
    </CENTER>
  </BODY>
</HTML>
```

Figure 4–2 shows the result of loading the `cssAbsolute.html` script.

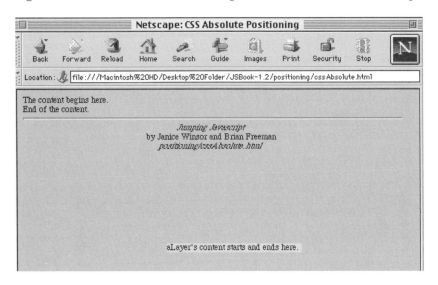

Figure 4–2 Result of loading the `cssAbsolute.html` script

Relative Positioning

The `relative` positioning property enables you to specify an offset for the layer relative to the natural position of the layer in the flow of the document.

The following `cssRelative.html` script indents the contents of the `aLayer` layer 25 pixels from the left and changes the background color to yellow.

```
<!--

                            cssRelative.html

     This script uses CSS positioning syntax to relatively
     position the content.

-->
<HTML>
  <HEAD>
    <TITLE>CSS Relative Positioning</TITLE>
    <STYLE TYPE="text/css">
      <!-- /* Hide from browsers that don't support */

      #aLayer {
                position:          relative;
                left:              25px;
                background-color:  yellow;
              }
      -->
    </STYLE>
  </HEAD>
<BODY>

  The content begins here.
  <DIV ID="aLayer">
    aLayer's content starts and ends here.
  </DIV>
  End of the content.

</BODY>
</HTML>
```

Figure 4–3 shows the result of loading the `cssRelative.html` script.

Figure 4–3 Result of loading the `cssRelative.html` script

The following `cssRelative2.html` script defines two relative layers: `outside` and `inside`. The `outside` layer indents the layer 15 pixels from the left and from the top, specifies a width of 100 pixels, and a background color of yellow. The `inside` layer specifies a background color of orange. Because no position is specified for the `inside` layer, it is displayed within the flow of the `outside` layer.

```
<!--

              cssRelative2.html

     This script uses CSS positioning syntax to relatively position
     content. "outside" positions the content and changes the
     background color to yellow. "inside" changes the background
     color to orange.

-->
<HTML>
  <HEAD>
    <TITLE>CSS Relative Positioning</TITLE>
    <STYLE TYPE="text/css">
      <!-- /* Hide from browsers that don't support */

      #outside {
                position:           relative;
                left:               15px;
                top:                15px;
                width:              100px;
                background-color:   yellow;
            }


      #inside {
                position:           relative;
                background-color:   orange;
            }
      -->
    </STYLE>
  </HEAD>
  <BODY>

    The content begins here.
    <DIV ID="outside">
      The outside content starts here.
      <DIV ID="inside">
    The inside content starts and ends here.
      </DIV>
      The outside content ends here.
    </DIV>
```

```
End of the content.

</BODY>
</HTML>
```

Figure 4–4 shows the result of loading the `cssRelative2.html` script.

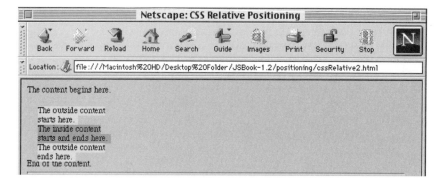

Figure 4–4 Result of loading the `cssRelative2.html` script

Notice that, in this example, the bottom of the background color of the `outside` layer overlaps the `End of the content` line.

You can position relative layers within other absolutely positioned layers. The following `cssAbsolute2.html` script positions the `outside` layer at 50,100 and changes the background color of the `inside` layer to orange.

```
<!--

        cssAbsolute2.html


    This script uses CSS positioning syntax to absolutely position
    content. "outside" positions the content and changes the
    background color to yellow. "inside" changes the background
    color to orange.

-->
<HTML>
  <HEAD>
    <TITLE>CSS Absolute Positioning</TITLE>
    <STYLE TYPE="text/css">
      <!-- /* Hide from browsers that don't support */

      #outside {
              position:            absolute;
              left:                 50px;
              top:                 100px;
              width:               100px;
              background-color:    yellow;
```

```
            }

    #inside {
            background-color:   orange;
            }
    -->
  </STYLE>
</HEAD>
<BODY>

  The content begins here.
  <DIV ID="outside">
    The outside content starts here.
    <DIV ID="inside">
  The inside content starts and ends here.
    </DIV>
    The outside content ends here.
  </DIV>
  End of the content.

  <CENTER><hr SIZE=3 WIDTH="100%">
    <DT><I>Jumping Javascript</I></DT>
    <DT>by Janice Winsor and Brian Freeman</DT>
    <DT><I>positioning/cssAbsolute2.html</I></DT>
  </CENTER>
  </BODY>
</HTML>
```

Figure 4–5 shows the result of loading the `cssAbsolute2.html` script.

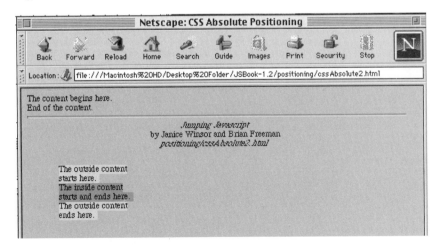

Figure 4–5 Result of loading the `cssAbsolute2.html` script

Positioning a Layer by Using the STYLE Attribute

You can position individual blocks of HTML content by defining a STYLE attribute for an individual HTML tag.

The following cssStyleAttribute.html script defines a style attribute by including the position property as part of the <DIV> HTML tag.

HTML Brushup — <DIV></DIV> Tags

This tag is a Netscape 2.0 extension that is a proposed replacement for the nonstandard <CENTER> tag. The <DIV> tag accepts the ALIGN attribute with the possible values of LEFT I RIGHT I CENTER. As with any HTML 4.0 tag, you can also use the STYLE attribute as part of its definition.

Below is an example of defining a style as part of the <DIV> tag

<DIV

STYLE="position:absolute;left:200px;top:200px;background-color:yellow">

A Layer definition contained in HTML starts and ends here.

</DIV>

```
<!--

            cssStyleAttribute.html

    This script uses CSS positioning syntax to absolutely position
    content.

-->
<HTML>
  <HEAD>
    <TITLE>CSS Absolute Positioning</TITLE>
  </HEAD>
  <BODY>

    The content begins here.
    <DIV
        STYLE="position:absolute;left:200px;top:200px;background-
color:yellow">
        A Layer definition contained in HTML starts and ends here.
    </DIV>
    End of the content.

    <CENTER><hr SIZE=3 WIDTH="100%">
      <DT><I>Jumping Javascript</I></DT>
```

```
        <DT>by Janice Winsor and Brian Freeman</DT>
        <DT><I>positioning/cssStyleAttribute.html</I></DT>
      </CENTER>
    </BODY>
  </HTML>
```

Figure 4–6 shows the result of loading the `cssStyleAttribute.html` script.

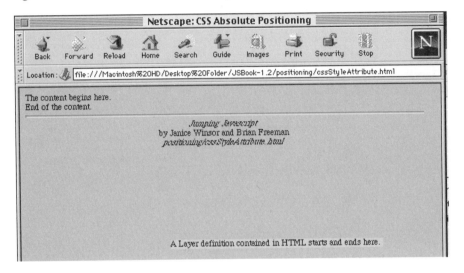

Figure 4–6 Result of loading the `cssStyleAttribute.html` script

Identifying Layers by Name

When you create named layers, you can use the layer's ID as a name to refer to the layer in the `layer` object. Because of the design of CSS-P, layers defined in CSS syntax are always named.

Use the following syntax to identify a CSS layer by name:

```
#layername {position:absolute;}
```

The *layername* ID must begin with an alphabetic character.

Controlling the Width of Layers

Use the `WIDTH` attribute to control the width of the layer at which the contents wrap. You can express the `WIDTH` value as an integer or as a percentage of the width of the containing layer.

When you do not specify a value for the `WIDTH` attribute, the contents of the layer wrap at the right boundary of the enclosing layer.

Note – If the layer contains elements, such as images, that cannot be wrapped, those elements extend beyond the specified width. The actual width of the layer expands to accommodate nonwrapping elements.

The following `cssWidth.html` script defines two layers, `outside` and `inside`. The width of the `outside` layer is set to 100 pixels. The width of the `inside` layer is set to 10 percent of the width of the enclosing `outside` layer, which is 10 pixels. When the script is loaded, the text wraps only at word boundaries. The longest word, `containing`, is wider than 10 pixels, so the layer expands from 10 pixels to accommodate the longest word.

```
<!--

                        cssWidth.html

    This example shows you can express width as an integer or as
    a percentage of the containing layer.

-->
<HTML>
  <HEAD>
    <TITLE>CSS width property</TITLE>
    <STYLE TYPE="text/css">
      <!-- /* Hide from browsers that don't support */

      #outside {
        position:          absolute;
        left:              100px;
        top:               100px;
        width:             100px;
        background-color:  yellow;
      }

      #inside {
        position:          relative;
        width:             10%;
        background-color:  salmon;
      }

      -->
    </STYLE>
  </HEAD>
  <BODY>
```

```
      <DIV ID="outside">
        The width of this layer, <CODE>outside</CODE>,
        is set to 100.
        <DIV ID="inside">
          This layer, <CODE>inside</CODE>, sets its
          width to 10 percent of the containing layer's
          width. The containing layer is <CODE>outside</CODE>.
        </DIV>
        The outside content ends here.
      </DIV>

      <CENTER><hr SIZE=3 WIDTH="100%">
        <DT><I>Jumping Javascript</I></DT>
        <DT>by Janice Winsor and Brian Freeman</DT>
        <DT><I>positioning/cssWidth.html</I></DT>
      </CENTER>
    </BODY>
  </HTML>
```

Figure 4–7 shows the result of loading the `cssWidth.html` script.

Figure 4–7 Result of loading the `cssWidth.html` script

Controlling the Height of Layers

Use the HEIGHT attribute to control the initial height of the clipping region of the layer. You can express the HEIGHT value as an integer or as a percentage of the height of the containing layer.

When you do not specify a value for the HEIGHT attribute, the height is the minimum height that contains all of the contents of the layer.

Note – If the layer contains elements, such as images, that cannot fit inside the specified height, the actual height of the layer expands to accommodate all of the contents.

The following cssHeight.html script defines two layers, outside and inside. The height of the outside layer is set to 100 pixels. The height of the inside layer is set to 300 percent of the height of the enclosing outside layer. Because the contents of the outside layer requires more than 100 pixels to display completely, the height becomes a reference for the child inside layer.

```
<!--

                cssHeight.html

    This example shows you can express height as an integer or as
    a percentage of the containing layer.

-->
<HTML>
  <HEAD>
    <TITLE>CSS height Attribute</TITLE>
    <STYLE TYPE="text/css">
      <!-- /* Hide from browsers that don't support */

      #outside {
        position:           absolute;
        left:               100px;
        top:                100px;
        width:              100px;
        height:             100px;
        background-color:   yellow;
        border-width:       1;
      }

      #inside {
        position:           relative;
        left:               100px;
```

```
          top:                100px;
          width:              100px;
          height:             300%;
          background-color:   salmon;
          border-width:       1;
        }

      -->
    </STYLE>
  </HEAD>
  <BODY>

    <DIV ID="outside">
      The height of this <CODE>outside</CODE> layer
      is set to 100.
      <DIV ID="inside">
        The height of this <CODE>inside</CODE> layer
        is set to 300 percent of the containing layer's
        height. The containing layer is <CODE>outside</CODE>.
      </DIV>
      Note that <CODE>outside</CODE>'s height is larger
      than 100 pixels. In this case, the <CODE>height</CODE>
      attribute acts as a reference for the
      child layer <CODE>inside</CODE>.
    </DIV>

    <CENTER><hr SIZE=3 height="100%">
      <DT><I>Jumping Javascript</I></DT>
      <DT>by Janice Winsor and Brian Freeman</DT>
      <DT><I>positioning/cssHeight.html</I></DT>
    </CENTER>
  </BODY>
</HTML>
```

Figure 4–8 shows the result of loading the `cssHeight.html` script.

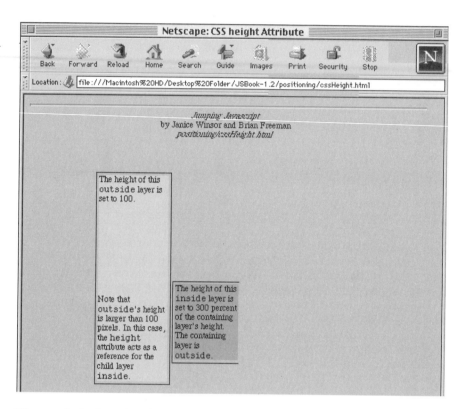

Figure 4–8 Result of loading the `cssHeight.html` script

Clipping Layers

Use the CLIP attribute to define the boundaries for the visible area of the layer. You define the values for the CLIP attribute as a comma-separated set of four numbers indicating left, top, right, and bottom values. Optionally, you can enclose the numbers in a quoted string. If you do not quote the string, do not include any white space between the numbers.

You specify the left and right values as the number of pixels from the left edge of the layer. You specify the top and bottom values as the number of pixels down from the top edge of the layer. The following example clips the layer at the right and bottom at 200 pixels.

```
#layerOne {
    position:          absolute;
    clip:              (0px,0px,200px,200px);
        background-color:  yellow;
}
```

If you want to clip only the right and bottom of the layer, you can specify a set of two numbers. The left and top values default to 0. The following example is equivalent to the one above.

```
#layerOne {
    position:           absolute;
    clip:               (200px,200px);
        background-color:  yellow;
}
```

Note – The CLIP attribute in Navigator 4.0 is buggy.

Controlling the Visibility of Layers

Use the VISIBILITY attribute to determine whether the layer is visible or not. By default, a layer has the same visibility as its parent layer. In other words, the default value of the VISIBILITY attribute is INHERIT. The HIDE value hides the layer, and SHOW shows the layer. You can omit the VISIBILITY attribute value if you want the layer to inherit its value from the parent layer, or you can explicitly set the value to INHERIT.

If the layer is the top layer, the default VISIBILITY value is SHOW because the body document is always visible.

Even if the visibility of a layer is set to SHOW, you can see the layer only if there are no other visible opaque layers stacked on top of it. When a layer is set to HIDE, its contents are not shown. However, the layer still takes up space in the document flow.

The following cssVisibility.html script defines four layers: one is the parent, one shows the layer, another hides the layer, and the fourth inherits the visibility attribute from the parent layer.

```
<!--

                    cssVisibility.html

    This example shows the different types of visibility a layer
    can be defined as. In all, four layers are defined
    here. layerOne is the parent of the other three layers.
    In turn, showLayer, hideLayer and inheritLayer set visibility
    to show, hide, and inherit.

-->
```

```html
<HTML>
  <HEAD>
    <TITLE>CSS Visibility property</TITLE>
    <STYLE TYPE="text/css">
      <!-- /* Hide from browsers that don't support */

      #layerOne {
        position:          absolute;
        top:               100;
        left:              200;
        background-color:  yellow;
      }

      #showLayer {
        position:          absolute;
        top:               25;
        left:              25;
        visibility:        show;
        background-color:  orange;
      }

      #hideLayer {
        position:          absolute;
        top:               50;
        left:              50;
        visibility:        hide;
        background-color:  lightblue;
      }

      #inheritLayer {
        position:          absolute;
        top:               75;
        left:              75;
        visibility:        inherit;
        background-color:  salmon;
      }

      -->
    </STYLE>
  </HEAD>
<BODY>
  <SPAN ID = "layerOne">
    <P>This layer is the parent.</P>
    <SPAN ID = "showLayer">
      <P>This layer is visible.</P>
    </SPAN>
    <SPAN ID = "hideLayer">
      <P>This layer is invisible.</P>
```

```
    </SPAN>
    <SPAN ID = "inheritLayer">
      <P>This layer inherits its visibility.</P>
    </SPAN>
  </SPAN>

  <CENTER><hr SIZE=3 WIDTH="100%">
    <DT><I>Jumping Javascript</I></DT>
    <DT>by Janice Winsor and Brian Freeman</DT>
    <DT><I>positioning/cssVisibility.html</I></DT>
  </CENTER>
 </BODY>
</HTML>
```

Figure 4–9 shows the result of loading the `cssVisibility.html` script.

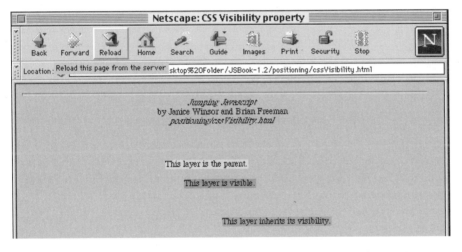

Figure 4–9 Result of loading the `cssVisibility.html` script

Specifying the Background Color of Layers

Use the `background-color` property to specify the solid background color for a block of HTML content. You can specify the background color by name or by specifying a hexadecimal RGB value.

If you specify no background color, the background of the layer is transparent.

When you define a background color by using the CSS syntax, the background color is applied only to the background for the specific content of the layer. By contrast, background color defined with the `<LAYER>` tag is applied to the rectangular region occupied by the layer.

The following example specifies a background color of lavender by using the color name:

```
#outside {
    position:           absolute;
    left:               100px;
    top:                100px;
    width:              100px;
    height:             100px;
    background-color:   lavender;
}
```

The following example specifies a background color of lavender by using its hexadecimal RGB value:

```
#outside {
    position:           absolute;
    left:               100px;
    top:                100px;
    width:              100px;
    height:             100px;
    background-color:   #E6E68C;
}
```

Specifying the Background Image of Layers

Use the `background-image` attribute to draw a tiled image across the background of a block of HTML content. The value for this property is the URL for an image. The size of the background image is determined by the amount of HTML content, not by the size of the layer.

If you specify no background image, the background of the layer is transparent.

Alternatively, you can also use the layer-backgound-image property, which is supported by Navigator 4.x but not approved by WC3. The `layer-background-image` property draws a tiled image across the background area specified by the left, top, width, and height attributes.

The following `backgroundImage.html` script uses CSS syntax to define two layers. Layer One uses the WC3-approved `background-image` property to use the `rainbow.gif` file as the background image. This property displays the background image behind the actual content of the layer only. Layer Two uses the `layer-background-image` property, which uses the size properties to determine where the background image is displayed.

```
<!--
            backgroundImage.html

    This script sets the background image with CSS syntax. It
    shows the style property; background-image; and the Navigator
    4.0 supported, non-W3C-approved property,
    layer-background-image, setting the background image.

-->
<HTML>
  <HEAD>
    <TITLE>Background Image Attribute</TITLE>
    <STYLE TYPE="text/css">
      <!-- /* Hide from browsers that don't support */

      #layerOne {
        position: absolute;
        top: 100;
        left: 200;
        width: 300;
        height: 216;
        background-image:url("../images/rainbow.gif");
      }

      #layerTwo {
        position: absolute;
        top: 300;
        left: 200;
        width: 300;
        height: 216;
        layer-background-image:url("../images/rainbow.gif");
      }

      -->
    </STYLE>
  </HEAD>
  <BODY>

    <SPAN ID="layerOne">
      <H1>Layer One</H1>
      <P>This layer is defined with CSS syntax.</P>
      <P>The background image is applied to the region occupied
by the layer by setting the <CODE>background-image</CODE>
property. The height is determined by the actual
content.</P>
    </SPAN>

    <SPAN ID="layerTwo">
```

```
<H1>Layer Two</H1>
<P>This layer is defined with CSS syntax.</P>
<P>The background image is applied to the region
occupied by the layer by setting the
<CODE>layer-background-image</CODE> property. The height
is determined by the value of the <CODE>height</CODE>
property. <CODE>layer-background-image</CODE> is not approved
by the W3C.</P>
</SPAN>

<CENTER><hr SIZE=3 WIDTH="100%">
  <DT><I>Jumping Javascript</I></DT>
  <DT>by Janice Winsor and Brian Freeman</DT>
  <DT><I>positioning/backgroundImage.html</I></DT>
</CENTER>
</BODY>
</HTML>
```

Figure 4–10 shows the result of loading the `backgroundImage.html` script.

Netscape: Background Image Attribute

Back | Forward | Reload | Home | Search | Guide | Images | Print | Security | Stop

Location: file:///MacintoshHD/Desktop%20Folder/JSBook-1.2/positioning/backgroundImage.html

Jumping JavaScript
by Janice Winsor and Brian Freeman
positioning/backgroundImage.html

Layer One

This layer is defined with CSS syntax.

The background image is applied to the region occupied by the layer by setting the `background-image` property. The height is determined by the actual content.

Layer Two

This layer is defined with CSS syntax.

The background image is applied to the region occupied by the layer by setting the `layer-background-image` property. The height is determined by the value of the `height` property. `layer-background-image` is not approved by the W3C.

Figure 4–10 Result of loading the `backgroundImage.html` script

Including Externally Specified Layers

Use the `source-include` attribute to specify an external file that contains HTML-formatted text that you want to display as part of the layer. The value for this attribute is a URL for the file.

Note – The `source-include` attribute is a Netscape extension and is not approved by WC3.

The following `cssSrc.html` script includes an HTML file containing text. Note that you can specify the layer formatting either as part of the included file or within the HTML file that calls the included file.

```
<!--
                 cssSrc.html

      This example shows the CSS include-source property. It does
      this by defining incHaiku to include haiku.html as its
      content.

-->
<HTML>
  <HEAD>
    <TITLE>CSS source-include property</TITLE>
    <STYLE TYPE="text/css">
      <!-- /* Hide from browsers that don't support */

      #incHaiku {
        position:absolute;
        top:150px;
        left:250px;
        include-source:url("haiku.html");
      }

      -->
    </STYLE>
  </HEAD>
  <BODY>

    <DIV ID="incHaiku"></DIV>

    <CENTER><hr SIZE=3 WIDTH="100%">
      <DT><I>Jumping Javascript</I></DT>
      <DT>by Janice Winsor and Brian Freeman</DT>
      <DT><I>positioning/cssSrc.html</I></DT>
    </CENTER>
  </BODY>
</HTML>
```

Figure 4–11 shows the result of loading the `cssSrc.html` script.

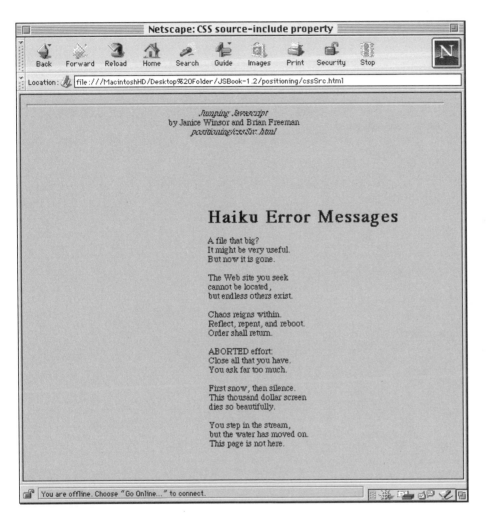

Figure 4–11 Result of loading the `cssSrc.html` script

Controlling the Stacking Order of Layers

Use the Z-INDEX attribute to specify the stacking order of layers that have the same parent layer. The Z-INDEX value is a positive integer, with higher-numbered values stacked above those with lower ones.

The following `cssZIndex.html` script creates four layers and assigns each one a different Z-INDEX value.

```
<!--
                    cssZIndex.html
```

This script shows the LAYER tag's Z-INDEX attribute by
changing the stacking order of the layers defined below.

```
-->
<HTML>
  <HEAD>
    <TITLE>Layer Tag Z-INDEX Attribute</TITLE>
    <STYLE TYPE="text/css">
      <!-- /* Hide from browsers that don't support */

        #layerOne {
          position: absolute;
          z-index: 3;
          top: 200;
          left: 250;
          width: 100;
          height: 100;
          border-width: 1;
          background-color: yellow;
        }

        #layerTwo {
          position: absolute;
          z-index: 4;
          top: 250;
          left: 300;
          width: 100;
          height: 100;
          border-width: 1;
          background-color: orange;
        }

        #layerThree {
          position: absolute;
          z-index: 1;
          top: 175;
          left: 325;
          width: 100;
          height: 100;
          border-width: 1;
          background-color: lightblue;
        }

        #layerFour {
          position: absolute;
          z-index: 2;
          top: 275;
          left: 225;
```

```
        width: 100;
        height: 100;
        border-width: 1;
        background-color: salmon;
      }

      -->
    </STYLE>
  </HEAD>
<BODY>
  <P>The LAYER tag's Z-INDEX attribute enables you to change the
    stacking order of the layers.</P>

  <SPAN ID="layerOne">
    This layer is layerOne.
  </SPAN>
  <SPAN ID="layerTwo">
    This layer is layerTwo.
  </SPAN>
  <SPAN ID="layerThree">
    This layer is layerThree.
  </SPAN>
  <SPAN ID="layerFour">
    This layer is layerFour.
  </SPAN>

  <CENTER><hr SIZE=3 WIDTH="100%">
    <DT><I>Jumping Javascript</I></DT>
    <DT>by Janice Winsor and Brian Freeman</DT>
    <DT><I>positioning/cssZIndex.html</I></DT>
  </CENTER>
  </BODY>
</HTML>
```

Figure 4–12 shows the result of loading the cssZIndex.html script.

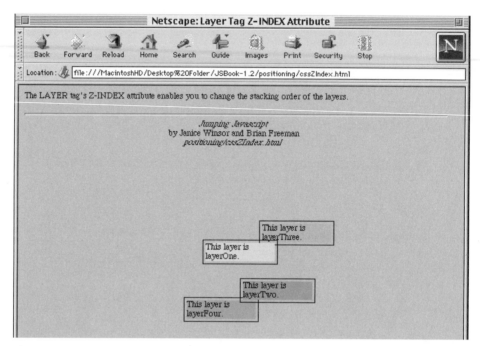

Figure 4–12 Result of loading the `cssZIndex.html` script

`<LAYER>` Tag Positioning

The Navigator 4.x release supports an alternative to the CSS syntax for positioning blocks of HTML context. This alternative extends HTML to include the `<LAYER></LAYER>` tags.

Because other browsers may not be able to handle layers that you define by using the `<LAYER>` tag properties, Netscape also provides `<NOLAYER></NOLAYER>` tags that enable you to provide alternative HTML for display in those browsers that may not support the `<LAYER>` tags.

In contrast to defining CSS layers, with the `<LAYER>` tags you specify the position and content of a layer of HTML inside a `<LAYER>` tag within the body of the page. The `<LAYER>` tag supports the attributes described in Table 4-1 on page 133. It also supports the following event handlers, which have no equivalent in CSS positioning:

- `onMouseOver`

- `onMouseOut`

- `onFocus`

- onBlur

- onLoad

For more information on using these event handlers with the <LAYER> tags, refer to Chapter 6, "Dynamic HTML."

The following ltag.html script uses the <LAYER> tag to position the footer for our script examples 100 pixels from the top, 175 pixels from the left, with a width of 400 pixels, and a font family of Courier.

```
<!--
                ltag.html

      This example positions the document footer with a LAYER tag.

-->
<HTML>
  <HEAD>
    <TITLE>Layer Tag</TITLE>
  </HEAD>
  <BODY>
    <LAYER
      id=              "aLayer"
      top=             "100px"
      left=            "175"
      width=           "400"
      fontFamily=      "Courier">
      <CENTER><hr SIZE=3 WIDTH="100%">
        <DT><I>Jumping Javascript</I></DT>
        <DT>by Janice Winsor and Brian Freeman</DT>
        <DT><I>positioning/ltag.html</I></DT>
      </CENTER>
    </LAYER>
  </BODY>
</HTML>
```

Figure 4–13 shows the result of loading the ltag.html script.

```
┌──────────────────────────── Netscape: Layer Tag ───────────────────────────┐
│  Back  Forward  Reload  Home  Search  Guide  Images  Print  Security  Stop  │  N
├─────────────────────────────────────────────────────────────────────────────┤
│  Location : file:///Macintosh%20HD/Desktop%20Folder/JSBook-1.2/positioning/ltag.html │
├─────────────────────────────────────────────────────────────────────────────┤
│                                                                             │
│                                                                             │
│                                                                             │
│                               Jumping JavaScript                            │
│                         by Janice Winsor and Brian Freeman                  │
│                               positioning/ltag.html                         │
└─────────────────────────────────────────────────────────────────────────────┘
```

Figure 4–13 Result of loading the `ltag.html` script

Absolute Positioning

You position a layer absolutely with the <LAYER> tags by including the TOP and LEFT attributes as part of the <LAYER> tag definition.

```
<LAYER
   ID = "layername"
   LEFT = "nnnpx"
   TOP = "nnnpx"
```

The following example positions the content of the aLayer layer 200 pixels from the top and left.

```
<LAYER
   id        = "aLayer"
   left      = "200px"
   top       = "200px"
   bgcolor   = "yellow">
   aLayer's content starts and ends here.
</LAYER>
```

Relative Positioning

<ILAYER> and </ILAYER> are the in-flow layer HMTL tags that you use to specify positioning for content that is contained within another context. The <ILAYER> content is positioned within the context for the outer layer.

The following example indents the contents 25 pixels.

```
<ILAYER
   id      = "aLayer"
   left    = "25px"
   bgcolor = "yellow">
   aLayer's content starts and ends here.
</ILAYER>
```

The following example specifies an outside absolute layer by using the <LAYER>
tags and an inside in-flow layer by using the <ILAYER> tags.

```
The content begins here.
<LAYER
   id      = "outside"
   left    = "50px"
   top     = "100px"
   width   = "100px"
   bgcolor = "yellow">
   The outside content starts here.
   <ILAYER ID = "inside" BGCOLOR = "orange">
The inside content starts and ends here.
   </ILAYER>
   The outside content ends here.
</LAYER>
End of the content.
```

Identifying Layers by Name

When you create named layers, you can use the layer's ID as a name to refer to
the layer both in HTML and from the layer object. By default, layers are not
named.

Use the following syntax to identify a <LAYER> layer by name:

```
<LAYER ID=layername>
```

The layername ID must begin with an alphabetic character.

Note – The ID attribute is a new identifier for the NAME attribute. Although the
NAME attribute is still supported, it applies only to the <LAYER> tag.

Controlling the Width of Layers

Use the WIDTH attribute to control the width of the layer at which the contents
wrap. You can express the WIDTH value as an integer or as a percentage of the
width of the containing layer.

When you do not specify a value for the WIDTH attribute, the contents of the layer wrap at the right boundary of the enclosing layer.

Note – If the layer contains elements, such as images, that cannot be wrapped, those elements extend beyond the specified width. The actual width of the layer expands to accommodate nonwrapping elements.

The following example defines two layers, outside and inside. The width of the outside layer is set to 100 pixels. The width of the inside layer is set to 10 percent of the width of the enclosing outside layer, which is 10 pixels. When the script is loaded, the text wraps only at word boundaries. The longest word, containing, is wider than 10 pixels, so the layer expands from 10 pixels to accommodate the longest word.

```
<LAYER
    id        = "outside"
    left      = "100"
    top       = "100"
    width     = "100"
    bgcolor   = "yellow">
The width of this layer, outside,
is set to 100.
    <LAYER
      id      = "inside"
      width   = "10%"
      bgcolor = "salmon">
      This layer, inside, sets its width to
      10 percent of the containing layer's width. The containing
      layer is outside.
    </LAYER>
</LAYER>
```

Controlling the Height of Layers

Use the HEIGHT attribute to control the initial height of the clipping region of the layer. You can express the HEIGHT value as an integer or as a percentage of the height of the containing layer.

When you do not specify a value for the HEIGHT attribute, the height is the minimum height that contains all of the contents of the layer.

Note – If the layer contains elements, such as images, that cannot fit inside the specified height, the actual height of the layer expands to accommodate all of the contents.

The following example defines two layers, outside and inside. The height of the outside layer is set to 100 pixels. The height of the inside layer is set to 300% of the height of the enclosing outside layer. Because the contents of the outside layer require more than 100 pixels to display completely, the height becomes a reference for the child inside layer.

```
<LAYER
   id        = "outside"
   left      = "100"
   top       = "100"
   width     = "100"
   height    = "100"
   bgcolor   = "yellow">
The height of this layer,outside,
is set to 100.
   <LAYER
    id        = "inside"
    left      = "100"
    top       = "100"
    width     = "100"
    height    = "300%"
    bgcolor   = "salmon">
    This layer, inside, sets its height to
    300 percent of the containing layer's height. The
    containing layer is outside.
   </LAYER>
Note that outside's height is larger than
100 pixels. In this case, the height property acts as a
reference for the child layer inside.
</LAYER>
```

Clipping Layers

Use the CLIP attribute to define the boundaries for the visible area of the layer. You define the values for the CLIP attribute as a comma-separated set of four numbers indicating left, top, right, and bottom values. Optionally, you can enclose the numbers in a quoted string. If you do not quote the string, do not include any white space between the numbers.

You specify the left and right values as the number of pixels from the left edge of the layer. You specify the top and bottom values as the number of pixels down from the top edge of the layer. The following example clips the layer at the right and bottom at 200 pixels.

```
<LAYER CLIP="0px,0px,200px,200px">
```

If you want to clip only the right and bottom of the layer, you can specify a set of two numbers. The left and top values default to 0. The following example is equivalent to the one above.

```
<LAYER CLIP="200px,200px">
```

Controlling the Visibility of Layers

Use the VISIBILITY attribute to determine whether the layer is visible or not. By default, a layer has the same visibility as its parent layer. In other words, the default value of the VISIBILITY attribute is INHERIT. The HIDE value hides the layer, and SHOW shows the layer. You can omit the VISIBILITY attribute value if you want the layer to inherit its value from the parent layer, or you can explicitly set the value to INHERIT.

If the layer is the top layer, the default VISIBILITY value is SHOW because the body document is always visible.

Even if the visibility of a layer is set to SHOW, you can see the layer only if there are no other visible opaque layers stacked on top of it. When a layer is set to HIDE, its contents are not shown. However, the layer still takes up space in the document flow.

The following example defines four layers: one is the parent, one shows the layer, another hides the layer, and the fourth inherits the visibility attribute from the parent layer.

```
<LAYER
    id = "layerOne"
    top = "100"
    left = "200"
    bgcolor = "yellow">
    <P>This layer is the parent.</P>
    <LAYER
id = "showLayer"
    top = "25"
    left = "25"
visibility = "show"
bgcolor = "orange">
<P>This layer is visible.</P>
    </LAYER>
    <LAYER
```

```
id = "hideLayer"
     top = "50"
     left = "50"
visibility = "hide"
bgcolor = "lightblue">
<P>This layer is invisible.</P>
   </LAYER>
   <LAYER
id = "inheritLayer"
     top = "75"
     left = "75"
visibility = "inherit"
bgcolor = "salmon">
<P>This layer inherits its visibility from the
parent layer</P>
   </LAYER>
 </LAYER>
```

Specifying the Background Color of Layers

Use the BGCOLOR property to specify the solid background color for a block of
HTML content. You can specify the background color by name or by specifying a
hexadecimal RGB value.

If you specify no background color, the background of the layer is transparent.

The following example specifies a background color of lavender by using the
color name:

```
<LAYER BGCOLOR="lavender>
```

The following example specifies a background color of lavender by using its
hexadecimal RGB value:

```
<LAYER BGCOLOR=#E6E68C>
```

When you define a background color by using the <LAYER> tag, the color is
applied to the rectangular region occupied by the layer. By contrast, a CSS
background color is applied only to the background for the specific content of the
layer.

Specifying the Background Image of Layers

Use the BACKGROUND attribute to draw a tiled image across the background of a
block of HTML content. The value for this property is the URL for an image.

If you specify no background image, the background of the layer is transparent.

The following example uses the BACKGROUND attribute to include the
rainbow.gif file as the background image for the layer.

```
<LAYER
   id = "layerOne"
   background = "../images/rainbow.gif"
   top = "100"
   left = "200"
   width  = "300"
   height = "432">
   <H1>Layer One</H1>
   <P>This layer is defined with a &lt;LAYER&gt; tag.</P>
   <P>The background image is applied to the region occupied
by the layer. The height is determined by the value of
the height property.</P>
</LAYER>
```

Including Externally Specified Layers

Use the SRC attribute to specify an external file that contains HTML-formatted text that you want to display as part of the layer. The value for this attribute is a URL for the file.

The following example includes an HTML file containing text. Note that you can specify the layer formatting either as part of the included file or within the HTML file that calls the included file.

```
<LAYER
   top  = "150"
   left = "250"
   src  = "haiku.html">
</LAYER>
```

Controlling the Stacking Order of Layers

Use the Z-INDEX attribute to specify the stacking order of layers that have the same parent layer. The Z-INDEX value is a positive integer, with higher-numbered values stacked above those with lower ones.

The following example creates four layers and assigns each one a different Z-INDEX value.

```
<LAYER
   id = "layerOne"
   z-index = "3"
   top = "200"
   left = "250"
   width = "100"
   height = "100"
   bgcolor = "yellow">
   This layer is layerOne.
</LAYER>
```

```
<LAYER
  id = "layerTwo"
  z-index = "4"
  top = "250"
  left = "300"
  width = "100"
  height = "100"
  bgcolor = "orange">
  This layer is layerTwo.
</LAYER>

<LAYER
  id = "layerThree"
  z-index = "1"
  top = "175"
  left = "325"
  width = "100"
  height = "100"
  bgcolor = "lightblue">
  This layer is layerThree.
</LAYER>

<LAYER
  id = "layerFour"
  z-index = "2"
  top = "275"
  left = "225"
  width = "100"
  height = "100"
  bgcolor = "salmon">
  This layer is layerFour.
</LAYER>
```

You can also use the ABOVE and BELOW attributes, which have no equivalents in CSS, to stack a layer on top of or below the newly created layer.

The following example creates four layers and uses the ABOVE attribute to position layerThree on top of layerFour.

```
<LAYER
  id = "layerOne"
  top = "200"
  left = "100"
  width = "100"
  height = "100"
  bgcolor = "yellow">
  This layer is layerOne.
</LAYER>
```

```
<LAYER
  id = "layerOne"
  top = "250"
  left = "150"
  width = "100"
  height = "100"
  bgcolor = "orange">
  This layer is layerTwo.
</LAYER>

<LAYER
  id = "layerThree"
  top = "200"
  left = "350"
  width = "100"
  height = "100"
  bgcolor = "lightblue">
  This layer is layerThree.
</LAYER>

<LAYER
  id = "layerFour"
  top = "250"
  left = "400"
  width = "100"
  height = "100"
  above = "layerThree"
  bgcolor = "salmon">
  This Layer is layerFour>. It contains an
  above attribute set to layerThree.
</LAYER>
```

Dynamic and Downloadable Fonts

▼ A WORD ABOUT ON-LINE FONTS

▼ INTRODUCING DYNAMIC FONTS

▼ HOW TO USE DOWNLOADABLE FONTS

One of the most frustrating things for Web page designers was the inability to control what fonts were displayed in the user's browser. With the Navigator 4 release, Web authors can include a `<LINK>` tag that instructs the browser to download a Bitstream TrueDoc font definition file as part of a Web page. Each file can contain more than one font definition. One reference to a font file can load all the necessary fonts for a page. For complete information about TrueDoc fonts, see `http://www.truedoc.com`.

This chapter discusses some issues of on-line fonts and terminology, describes how to create font definition files, link the definition into the document, and use the font. It also shows how to link directly to the TrueDoc server so that you can use definitions for fonts that you do not already own in your Web page designs.

A Word About On-line Fonts

Style sheets provide the flexibility to enable Web designers to specify on-line fonts. Fonts used in desktop publishing are usually designed for specific platforms, and the emphasis is primarily on producing printed output.

On-line font design has a different set of issues than fonts designed for the printed page. Traditional fonts that work well in print may have definitions that are too fine, don't scale well at different sizes, or have shapes that are too round and lines that are too thin to display well with the pixels on a computer screen.

If you are familiar with typography and print fonts, you may find the transition to on-line fonts a bit confusing.

Font Families

In the Web environment, the term *font family* can mean one of the following generic families that you can use in designating fonts in HTML documents:

- Serif
- Sansserif
- Monospace
- Cursive
- Fantasy

It can also mean the specific *typeface* implementation such as Times Roman or Palatino.

A *serif* is a small line used to finish off a main stroke of a letter, as at the top and bottom of M. For printed documents, serif fonts, such as Times Roman, are considered the most readable for general use, although on-line serif fonts may not necessarily be easily readable.

Sansserif fonts lack the additional embellishments and may be easier to read on-line.

Monospace fonts are those that imitate old-fashioned typewriters or computer display fonts such as Courier. Each letter takes up the same space, regardless of its width. An i takes up the same space as an m. Monospace fonts are useful for numerical outputs and for program listings to ensure that items line up properly in columns.

Cursive fonts, such as Zapf-Chancery, imitate handwriting. They are used almost exclusively for artistic effect and can be difficult to read on-line.

Fantasy fonts such as Blippo Bold are also used for artistic effect. They may cause difficulties in use on-screen because one fantasy font cannot easily substitute for another.

Pixels and Point Sizes

Typographers normally specify type in point size. A *point* is the equivalent of 1/72 inch. The natural unit of size on a computer monitor is a *pixel*, which is a contraction for picture element. A pixel is a single dot on a display screen. The number of pixels on a monitor can vary widely. A Macintosh system monitor has 72 pixels to the inch. A typical non-Mac PC monitor has 96 pixels per inch. High-resolution monitors may have 120 pixels per inch. Some monitors are scalable, and users can choose one of several different screen resolutions. What this variation in pixel resolution and size means is that, depending on the monitor, fonts may look 2 to 3 points larger on one monitor than on the next.

Font Sizes

It's important to understand exactly how the browser interprets the font sizes you specify. You can specify fonts in either absolute or relative sizes. When you specify a font size from 1 to 7 in the SIZE attribute of the FONT tag, you are specifying *relative sizes*. In style sheets, these values are converted as shown in Table 5-1.

Table 5-1 Font SIZE Attributes

Attribute	Style Sheet Values
1	xx-small
2	x-small
3	small
4	medium
5	large
6	x-large
7	xx-large

Note – The SIZE attributes do not correspond to traditional typographical point size.

When you specify a point size such as 12pt, you are specifying *absolute sizes*. Even on the printed page, different font families of the same point size display differently, as shown in Figure 5–1. The point size for each font is determined by the *x-height*: the height of the lowercase letter x in the particular implementation.

Palatino 12pt

Times Roman 12pt

Courier 12pt

Avant Garde 12pt

Bookman 12pt

Helvetica 12pt

New Century Schoolbook 12pt

Figure 5–1 Different size characteristics of fonts set to the same point size

For more information about on-line font issues and discussions, refer to:
`http://www.w3.org/Fonts/`

For a glossary of type terminology, refer to:
`http://www.adobe.com/supportservice/devrelations/typeforum/`
`glossary.html`

Introducing Dynamic Fonts

If you want users to see your documents in the way you designed them, use dynamic fonts. *Dynamic fonts* is the term that Bitstream uses to describe the technology behind their TrueDoc fonts.

TrueDoc fonts are designed and stored in a compact data structure called a *portable font resource* (PFR). The PFR for each font contains a limited font description that is relevant only to the current document. PFR files are relatively small and easy to download, and you only need to download the PFR file once per document.

According to Bitstream, dynamic fonts provide the following benefits:

* Uses standard HTML tags
* Enables Web authors to format text without using bitmap graphics in the form of GIF or JPEG files
* Reduces download time
* Preserves text so that users can search through it
* Enables search engines to include the text you have preserved in their databases

- Dynamically displays text on the user's browser.

TrueDoc dynamic fonts have two main components:

- The Character Shape Player(CSP)
- The Character Shape Recorder (CSR)

Web authoring tools are including the CSP as part of their product. The CSP enables a browser or authoring tools to display PFR fonts. Netscape has included CSP as part of the Navigator 4 release.

The CSR authoring tools enables users to create PSR files from TrueType and PostScript Type 1 fonts they already own. The CSR authoring tool is available as a plug-in to Netscape Composer. Other HTML editors are also incorporating the font recorder in their software.

Two currently-available stand-alone TrueDoc authoring tools are:

- HexMac Typograph
- Extensis BeyondPress

You create TrueDoc PFR files by using a TrueDoc-capable authoring tool to incorporate the TrueType and PostScript Type 1 fonts that you already have. When creating a PFR, most dynamic font tools create a document-specific file that includes only the characters used in the document, omitting the unused ones. The PFR file can be much smaller than a complete font definition file because a PFR file does not contain the complete set of characters, making it faster to download. Some authoring tools enable you to record the entire character set or the "lower 128," which can be useful in creating PFRs to share between documents.

Nobody can steal your fonts because they are protected by the TrueDoc DocLock security keys.

If you don't want to create your own fonts, Bitstream provides a set of PFR files on `http://www.truedoc.com` that you can link into your Web pages.

How to Use Downloadable Fonts

Before you can create PFR files from your own fonts, you must have a TrueDoc-capable authoring tool. This section describes the steps you follow to incorporate your own PFR files and assumes that you have such a tool available. To create PFR files, follow the instructions for the authoring tool you have.

To use downloadable fonts, you must perform the following tasks:

- Create the PFR files using the a Character Shape Recorder authoring tool, or identify a PFR file on the TrueDoc Web page.

- Link the font definition into the document by using the <LINK > tag.

- Use the font definition by specifying the font as part of a CSS style sheet or by using the <FONT></FONT> HTML tags.

- Make sure that the server has the right MIME types installed.

HTML Brushup — <LINK> Tag

Use the <LINK> tag to import an external document or a PFR font file into a Web page.

<LINK>	Import an external document
REL	Define the relationship of the document. For style sheets, you specify the value REL="stylesheet". Other possible values are Alternate, Start, Next, Prev, Contents, Index, Glossary, Copyright, Section, Subsection, Appendix, Help, and Bookmark.
TYPE	The type of style sheet, either "text/css" or "text/JavaScript"
HREF	The URL for the style sheet you are importing
TITLE	The name of the style sheet

The following example uses the <LINK> tag to import first a CSS and then a JavaScript style sheet:

<LINK REL="stylesheet" TYPE="text/css" HREF="style.css">

<LINK REL="stylesheet" TYPE="text/javascript" HREF="style2.jss">

Linking the Font Definition into the Document

You link the font definition into the document by including it as part of a <LINK> tag that you put between the <HEAD> and </HEAD> tags at the top of an HTML document.

The following example links a font named Calligraph421 from the TrueDoc Web site.

```
<LINK REL=FONTDEF
SRC="http://www.truedoc.com/pfrs/Calligraph421.pfr">
```

The REL attribute specifies that the linked file is a font definition. The SRC attribute specifies the source for the font definition, in this case, the PFR file.

The PFR files on the TrueDoc server contain representations of all of the characters in the font.

If you have a local PFR font file, you use the SRC attribute to include the path to the file.

Using the Font Definition

You can specify where the font is used either by including it as part of a CSS style sheet or by using the <FONT></FONT> HTML tags.

Cascading Style Sheets

When you use CSS to define styles, you also must include the font definition in your style sheets for those elements that you want to use that particular font. In the following example, the font family is included in the fancy class and is used for <H1> tags.

```
<STYLE TYPE="text/css">

    P.fancy   {font-family:"Calligraph421 BT";
               font-size:24pt}
    H1        {font-family:"Calligraph421 BT";
               font-size:24pt}
</STYLE>
```

A TrueDoc-enabled browser such as Netscape Communicator or Internet Explorer 4 for Windows can download this font. Browsers that cannot handle that particular format or that don't download fonts use the user's default font for <H1> tags.

Figure 5–2 shows the result of using this font definition.

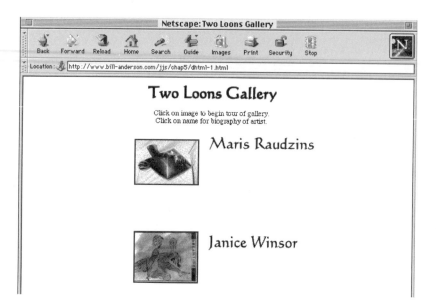

Figure 5–2 Page using TrueDoc fonts

For the complete script of this example, see "Putting It All Together" on page 199 in Chapter 6.

HTML Brushup — Specifying Fonts

You specify fonts by using the <FONT></font> tags to enclose text that you want to display in a specific font.

<FONT

COLOR=*"colorTripletOrName"*

FACE=*"FontFaceName"*

ID=*"identifier"*

POINT-SIZE=*"positiveInteger"*

SIZE=*"positiveInteger"*

STYLE=*"styleSheetProperties*

WEIGHT=*"positiveInteger between 100 and 900 in increments of 100"*

</FONT>

<FONT > </FONT> tags

If you don't have a lot of text to mark up or if the document is small, you can use the <FONT></FONT> HTML tags.

The following example uses the Calligraph421 font for the Two Loons Gallery heading.

```
<FONT FACE="Calligraph421 BT" POINT-SIZE="24">
Two Loons Gallery
</FONT>
```

Specifying the PFR MIME Type on the Server

For users to be able to download and view TrueDoc PFRs from their TrueDoc-enabled web browsers, system administrators must set up their Web servers to recognize the PFR MIME type.

The MIME type is:

```
application/font-tdpfr
```

The file extension is

```
pfr
```

The complete definition for the mime.types file of Netscape Suitespot server is:

```
type=application/font-tdpfr exts=pfr
```

If you are using a Windows NT or UNIX server, the gopher type is:

```
5:REG_SZ:
```

For a Windows NT or UNIX server, the entire key looks like this:

```
application/font-tdpfr,pfr,,5:REG_SZ:
```

Depending on the Web server, the system administrator may need to enter the extension in upper case or lower case (or both) and put a period before the extension.

Note that, in the future, you may also have to specify an additional MIME type, as follows:

```
/font/truedoc
```

For more information refer to the TrueDoc Web page at:

```
http://www.truedoc.com
```

Dynamic HTML

▼ WHAT IS DHTML?

▼ THE JAVASCRIPT LAYER OBJECT

▼ LAYER OBJECT EVENT HANDLERS

▼ PUTTING IT ALL TOGETHER

Dynamic HTML (DHTML) enables Web authors to download an entire set of page elements when a user specifies a URL. The user can then manipulate the elements in whatever ways the Web authors have scripted without having to refer back to the server.

DHML enables Web authors to go beyond the limits of pages designed with HTML. The basic concept of DHTML is simple. It breaks the document into containers of information that Web authors can address and modify separately. Scripts are no longer static. With DHTML. the Web author can dynamically control and change style elements, positioning, fonts, and layers, modifying the HTML code directly.

This chapter first describes the elements of DHTML and then focuses on how you can use the new JavaScript `layer` object and event model to create dynamic Web pages.

181

What Is DHTML?

There is no single specification for DHTML. Instead, it is an aggregation of specifications that come from a variety of standards bodies and proprietary development. To complicate the picture further, standards bodies make recommendations, but browsers do not need to follow those recommendations. Implementations of standards for each of the parts of DHTML can differ from browser to browser.

DHTML Standards Bodies

If you look at the technologies that combine to make DHTML work from a standards perspective, the list would look like this:

- HTML standards provide the basic structural elements of a Web page.

- ECMAScript is the European Computer Manufacturers Association standardization of Netscape's implementation of the client-side JavaScript 1.1 language. In addition to core JavaScript functionality, which provides data types, variables, control structures, and so on, ECMAScript also includes the new `layer` object and the new event model that enables Web authors to programmatically manipulate DHTML Web pages.

- CSS1 standards provide a way to define style sheets that control the look of the content. Netscape complies with CSS1 and also provides its own style sheet syntax that works only in Netscape browsers.

- CSS-P standards define positioning of blocks of HTML, both text and graphics. Netscape supports the working draft CSS-P recommendation available when Navigator 4 was under development. Netscape also provides its own `<LAYER>` and `<ILAYER>` tags that work only in Netscape browsers.

- CSS2 standards is the next evolution of cascading style sheet syntax; it combines CSS1 and CSS-P standards.

- The *document object model* (DOM) standards define what constitutes a document. DOM specifies which scriptable entities are maintained in a browser's memory when a document is loaded. Scripts can dynamically access the objects that are an inherent part of that document without referring back to the server for more data. Because DOM standards were late in evolving, both Netscape and Microsoft implemented their own versions of DOM in their release 4 browsers. Navigator 4 has no automatic refresh or content reflow and is much more limited in the HTML tags that enable scriptable access. Internet Explorer 4 provides a much richer feature set, enabling Web authors to access virtually any HTML element as part of its DOM. However, the MSIE object model is not clearly documented and is not internally consistent.

- And coming soon, extensible markup language (XML), which is being touted as the next solution to Web programming. XML is a subset of the standard generalized markup language (SGML). Advocates tout it as simple, extensible, interoperable, and open. If you're familiar at all with SGML, you'll be rightly skeptical of the claims of simplicity.

DHTML Functionality and Features

If you slice up DHTML differently and look at the functionality and features that are available to Web authors on specific browsers as a result of the collection of standards, your DHTML list might look like this:

- DOM standards (quite different in Netscape and Microsoft)

- Style sheets (Netscape and Microsoft)

- Absolute content positioning (Netscape and Microsoft)

- Downloadable fonts (Netscape)

- The new JavaScript event model (quite different in Netscape and Microsoft). The Netscape JavaScript model passes events down the hierarchy. The Microsoft JScript model bubbles events up through the object hierarchy.

- Scripting language such as JavaScript (Netscape) or JScript and VBScript (Microsoft). Both JavaScript 1.2 and 1.3 and JScript have extensions that go far beyond the W3C ECMAScript standard.

Problems with Cross-Browser Scripting

Because standards were emerging at the time both Microsoft and Netscape were developing their release 4 browsers, you're likely to encounter problems if you write scripts for either Navigator 4 or Internet Explorer 4 and expect the scripts to work properly on the other browser. The biggest difference is in the implementations of the DOM and in how you programmatically access them.

How can you deal with this problem? You can write code for one browser or the other, or you can determine what works in both browsers and code to that subset.

Many Web authors are dealing with cross-browser scripting problems by writing libraries that avoid some of the browser-specific features and hide some of the incompatibilities.

The JavaScript layer Object

The `layer` object is a Netscape addition to the JavaScript 1.2 release to enable you to programmatically manipulate layers. You create the `layer` object by using cascading style sheet syntax or by using the HTML `<LAYER>` `</LAYER>` or `<ILAYER>` `</ILAYER>` tags. The browser creates a `layer` object that corresponds to each layer in your document, storing the objects in an array in the `document.layers` property. You access a `layer` object by indexing into the array.

To define a layer, use CSS syntax and include the `position` property as shown in the following example.

```
#aLayer {
   position:     absolute;
   top:          100px;
   left:         175px;
   width:        400px;
   font-family:  Courier;
}
```

Alternatively, you can create a layer by using the HTML `<LAYER>` `</LAYER>` or `<ILAYER>` `</ILAYER>` tags, although these tags are supported only by Netscape. Refer to the HTML brushup box for more details.

HTML Brushup — Creating Layers

You create layers by using the <LAYER> </LAYER> tags to define a layer of content within a document. You can use the <ILAYER> </ILAYER> tags to define an inline layer of content within a text flow. The attributes are the same for both the <LAYER> and <ILAYER> tags:

<LAYER

ABOVE=*name*

BACKGROUND=*URL*

BELOW=*name*

BGCOLOR=*color*

CLASS=*name*

CLIP=*edge*

LEFT=*n*

ID or NAME=*name*

SRC=*URL*

STYLE=*style*

TOP=*n*

VISIBILITY=*value*

WIDTH=*n*

Z-INDEX=*n* >

body_content

</LAYER>

The properties, methods, and event handlers for the layer object are listed in alphabetical order in Table 6-1.

Table 6-1 Properties, Methods, and Event Handlers for the layer Object

Properties	Methods	Event Handlers
above	captureEvents	onBlur
background	handleEvent	onFocus
below	load	onLoad

Table 6-1 Properties, Methods, and Event Handlers for the layer Object (Continued)

Properties	Methods	Event Handlers
bgColor	moveAbove	onMouseDown
clip.bottom	moveBelow	onMouseOut
clip.height	moveBy	onMouseOver
clip.left	moveTo	onMouseUp
clip.right	moveToAbsolute	
clip.top	releaseEvents	
clip.width	resizeBy	
document	resizeTo	
id	routeEvent	
left		
name		
pageX		
pageY		
parentLayer		
siblingAbove		
siblingBelow		
src		
top		
visibility		
zIndex		

You can access a layer from JavaScript by the layer's ID or by the index number in the following ways:

```
document.layername
document.layers[layername]
document.layers[index]
```

As with any JavaScript object, you can access the properties of the `layer` object by using the following syntax:

```
layerObject.propertyName
```

Property names are case sensitive.

Naming Layers

If the layers have been assigned a name, you can use the `id` or `name` property to reference layers by name, using the format:

```
document.layers[n].id
```

Property	Value	Gettable	Settable
id or name	string	Yes	No

Referencing the Layer's Document

Each `layer` object contains its own `document` object. You can use this object to access the layers, images, applets, embeds, links, and anchors contained within the layer. You can also use methods of the `document` object to change the contents of the layer.

Property	Value	Gettable	Settable
document	string	Yes	No

Referencing the Layer's Source Document

If the layer has been assigned a source with the `SRC` attribute, you can use the `src` property to reference the URL string that specifies the source of the layer's content. You can also change the source for the layer by using this property.

Property	Value	Gettable	Settable
src	URL	Yes	Yes

Positioning Layers

You use the properties listed in the table below to position a layer within the document and to refer to layers above and below the current layer.

Property	Value	Gettable	Settable
top	number	Yes	Yes
left	number	Yes	Yes
above	array index	Yes	No
below	array index	Yes	No
parentLayer	layerName or windowName	Yes	No
siblingAbove	array index	Yes	No
siblingBelow	array index	Yes	No
pageX	number (pixels)	Yes	Yes
pageY	number (pixels)	Yes	Yes
zIndex	array	Yes	Yes

The top and left properties specify the position of the top or left edge of the layer in relation to the origin of its parent layers for layers with absolute position or relative to the natural flow position for layers with relative positions. The value is an integer, in pixels, or a percentage of the size of the layer.

The above, below, siblingAbove, siblingBelow, and zIndex properties specify relative positions of the layer object above or below in the z-order, or the stacking order, of the layer above or below the current layer. The value is either the index number of the layer or the name of a layer. For the zIndex property, the value is the relative order of this layer with respect to other layers. Layers with lower zIndex numbers are stacked beneath this layer. Higher zIndex values put the layer closer to the viewer. For example, a layer with a zIndex of 30 would overlay a layer with a zIndex of 20.

The pageX and pageY properties specify the horizontal and vertical position of the layer relative to the page. The value is an integer in pixels.

Setting the Background Color or Image of a Layer

You use the properties listed in the table below to specify the background color or background image for a layer.

Property	Value	Gettable	Settable
background	URL	Yes	Yes
bgColor	hexadecimal string or predefined JavaScript color	Yes	Yes

You can set the background color for a layer or provide a background image. If the background image is smaller than the layer, it is tiled to repeat itself. Images larger than the rectangle are clipped to the rectangle of the layer. You can change both the background color and image on the fly. The following functions change the background color of a layer.

```
function preClick(evt) {
    oldColor = evt.target.bgColor
    evt.target.bgColor = "yellow"
    return false
}

function clrClick(evt) {
    evt.target.bgColor = oldColor
    return false
}

function beginClick(evt) {
    // Ignore any other mouse button
    if (evt.which != 1) return false
    evt.target.bgColor = "lightgreen"
    return false
}
```

See "Putting It All Together" on page 199 for the complete script.

Clipping Layers

You use the properties listed in the table below to show part of a layer while hiding another part. Values can be negative, 0, or positive integers.

Property	Value	Gettable	Settable
clip.top	pixels	Yes	Yes
clip.bottom	pixels	Yes	Yes
clip.left	pixels	Yes	Yes
clip.right	pixels	Yes	Yes
clip.height	pixels	Yes	Yes
clip.width	pixels	Yes	Yes

The following function extracted from the dhtml-2.html script uses clip properties to create a transition effect when images are changed. It also uses the visibility property to show and hide different layers. See "Putting It All Together" on page 199 for the complete script.

```
// horizWipe is a generic routine that handles both the closing
// and opening of a layer.

function horizWipe(lyrStr, nextStr, pxRate, theWidth, delay) {

   var lyrID = eval(lyrStr)

   if ((lyrID.clip.width + pxRate) > theWidth){
      lyrID.clip.width = theWidth
      return
   }

   lyrID.clip.left += -(pxRate/2)
   lyrID.clip.right += (pxRate/2)

// checking for zero prevents an endless loop, since the browser
// doesn't allow a width of less than zero.

   if (lyrID.clip.width <= 0) {
      lyrID.clip.width = 0
      lyrID.visibility = "hide"

// After closing one picture, it is time to set up for opening
// the next picture. The trick is to start with clip.right and
```

```
// clip.left equal to half the layer width.

    pxRate = -pxRate
    lyrStr = nextStr
    var nextLyr = eval(lyrStr)
    nextLyr.clip.left = theWidth / 2
    nextLyr.clip.right = theWidth / 2
    nextLyr.visibility = "show"
}
```

Controlling Visibility

Use the `visibility` property to control whether the layer is visible and whether it inherits the visibility of the parent layer. The default is to inherit the visibility of the parent layer.

Property	Value	Gettable	Settable
visibility	show | hide | inherit	Yes	Yes

The `visibility` property is set by the `VISIBILITY` attribute. The attribute can be set to one of three values:

- SHOW displays the layer in the normal way.
- HIDE makes the layer invisible.
- INHERIT makes the layer's visibility the same as that of its parent layer.

Moving Layers

You can use the methods listed below to move layers in specific ways.

Method

moveBelow(*alayer*)

moveBy(horizontal, vertical)

moveTo(x-coordinate, y-coordinate)

moveToAbsolute(x, y)

Returns

Nothing

Use the `moveBelow` method to stack the layer below the specified layer without changing the horizontal or vertical position of either layer. After restacking, both layers share the same parent layer.

Use the `moveBy` method to change the layer position horizontally and vertically by the specified number of pixels.

Use the `moveTo` method to move the top-left corner of the element to the specified screen coordinates within the enclosing container. If the enclosing container is another layer, then the inner layer moves according to the coordinates of the enclosing layer. For example, `moveTo(0,0)` positions the top-left corner of the layer in the top-left corner of the window.

Use the `moveToAbsolute` to change the position of the layer to the specified pixel coordinates within the page, instead of within the containing layer. Using this method is equivalent to setting both the `pageX` and `pageY` properties of the `layer` object.

The following function extracted from the `dhtml-3.html` script uses the `moveBy()` method to move images around on the screen. See "Putting It All Together" on page 199 for the complete script.

```
function swapImg(workImg, nextImg, pxRate, delay) {
    lyrRef = eval("document.imgLayer.document.img" + workImg)
    snootObj.moveBy(pxRate,0)
    lyrRef.moveBy(pxRate, 0)

    if (pxRate < 0 & -lyrRef.left >= lyrRef.clip.width) {
        snootObj.visibility = "hide"
        lyrRef.visibility = "hide"
        var newLyr = eval("document.imgLayer.document.img" +
nextImg)
        newLyr.left = -newLyr.clip.width
        newLyr.visibility = "show"
        pxRate = -pxRate
        workImg = nextImg
        snootObj = rightSnoot
        snootObj.left = 5
        snootObj.visibility = "show"
    }

    else if (pxRate > 0 & lyrRef.left >= 0) {
        lyrRef.left = 5
        oldText = eval(slctTitle + currImage)
        oldText.visibility = "hide"
        newText = eval(slctTitle + nextImg)
        newText.visibility = "show"
        snootObj.visibility = "hide"
```

```
        currImage = nextImg
        return
}
```

Capturing and Releasing Events

You can use the `captureEvents` and `releaseEvents` methods to capture events in pages loaded from different locations and to release them when you are done. Use these methods in combination with the `routeEvent` and `handleEvent` methods.

Method

captureEvents(*eventType*)

releaseEvents(*eventType*)

handleEvent(*event*)

routeEvent(*event*)

Returns

Nothing

These methods require special parameters, which are static properties of the Event object (with a capital E). You can specify a single event or provide a list of multiple events separated by the bitwise OR operator (|). The following list shows the syntax for specifying the events that you can capture.

- Event.MOUSEDOWN
- Event.MOUSEMOVE
- Event.MOUOSEOUT
- Event.MOUSEOVER
- Event.MOUSEUP

The following example uses the `captureEvents()` method as part of event handling in the `dhtml-2.html` script. See "Putting It All Together" on page 199 for the complete script.

```
    slctBtn.captureEvents(Event.MOUSEDOWN | Event.MOUSEUP)
```

Of course, in addition to using these methods, you also need to provide an event handler for each event assigned to the object.

Changing the Source of a Layer

Use the load() method to change the source of a layer to the contents of a specified file and at the same time change the width at which the HTML contents of the layer are wrapped.

Method

load(*sourcestring, width*)

Returns

Nothing

layer Object Event Handlers

An event handler is a JavaScript structure that responds to a specific event such as a mouse click in a certain location. The response is that the script performs an action defined by specific event handler attributes. In the JavaScript 1.2 release, Netscape has expanded the event handler model to provide the capabilities for a window or document to capture certain types of events before they reach their intended target.

It's difficult to write DHTML scripts without using event handlers, and you'll see lots of events in the scripts in "Putting It All Together" on page 199. This section provides a brief introduction to some of the elements of the new event model. For a complete description of the new event model and the event object, see Chapter 9, "New Event Model."

The layer object provides the following event handlers:

- onBlur
- onFocus
- onLoad
- onMouseOut
- onMouseUp

Note – These event handlers are also available in the Netscape <LAYER> tag. They are not available for use with the <ILAYER> tag. Although Netscape's syntax specification implies that relative layers support events, in actual practice they do not.

Using Event Handlers to Control Window Focus

The layer object provides onBlur and onFocus event handlers to complement the blur() and focus() methods.

Event Handler

onBlur

Syntax

<BODY (*other attributes*) onBlur = "*JavaScript code*">

<FRAMESET (*other attributes*) onBlur="*JavaScript code*">

Use the onBlur event handler to perform an action when the user clicks away from the window. You include the onBlur event handler as an attribute of a <BODY> tag for a single-frame document or as an attribute of a <FRAMESET> tag for the top window of a multiple-frame document.

Event Handler

onFocus

Syntax

<BODY (*other attributes*) onFocus = "*JavaScript code*">

<FRAMESET (*other attributes*) onFocus="*JavaScript code*">

Use the onFocus event handler to perform an action when the user clicks in the window to set the input focus. You include the onFocus event handler as an attribute of a <BODY> tag for a single-frame document or as an attribute of a <FRAMESET> tag for the top window of a multiple-frame document.

Note – Window managers on each platform have different abilities to handle onBlur and onFocus events. Because of inconsistent behavior across all platforms, we suggest that you do not rely on the use of onBlur and onFocus event handlers in your scripts.

The Macintosh platform is the most limited of the platforms because it is a single-user, click-to-type platform. You can have only one active window at a time, and regardless of where you move the pointer, the active window gets all of the events. The Macintosh platform cannot respond to onBlur and onFocus events at the window level.

The X11 and Windows 95 platforms do respond to onBlur and onFocus event handlers, but these handlers behave differently on each of these platforms. The differences between X11 and Windows 95/98/NT arise from the handling of focus. In X11, including the Common Desktop Environment (CDE), the difficulty is that the window does not rise to the top when it receives the focus. In Windows, the window is raised to the top. CDE enables a user to specify explicit focus and raise the window to the top. When the user specifies this preference, then CDE and Windows behave the same.

Using Event Handlers on Load

The onLoad event handler enables you to perform scripting actions when file load events occur. The load event occurs when the browser finishes loading the window or all of the frames in a frameset. The onLoad event handler enables you to execute JavaScript code when the event occurs.

You include the onLoad event handler as an attribute of a <BODY> tag for a single-frame document or as an attribute of a <FRAMESET> tag for the top window of a multiple-frame document. When you use onLoad as an attribute of <FRAMESET>, the event triggers only after all frames defined by that frameset have loaded completely.

Event Handler

onLoad

Syntax

<BODY (*other attributes*) onload = "*JavaScript code*">

<FRAMESET (*other attributes*) onLoad = "*JavaScript code*">

Capturing Events on Mouse Out and on Mouse Up

The onMouseOut and onMouseUp events are part of the new event model with the JavaScript 1.2 release. Because these events respond to a click of a mouse button rather than an action that is performed on a specific user interface element, you script them in a slightly different way.

When a user clicks a mouse button to initiate an event that is targeted at a page element in the Navigator 4 release, the event moves down through the object hierarchy from the window, document, and layer objects that lead to the ultimate target. These intervening objects pass the event through without taking any action unless you instruct an object to intercept the event at a specific level.

To instruct an object to intercept an event, you use the captureEvents() method. The captureEvents() method uses the following syntax.

```
captureEvents(Event.EVENTTYPE | Event.EVENTTYPE)
```

See "Capturing and Releasing Events" on page 193 for a list of event types.

Event Handler
onMouseOut
onMouseUp
Syntax
document.onmouseout = *function*
document.onmouseup = *function*

The following excerpt from the `dhtml-2.html` script uses the `captureEvents()` method and shows the statements and functions for handling these events. See "Putting It All Together" on page 199 for the complete script.

```
// Event handlers for individual layers

marisResume.captureEvents(Event.MOUSEOVER | Event.MOUSEOUT |
Event.MOUSEDOWN | Event.MOUSEUP)

marisResume.onmouseover=preClick
marisResume.onmouseout=clrClick
marisResume.onmousedown=beginClick
marisResume.onmouseup=doMClick

janiceResume.captureEvents(Event.MOUSEOVER | Event.MOUSEOUT |
Event.MOUSEDOWN | Event.MOUSEUP)

janiceResume.onmouseover=preClick
janiceResume.onmouseout=clrClick
janiceResume.onmousedown=beginClick
janiceResume.onmouseup=doJClick

//
// Process Events

function preClick(evt) {
    oldColor = evt.target.bgColor
    evt.target.bgColor = "yellow"
    return false
}
```

```
function clrClick(evt) {
    evt.target.bgColor = oldColor
    return false
}

function beginClick(evt) {
    // Ignore any other mouse button
    if (evt.which != 1) return false
    evt.target.bgColor = "lightgreen"
    return false
}

//
// The evt.target object reference lacks the name property, so the
// script needs two event handlers - one for Maris and one for
Janice.

function doMClick(evt) {
    if (evt.which != 1) return false
    evt.target.bgColor = "lightsalmon"
    window.open("resume-maris.html", "marisWin",
      "titlebar,scrollbars")
    return false
}

function doJClick(evt) {
    if (evt.which != 1) return false
    evt.target.bgColor = "lightsalmon"
    window.open("resume-janice.html", "janiceWin",
      "titlebar,scrollbars")
    return false
}
```

Putting It All Together

This section provides a complete example of a virtual art gallery that uses DHTML to put it all together. The example is divided into three separate HTML files and includes external text files and graphics that are not included here. All of the files are available on the CD-ROM, however.

The first script in the example, dhtml-1.html, starts the tour of the Two Loons virtual art gallery. The script defines two functions. The displayLayer() function hides the old layer and shows the new one. The revealScr() function reveals the screen. It then creates the layers and includes the references for external documents. Event management routines and functions are positioned at the end of the script to avoid generating references to objects before the browser has defined them. The scripts also use downloadable fonts. For more information about downloadable fonts, see Chapter 5, "Dynamic and Downloadable Fonts."

```
<!--

                 dhtml-1.html


      An example of using DHTML.

-->
<HTML>
    <HEAD>
    <TITLE>Two Loons Gallery</TITLE>

<SCRIPT LANGUAGE="JavaScript">
<!--
//
// Get the size of the screen
scrWidth = window.innerWidth
scrCenter = scrWidth / 2
scrHeight = window.innerHeight

//
// Hide the old layer and show the new layer.

function displayLayer(oldLayer, newLayer) {
    if (oldLayer) oldLayer.visibility = "hide"
    layerRef = eval("document." + newLayer)
    layerRef.visibility = "show"
}

//
// Reveal the screen.
// Full object references are used as an example.
// The event management section shows a shorter method
// for referencing objects.

function revealScr() {
    document.Maris.clip.width = scrWidth
    document.Maris.clip.height = scrHeight
    document.Maris.document.Maris1.left = scrCenter - 140
    document.Maris.document.Maris2.left = scrCenter - 20
    displayLayer("", "Maris")
    document.Janice.clip.width = scrWidth
    document.Janice.clip.height = scrHeight
    document.Janice.document.Janice1.left = scrCenter - 140
    document.Janice.document.Janice2.left = scrCenter - 20
    displayLayer("", "Janice")
```

```
}

//-->
</SCRIPT>

<LINK REL=FONTDEF
SRC="http://www.truedoc.com/pfrs/Calligraph421.pfr">

<STYLE TYPE="text/css">
    P.fancy  {font-family:"Calligraph421 BT";
              font-size:24pt}
    H1       {font-family:"Calligraph421 BT";
              font-size:24pt}
    #Maris   {position:absolute;
              visibility:hide}
    #Maris1  {position:absolute;
              top:10;
              width:120;
              visibility:inherit}
    #Maris2  {position:absolute;
              width:200;
              visibility:inherit}
    #Janice  {position:absolute;
              top:240;
              visibility:hide}
    #Janice1 {position:absolute;
              width:120;
              visibility:inherit}
    #Janice2 {position:absolute;
              width:160;
              visibility:inherit}
</STYLE>
  </HEAD>

  <BODY BGCOLOR="white" ONLOAD="revealScr()">

    <H1 ALIGN="CENTER">Two Loons Gallery</H1>

    <P ALIGN="CENTER">Click on image to begin tour of
      gallery.<BR>
        Click on name for biography of artist.</P>
    <DIV ID="Maris">

    <P ID="Maris1"><A HREF="dhtml-2.html" NAME="mgallery"><IMG
SRC="images/Birth-1s.jpeg" ALT="Birth-1 (small)" WIDTH="100"
HEIGHT="68"></A></P>

    <P ID="Maris2" CLASS=fancy>Maris Raudzins</P> </DIV>
```

```
     <DIV ID="Janice">

     <P ID="Janice1"><A HREF="dhtml-3.html" NAME="jgallery"><IMG
SRC="images/Dreamtime-s.jpeg" ALT="Dreamtime (small)" WIDTH="100"
HEIGHT="77"></A></P>

     <P ID="Janice2" CLASS=fancy>Janice Winsor</P> </DIV>

<SCRIPT LANGUAGE="JavaScript">
<!--

//
// Event management routines are at the end to avoid generating any
// references to objects before the browser defines the object.
//
//
// Save the old color.

oldColor=""

//
// Define layer references

marisResume = document.Maris.document.Maris2
janiceResume = document.Janice.document.Janice2

//
// Define event handlers
//
// A standard event handler for dealing with the resizing of a
// Navigator window, since Netscape Navigator fails to
// correctly handle resizing.

window.captureEvents(Event.RESIZE)
window.onresize=resizeLayers

function resizeLayers() {
   location.reload()
   return false
}

//
// Event handlers for individual layers

marisResume.captureEvents(Event.MOUSEOVER | Event.MOUSEOUT |
Event.MOUSEDOWN | Event.MOUSEUP)

marisResume.onmouseover=preClick
```

```
marisResume.onmouseout=clrClick
marisResume.onmousedown=beginClick
marisResume.onmouseup=doMClick

janiceResume.captureEvents(Event.MOUSEOVER | Event.MOUSEOUT |
Event.MOUSEDOWN | Event.MOUSEUP)

janiceResume.onmouseover=preClick
janiceResume.onmouseout=clrClick
janiceResume.onmousedown=beginClick
janiceResume.onmouseup=doJClick

//
// Process events.

function preClick(evt) {
    oldColor = evt.target.bgColor
    evt.target.bgColor = "yellow"
    return false
}

function clrClick(evt) {
    evt.target.bgColor = oldColor
    return false
}
function beginClick(evt) {
    // Ignore any other mouse button.
    if (evt.which != 1) return false
    evt.target.bgColor = "lightgreen"
    return false
}


//
// The evt.target object reference lacks the name property, so the
// script needs two event handlers - one for Maris and one
// for Janice.

function doMClick(evt) {
    if (evt.which != 1) return false
    evt.target.bgColor = "lightsalmon"
    window.open("resume-maris.html", "marisWin",
"titlebar,scrollbars")
    return false
}

function doJClick(evt) {
    if (evt.which != 1) return false
    evt.target.bgColor = "lightsalmon"
```

```
    window.open("resume-janice.html", "janiceWin",
"titlebar,scrollbars")
    return false
}


//-->
</SCRIPT>
  </BODY>
</HTML>
```

Figure 6-1 shows the result of loading the `dhtml-1.html` script.

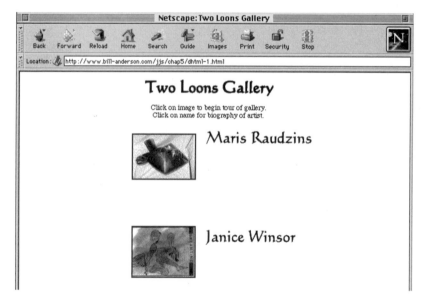

Figure 6–1 Result of loading the `dhtml-1.html` script

When you move the pointer over the names of the artists, the event handler changes the background color. Clicking on each name opens a new window with information about the artist. Clicking on the image opens the gallery for the individual artist.

The following `dhtml-2.html` script opens Maris's gallery. This script shows examples of how to show and hide layers dynamically. It also creates a transition effect by using the clip properties to gradually reduce the sides of each image and then expand the underlying image to display it in the same location. Moving the pointer over the name of the sculpture displays a popup window with more information about each sculpture as a new layer on top of the image. The popup window has a timeout and is hidden again when the time expires.

Event handlers manage the background color changes for the Next View text and
also control the transition effects.

```
<!--
                dhtml-2.html

    An example of using DHTML.

-->
<HTML>
  <HEAD>
    <META NAME="GENERATOR"
    CONTENT="NetObjects ScriptBuilder 2.01">

    <LINK REL=FONTDEF
SRC="http://www.truedoc.com/pfrs/Calligraph421.pfr">

    <TITLE>Maris's Gallery</TITLE>

    <STYLE TYPE="text/css">
        P.title {font-family:"Calligraph421 BT";
                 font-size:12pt}
        H1       {font-family:"Calligraph421 BT";
                 font-size:24pt}
        #Birth  {position:absolute;
                 visibility: visible}
        #Birth1 {position:absolute;
                 left:140;
                 visibility:inherit}
        #Birth2 {position:relative;
                 top:30;
                 visibility:inherit}
        #Birth21 {position:absolute;
                  visibility:inherit}
        #Birth22 {position:absolute;
                  visibility:hide}
        #Birth23 {position:absolute;
                  visibility:hide}
        #Birth3 {position:absolute;
                 left:140;
                 top:273;
                 visibility:inherit}
        #Birth4 {position:absolute;
                 top:30;
                 background-color:yellow;
                 border-style:ridge;
                 border-width:thin;
                 visibility:hide}
```

```
#Entw   {position:absolute;
         left:340;
         visibility: visible}
#Entw1  {position:absolute;
         left:120;
         visibility:inherit}
#Entw2  {position:relative;
         top:30;
         visibility:inherit}
#Entw21 {position:absolute;
         visibility:inherit}
#Entw22 {position:absolute;
         visibility:hide}
#Entw23 {position:absolute;
         visibility:hide}
#Entw3  {position:absolute;
         left:120;
         top:273;
         visibility:inherit}
#Entw4  {position:absolute;
         top:30;
         background-color:yellow;
         border-style:ridge;
         border-width:thin;
         visibility:hide}
#Extn   {position:absolute;
         top:400;
         z-index:40;
         visibility: visible}
#Extn1  {position:absolute;
         left:130;
         visibility:inherit}
#Extn2  {position:relative;
         top:30;
         visibility:inherit}
#Extn21 {position:absolute;
         visibility:inherit}
#Extn22 {position:absolute;
         visibility:hide}
#Extn23 {position:absolute;
         visibility:hide}
#Extn24 {position:absolute;
         visibility:hide}
#Extn3  {position:absolute;
         left:130;
         top:253;
         visibility:inherit}
#Extn4  {position:absolute;
```

```
                top:30;
                width:200;
                background-color:yellow;
                border-style:ridge;
                border-width:thin;
                visibility:hide}
      #Invit   {position:absolute;
                left:340;
                top:400;
                z-index:10;
                visibility: visible}
      #Invit1 {position:absolute;
                left:130;
                visibility:inherit}
      #Invit2 {position:relative;
                top:30;
                visibility:inherit}
      #Invit21 {position:absolute;
                 visibility:inherit}
      #Invit22 {position:absolute;
                 visibility:hide}
      #Invit3 {position:absolute;
                left:130;
                top:253;
                visibility:inherit}
      #Invit4 {position:absolute;
                top:30;
                background-color:yellow;
                border-style:ridge;
                border-width:thin;
                visibility:hide}
    </STYLE>
  </HEAD>

  <BODY BGCOLOR="white" ONLOAD="startIt()">
    <H1 ALIGN="CENTER">Maris Raudzin's Gallery</H1>

    <DIV ID="Birth">
      <P ID="Birth1" CLASS=title>Birth</P>
      <DIV ID="Birth2">
      <P ID="Birth21"><IMG SRC="images/Birth-1.jpeg" ALT="Birth"
ALIGN="MIDDLE" WIDTH="300" HEIGHT="211"></P>
      <P ID="Birth22"><IMG SRC="images/Birth-2.jpeg" ALT="Birth"
ALIGN="MIDDLE" WIDTH="300" HEIGHT="210"></P>
      <P ID="Birth23"><IMG SRC="images/Birth-3.jpeg" ALT="Birth"
ALIGN="MIDDLE" WIDTH="300" HEIGHT="210"></P>
      </DIV>
```

```
        <P ID="Birth3" CLASS=title>Next View</P>

        <DIV ID="Birth4">
          <P>Birth</P>
          <P>Bronze<BR>
             14 inches long<BR>
             8 1/2 inches high<BR>
             11 inches wide</P>
        </DIV>
      </DIV>

      <DIV ID="Entw">
        <P ID="Entw1" CLASS=title>Entwined</P>
        <DIV ID="Entw2">
          <P ID="Entw21"><IMG SRC="images/Entwined-1.jpeg"
ALT="Entwined" ALIGN="MIDDLE" WIDTH="300" HEIGHT="219"></P>
          <P ID="Entw22"><IMG SRC="images/Entwined-2.jpeg"
ALT="Entwined" ALIGN="MIDDLE" WIDTH="300" HEIGHT="219"></P>
          <P ID="Entw23"><IMG SRC="images/Entwined-3.jpeg"
ALT="Entwined" ALIGN="MIDDLE" WIDTH="300" HEIGHT="219"></P>
        </DIV>

        <P ID="Entw3" CLASS=title>Next View</P>

        <DIV ID="Entw4">
          <P>Entwined</P>
          <P>Two-piece Bronze<BR>
             9 inches long<BR>
             5 inches high<BR>
             6 inches wide</P>
        </Div>
      </DIV>

      <DIV ID="Extn">
        <P ID="Extn1" CLASS=title>Extinct</P>
        <DIV ID="Extn2">
          <P ID="Extn21"><IMG SRC="images/Extinct-1.jpeg"
ALT="Extinct" ALIGN="MIDDLE" WIDTH="300" HEIGHT="202"></P>
          <P ID="Extn22"><IMG SRC="images/Extinct-2.jpeg"
ALT="Extinct" ALIGN="MIDDLE" WIDTH="300" HEIGHT="202"></P>
          <P ID="Extn23"><IMG SRC="images/Extinct-3.jpeg"
ALT="Extinct" ALIGN="MIDDLE" WIDTH="300" HEIGHT="202"></P>
          <P ID="Extn24"><IMG SRC="images/Extinct-4.jpeg"
ALT="Extinct" ALIGN="MIDDLE" WIDTH="300" HEIGHT="202"></P>
        </DIV>

        <P ID="Extn3" CLASS=title>Next View</P>
```

```
        <DIV ID="Extn4">
          <P>Extinct</P>
          <P>Four-piece Plane Timber<BR>
              18 inches long, 10 1/2 inches high, 15 inches wide<BR>
              24 inches long, 9 inches high, 12 inches wide<BR>
              19 inches long, 8 inches high, 10 inches wide<BR>
              22 inches long, 10 inches high 15 inches wide</P>
          <P>This sculpture can be positioned in an amazing array of
              positions. Each new grouping brings fresh new life to
each
              of the four pieces.</P>
        </DIV>
      </DIV>

      <DIV ID="Invit">
        <P ID="Invit1" CLASS=title>Invitation</P>
        <DIV ID="Invit2">
          <P ID="Invit21"><IMG SRC="images/Invitation-1.jpeg"
ALT="Invitation" ALIGN="MIDDLE" WIDTH="300" HEIGHT="200"></P>
          <P ID="Invit22"><IMG SRC="images/Invitation-2.jpeg"
ALT="Invitation" ALIGN="MIDDLE" WIDTH="300" HEIGHT="200"></P>
        </DIV>

        <P ID="Invit3" CLASS=title>Next View</P>

        <DIV ID="Invit4">
          <P>Invitation</P>
          <P>Jarrah Timber<BR>
              27 inches long<BR>
              11 inches high<BR>
              17 inches wide</P>
        </DIV>
      </DIV>
    </BODY>

<SCRIPT LANGUAGE="JavaScript">
<!--
//
// Layer Object References
// work with the image layer reference as a string to allow
// modification and to allow passing of the string to the
// setTimeout() method.

var birthPics = "document.Birth.document.Birth2.document.Birth2"
var birthNext = document.Birth.document.Birth3
var birthPop = document.Birth.document.Birth1
var birthDesc = "document.Birth.document.Birth4"
var entwPics = "document.Entw.document.Entw2.document.Entw2"
```

```
var entwNext = document.Entw.document.Entw3
var entwPop = document.Entw.document.Entw1
var entwDesc = "document.Entw.document.Entw4"
var extnPics = "document.Extn.document.Extn2.document.Extn2"
var extnNext = document.Extn.document.Extn3
var extnPop = document.Extn.document.Extn1
var extnDesc = "document.Extn.document.Extn4"
var invitPics = "document.Invit.document.Invit2.document.Invit2"
var invitNext = document.Invit.document.Invit3
var invitPop = document.Invit.document.Invit1
var invitDesc = "document.Invit.document.Invit4"

//
// Event handlers
//

birthNext.captureEvents(Event.MOUSEOVER | Event.MOUSEOUT |
Event.MOUSEDOWN | Event.MOUSEUP)

birthNext.onmouseover=preClick
birthNext.onmouseout=clrClick
birthNext.onmousedown=beginClick
birthNext.onmouseup=doBirth
birthPop.captureEvents(Event.MOUSEOVER)
birthPop.onmouseover=doBirthPop

entwNext.captureEvents(Event.MOUSEOVER | Event.MOUSEOUT |
Event.MOUSEDOWN | Event.MOUSEUP)

entwNext.onmouseover=preClick
entwNext.onmouseout=clrClick
entwNext.onmousedown=beginClick
entwNext.onmouseup=doEntw

entwPop.captureEvents(Event.MOUSEOVER)
entwPop.onmouseover=doEntwPop

extnNext.captureEvents(Event.MOUSEOVER | Event.MOUSEOUT |
Event.MOUSEDOWN | Event.MOUSEUP)

extnNext.onmouseover=preClick
extnNext.onmouseout=clrClick
extnNext.onmousedown=beginClick
extnNext.onmouseup=doExtn

extnPop.captureEvents(Event.MOUSEOVER)
extnPop.onmouseover=doExtnPop
```

```
invitNext.captureEvents(Event.MOUSEOVER | Event.MOUSEOUT |
Event.MOUSEDOWN | Event.MOUSEUP)

invitNext.onmouseover=preClick
invitNext.onmouseout=clrClick
invitNext.onmousedown=beginClick
invitNext.onmouseup=doInvit

invitPop.captureEvents(Event.MOUSEOVER)
invitPop.onmouseover=doInvitPop

//
// Process Events
var btnColor = "lightgrey"
var birthIdx = 1
var entwIdx = 1
var extnIdx = 1
var invitIdx = 1
var lyrWidth = 0

function startIt() {
    birthNext.bgColor = btnColor
    entwNext.bgColor = btnColor
    extnNext.bgColor = btnColor
    invitNext.bgColor = btnColor
}

function preClick(evt) {
    evt.target.bgColor = "yellow"
    return false
}

function clrClick(evt) {
    evt.target.bgColor = btnColor
    return false
}

function beginClick(evt) {
    // Ignore any other mouse button.
    if (evt.which != 1) return false
    evt.target.bgColor = "lightgreen"
    return false
}

//
// The evt.target object reference lacks the name property, so
the
// script needs separate event handlers for each image.
```

```
function doBirth(evt) {
    if (evt.which != 1) return false
    evt.target.bgColor = "lightsalmon"
    var currPic = birthPics + birthIdx
    var lyrTarget = eval(currPic)
    lyrWidth = lyrTarget.clip.width
    birthIdx += 1

    if (birthIdx > 3) birthIdx = 1
    var nextPic = birthPics + birthIdx
    horizWipe(currPic, nextPic, -4, lyrWidth, 20)
    return false
}

function doEntw(evt) {
    if (evt.which != 1) return false
    evt.target.bgColor = "lightsalmon"
    var currPic = entwPics + entwIdx
    var lyrTarget = eval(currPic)
    lyrWidth = lyrTarget.clip.width
    entwIdx += 1

    if (entwIdx > 3) entwIdx = 1
    var nextPic = entwPics + entwIdx
    horizWipe(currPic, nextPic, -4, lyrWidth, 20)
    return false
}

function doExtn(evt) {
    if (evt.which != 1) return false
    evt.target.bgColor = "lightsalmon"
    var currPic = extnPics + extnIdx
    var lyrTarget = eval(currPic)
    lyrWidth = lyrTarget.clip.width
    extnIdx += 1

    if (extnIdx > 4) extnIdx = 1
    var nextPic = extnPics + extnIdx
    horizWipe(currPic, nextPic, -4, lyrWidth, 20)
    return false
}

function doInvit(evt) {
    if (evt.which != 1) return false
    evt.target.bgColor = "lightsalmon"
    var currPic = invitPics + invitIdx
    var lyrTarget = eval(currPic)
```

```
        lyrWidth = lyrTarget.clip.width
        invitIdx += 1

        if (invitIdx > 2) invitIdx = 1
        var nextPic = invitPics + invitIdx
        horizWipe(currPic, nextPic, -4, lyrWidth, 20)
        return false
}

// horizWipe is a generic routine that handles both the closing
// and opening of a layer.

function horizWipe(lyrStr, nextStr, pxRate, theWidth, delay) {
    var lyrID = eval(lyrStr)

    if ((lyrID.clip.width + pxRate) > theWidth){
        lyrID.clip.width = theWidth
        return
    }

    lyrID.clip.left += -(pxRate/2)
    lyrID.clip.right += (pxRate/2)

    // Checking for zero prevents an endless loop, since the
browser
    // doesn't allow a width of less than zero.

    if (lyrID.clip.width <= 0) {
        lyrID.clip.width = 0
        lyrID.visibility = "hide"
    // After closing one picture, it is time to set up for opening
    // the next picture. The trick is to start with clip.right and
    // clip.left equal to half the layer width.
        pxRate = -pxRate
        lyrStr = nextStr
        var nextLyr = eval(lyrStr)
        nextLyr.clip.left = theWidth / 2
        nextLyr.clip.right = theWidth / 2
        nextLyr.visibility = "show"
    }

    // The layer references must be passed as strings. This
requires
    // the passing of the double quotes, which must be enclosed in
    // single quotes.

    var timerID = setTimeout('horizWipe("'+lyrStr+'",
"'+nextStr+'", '
```

```
        +pxRate+", "+theWidth+", "+delay+")", delay)
}

function doBirthPop(evt) {
    var birthRef = eval(birthDesc)
    birthRef.visibility = "show"
    var timerID = setTimeout('clrPop("'+birthDesc+'")', 5000)
    return false
}

function doEntwPop(evt) {
    var entwRef = eval(entwDesc)
    entwRef.visibility = "show"
    var timerID = setTimeout('clrPop("'+entwDesc+'")', 5000)
    return false
}

function doExtnPop(evt) {
    var extnRef = eval(extnDesc)
    extnRef.visibility = "show"
    var timerID = setTimeout('clrPop("'+extnDesc+'")', 5000)
    return false
}

function doInvitPop(evt) {
    var invitRef = eval(invitDesc)
    invitRef.visibility = "show"
    var timerID = setTimeout('clrPop("'+invitDesc+'")', 5000)
    return false
}

function clrPop(lyrRef) {
    var clrLyr = eval(lyrRef)
    clrLyr.visibility = "hide"
    return
}

//-->
</SCRIPT>

</HTML>
```

Figure 6–2 shows the result of clicking on the icon to load the dhtml-2.html
script for Maris's gallery.

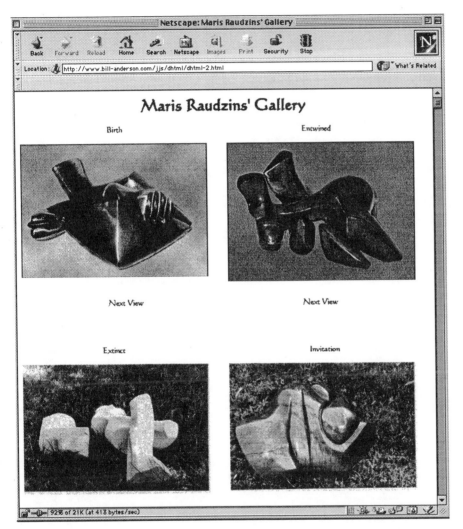

Figure 6–2 Result of loading the `dhtml-2.html` script

Figure 6–3 shows two of the timed popup layers that are displayed on top of an image when you move the pointer over the name of the sculpture. The figure shows the transition effect created by clipping to the sides of the first Birth image and the background color change for the text. Of course, the page cannot show the gradual changes as the sides of the image are clipped away.

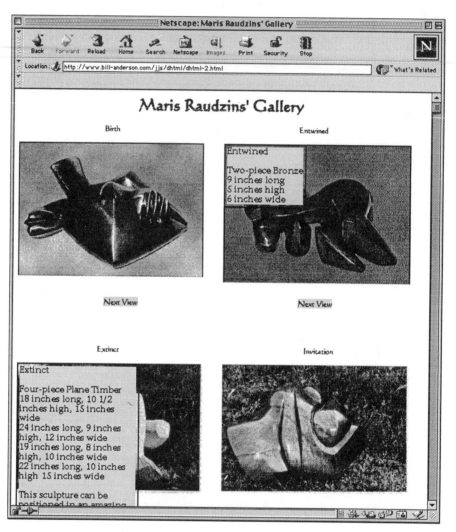

Figure 6–3 Timed popup layers in the `dhtml-2.html` script

Figure 6–4 shows the transition effect created by clipping to the sides of the first Birth image and the background color change for the text. Of course, the figure cannot show the gradual changes as the sides of the image are clipped away.

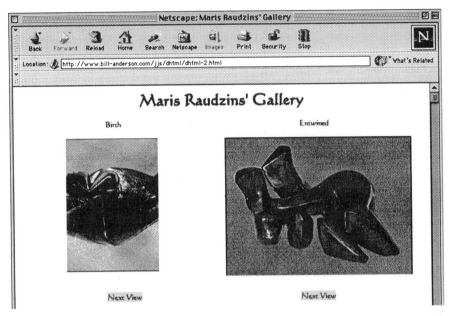

Figure 6–4 Contracting clipping effect in the `dhtml-2.html` script

Figure 6–5 shows the underlying image gradually being revealed as the sides of the new layer are clipped to expand.

Figure 6–5 Expanding clipping effect in the `dhtml-2.html` script

The following `html-3.html` script is loaded by clicking on the Dreamtime painting in the opening page of the gallery. This script uses a drop-down menu to enable gallery visitors to view a series of paintings. The images are specified as layers and are hidden or shown depending on the item chosen from the menu. In addition, Mr. Snoot, the Western brown bandicoot, helps out in the gallery. The `moveBy()` method helps Mr. Snoot push the old painting off the left edge of the screen and pull the new one behind him into view. Clicking on the image displays more information about each painting. Clicking on the link at the bottom of the page opens a new window with information about a related book by the artist. A series of event handler functions coordinate and execute the actions.

```
<!--
                 dhtml-3.html

     An example of using DHTML.

-->
<HTML>

<HEAD>
<TITLE>Janice's Gallery</TITLE>

<LINK REL=FONTDEF
SRC="http://www.truedoc.com/pfrs/Calligraph421.pfr">

<STYLE TYPE="text/css">
  P.title    {font-family:"Calligraph421 BT";
              font-size:12pt}
  H1         {font-family:"Calligraph421 BT";
              font-size:24pt}
  #imgSelect {position:absolute;
              z-index:30;
              visibility:show}
  #imgTitle  {position:absolute;
              width:200;
                  height:20;
              border-style:solid;
                  border-color:black;
                  border-width:thin;
              visibility:show}
  #txtDream  {position:absolute;
              top:5;
              left:10;
              visibility:show}
  #txtDark   {position:absolute;
              top:5;
              left:10;
```

```
                   visibility:hide}
#txtLunacy {position:absolute;
               top:5;
               left:10;
               visibility:hide}
#txtBest   {position:absolute;
               top:5;
               left:10;
               visibility:hide}
#txtBroken {position:absolute;
               top:5;
               left:10;
               visibility:hide}
#slctBtn   {position:absolute;
               left:206;
                   height:20;
                   border-style:solid;
                   border-color:black;
                   border-width:thin;
               visibility:show}
#slctList  {position:absolute;
               left:0;
               top:30;
               width:200;
               height:100;
                   border-style:solid;
                   border-color:black;
                   border-width:thin;
               visibility:hide}
#opt1      {position:absolute;
               top:10;
               left:10;
               height:20;
               visibility:inherit}
#opt2      {position:absolute;
               top:30;
               left:10;
               height:20;
               visibility:inherit}
#opt3      {position:absolute;
               top:50;
               left:10;
               height:20;
               visibility:inherit}
#opt4      {position:absolute;
               top:70;
               left:10;
               height:20;
```

```
                      visibility:inherit}
#opt5         {position:absolute;
               top:90;
               left:10;
               height:20;
               visibility:inherit}
#imgLayer     {position:absolute;
               left:0;
                   top:170;
                   z-index:10;
               visibility:show}
#imgDream     {position:absolute;
               left:5;
               visibility:inherit}
#imgDark      {position:absolute;
               left:5;
               visibility:hide}
#imgLunacy    {position:absolute;
               left:5;
               visibility:hide}
#imgBest      {position:absolute;
               left:5;
               visibility:hide}
#imgBroken    {position:absolute;
               left:5;
               visibility:hide}
#snootLeft    {position:absolute;
               visibility:hide}
#snootRght    {position:absolute;
               visibility:hide}
#popDream     {position:absolute;
               top:140;
               left:400;
                   border-style:solid;
                   border-color:black;
                   border-width:thin;
                   background-color:lightyellow;
               visibility:hide}
#popDark      {position:absolute;
               top:140;
               left:400;
                   border-style:solid;
                   border-color:black;
                   border-width:thin;
                   background-color:lightyellow;
               visibility:hide}
#popLunacy    {position:absolute;
               top:140;
```

```
                   left:400;
                        border-style:solid;
                        border-color:black;
                        border-width:thin;
                        background-color:lightyellow;
                   visibility:hide}
  #popBest      {position:absolute;
                   top:140;
                   left:400;
                        border-style:solid;
                        border-color:black;
                        border-width:thin;
                        background-color:lightyellow;
                   visibility:hide}
  #popBroken   {position:absolute;
                   top:140;
                   left:400;
                        border-style:solid;
                        border-color:black;
                        border-width:thin;
                        background-color:lightyellow;
                   visibility:hide}
  #popAsk       {position:absolute;
                   top:140;
                   left:400;
                   visibility:hide}
  #popSnoot    {position:absolute;
                   top:180;
                   left:400;
                   visibility:hide}
  #dreamDoor   {position:absolute;
                   top:610;
                   visibility:show}
</STYLE>
</HEAD>

<BODY BGCOLOR="white">
<H1 ALIGN="CENTER">Janice Winsor's Gallery</H1>
<P ALIGN="CENTER"><I>(Click on image to display a
description.)</I></P>

<DIV ID="imgSelect">
  <DIV ID="imgTitle">
    <IMG SRC="images/listBack.jpeg" ALT="list Background"
BORDER="0" WIDTH="200"
        HEIGHT="20">
    <P ID="txtDream" CLASS=title>DreamTime</P>
    <P ID="txtDark" CLASS=title>Dark Power</P>
```

```
      <P ID="txtLunacy" CLASS=title>Lunacy</P>
      <P ID="txtBest" CLASS=title>Best of Times</P>
      <P ID="txtBroken" CLASS=title>Broken</P>
   </DIV>

   <DIV ID="slctBtn">
     <IMG SRC="images/bluesquares09.gif" ALT="Down Arrow" BORDER="0"
WIDTH="16"
          HEIGHT="20">
   </DIV>

   <DIV ID="slctList">
     <IMG SRC="images/listBack.jpeg" ALT="list Background" BORDER="0"
WIDTH="200"
          HEIGHT="140">
     <P ID="opt1">Dreamtime</P>
     <P ID="opt2">Dark Power</P>
     <P ID="opt3">Lunacy</P>
     <P ID="opt4">Best of Times</P>
     <P ID="opt5">Broken</P>
   </DIV>
</DIV>

<DIV ID="imgLayer">
   <P ID="imgDream"><IMG SRC="images/Dreamtime.jpeg" ALT="Dreamtime"
ALIGN="TOP"
       BORDER="0" WIDTH="540" HEIGHT="415"></P>
   <P ID="imgDark"><IMG SRC="images/DarkPower.jpeg" ALT="Dark Power"
ALIGN="TOP"
       BORDER="0" WIDTH="323" HEIGHT="415"></P>
   <P ID="imgLunacy"><IMG SRC="images/Lunacy.jpeg" ALT="Lunacy"
       ALIGN="TOP" BORDER="0" WIDTH="600" HEIGHT="415"></P>
   <P ID="imgBest"><IMG SRC="images/BestOfTimes.jpeg" ALT="Best of
Times"
       ALIGN="TOP" BORDER="0" WIDTH="553" HEIGHT="415"></P>
   <P ID="imgBroken"><IMG SRC="images/Broken.jpeg" ALT="Broken"
       ALIGN="TOP" BORDER="0" WIDTH="323" HEIGHT="415"></P>
   <P ID="snootLeft"><IMG SRC="images/Snoot-1sl.jpeg" ALT="Snoot Left"
       ALIGN="TOP" BORDER="0" WIDTH="200" HEIGHT="133"></P>
   <P ID="snootRght"><IMG SRC="images/Snoot-1sr.jpeg" ALT="Snoot
Right"
       ALIGN="TOP" BORDER="0" WIDTH="200" HEIGHT="133"></P>
</DIV>

<DIV ID="popDream">
   <P>Paper and cyanotype</P>
   <P>19 inches by 25 inches</P>
   <P>Dreamtime resulted from a dream that the artist had about living
```

```
in Australia in the dreamtime. It represents the connection that
each of us has with each other and with the planet.</P>
</DIV>

<DIV ID="popDark">
  <P>Paper stencil and spray paint</P>
  <P>19 inches by 25 inches</P>
  <P>Dark Power represents the interplay of the dark and light side of
mankind. The yin-yang symbol in the background represents the
balance of masculine and feminine energy. The jester's face
represents lightness and humor and not taking things too
seriously. It also represents the darker side that humor can
take in laughing at the expense of others. The line of
marching soldiers represents the shadow of military
oppression and the threat of death.</P>
</DIV>

<DIV ID="popLunacy">
  <P>Photograph and spray paint on glass</P>
  <P>19 inches by 25 inches</P>
  <P>Lunacy has a very dreamlike feeling. It's about life and death.
The shadow of the raven represents death and the dark forces.
The eggs represent the generative power of new life. The figure
curled in on herself represents looking within to understand the
meaning of life.  It also represents the apprehension and fear
that many people experience when forced to deal with issues
of life and death.</P>
</DIV>

<DIV ID="popBest">
  <P>Paper stencil</P>
  <P>19 inches by 25 inches</P>
  <P>The Best of Times resulted from a photo safari that the artist
took to Kenya. It distills the essence of life and death on the
Serengeti Plain.</P>
</DIV>

<DIV ID="popBroken">
  <P>Photograph and spray paint on glass</P>
  <P>19 inches by 25 inches</P>
  <P>Broken reminds me of a brass plaque I used to own that said "?
collision at sea can ruin your whole day." It represents survival
in the face of events that, at the time, seem to shatter your life.</
</DIV>

<DIV ID="popAsk">
  <P CLASS=title>What was that?</P>
</DIV>
```

```
<DIV ID="popSnoot">
  <P><IMG SRC="images/Snoot-1sr.jpeg" ALT="Snoot Right"
     ALIGN="TOP" BORDER="0" WIDTH="200" HEIGHT="133"></P>
  <P>Mr. Snoot, the Australian western brown bandicoot, helps out
  in the gallery by rearranging the pictures. Bandicoots are
  solitary, nocturnal marsupials. Their long, sensitive
  snouts detect food in the form of insects, worms, seeds,
  and berries. Bandicoots are about eight inches long,
  with a four-inch tail. However, they have ferocious
  temperaments.
     Early this century, eight bandicoots from a remote area
  were sent in the same cage by train to Adelaide. When
  they arrived, all were hairless and dead, having fought
  and killed each other on the way. In the wild, many
  bandicoots are partially or completely tailless after an
  altercation with another of their species. Although you
  can't see it in the photo, Mr. Snoot's tail is only
  three-quarters of an inch long.</P>
</DIV>

<DIV ID="dreamDoor">
  <A HREF="Dreamdoor.html"><P><IMG SRC="images/DreamDoor-i.jpeg"
ALT="Dream Door"
     ALIGN="MIDDLE" BORDER="0" WIDTH="50" HEIGHT="77"
HSPACE="14">Click to open the Dream Door</P></A>
</DIV>

<SCRIPT LANGUAGE="JavaScript">

//
// Global Variables

var listOpen = false
var oldColor = ""
var currImage = "Dream"
var firstChg = true

//
// Object References

var slctTitle = "document.imgSelect.document.imgTitle.document.txt"
var slctBtn = document.imgSelect.document.slctBtn
var optList = document.imgSelect.document.slctList
var optDream = document.imgSelect.document.slctList.document.opt1
var optDark = document.imgSelect.document.slctList.document.opt2
var optLun = document.imgSelect.document.slctList.document.opt3
var optBest = document.imgSelect.document.slctList.document.opt4
```

```
var optBrk = document.imgSelect.document.slctList.document.opt5
var leftSnoot = document.imgLayer.document.snootLeft
var rightSnoot = document.imgLayer.document.snootRght
var snootObj = leftSnoot
var snootAsk = document.popAsk
var snootDesc = document.popSnoot
var winDream = document.imgLayer.document.imgDream
var descDream = "document.popDream"
var winDark = document.imgLayer.document.imgDark
var descDark = "document.popDark"
var winLunacy = document.imgLayer.document.imgLunacy
var descLunacy = "document.popLunacy"
var winBest = document.imgLayer.document.imgBest
var descBest = "document.popBest"
var winBrk = document.imgLayer.document.imgBroken
var descBrk = "document.popBroken"
var openDoor = document.dreamDoor

//
// Event Handlers

slctBtn.captureEvents(Event.MOUSEDOWN | Event.MOUSEUP)

slctBtn.onmousedown=killEvent
slctBtn.onmouseup=showList

function killEvent(evt) {
   return false
}

function showList(evt) {
   if (listOpen) {
      optList.visibility = "hide"
      listOpen = false
   }
   else {
      optList.visibility = "show"
      listOpen = true
   }
   return false
}

optDream.captureEvents(Event.MOUSEOVER | Event.MOUSEOUT |
Event.MOUSEDOWN | Event.MOUSEUP)

optDream.onmouseover=preClick
optDream.onmouseout=clrClick
optDream.onmousedown=beginClick
```

```
optDream.onmouseup=doDream

winDream.captureEvents(Event.MOUSEDOWN | Event.MOUSEUP)
winDream.onmousedown=killEvent
winDream.onmouseup=doDreamPop

optDark.captureEvents(Event.MOUSEOVER | Event.MOUSEOUT |
Event.MOUSEDOWN | Event.MOUSEUP)

optDark.onmouseover=preClick
optDark.onmouseout=clrClick
optDark.onmousedown=beginClick
optDark.onmouseup=doDark

winDark.captureEvents(Event.MOUSEDOWN | Event.MOUSEUP)
winDark.onmousedown=killEvent
winDark.onmouseup=doDarkPop

optLun.captureEvents(Event.MOUSEOVER | Event.MOUSEOUT |
Event.MOUSEDOWN | Event.MOUSEUP)

optLun.onmouseover=preClick
optLun.onmouseout=clrClick
optLun.onmousedown=beginClick
optLun.onmouseup=doLunacy

winLunacy.captureEvents(Event.MOUSEDOWN | Event.MOUSEUP)
winLunacy.onmousedown=killEvent
winLunacy.onmouseup=doLunPop

optBest.captureEvents(Event.MOUSEOVER | Event.MOUSEOUT |
Event.MOUSEDOWN | Event.MOUSEUP)

optBest.onmouseover=preClick
optBest.onmouseout=clrClick
optBest.onmousedown=beginClick
optBest.onmouseup=doBest

winBest.captureEvents(Event.MOUSEDOWN | Event.MOUSEUP)
winBest.onmousedown=killEvent
winBest.onmouseup=doBestPop

optBrk.captureEvents(Event.MOUSEOVER | Event.MOUSEOUT |
Event.MOUSEDOWN | Event.MOUSEUP)

optBrk.onmouseover=preClick
optBrk.onmouseout=clrClick
optBrk.onmousedown=beginClick
```

```
optBrk.onmouseup=doBroken

winBrk.captureEvents(Event.MOUSEDOWN | Event.MOUSEUP)
winBrk.onmousedown=killEvent
winBrk.onmouseup=doBrokenPop

openDoor.captureEvents(Event.MOUSEDOWN | Event.MOUSEUP)
openDoor.onmousedown=killEvent
openDoor.onmouseup=doDreamDoor

function preClick(evt) {
    oldColor = evt.target.bgColor
    evt.target.bgColor = "yellow"
    return false
}

function clrClick(evt) {
    evt.target.bgColor = oldColor
    return false
}

function beginClick(evt) {
    // Ignore any other mouse button.
    if (evt.which != 1) return false
    evt.target.bgColor = "lightgreen"
    return false
}

function doDream(evt) {
    // Ignore any other mouse button.

    if (evt.which != 1) return false
    evt.target.bgColor = "lightsalmon"
    showList(evt) // Hide the popup menu.

    if (currImage != "Dream") {
        setSnoot(currImage)
        swapImg(currImage, "Dream", -5, 20)
    }
    return false
}

function doDark(evt) {
    // Ignore any other mouse button.

    if (evt.which != 1) return false
    evt.target.bgColor = "lightsalmon"
    showList(evt) // Hide the popup menu.
```

```
       if (currImage != "Dark") {
          setSnoot(currImage)
          swapImg(currImage, "Dark", -5, 20)
       }
       return false
    }


    function doLunacy(evt) {
       // Ignore any other mouse button.

       if (evt.which != 1) return false
       evt.target.bgColor = "lightsalmon"
       showList(evt) // Hide the popup menu.

       if (currImage != "Lunacy") {
          setSnoot(currImage)
          swapImg(currImage, "Lunacy", -5, 20)
       }
       return false
    }

    function doBest(evt) {
       // Ignore any other mouse button.

       if (evt.which != 1) return false
       evt.target.bgColor = "lightsalmon"
       showList(evt) // Hide the popup menu.

       if (currImage != "Best") {
          setSnoot(currImage)
          swapImg(currImage, "Best", -5, 20)
       }
       return false
    }

    function doBroken(evt) {
       // Ignore any other mouse button.

       if (evt.which != 1) return false
       evt.target.bgColor = "lightsalmon"
       showList(evt) // Hide the popup menu.

       if (currImage != "Broken") {
          setSnoot(currImage)
          swapImg(currImage, "Broken", -5, 20)
       }
       return false
```

```
   }

   function setSnoot(workImg) {
      var imgRef = eval("document.imgLayer.document.img" + workImg)
      leftSnoot.left = imgRef.clip.width + 5
      snootObj = leftSnoot
      leftSnoot.visibility = "show"
   }

   function swapImg(workImg, nextImg, pxRate, delay) {
      lyrRef = eval("document.imgLayer.document.img" + workImg)
      snootObj.moveBy(pxRate,0)
      lyrRef.moveBy(pxRate, 0)

      if (pxRate < 0 & -lyrRef.left >= lyrRef.clip.width) {
         snootObj.visibility = "hide"
         lyrRef.visibility = "hide"
         var newLyr = eval("document.imgLayer.document.img" +
nextImg)
         newLyr.left = -newLyr.clip.width
         newLyr.visibility = "show"
         pxRate = -pxRate
         workImg = nextImg
         snootObj = rightSnoot
         snootObj.left = 5
         snootObj.visibility = "show"
      }

      else if (pxRate > 0 & lyrRef.left >= 0) {
         lyrRef.left = 5
         oldText = eval(slctTitle + currImage)
         oldText.visibility = "hide"
         newText = eval(slctTitle + nextImg)
         newText.visibility = "show"
         snootObj.visibility = "hide"
         currImage = nextImg

         if (firstChg) {
            firstChg = false
            snootAsk.visibility = "show"  ·
            var timerID = setTimeout('clrPop("document.popAsk")',
   5000)
            snootDesc.visibility = "show"
            var timerID = setTimeout('clrPop("document.popSnoot")',
   20000)
         }
         return
      }
      var timerID = setTimeout('swapImg("'+workImg+'",
```

```
          "'+nextImg+'", '+pxRate+", "+delay+")", delay)
      }

function doDreamPop(evt) {
   var dreamRef = eval(descDream)
   dreamRef.visibility = "show"
   var timerID = setTimeout('clrPop("'+descDream+'")', 5000)
   return false
}

function doDarkPop(evt) {
   var darkRef = eval(descDark)
   darkRef.visibility = "show"
   var timerID = setTimeout('clrPop("'+descDark+'")', 5000)
   return false
}

function doLunPop(evt) {
   var lunRef = eval(descLunacy)
   lunRef.visibility = "show"
   var timerID = setTimeout('clrPop("'+descLunacy+'")', 5000)
   return false
}

function doBestPop(evt) {
   var bestRef = eval(descBest)
   bestRef.visibility = "show"
   var timerID = setTimeout('clrPop("'+descBest+'")', 5000)
   return false
}

function doBrokenPop(evt) {
   var brkRef = eval(descBrk)
   brkRef.visibility = "show"
   var timerID = setTimeout('clrPop("'+descBrk+'")', 5000)
   return false
}

function clrPop(lyrRef) {
   var clrLyr = eval(lyrRef)
   clrLyr.visibility = "hide"
   return
}

function doDreamDoor(evt) {
   if (evt.which != 1) return false
   evt.target.bgColor = "lightsalmon"
   window.open("Dreamdoor.html", "DreamDoor",
```

```
"titlebar,scrollbars")
    return false
}
</SCRIPT>
</BODY>
</HTML>
```

Figure 6–6 shows the result of loading the `dhtml-3.html` script.

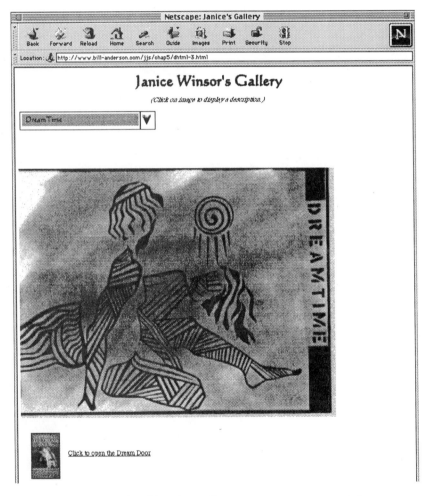

Figure 6–6 Result of loading the `dhtml-3.html` script

Figure 6–7 shows the drop-down menu with the list of paintings.

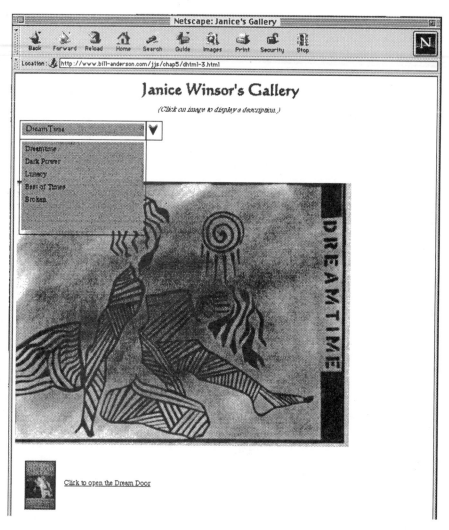

Figure 6–7 The drop-down menu in the `dhtml-3.html` script

When you choose a painting from the menu, Mr. Snoot pushes the painting off the left edge of the screen, as shown in Figure 6–8.

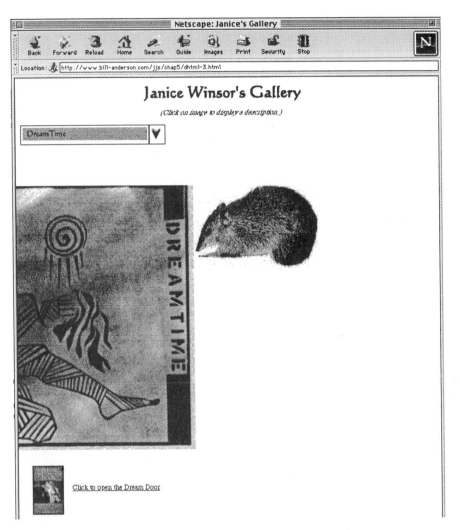

Figure 6–8 Using the `moveBy()` method in the `dhtml-3.html` script

The first time Mr. Snoot helps out in the gallery, a "What was that?" message is displayed when he completes his transit from left to right, as shown in Figure 6–9. The message has a timeout, and the layer containing the text is hidden when the time is up. The bandicoot has a longer timeout.

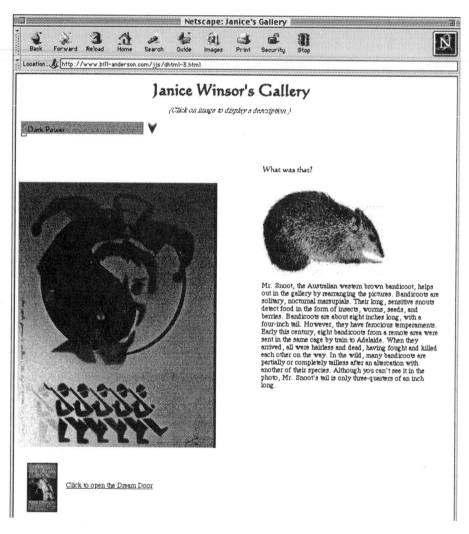

Figure 6–9 Additional layer showing information about Mr. Snoot

As you can see from this example, there are many ways you can put the elements of DHTML together to put action and movement into your Web pages.

Regular Expressions

▼ CREATING A REGULAR EXPRESSION

▼ WRITING A SIMPLE PATTERN

▼ USING THE REGEXP OBJECT

▼ USING STRING OBJECT METHODS

Regular expressions provide you with a powerful way to search for and manipulate text. You first create patterns to match character combinations. Then, you can use these patterns to find, copy, and replace pieces of text.

In JavaScript, regular expressions are also objects. Whenever you create a regular expression, JavaScript creates a `RegExp` object, which has methods you can use to execute a match against a string. You can also pass the regular expression as arguments to the `String` object methods `match()`, `replace()`, `search()`, and `split()`. The `RegExp` construction object has properties most of which are set when a match is successful. For example, the `lastMatch` property specifies the last successful match.

In addition to the `RegExp` object, the Communicator 4.x release adds new properties to the `Array` object that provide information about a successful match.

Creating a Regular Expression

You create a regular expression pattern in one of two ways:

- Using literal notation with the format

  `/pattern/flags`

  Use literal notation for better performance when the pattern remains constant.

- Calling the constructor function of the `RegExp` object with the format

  `new RegExp ("pattern", "flags")`

  Use the constructor function when you know the pattern will change or when you don't know the pattern and are getting it from another source such as user input.

Flags

You can specify optional flags for regular expressions with one of the following three value:

- `g` — Global match
- `i` — Ignore case
- `gi` — Match globally and ignore case

Literal Notation

The literal notation syntax is to define the regular expression between two slashes (/) without using any quotation marks, followed by any optional flags. The following example creates a regular expression for the string `apricots` and specifies a global match.

```
/apricots/g
```

When you create a regular expression with literal notation, the regular expression is compiled when the script is evaluated.

RegExp Constructor Function

The construction function syntax uses the `new` statement to create a new instance of the `RegExp` object. The expression is enclosed in parentheses and surrounded with double quotation marks. The following expression creates the same regular expression as `/apricots/g`.

```
new RegExp ("apricots", "g")
```

Each window has a separate predefined `RegExp` object. Because each script runs to completion in each window, you can be assured that different scripts do not overwrite values of the `RegExp` object.

Writing a Simple Pattern

The simplest regular expression defines the exact string to be used in a search and uses a direct match. For example, the following regular expression globally matches `rose` in the string `"A rose is a rose."`

```
re2=/rose/g
```

When the `re2` value is supplied as a parameter to the `replace()` method described later in this chapter, the replacement is done gobally, through the entire string, instead of just once on the first match found.

Using Special Characters

Regular expressions in JavaScript are based on the Perl language. The JavaScript 1.2 regular expression syntax is based on Perl 4 regular expressions. The JavaScript 1.3 regular expression syntax is based on Perl 5 regular expressions. If you want to do sophisticated pattern matching, you may find a Perl manual helpful. A good reference is the O'Reilly book, *Mastering Regular Expressions*, by Jeffrey E. F. Friedl, 1997.

When you create regular expressions, each character matches itself unless it is one of the following special characters:

- + (plus)
- ? (question mark)
- . (period)
- * (asterisk)
- ^ (caret)
- $ (dollar sign)
- ( ) (parentheses)
- [ ] (square brackets)
- { } (curly braces)
- | (pipe)
- \ (backslash)

You can put a backslash (\) before each character to escape it so that it is matched as a literal character.

Table 7-1 shows the syntax for basic pattern matching in regular expressions.

Table 7-1 Basic Pattern Matching in Regular Expressions

Character	Meaning
^	Matches beginning of input or line. For example, /^A/ does not match the A in any A, but does match it in Any A.
$	Matches end of input or line. For example, /g$/ does not match the g in froggie, but does match it in frog.
.	The decimal point matches any single character except the newline character. For example, /.n/ matches on in now you are on time, but not now because there is no character preceding the n.
(x)	Matches x and remembers the match. For example, /(foo)/ matches and remembers foo in foo bar.
x|y	Matches either x or y. For example, /used|new/ matches used in used car and new in new car.
[xyz]	A character set. Matches any one of the enclosed characters. You can specify a range of characters by using a hyphen. For example, [wxyz] is the same as [w-z]. They match the xy in xylophone and the z in zoo.
[^xyz]	A negated or complemented character set. Matches anything that is not enclosed in the brackets. You can specify a range of characters by using a hyphen. For example, [^xyz] is the same as [^x-z]. They initially match the l in xylophone and the first o in zoo.
\n	Where n is a positive integer. A back reference to the last substring matching the n parenthetical in the regular expression (counting left parentheses). For example, /apple(,)\sorange\1/ matches apple, orange, in apple, orange, cherry, peach. Note: If the number of left parentheses is less than the number specified in \n, the \n is taken as an octal escape as described in the next row.
\o *octal* \x *hex*	Where \o *octal* is an octal escape value or \x is a hexadecimal escape value. Enables you to embed ASCII codes into regular expressions.

You can create subpatterns by using one or more of the quantifiers described in Table 7-2 to match the preceding element as many times as possible.

Table 7-2 Quantifiers for Matching Subpatterns in Regular Expressions

Character	Meaning
*	Matches the preceding character 0 or more times. For example, /ko*/ matches koo in Laugh kookaburra and k in I like it, but nothing in The cow mooed.
+	Matches the preceding character 1 or more times. Equivalent to {1,}. For example, /a+/ matches the a in car and all the a's in aaaarghh.
?	Matches the preceding character 0 or 1 time. For example, /e?le?/ matches the el in angel and the le in angle.
{n}	Where n is a positive integer. Matches exactly n occurrences of the preceding character. For example, /o{2}/ doesn't match the o in hot, but it matches all of the o's in book, and the first two o's in ooooh.
{n,}	Where n is a positive integer. Matches at least n occurrences of the preceding character. For example, /o{2,}/ doesn't match the o in hot, but it matches all of the o's in book and ooooh.
{n,m}	Where n and m are positive integers. Matches at least n and at most m occurrences of the preceding character. For example, /o{1,3}/ matches nothing in hat, the o in hot, the first two o's in hoot, and the first three o's in ooooooh Notice that when matching ooooooh, the match is ooo, even though the original string had more o's in it.
\n	Where n is a positive integer. A back reference to the last substring matching the n parenthetical in the regular expression (counting left parentheses). For example, /apple(,)\sorange\1/ matches apple, orange, in apple, orange, cherry, peach. Note: If the number of left parentheses is less than the number specified in \n, the \n is taken as an octal escape.

A backslash preceding a special, nonalphanumeric character escapes it to match its literal meaning. However, putting a backslash in front of most alphanumeric characters turns them into special symbols in regular expression patterns. Table 7-3 describes the escaped special characters.

Table 7-3 Special Characters in Regular Expressions

Character	Meaning
\	Escapes a special character to match it literally. For example, * is a special character that matches 0 or more occurrences of the preceding character. To match a literal asterisk, precede it with a backslash.
	Alternatively, escapes a literal character to interpret it as a special character. For example, /b/ matches the character b, but /\b/ matches a word boundary.
[\b]	Matches a backspace.
\b	Matches a word boundary such as a space. For example, /\bt/ matches the t in today;/t\b/ matches the t in me too.
\B	Matches a nonword boundary. For example, /\Bt/ matches the middle t in total, and /o\B/ matches the o in me hot.
\c *X*	Where *X* is a control character. Matches a control character in a string. For example, /\cM/ matches control-M in a string.
\d	Matches a digit. Equivalent to [0-9]. For example, /\d/ or /[0-9]/ matches 2 in Tea for 2.
\D	Matches any nondigit character. Equivalent to [^0-9]. For example, /\D/ or /[^0-9]/ matches B in B2 is the suite number.
\f	Matches a form-feed.
\n	Matches a linefeed.
\r	Matches a carriage return.
\s	Matches a single whitespace character, including space, tab, form feed, line feed. Equivalent to [\f\n\r\t\v].
\S	Matches a single character other than white space. Equivalent to [^ \f\n\r\t\v].
\t	Matches a tab.
\v	Matches a vertical tab.

Table 7-3 Special Characters in Regular Expressions (Continued)

Character	Meaning
\w	Matches any alphanumeric character including the underscore. Equivalent to [A-Za-z0-9_]. For example, /\w/ matches a in apple, 5 in $5.28, and 3 in 3D.
\W	Matches any nonword character. Equivalent to [^A-Za-z0-9_]. For example, /\W/ or /[^$A-Za-z0-9_]/ matches % in 50%.
\o *octal* \x *hex*	Where \o *octal* is an octal escape value or \x is a hexadecimal escape value. Allows you to embed ASCII codes into regular expressions.

Using the RegExp Object

The RegExp object is a built-in object used to create patterns and work with regular expressions. You create a new pattern by using the syntax:

```
new RegExp ("pattern", "flags")
```

The properties, methods, and event handlers for the RegExp object are listed in alphabetical order in Table 7-4.

Table 7-4 Properties, Methods, and Event Handlers for the RegExp Object

Properties	Methods	Event Handlers
$1, ... $9`	compile	None
$_ (input)	exec	
$* (multiline)	test	
$& (lastMatch)		
$+ (lastParen)		
$` (leftContext)		
$' (rightContext)		
global		
ignoreCase		
input		

Table 7-4 Properties, Methods, and Event Handlers for the
RegExp Object (Continued)

Properties	Methods	Event Handlers
lastIndex		
lastMatch		
lastParen		
leftContext		
multiline		
rightContext		
source		

Getting Remembered Substring Matches

When you use parentheses to remember a matched string, you can get the last
nine of those values by using the $1, ... $9 properties of the RegExp object.

Property	Value	Gettable	Settable
$1, ... $9	string	Yes	No

You can store an unlimited number of parenthesized substrings; however, the
predefined RegExp object holds only the last nine. You can access all of the
parenthesized substrings by using the indexes for the returned array.

You can use the values from these properties as replacement text for the
String.replace method. When you use them with the String object, you do
not use the RegExp object name as part of the syntax.

When parentheses are not included in the regular expression, the script interprets
$*n* literally

Because input is a property of the RegExp constructor itself, it is not a property of
an individual regular expression object. You always call it as RegExp.input. For
an example of using remembered substring matches, see "Replacing Substrings in
a String" on page 257.

Determining If the Global Flag Is Set

Use the `global` property to determine whether the global flag was set for an individual regular expression object.

Property	Value	Gettable	Settable
global	Boolean	Yes	No

The value of the `global` property is `true` if the g flag was used. Otherwise, the value is `false`. The g flag indicates that the regular expression should be tested against all possible matches in a string.

You cannot change this property directly. However, you can change it indirectly by calling the `compile` method.

Determining If Case Sensitivity Is Set

Use the `ignoreCase` property to determine whether the ignore case flag was set for an individual regular expression object.

Property	Value	Gettable	Settable
ignoreCase	Boolean	Yes	No

The value of the `ignoreCase` property is `true` if the i flag was used. Otherwise, the value is `false`. The i flag indicates that case should be ignored while matching a string.

You cannot change this property directly. However, you can change it indirectly by calling the `compile` method. For an example of determining if case sensitivity is set, see "Example of Executing the Search for a Match in a Specified String" on page 248.

Setting the Matching String

Use the `input` property to set the string against which a regular expression is matched. $_ is the Perl shortcut name for the same property.

Property	Value	Gettable	Settable
input	string	Yes	No
$_	string	Yes	No

Because `input` is static, it is not a property of an individual regular expression object. Instead, you always call it as `RegExp.input`.

If you do not provide a string argument to `RegExp exec()` or `test()` methods and if `RegExp.input` has a value, its value is used as the argument to that method.

The event handlers for the `text`, `textarea`, `select`, and `anchor` objects set input to the value of the string they contain.

Getting the Index to Start the Next Match

Use the `lastIndex` property to get the index at which to start the next match.

Property	Value	Gettable	Settable
lastIndex	integer	Yes	Yes

The `lastIndex` property is set only if the regular expression used the g flag to indicate a global search. The following rules apply:

- If `lastIndex` is greater than the length of the string, `RegExp.test` and `RegExp.exec` fail and `lastIndex` is set to 0.

- If `lastIndex` is equal to the length of the string and if the regular expression matches the empty string, then the regular expression matches input starting at `lastIndex`.

- If `lastIndex` is equal to the length of the string and if the regular expression does not match the empty string, then the regular expression mismatches input and `lastIndex` is reset to 0.

- Otherwise, `lastIndex` is set to the next position following the most recent match.

Getting the Last Match

Use the `lastMatch` property to get the last matched string. `$&` is the Perl shortcut name for the same property.

Property	Value	Gettable	Settable
lastMatch	string	Yes	No
$&	string	Yes	No

Because `lastMatch` is static, it is not a property of an individual regular expression object. Instead, you always call it as `RegExp.lastMatch`.

Getting the Last Parenthesized Substring Match

Use the `lastParen` property to get the last parenthesized substring match. `$+` is the Perl shortcut name for the same property.

Property	Value	Gettable	Settable
lastParen	string	Yes	No
$+	string	Yes	No

Because `lastParen` is static, it is not a property of an individual regular expression object. Instead, you always call it as `RegExp.lastParen`. For an example of getting the last parenthesized substring match, see "Testing the Search for a Match (Index)" on page 254.

Getting the Substring Preceding the Most Recent Match

Use the `leftContent` property to get the substring preceding the most recent match. `$`` (dollar single backquote) is the Perl shortcut name for the same property.

Property	Value	Gettable	Settable
leftContent	string	Yes	No
$`	string	Yes	No

Because `leftContent` is static, it is not a property of an individual regular expression object. Instead, you always call it as `RegExp.leftContent`.

Determining Whether to Search Across Multiple Lines

Use the `multiline` property to determine whether the regular expression is set to search across multiple lines. `$*` is the Perl shortcut name for the same property.

Property	Value	Gettable	Settable
multiline	Boolean	Yes	No
$*	Boolean	Yes	No

Because `multiline` is static, it is not a property of an individual regular expression object. Instead, you always call it as `RegExp.multiline`.

The `multiline` property returns a value of `true` if multiple lines are searched; `false` if searches must stop at line breaks.

The `multiline` property can be set either by a script or by the browser.

Note – When an event handler is called for a `TEXTAREA` form element, the browser automatically sets `multiline` to `true`. After the event handler completes, the `multiline` value is cleared. Consequently, if you present `multiline` to `true`, it is reset to `false` after the execution of any `TEXTAREA` event handler.

Getting the Substring Following the Most Recent Match

Use the `rightContent` property to get the substring following the most recent match. `$'` (dollar single quote) is the Perl shortcut name for the same property.

Property	Value	Gettable	Settable
rightContent	string	Yes	No
$'	string	Yes	No

Because `rightContent` is static, it is not a property of an individual regular expression object. Instead, you always call it as `RegExp.rightContent`.

Getting the Text of the Pattern

Use the `source` property to get the text of the pattern, excluding the forward slashes and any flags.

Property	Value	Gettable	Settable
source	string	Yes	No

You cannot change this property directly, However, you can change its value by calling the `compile` method.

For an example of using the `source` property, see "Testing the Search for a Match (Boolean)" on page 250.

Compiling a Regular Expression During Script Execution

Use the `compile` method to compile a regular expression that is created with the `RegExp` constructor function and that will remain constant after getting its pattern. This method forces compilation of the regular expression once only.

You can also use the `compile` method to change the regular expression during script execution and recompile for more efficient repeated use.

Calling the `compile` method changes the value of the `source`, `global`, and `ignoreCase` properties for the regular expression.

Method

regexp.compile(pattern, flags)

Returns

Nothing.

Executing the Search for a Match in a Specified String

Use the `exec()` method to execute the search for a match in a specified string. The `exec()` method returns an array with the results of the match. You can call the `exec()` method either directly with *regexp.exec(string)* or indirectly with *regexp(string)*. *regexp* can be either a variable name or a literal. The string argument is optional. If you do not specify a string, the value of `RexExp.input` is used.

If the match succeeds, the `exec` method returns an array and updates the properties of the regular expression object and the predefined `RegExp` object. If the match fails, the `exec` method returns `null`.

Method

regexp.exec(string)

regexp(string)

Returns

Array of match results if successful; if the match fails, returns null.

Note – If you want a true or false answer to the match, use either the test() method or the String.search method instead of the exec() method.

If your regular expression uses the g flag, you can use the exec() method in combination with the lastIndex property to find successive matches in the same string.

Example of Executing the Search for a Match in a Specified String

The following exec.html script uses the exec() method for regular expressions. It also uses the $1, global and ignoreCase properties.

```
<!--


                        exec.html

Example of using the exec() method for regular expressions.

-->

<HTML>
  <HEAD>

    <TITLE>Using the exec() Method</TITLE>


<SCRIPT LANGUAGE="JavaScript1.2">
<!--

testStr="Checking for all Apples and Apricots."
nfre=/(\bA\w+)/
gfre=/(\bA\w+)/g
ifre=/(\bA\w+)/i
gifre=/(\bA\w+)/gi
//-->

</SCRIPT>
  </HEAD>

  <BODY>

<SCRIPT LANGUAGE="JavaScript1.2">

<!--
```

```
nTest=nfre.exec(testStr)

with (document) {
    write("The test String is: "+nTest.input+"<BR>")
    write("pattern: "+nfre.source+" produces: "+nTest)
    write(" at index: "+nTest.index+"<BR>")
    write("global flag: "+nfre.global)
    write(", ignore case flag: "+nfre.ignoreCase+"<BR>")
    write("lastParen: "+RegExp.lastParen+", $1: "+RegExp.$1+"<BR>")
    write("<HR>")
}


gTest=gfre.exec(testStr)

with (document) {
    write("The test String is: "+gTest.input+"<BR>")
    write("pattern: "+gfre.source+" produces: "+gTest)
    write(" at index: "+gTest.index+"<BR>")
    write("global flag: "+gfre.global)
    write(", ignore case flag: "+gfre.ignoreCase+"<BR>")
    write("lastParen: "+RegExp.lastParen+", $1: "+RegExp.$1+"<BR>")
    write("<HR>")
}


iTest=ifre.exec(testStr)

with (document) {
    write("The test String is: "+iTest.input+"<BR>")
    write("pattern: "+ifre.source+" produces: "+iTest)
    write(" at index: "+iTest.index+"<BR>")
    write("global flag: "+ifre.global)
    write(", ignore case flag: "+ifre.ignoreCase+"<BR>")
    write("lastParen: "+RegExp.lastParen+", $1: "+RegExp.$1+"<BR>")
    write("<HR>")
}


giTest=gifre.exec(testStr)

with (document) {
    write("The test String is: "+giTest.input+"<BR>")
    write("pattern: "+gifre.source+" produces: "+giTest)
    write(" at index: "+giTest.index+"<BR>")
    write("global flag: "+gifre.global)
    write(" ignore case flag: "+gifre.ignoreCase+"<BR>")
    write("lastParen: "+RegExp.lastParen+", $1: "+RegExp.$1+"<BR>")
}

//-->
```

```
    </SCRIPT>
      </BODY>
    </HTML>
```

Figure 7–1 shows the result of loading the `exec.html` script.

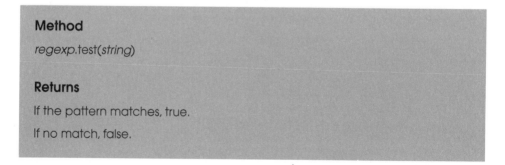

Figure 7–1 Result of loading the `exec.html` script

Testing the Search for a Match (Boolean)

Use the `test` method to determine whether a regular expression matches a specified string. The `test` method returns a value of either `true` or `false`. If you do not specify a string for the `test` method, the value of `RegExp.input` is used.

Method

regexp.test(string)

Returns

If the pattern matches, true.

If no match, false.

Example of Testing the Search for a Match

The following `test.html` script uses the `test()` method and the `source` and `ignoreCase` properties to test the search for a match. It also uses the `search()` method of the `String` object on the same strings to return an index of the regular expression inside the string.

```
<!--


                  test.html


Example of the test() method for regular expressions.


-->


<HTML>
  <HEAD>

    <TITLE>Testing for a Match in a String</TITLE>

<SCRIPT LANGUAGE="JavaScript1.2">

<!--

testStr="Checking for all Apples and Apricots."
failStr="Nothing here but carrots and spinach."

nfre=/(\bA\w+)/
ifre=/(\bA\w+)/i

function listResults(inStr, pattern, caseFlag, tstRes) {
    with (document) {
        write("The test String is: "+inStr+"<BR>")
        write("pattern: "+pattern)
        write(" Ignore Case: "+caseFlag)
        write(" produces: "+tstRes+"<BR>")
        write("<HR>")
    }
}

//-->
</SCRIPT>
  </HEAD>

  <BODY>

    <P>Testing for a match in a string using the test() method.</P>
```

```
<SCRIPT LANGUAGE="JavaScript1.2">
<!--

results=nfre.test(testStr)
listResults(testStr, nfre.source, nfre.ignoreCase, results)
results=ifre.test(testStr)
listResults(testStr, ifre.source, ifre.ignoreCase, results)
results=nfre.test(failStr)
listResults(failStr, nfre.source, nfre.ignoreCase, results)

//-->
</SCRIPT>

    <P>Testing for a match in a string using the search() method.</P>

<SCRIPT LANGUAGE="JavaScript1.2">

<!--

results=testStr.search(nfre)
listResults(testStr, nfre.source, nfre.ignoreCase, results)
results=testStr.search(ifre)
listResults(testStr, ifre.source, ifre.ignoreCase, results)
results=failStr.search(nfre)
listResults(failStr, nfre.source, nfre.ignoreCase, results)

//-->
</SCRIPT>
  </BODY>
</HTML>
```

Figure 7–2 shows the result of loading the `test.html` script.

```
┌─────────────────────────────────────────────────────────────────────┐
│ ▤▤       Netscape: Testing for a Match in a String        ▤         │
│  ◀       ▶       ↻       ⌂      ✐      ⇱      🖼     🖨      🔓     ▥  │ ⎸N⎹│
│ Back  Forward  Reload  Home  Search  Guide  Images  Print  Security Stop │
│ ─────────────────────────────────────────────────────────────────── │
│ Location :  🔖 http://www.bill-anderson.com/jjs/chap7/test.html      │
│ ─────────────────────────────────────────────────────────────────── │
│ Testing for a match in a string using the test() method.          ⬆ │
│                                                                      │
│ The test String is: Checking for all Apples and Apricots.            │
│ pattern: (\bA\w+) Ignore Case: false produces: true                 │
│ ──────────────────────────────────────────────────────────         │
│ The test String is: Checking for all Apples and Apricots.            │
│ pattern: (\bA\w+) Ignore Case: true produces: true                  │
│ ──────────────────────────────────────────────────────────         │
│ The test String is: Nothing here but carrots and spinach.            │
│ pattern: (\bA\w+) Ignore Case: false produces: false                │
│ ──────────────────────────────────────────────────────────         │
│ Testing for a match in a string using the search() method.          │
│                                                                      │
│ The test String is: Checking for all Apples and Apricots.            │
│ pattern: (\bA\w+) Ignore Case: false produces: 17                   │
│ ──────────────────────────────────────────────────────────         │
│ The test String is: Checking for all Apples and Apricots.            │
│ pattern: (\bA\w+) Ignore Case: true produces: 13                    │
│ ──────────────────────────────────────────────────────────         │
│ The test String is: Nothing here but carrots and spinach.            │
│ pattern: (\bA\w+) Ignore Case: false produces: -1                 ⬇ │
│ ─────────────────────────────────────────────────────────────────── │
│ 🔒 ▭                                       ▨▨ ▦ ▥ ✐ ▣            │
└─────────────────────────────────────────────────────────────────────┘
```

Figure 7-2 Result of loading the `test.html` script

Using String Object Methods

The Navigator 4 release also provides the new methods `match()`, `replace()`, `search()`, and `split()` for the `String` object that are used with regular expressions.

Method

string.search(regexp)

string.match(regexp)

string.replace(regexp, newSubstring)

string.split(separator, limit)

Returns

search() returns the index of the regular expression inside the string if successful. Otherwise, returns -1.

match() returns the string matched.

replace() returns a new substring that replaces the matched substring with a new substring.

split() returns an array of substrings with the separator removed.

Searching the String

The `search()` method of the `String` object is similar to the *string*.`indexOf()` method. Both methods return the index of the character number where the string begins. The difference, of course, is that the matching string for the *string*.`search()` method is a regular expression. See "Testing the Search for a Match (Boolean)" on page 250 for an example of the `search()` method.

Testing the Search for a Match (Index)

You have the option of using either the `RegExp` object `test()` method or the String `match()` method to test for a match. The `test()` method returns a value of `true` or `false`. The `match()` method returns an array of matches.

The following `match.html` script uses the `match()` method to search for a match. It also uses the `source`, `global`, `ignoreCase`, and `lastParen` properties of the `RegExp` object to display more information about the match.

```
<!--

                    match.html

Example using the match() method for regular expressions.

-->

<HTML>
  <HEAD>

    <TITLE>Using the match() Method</TITLE>

<SCRIPT LANGUAGE="JavaScript1.2">

<!--

testStr="Checking for all Apples and Apricots."

nfre=/(\bA\w+)/
gfre=/(\bA\w+)/g
ifre=/(\bA\w+)/i
gifre=/(\bA\w+)/gi

//-->

</SCRIPT>

  </HEAD>

  <BODY>

<SCRIPT LANGUAGE="JavaScript1.2">

<!--

nTest=testStr.match(nfre)

with (document) {
    write("The test String is: "+nTest.input+"<BR>")
    write("pattern: "+nfre.source+" produces: "+nTest)
    write(" at index: "+nTest.index+"<BR>")
    write("global flag: "+nfre.global)
    write(", ignore case flag: "+nfre.ignoreCase+"<BR>")
    write("lastParen: "+RegExp.lastParen+", $1: "+RegExp.$1+"<BR>")
    write("<HR>")
}
```

```
gTest=testStr.match(gfre)

with (document) {
    write("The test String is: "+gTest.input+"<BR>")
    write("pattern: "+gfre.source+" produces: "+gTest)
    write(" at index: "+gTest.index+"<BR>")
    write("global flag: "+gfre.global)
    write(", ignore case flag: "+gfre.ignoreCase+"<BR>")
    write("lastParen: "+RegExp.lastParen+", $1: "+RegExp.$1+"<BR>")
    write("<HR>")
}

iTest=testStr.match(ifre)

with (document) {
    write("The test String is: "+iTest.input+"<BR>")
    write("pattern: "+ifre.source+" produces: "+iTest)
    write(" at index: "+iTest.index+"<BR>")
    write("global flag: "+ifre.global)
    write(", ignore case flag: "+ifre.ignoreCase+"<BR>")
    write("lastParen: "+RegExp.lastParen+", $1: "+RegExp.$1+"<BR>")
    write("<HR>")
}

giTest=testStr.match(gifre)

with (document) {
    write("The test String is: "+giTest.input+"<BR>")
    write("pattern: "+gifre.source+" produces: "+giTest)
    write(" at index: "+giTest.index+"<BR>")
    write("global flag: "+gifre.global)
    write(" ignore case flag: "+gifre.ignoreCase+"<BR>")
    write("lastParen: "+RegExp.lastParen+", $1: "+RegExp.$1+"<BR>")
}

//-->
</SCRIPT>
  </BODY>
</HTML>
```

Figure 7–3 shows the result of loading the `match.html` script. Compare the results of this script with Figure 7–2 on 253, which uses the `test()` method of the `RegExp` object.

```
┌─────────────────────────────────────────────────────────────────────┐
│              Netscape: Using the match() Method                    ☰ │
├─────────────────────────────────────────────────────────────────────┤
│   🔙      🔜      🔄     🏠      🔍     📖    🖼️     🖨️    🔒    ⏹️   │   N   │
│  Back   Forward  Reload  Home   Search  Guide Images  Print Security Stop│
├─────────────────────────────────────────────────────────────────────┤
│ Location: 🔖 http://www.bill-anderson.com/jjs/chap7/match.html       │
├─────────────────────────────────────────────────────────────────────┤
│ The test String is: Checking for all Apples and Apricots.           │
│ pattern: (\bA\w+) produces: ["Apples", "Apples"] at index: 17       │
│ global flag: false, ignore case flag: false                         │
│ lastParen: Apples, $1: Apples                                       │
│                                                                     │
│ The test String is: undefined                                       │
│ pattern: (\bA\w+) produces: ["Apples", "Apricots"] at index: undefined│
│ global flag: true, ignore case flag: false                          │
│ lastParen: Apricots, $1: Apricots                                   │
│                                                                     │
│ The test String is: Checking for all Apples and Apricots.           │
│ pattern: (\bA\w+) produces: ["all", "all"] at index: 13             │
│ global flag: false, ignore case flag: true                          │
│ lastParen: all, $1: all                                             │
│                                                                     │
│ The test String is: undefined                                       │
│ pattern: (\bA\w+) produces: ["all", "Apples", "and", "Apricots"] at index: undefined│
│ global flag: true ignore case flag: true                            │
│ lastParen: Apricots, $1: Apricots                                   │
│                                                                     │
└─────────────────────────────────────────────────────────────────────┘
```

Figure 7–3 Result of loading the `match.html` script

Replacing Substrings in a String

You can use the `String` object `replace()` method to replace substrings within a string. The following `replace.html` script uses the `replace()` method to replace `holiday` with `vacation` and `rose` with `flower`. It also uses the $1 and $2 properties of the `RegExp` object to swap the order of a remembered first and last name by using the `replace()` method..

```
<!--

                      replace.html

Example of how to use the replace() method in regular expressions.

-->
<HTML>
  <HEAD>
    <TITLE>Replacing a Substring with Another String</TITLE>

<SCRIPT LANGUAGE="JavaScript1.2">
<!--

testStr1="There is nothing like a holiday."
testStr2="A rose is a rose."
testStr3="John Smith"
```

```
re2=/rose/g
re3=/(\w+)\s(\w+)/

//-->
</SCRIPT>
  </HEAD>

  <BODY>

    <P>Replacing matches:</P>

<SCRIPT LANGUAGE="JavaScript1.2">

<!--

document.write("Old String: "+testStr1+"<BR>")
document.write("Replace holiday with vacation<BR>")
testRes1=testStr1.replace(/holiday/, "vacation")
document.write("New String:: "+testRes1+"<BR>")
document.write("<HR>")
document.write("Old String: "+testStr2+"<BR>")
document.write("Replace all occurrences of rose with flower<BR>")
testRes2=testStr2.replace(re2, "flower")
document.write("New String:: "+testRes2+"<BR>")
document.write("<HR>")

//-->
</SCRIPT>

    <P>Replacing remembered substrings:</P>

<SCRIPT LANGUAGE="JavaScript">

<!--

document.write("Old String: "+testStr3+"<BR>")
document.write("Swap the order.<BR>")
testRes3=testStr3.replace(re3, "$2, $1")
document.write("New String: "+testRes3+"<BR>")

//-->
</SCRIPT>
  </BODY>
</HTML>
```

Figure 7–4 shows the result of loading the `replace.html` script.

```
┌─────────────────────────────────────────────────────────────────────┐
│  ═══════  Netscape: Replacing a Substring with another String  ═══  ▣ │
│ ┌──┐ ┌─────┐                                                          │
│  Back  Forward  Reload  Home  Search  Guide  Images  Print  Security  Stop   N │
│ ─────────────────────────────────────────────────────────────────────│
│ Location:  file:///MacintoshHD/Desktop%20Folder/replace.html         │
│ ─────────────────────────────────────────────────────────────────────│
│  Replacing matches:                                                   │
│                                                                       │
│  Old String: There is nothing like a holiday.                         │
│  Replace holiday with vacation                                        │
│  New String:: There is nothing like a vacation.                       │
│  ──────────────────────────────────────────────────────────────      │
│  Old String: A rose is a rose.                                        │
│  Replace all occurrences of rose with flower                          │
│  New String:: A flower is a flower.                                   │
│  ──────────────────────────────────────────────────────────────      │
│                                                                       │
│  Replacing remembered substrings:                                     │
│                                                                       │
│  Old String: John Smith                                               │
│  Swap the order.                                                      │
│  New String: Smith, John                                              │
│                                                                       │
│                                                                       │
└─────────────────────────────────────────────────────────────────────┘
```

Figure 7–4 Result of loading the `replace.html` script

Object Signing

▼ OBTAINING OBJECT SIGNING TOOLS

▼ PREPARING A SCRIPT FOR SIGNING

▼ RUNNING THE PAGE SIGNING SCRIPT

▼ MOVING OR EDITING SIGNED SCRIPT FILES

▼ SUMMARY OF THE OBJECT SIGNING PROCESS

With the JavaScript 1.2 release, Netscape supports a set of tools and technologies called *object signing*. With object signing, Navigator 4 can permit Java applets and JavaScript objects to selectively access system resources that would otherwise have to remain off limits for security reasons. The objects signed with this technology can be JavaScript scripts, plug-ins, applets, Java code, or any kind of file. The signature is a digital signature.

The digital signature enables the user to confirm the identity of the creator/author of the script, that the script was not tampered with since the creatur/author signed it, and that the creator/author takes responsibility for the script.

An important point is that identity does not equal trust. Just because you know the identity of the creator/author of some code and that they take responsibility for it doesn't mean you necessarily trust what that code will do. For example, suppose the author of the code is HackersRus. Just because you know HackersRus created the code doesn't necessarily mean you want to run that code.

Thus, the privilege security model enables the user to grant privileges to those they trust and deny privileges to those they don't.

Obtaining Object Signing Tools

Before you can create signed scripts, you need to obtain a security certificate that verifies your digital signature. To be able to incorporate that digital signature into your scripts, you also need what is called a JAR packager.

Digital Certificate

Before you can sign a script or other object, you must apply for a *digital certificate*. A digital certificate is a small piece of data that gets downloaded and bound to an individual copy of the Navigator 4 browser on a specific computer.

You can get two types of Netscape Object Signing certificate:

- The Class 2 Netscape Object Signing certificate for individual software authors costs $20 per year.

- The Class 3 Netscape Object Signing certificate for commercial software developers costs $400 per year.

Each certificate is displayed in the list of certificates in the Navigator 4 Security Information window in the Yours category. If you have no certificates, the list is empty, as shown in Figure 8–1.

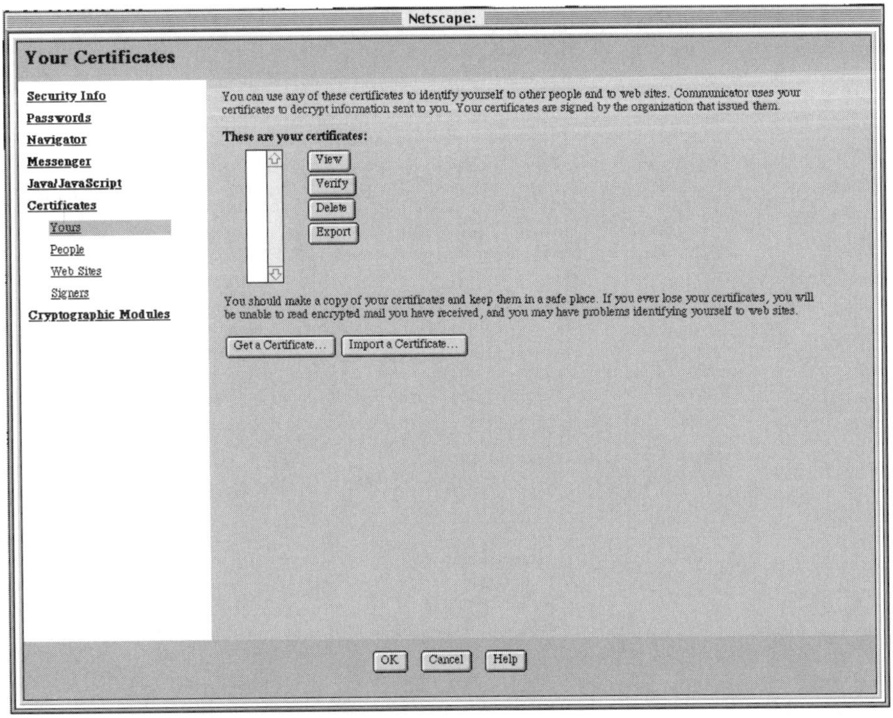

Figure 8–1 Netscape Your Certificates Window with no certificates

Figure 8–2 shows the Netscape Security Your Certificates window with certificates in a Windows NT browser.

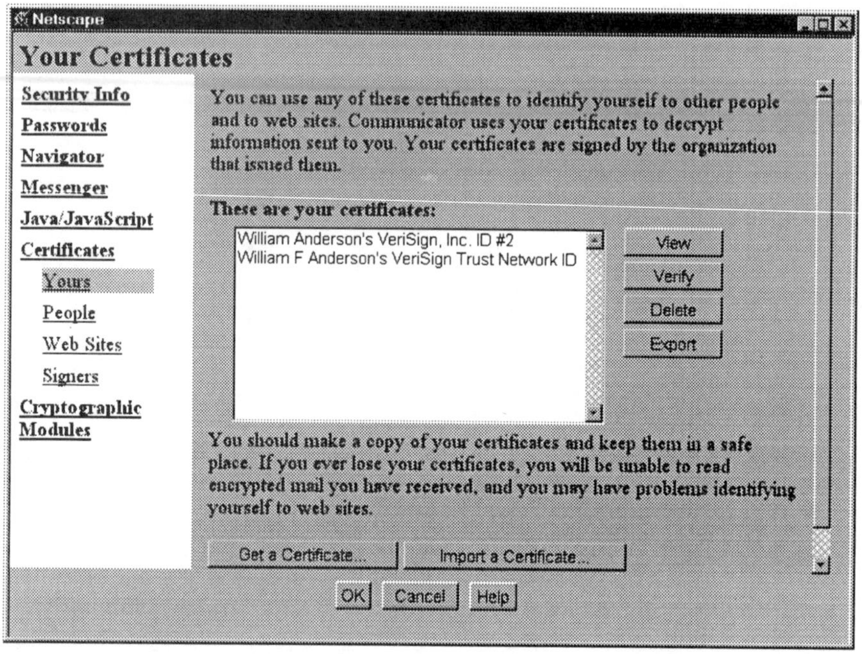

Figure 8–2 Netscape Your Certificates Window with certificates

Netscape provides you with an easy way to access certificate authorities. When you click on the Get a Certificate button at the bottom of the Your Certificates window, a help page at Netscape's Web site is displayed. That page provides several links to certificate authorities.

The primary certificate authority is a company named VeriSign, which was the first company to declare itself a certificate authority. It is also the first link on Netscape's page, as shown in Figure 8–3.

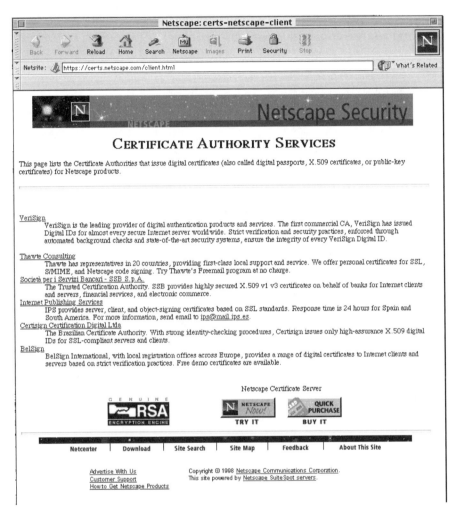

Figure 8–3 Netscape's links to certificate authorities

If you prefer to go directly to the VeriSign Web page, you can find it at:

```
http://digitalid.verisign.com/nosintro.htm
```

Although we do not necessarily recommend VeriSign over other certificate authorities, it is the company that we used for our signing certificate.

When you pick up a certificate, it is downloaded and incorporated to the browser that you are using. When you are ready to pick up your certificate, be sure you connect to the certificate authority with the browser you will use to sign your pages.

To obtain your certificate, you fill out a form with personal information such as your name and address and a driver's license number and pay with a secure credit card transaction. After VeriSign processes the application, they send you an e-mail message with a code number that you use to pick up your certificate.

When you pick up the certificate, it is downloaded and added to your list of certificates for the browser. You can view the details of the certificate by clicking on the Verify button.

Note – A bug in Navigator 4 may show you that your certificate is not valid when you click on the Verify button, even though it is valid. You can verify your certificate directly with VeriSign, as described below.

You can verify your certificate with VeriSign. With your certificate number handy, connect to VeriSign's Digital ID Center at `http://digitalid.verisign.com/status.htm`. Figure 8–4 shows the VeriSign Digital ID Center's Web page.

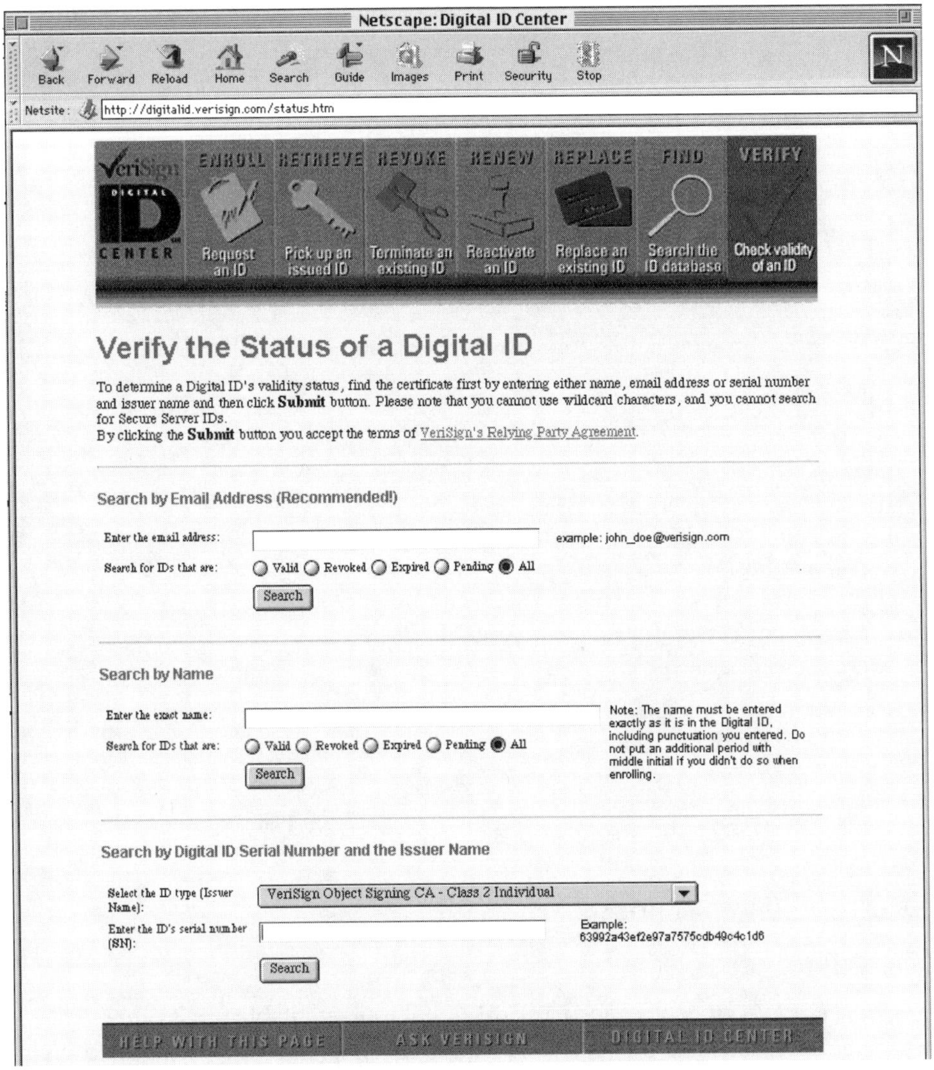

Figure 8-4 VeriSign Digital ID Center

You can search by e-mail address, by complete name, or by individual serial number and certificate type. If you use your certificate number to search, type it without any punctuation and type any letters as lower case. Figure 8–5 shows the result of searching for all certificates by an e-mail address.

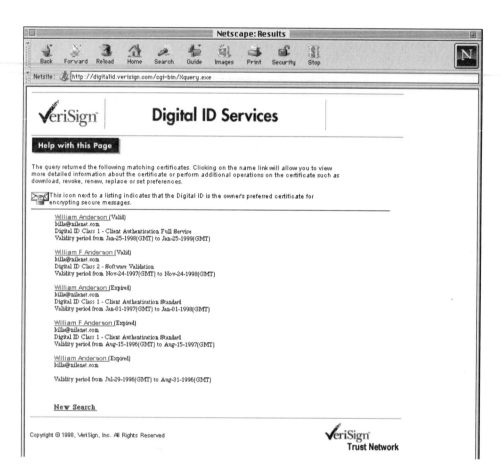

Figure 8–5 Results of Digital ID search

JAR Packager

To create signed scripts, you need an additional tool, available free from
Netscape, called a *Java Archive (JAR) packager*. The JAR packager, also called the
Netscape *Signing Tool*, is a stand-alone, command-line tool that you use to create
digital signatures. The Signing Tool places the digital signature and the associated
scripts in a JAR file, which always has a `.jar` suffix.

The JAR file type is a registered Internet MIME type that is based on the standard
cross-platform ZIP archive. The JAR file acts as a digital envelope for a
compressed collection of files. The format is a set of conventions for associating
digital signatures, installer scripts, and other information with files in a package.
Actually, the JAR format does not require the digital signature to be stored
physically inside the file.

The digital signatures enable Communicator and users of your Web pages to confirm the identity of the individual, company, or other entity whose digital signature is associated with the files. It also enables Communicator to check whether the files have been tampered with since they were signed.

When you run the JAR packager, it creates a manifest containing a list of items that are zipped together in the file. The manifest contains certificate information and creates a hash table of the elements of the script that are marked for signing. The hash table is like a checksum. If the document links in an external `.js` script library file, that file is also packaged in the JAR file.

When the user loads the file into a browser, Navigator checks the hash table against the signed items in the script to verify that no changes were made to the source code since it was signed.

Note – Early versions of the JAR packager were not able to sign script-enabled pages, so Netscape provided a separate Perl script utility named `zigbert.exe` that was run from a command line. Because `zigbert` was a Perl script, you also needed to have a Perl interpreter available on your system.

The JAR packager version 1.1 that is now available from Netscape can now sign script-enabled pages. If you use the 1.1 JAR packager, you no longer need to run `zigbert` or have a Perl interpreter.

The JAR packager is available for the following platforms:

- AIX 4.2.1
- HP-UX 10.10
- HP-UX 11.00
- IRIX 6.2
- Linux 2.0 ELF
- OSF V4.0
- Solaris 2.5.1 (OS 5.5.1)
- Windows 95
- Windows NT 4.0

Note – None of the versions of the JAR packager are available for Macintosh platforms.

You can download the JAR packager from Netscape at:

```
http://developer.netscape.com/software/signedobj/jarpack.html
```

Preparing a Script for Signing

When you write a signed script, you need to provide additional information that the Signing Tool uses in the following ways:

- To identify the items in a file that are to be signed and stored in the JAR file

- To identify to the browser which items in the file must be run through the hash routine again to compare against the values stored in the JAR file

In addition, you use a set of Java classes that are provided with Navigator 4 in the `netscape.security.PrivilegeManager` class to turn on privileges and identify the type of privileges that you are willing to grant.

Creating and Identifying the Archive

The first step in creating a signed script is to identify the name of the JAR file to be associated with the script and to give it an ID string. You create the archive and the ID by including the following two attributes as part of the first `<SCRIPT>` tag in the signed script, preferably in the `<HEAD>` section:

- An `ARCHIVE` attribute, whose value is the name of the JAR file that contains the digital signature for the script

- Either an `ID` attribute, whose value is a string that is used to associate the script with a digital signature in the JAR file, or an `SRC` attribute that retrieves a script from the JAR file

The following example from the `sobject-1.html` script example shown in "Examples of Signed Scripts" on page 274, gives the `.jar` file the same name as the script. It also uses a numerical value for the `ID` attribute.

```
<SCRIPT LANGUAGE="JavaScript1.2" ARCHIVE="sobject-1.jar" ID=1>
```

The value for the `ID` attribute can be any string that you choose that is unique in the script. However, because it's common practice to sequentially number the other `ID` attributes in a signed script, it makes sense to use an `ID=1` value in the `<SCRIPT>` tag.

ID Attribute

In addition to identifying the script itself as a signed script, you also must add a unique ID attribute to each event handler or script element that you want signed.

For other <SCRIPT> tags, include the ID attribute anywhere within the opening tag, as shown below:

```
<SCRIPT LANGUAGE="JavaScript" ID=2>
JavaScript code
</SCRIPT>
```

For an event handler, include the ID attribute after the event handler inside the object tag, as shown in the following examples from the sobject-1.html script.

```
<P><INPUT TYPE="BUTTON" NAME="readBtn" VALUE="Read User Preferences"
ONCLICK="getPref()" ID=2></P>

<P><INPUT TYPE="BUTTON" NAME="updateBtn" VALUE="Update User
Preferences" ONCLICK="setPref()" ID=3></P>
```

PrivilegeManager Classes

Before the browser will allow access to protected properties and methods, you must enable privileges. The user is the only one who can grant permission to enable privileges, but you must include requests for those privileges as part of your code. The netscape.security.PrivilegeManager Java class that is provided with Navigator 4 has the following three methods:

```
netscape.security.PrivilegeManager.enablePrivilege(["target"])
netscape.security.PrivilegeManager.revertPrivilege(["target"])
netscape.security.PrivilegeManager.disablePrivilege(["target"])
```

When you use the enablePrivilege() method, the browser displays an alert for users, as shown in Figure 8–6, asking them whether they are willing to grant privileged access.

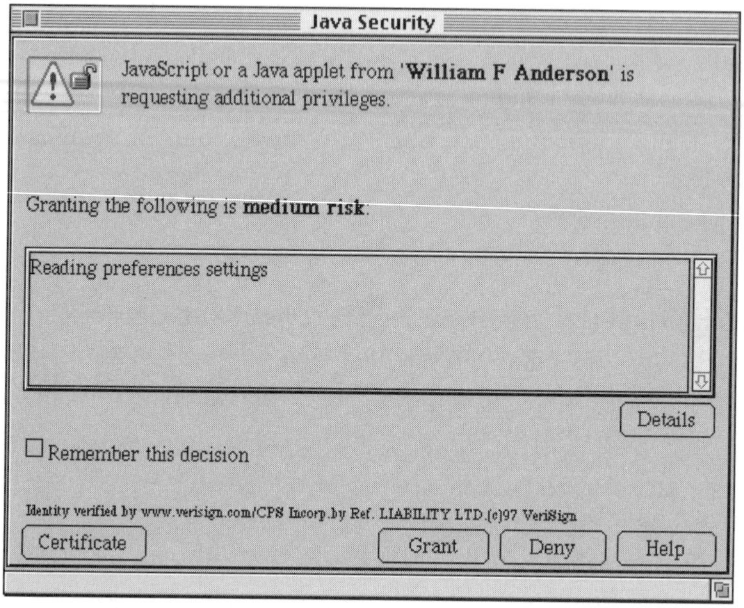

Figure 8–6 Java security alert

If the user grants the privilege, the script processes the next statement. If the user denies access, the script stops and an error message is displayed. The value for the risk is determined by the specific target that is included as part of the `enablePrivilege()` method.

Object Signing Targets

The object signing security model defines a set of narrow capabilities that are opened up when privileges are granted. Each set of capabilities is called a *target*. Netscape has produced two categories of targets: *primitive* and *macro*.

A primitive target is more limited. It usually enables either reading or writing of a specific kind of data. A macro target usually combines two or more primitive targets to reduce the number of security dialog boxes presented to the user.

Table 8-1 describes the most commonly used privilege targets.

Table 8-1 Most Commonly Used Privilege Targets

Target Name	Risk	Description
UniversalBrowserAccess	High	Reading or modifying browser data that may be considered private. Such information can include access to history lists or content of forms the user has filled out. Modification can also include positioning windows anywhere on the screen or creating custom windows.
UniversalBrowserRead	High	Reading browser data that may be considered private. Such information can include access to history lists or content of forms the user has filled out.
UniversalBrowserWrite	High	Modifying the browser in a potentially dangerous way. Such modifications can include positioning windows off the screen, creating windows smaller than 100 x 100 pixels, or suppressing user interface elements such as scrollbars and title bars.
UniversalFileAccess	High	Reading, modifying, or deleting any user files.
UniversalFileRead	High	Reading files stored in the user's computer.
UniversalFileWrite	High	Modifying files stored in the user's computer.
UniversalPreferencesRead	Medium	Reading user preference settings.
UniversalPreferencesWrite	High	Modifying user preference settings.
UniversalSendMail	Medium	Sending e-mail messages on the user's behalf.

The risk assessment classifications were created by Netscape and are considered to be guidelines only. Different users may have different opinions about the level of risk for any specific target.

For a complete list of targets, refer to:

```
http://developer.netscape.com/docs/manuals/signedobj/
targets/index.htm
```

Examples of Signed Scripts

This section shows two complete examples of signed scripts. The first script enables the user to modify user preferences. The second script enables the user to modify the properties of the current screen.

The following `sobject-1.html` script modifies user preferences.

```
<!--


                          sobject-1.html


Modify user preference for Navigator, using a signed object.


-->


<HTML>
  <HEAD>

    <TITLE>Modifying User Preferences</TITLE>

<SCRIPT LANGUAGE="JavaScript1.2" ARCHIVE="sobject-1.jar" ID=1>

<!--

function getPref() {
   netscape.security.PrivilegeManager.enablePrivilege
("UniversalPreferencesRead")
   document.userPref.autoLoad.checked=navigator.preference
("general.always_load_images")
   document.userPref.enableJava.checked=navigator.preference
("security.enable_java")
   document.userPref.enableJS.checked=navigator.preference
("javascript.enabled")
   document.userPref.enableCSS.checked=navigator.preference
("browser.enable_style_sheets")
   document.userPref.autoUpdate.checked=navigator.preference
("autoupdate.enabled")
   document.userPref.cookieBtn[navigator.preference
("network.cookie.cookieBehavior")].checked=true
   document.userPref.warnCookie.checked=navigator.preference
("network.cookie.warnAboutCookies")
}

function setPref() {

netscape.security.PrivilegeManager.enablePrivilege("UniversalPreferencesWrite")
```

```
    navigator.preference("general.always_load_images",
document.userPref.autoLoad.checked)

    navigator.preference("security.enable_java",
document.userPref.enableJava.checked)

    navigator.preference("javascript.enabled",
document.userPref.enableJS.checked)

    navigator.preference("browser.enable_style_sheets",
document.userPref.enableCSS.checked)

    navigator.preference("autoupdate.enabled",
document.userPref.autoUpdate.checked)

   for (var i=0; i<3; i++) {

     if (document.userPref.cookieBtn[i].checked) {
        navigator.preference("network.cookie.cookieBehavior", i)
        break
     }
   }

    navigator.preference("network.cookie.warnAboutCookies",
document.userPref.warnCookie.checked)

}

//-->
</SCRIPT>
  </HEAD>
  <BODY>

  <P>This example uses a signed script and the navigator.preference()
method to read or update user preferences.</P>

    <FORM NAME="userPref">
    <TABLE>
      <TR>
        <TD WIDTH="36">
        <P><INPUT TYPE="CHECKBOX" NAME="autoLoad"></P></TD>
        <TD WIDTH="455">Automatically load images</TD>
      </TR>

      <TR>
        <TD WIDTH="36">
        <P><INPUT TYPE="CHECKBOX" NAME="enableJava"></P></TD>
        <TD WIDTH="455">Enable Java</TD>
```

```
        </TR>

      <TR>
        <TD WIDTH="36">
        <P><INPUT TYPE="CHECKBOX" NAME="enableJS"></P></TD>
        <TD WIDTH="455">Enable JavaScript</TD>
      </TR>

      <TR>
        <TD WIDTH="36">
        <P><INPUT TYPE="CHECKBOX" NAME="enableCSS"></P></TD>
        <TD WIDTH="455">Enable Style Sheets</TD>
      </TR>

      <TR>
        <TD WIDTH="36">

        <P><INPUT TYPE="CHECKBOX" NAME="autoUpdate"></P></TD>
        <TD WIDTH="455">Enable SmartUpdate</TD>
      </TR>

      <TR>
        <TD WIDTH="36">
        <P><INPUT TYPE="RADIO" NAME="cookieBtn" VALUE="0"
CHECKED="CHECKED"></P></TD>

        <TD WIDTH="455">Accept all cookies</TD>
      </TR>

      <TR>
        <TD WIDTH="36">
        <P><INPUT TYPE="RADIO" NAME="cookieBtn" VALUE="1"></P></TD>
        <TD WIDTH="455">Accept cookies only from originating
server</TD>
      </TR>

      <TR>
        <TD WIDTH="36">
        <P><INPUT TYPE="RADIO" NAME="cookieBtn" VALUE="2"></P></TD>
        <TD WIDTH="455">Disable cookies</TD>
      </TR>

      <TR>
        <TD WIDTH="36">
        <P><INPUT TYPE="CHECKBOX" NAME="warnCookie"></P></TD>
        <TD WIDTH="455">Warn before accepting cookies</TD>
      </TR>
```

```
    </TABLE>

    <P><INPUT TYPE="BUTTON" NAME="readBtn" VALUE="Read User
Preferences" ONCLICK="getPref()" ID=2></P>

    <P><INPUT TYPE="BUTTON" NAME="updateBtn" VALUE="Update User
Preferences" ONCLICK="setPref()" ID=3></P>

    </FORM>
  </BODY>
</HTML>
```

Figure 8–7 shows the result of loading the `sobject-1.html` script.

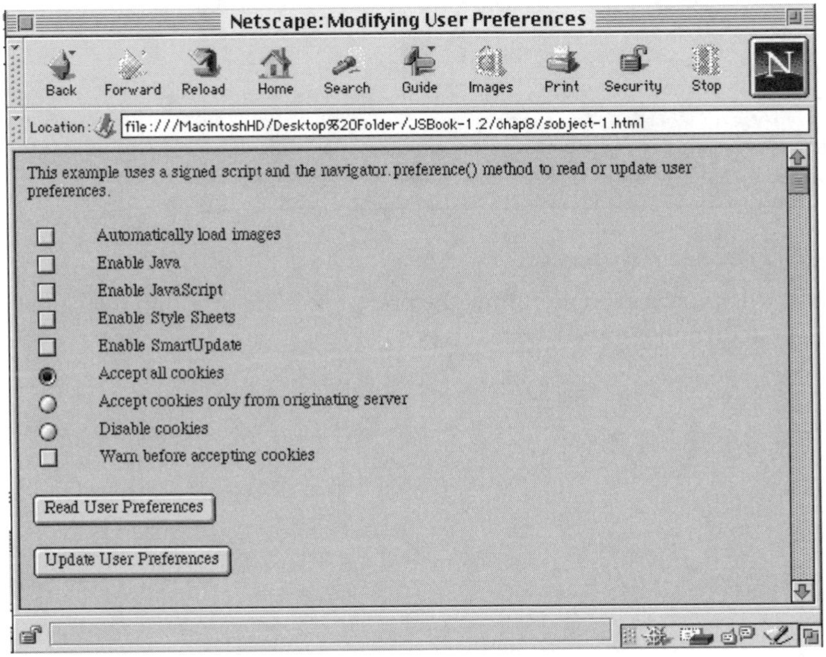

Figure 8–7 Result of loading the `sobject-1.html` script

When the user clicks on the Read User Preferences button, the Java alert window shown in Figure 8–8 is displayed. Notice that reading preferences is considered to be a medium risk.

```
┌─────────────────────────────────────────────────────────────┐
│ ■                    Java Security                           │
├─────────────────────────────────────────────────────────────┤
│  ⚠🔓    JavaScript or a Java applet from 'William F Anderson' is │
│         requesting additional privileges.                   │
│                                                             │
│                                                             │
│  Granting the following is medium risk:                     │
│  ┌───────────────────────────────────────────────────┐ ⬆   │
│  │Reading preferences settings                       │     │
│  │                                                   │     │
│  │                                                   │     │
│  │                                                   │ ⬇   │
│  └───────────────────────────────────────────────────┘     │
│                                          ┌─────────┐        │
│                                          │ Details │        │
│  □ Remember this decision                └─────────┘        │
│                                                             │
│  Identity verified by www.verisign.com/CPS Incorp.by Ref. LIABILITY LTD.(c)97 VeriSign │
│  ┌────────────┐            ┌───────┐ ┌───────┐ ┌───────┐   │
│  │ Certificate │            │ Grant │ │ Deny  │ │ Help  │   │
│  └────────────┘            └───────┘ └───────┘ └───────┘   │
└─────────────────────────────────────────────────────────────┘
```

Figure 8–8 Java security alert

When the user clicks on the Grant button, the preferences are read and displayed on the page, as shown in Figure 8–9.

Preparing a Script for Signing

```
┌─────────────────────────────────────────────────────────────────────┐
│ ▓▓▓▓▓▓▓▓▓▓▓▓▓ Netscape: Modifying User Preferences ▓▓▓▓▓▓▓▓▓▓▓▓▓     │
├─────────────────────────────────────────────────────────────────────┤
│   ⤓        ⤴        ⤶       ⌂        🔍       📖      🎞️      🖨️     🔓     🛑       │ N │
│  Back   Forward   Reload   Home    Search   Guide   Images   Print  Security  Stop   │
├─────────────────────────────────────────────────────────────────────┤
│ Location : 🔖 http://www.bill-anderson.com/jjs/chap8/sobject-1.html              │
├─────────────────────────────────────────────────────────────────────┤
│                                                                       │
│  This example uses a signed script and the navigator.preference() method to read or update user preferences. │
│                                                                       │
│     ☒      Automatically load images                                  │
│     ☒      Enable Java                                                 │
│     ☒      Enable JavaScript                                          │
│     ☒      Enable Style Sheets                                        │
│     ☒      Enable SmartUpdate                                         │
│     ◉      Accept all cookies                                         │
│     ○      Accept cookies only from originating server               │
│     ○      Disable Cookies                                           │
│     ☐      Warn before accepting cookies                             │
│                                                                       │
│   ┌──────────────────────┐                                           │
│   │  Read User Preferences │                                          │
│   └──────────────────────┘                                           │
│                                                                       │
│   ┌──────────────────────┐                                           │
│   │ Update User Preferences │                                         │
│   └──────────────────────┘                                           │
│                                                                       │
│                                                                       │
└─────────────────────────────────────────────────────────────────────┘
```

Figure 8–9 Result of reading user preferences

If you change any of the preferences and click on the Update User Preferences button, another Java security alert window is displayed, as shown in Figure 8–10. Notice that the risk of changing user preferences is considered to be high.

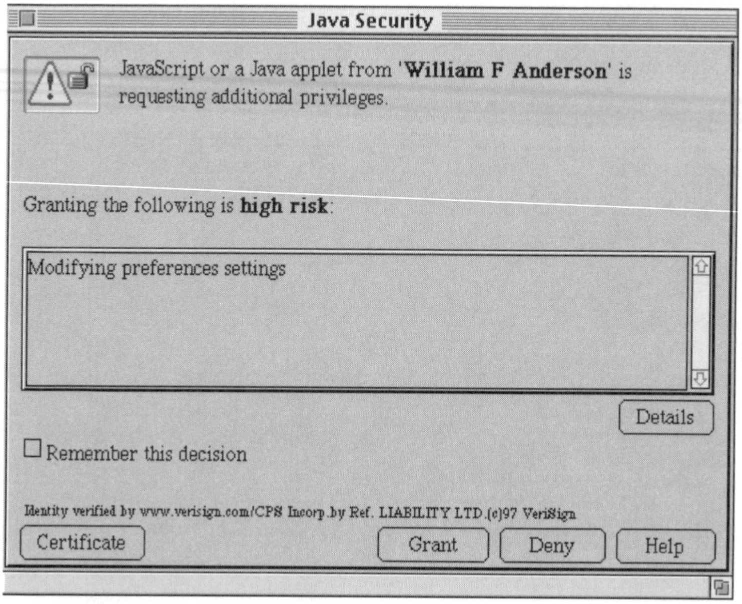

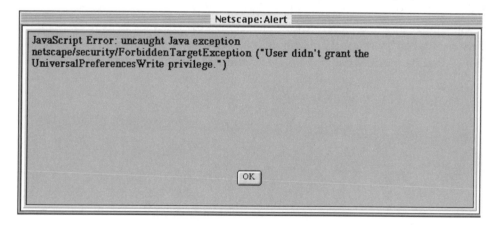

Figure 8–10 Java security alert

Clicking on the Grant button grants access to make the changes. If the user clicks on the Deny button, an error message is displayed, as shown in Figure 8–11.

Figure 8–11 Error message when user denies access

The following `sobject-2.html` script enables the user to set the parameters for the current window.

```
<!--

        sobject-2.html

Modify the properties of the current screen.

-->
<HTML>
<HEAD>

<TITLE>Opening and Closing Windows</TITLE>

<SCRIPT LANGUAGE="JavaScript" ARCHIVE="sobject-2.jar" ID=1>
<!--

var parentName="undefined"

var win_obj=new Array()
var winNameErr="Please enter a name for the window."
var errNum="Not an integer."
var errConflict="Always Raised already checked."
var intPat=/^\d+$/

function warnError (fieldObj, errMsg) {
   alert(errMsg)
   fieldObj.focus()
   fieldObj.select()
   return false
}

function isEmpty(str) {
   return(str==null || str=="")
}

function isInteger(str) {
   return intPat.test(str)
}

function needComma(str) {
   if (str!="") return ","
   return ""
}

function openWin(frmObj) {
   if (isEmpty(frmObj.winName.value))
```

```
            return warnError(frmObj.winName, winNameErr)
        if (!frmObj.winFeatures.checked) {
            win_obj[win_obj.length]=window.open("sobject-2.htm",
frmObj.winName.value)
            return true
        }


netscape.security.PrivilegeManager.enablePrivilege("UniversalBrowser
Write")
    var featureStr=""

    if (frmObj.winDependent.checked)
        featureStr+="dependent=yes"

    if (frmObj.winDirectories.checked)
        featureStr+=needComma(featureStr)+"directories=yes"

    if (frmObj.winHotkeys.checked)
        featureStr+=needComma(featureStr)+"hotkeys=yes"

    if (frmObj.winLocation.checked)
        featureStr+=needComma(featureStr)+"location=yes"

    if (frmObj.winMenubar.checked)
        featureStr+=needComma(featureStr)+"menubar=yes"

    if (frmObj.winResizable.checked)
        featureStr+=needComma(featureStr)+"resizable=yes"

    if (frmObj.winScrollbars.checked)
        featureStr+=needComma(featureStr)+"scrollbars=yes"

    if (frmObj.winStatus.checked)
        featureStr+=needComma(featureStr)+"status=yes"

    if (frmObj.winTitlebar.checked)
        featureStr+=needComma(featureStr)+"titlebar=yes"

    else
        featureStr+=needComma(featureStr)+"titlebar=no"

    if (frmObj.winToolbar.checked)
        featureStr+=needComma(featureStr)+"toolbar=yes"

    if (frmObj.winAlwaysRaised.checked)
        featureStr+=needComma(featureStr)+"alwaysRaised=yes"
```

```
    if (frmObj.winAlwaysLowered.checked) {
       if (frmObj.winAlwaysRaised.checked)
          return warnError(frmObj.winAlwaysLowered, errConflict)

       else
          featureStr+=needComma(featureStr)+"alwaysLowered=yes"
    }

    if (frmObj.winZlock.checked)
       featureStr+=needComma(featureStr)+"z-lock=yes"

    if (!isEmpty(frmObj.winInnerHeight.value)) {
       if (isInteger(frmObj.winInnerHeight.value)) {
          featureStr+=needComma(featureStr)+"innerHeight="
          featureStr+=frmObj.winInnerHeight.value
       }

       else return warnError(frmObj.winInnerHeight, errNum)
    }

    if (!isEmpty(frmObj.winInnerWidth.value)) {
       if (isInteger(frmObj.winInnerWidth.value)) {
          featureStr+=needComma(featureStr)+"innerWidth="
          featureStr+=frmObj.winInnerWidth.value
       }

       else return warnError(frmObj.winInnerWidth, errNum)
    }

    if (!isEmpty(frmObj.winOuterHeight.value)) {
       if (isInteger(frmObj.winOuterHeight.value)) {
          featureStr+=needComma(featureStr)+"outerHeight="
          featureStr+=frmObj.winOuterHeight.value
       }

       else return warnError(frmObj.winOuterHeight, errNum)
    }

    if (!isEmpty(frmObj.winOuterWidth.value)) {
       if (isInteger(frmObj.winOuterWidth.value)) {
          featureStr+=needComma(featureStr)+"outerWidth="
          featureStr+=frmObj.winOuterWidth.value
       }

       else return warnError(frmObj.winOuterWidth, errNum)
    }

    if (!isEmpty(frmObj.winScreenX.value)) {
```

```
        if (isInteger(frmObj.winScreenX.value)) {
            featureStr+=needComma(featureStr)+"screenX="
            featureStr+=frmObj.winScreenX.value
        }

        else return warnError(frmObj.winScreenX, errNum)
    }

    if (!isEmpty(frmObj.winScreenY.value)) {
        if (isInteger(frmObj.winScreenY.value)) {
            featureStr+=needComma(featureStr)+"screenY="
            featureStr+=frmObj.winScreenY.value
        }

        else return warnError(frmObj.winScreenY, errNum)
    }

    win_obj[win_obj.length]=window.open("sobject-2.html",
frmObj.winName.value, featureStr)

    return true
}

function checkParent() {
    if (window.opener==null) {
        alert("There is no parent window.")
        return false
    }

    if (window.opener.closed)
        alert("Window "+window.opener.name+" closed.")
    else alert("Window "+window.opener.name+" open.")
    return true
}

function relParent() {
    if (window.opener==null) return false
    if (window.opener.closed) window.opener=null
    return true
}

//-->
</SCRIPT>

</HEAD>

<BODY ONLOAD="document.winTest.winName.focus()" ID=3>
```

```
<SCRIPT LANGUAGE="JavaScript" ARCHIVE="sobject-2.jar" ID=2>
<!--

if (self.opener) parentName=self.opener.name
document.write("The parent window name is: "+parentName+"<BR>")
while (self.name==null || self.name=="") {
   self.name=prompt("Please enter a name for this window", "")
}

document.write("The current window name is: "+self.name)
//-->
</SCRIPT>
<P>Select the features you want for a new window:</P>
<FORM NAME="winTest">
<TABLE WIDTH="100%" BORDER="1">
<TR>
<TD WIDTH="25%">Name:</TD>
<TD COLSPAN="3" WIDTH="25%"> <P>
<INPUT TYPE="TEXT" NAME="winName" SIZE="20" VALUE=""></P>
</TD>

</TR>
<TR>
<TD WIDTH="25%">Set features:</TD>
<TD COLSPAN="3" WIDTH="25%"><P>
<INPUT TYPE="CHECKBOX" NAME="winFeatures" CHECKED="CHECKED"></P>
</TD>
</TR>

<TR>
<TD WIDTH="25%">dependent:</TD>
<TD WIDTH="25%"> <P><INPUT TYPE="CHECKBOX" NAME="winDependent"
VALUE="yes"></P>
</TD>
<TD WIDTH="25%">titlebar:</TD>
<TD WIDTH="162"><P>
<INPUT TYPE="CHECKBOX" NAME="winTitlebar" VALUE="yes"
CHECKED="CHECKED"></P>
</TD>
</TR>

<TR>
<TD WIDTH="25%">hotkeys:</TD>
<TD WIDTH="25%"><P>
<INPUT TYPE="CHECKBOX" NAME="winHotkeys" VALUE="yes"
CHECKED="CHECKED"></P>
</TD>
<TD WIDTH="25%">menubar:</TD>
```

```
<TD WIDTH="162"><P>
<INPUT TYPE="CHECKBOX" NAME="winMenubar" VALUE="yes"
CHECKED="CHECKED"></P>
</TD>
</TR>

<TR>
<TD WIDTH="25%">innerHeight:</TD>
<TD WIDTH="25%"><P>
<INPUT TYPE="TEXT" NAME="winInnerHeight" SIZE="4" MAXLENGTH="4"></P>
</TD>
<TD WIDTH="25%">toolbar:</TD>
<TD WIDTH="162"><P>
<INPUT TYPE="CHECKBOX" NAME="winToolbar" VALUE="yes"
CHECKED="CHECKED"></P>
</TD>
</TR>

<TR>
<TD WIDTH="25%">innerWidth:</TD>
<TD WIDTH="25%"><P>
<INPUT TYPE="TEXT" NAME="winInnerWidth" SIZE="4" MAXLENGTH="4"></P>
</TD>
<TD WIDTH="25%">location:</TD>
<TD WIDTH="162"><P>
<INPUT TYPE="CHECKBOX" NAME="winLocation" VALUE="yes"
CHECKED="CHECKED"></P>
</TD>
</TR>

<TR>
<TD WIDTH="25%">outerHeight:</TD>
<TD WIDTH="25%"><P>
<INPUT TYPE="TEXT" NAME="winOuterHeight" SIZE="4" MAXLENGTH="4"></P>
</TD>
<TD WIDTH="25%">personal:</TD>
<TD WIDTH="162"><P>
<INPUT TYPE="CHECKBOX" NAME="winDirectories" CHECKED="CHECKED"
VALUE="yes"></P>
</TD>
</TR>

<TR>
<TD WIDTH="25%">outerWidth:</TD>
<TD WIDTH="25%"><P>
<INPUT TYPE="TEXT" NAME="winOuterWidth" SIZE="4" MAXLENGTH="4"></P>
</TD>
<TD WIDTH="25%">scrollbars:</TD>
```

```
<TD WIDTH="162"><P>
<INPUT TYPE="CHECKBOX" NAME="winScrollbars" VALUE="yes"
CHECKED="CHECKED"></P>
</TD>
</TR>

<TR>
<TD WIDTH="25%">screenX:</TD>
<TD WIDTH="25%"><P><INPUT TYPE="TEXT" NAME="winScreenX" SIZE="4"
MAXLENGTH="4">
</P>
</TD>
<TD WIDTH="25%">status:</TD>
<TD WIDTH="162"><P>
<INPUT TYPE="CHECKBOX" NAME="winStatus" VALUE="yes"
CHECKED="CHECKED"></P>
</TD>
</TR>

<TR>
<TD WIDTH="25%">screenY:</TD>
<TD WIDTH="25%"><P><INPUT TYPE="TEXT" NAME="winScreenY" SIZE="4"
MAXLENGTH="4">
</P>
</TD>
<TD WIDTH="25%">resizable:</TD>
<TD WIDTH="162"><P>
<INPUT TYPE="CHECKBOX" NAME="winResizable" CHECKED="CHECKED"
VALUE="yes"></P>
</TD>
</TR>

<TR>
<TD WIDTH="25%">always raised:</TD>
<TD WIDTH="25%"><P><INPUT TYPE="CHECKBOX" NAME="winAlwaysRaised"
VALUE="yes">
</P>
</TD>
<TD WIDTH="25%">z-lock:</TD>
<TD WIDTH="25%"><P><INPUT TYPE="CHECKBOX" NAME="winZlock"
VALUE="yes"></P>
</TD>
</TR>

<TR>
<TD WIDTH="25%">always lowered:</TD>
<TD WIDTH="25%"><P><INPUT TYPE="CHECKBOX" NAME="winAlwaysLowered"
VALUE="yes">
```

```
</P>
</TD>
<TD WIDTH="25%"></TD>
<TD WIDTH="25%"></TD>
</TR>

<TR>
<TD WIDTH="25%" COLSPAN="2"> <P>
<INPUT TYPE="BUTTON" NAME="openBtn" VALUE="Open New Window"
 ONCLICK="openWin(this.form)" ID=4></P>
</TD>
<TD WIDTH="25%" COLSPAN="2"> <P>
<INPUT TYPE="BUTTON" NAME="winCloseBtn" VALUE="Close Current Window"
 ONCLICK="window.close()" ID=5></P>
</TD>
</TR>

<TR>
<TD WIDTH="25%" COLSPAN="2"> <P>
<INPUT TYPE="BUTTON" NAME="closeParentBtn" VALUE="Close Parent
Window"
 ONCLICK="if (window.opener!=null) window.opener.close()" ID=6></P>
</TD>
<TD WIDTH="25%" COLSPAN="2"> <P>
<INPUT TYPE="BUTTON" NAME="checkParentBtn" VALUE="Check Parent
Window"
 ONCLICK="checkParent()" ID=7></P>
</TD>
</TR>

<TR>
<TD WIDTH="25%" COLSPAN="2"> <P>
<INPUT TYPE="BUTTON" NAME="relParentBtn" VALUE="Release Parent
Window"
 ONCLICK="relParent()" ID=8></P>
</TD>
<TD WIDTH="25%" COLSPAN="2"></TD>
</TR>

</TABLE>
</FORM>
</BODY>
</HTML>
```

When you load the `sobject-2.html` script, you are asked to give the window a name, as shown in Figure 8–12.

www.bill-anderson.com – [JavaScript Applicatio

Please enter a name for this window

[   ]

Cancel   OK

Figure 8–12 Initial input window for `sobject-2.html` script

If you do not give the window a name and click on the OK button, it is assigned the name `undefined`. When you click on the OK button, the window shown in Figure 8–13 is displayed.

Netscape: Opening and Closing Windows

Back Forward Reload Home Search Guide Images Print Security Stop

Location: http://www.bill-anderson.com/jjs/chap8/sobject-2.html

The parent window name is: undefined
The current window name is: Fred

Select the features you want for a new window:

Name:			
Set features:	☒		
dependent:	☐	titlebar:	☒
hotkeys:	☒	menubar:	☒
innerHeight:		toolbar:	☒
innerWidth:		location:	☒
outerHeight:		personal:	☒
outerWidth:		scrollbars:	☒
screenX:		status:	☒
screenY:		resizable:	☒
always raised:	☐	z-lock:	☐
always lowered:	☐		

Open New Window	Close Current Window
Close Parent Window	Check Parent Window
Release Parent Window	

Figure 8–13 Result of loading the `sobject-2.html` script

Setting the parameters for a window and clicking on the Open New Window button displays the Java security alert shown in Figure 8–14. Notice that modifying the browser is considered to be high risk.

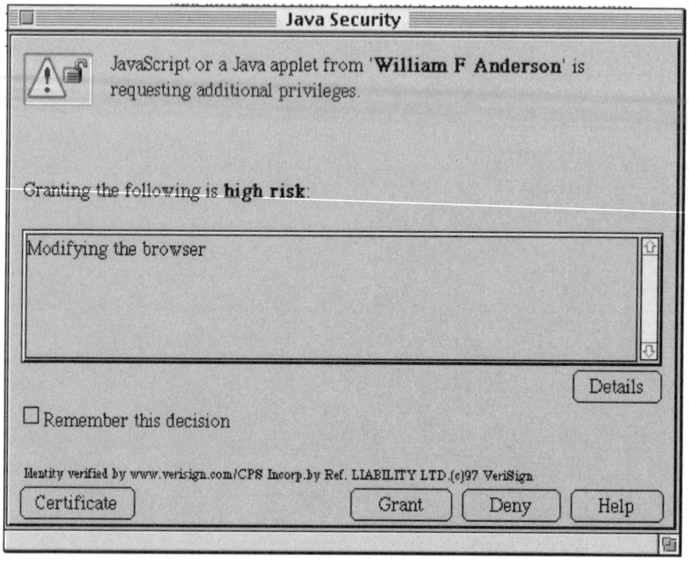

Figure 8–14 Java security alert

The defined window is lacking scrollbars and is fairly small, as shown in
Figure 8–15. Even though it's what was specified, it's no longer possible for the
user to get at the buttons at the bottom of the window.

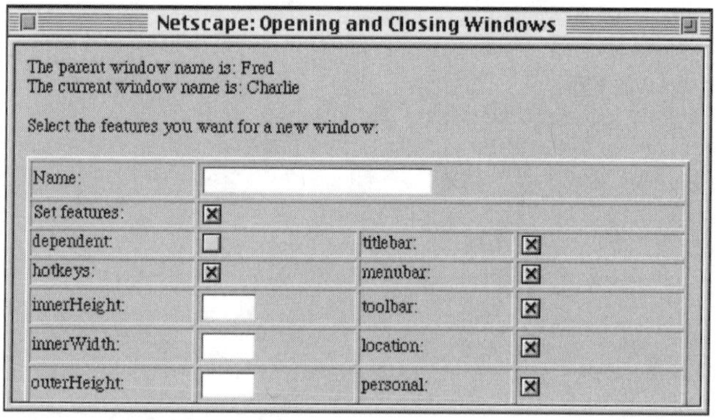

Figure 8–15 New browser window

Running the Page Signing Script

Before running the Netscape Signing Tool, you need the following software in place:

- The installed `signtool` executable.

- The path to the `signtool` executable included in your path environment variable.

- An object signing certificate.

  If you do not have an object signing certificate, the Netscape Signing Tool has an option that enables you to generate an object signing certificate for testing purposes. Refer to the Netscape documentation for information about how to create a test certificate.

Rather than trying to explain all of the complexities of how to use `signtool`, we suggest that you refer to the documentation for the Netscape Signing Tool. Instead, we'll show you what we did to create the examples in this chapter.

First, we set the following parameters in a file named `sign.txt`:

```
certdir=d:\netscape\Users\billa
certname=William F Anderson's VeriSign Trust Network ID
signdir=chap8
outfile=results.txt
```

The command line used to create the signed objects was:

```
signtool -f sign.txt -J --leavearc
```

The results of running `signtool` that were stored in the `results.txt` file are shown below.

```
using certificate directory: d:\netscape\Users\billa
removing: chap8/sobject-1.arc
removing: chap8/sobject-2.arc

Generating inline signatures from HTML files in: chap8
Processing HTML file: sobject-1.html
Processing HTML file: sobject-2.html

signing: chap8/sobject-1.jar
Generating chap8/sobject-1.arc/META-INF/manifest.mf file..
--> inlineScripts/1
--> inlineScripts/2
--> inlineScripts/3
Generating zigbert.sf file..
adding chap8/sobject-1.arc/META-INF/manifest.mf to
chap8/sobject-1.jar...(deflated 46%)
adding chap8/sobject-1.arc/META-INF/zigbert.sf to
```

```
chap8/sobject-1.jar...(deflated 41%)
adding chap8/sobject-1.arc/META-INF/zigbert.rsa to
chap8/sobject-1.jar...(deflated 40%)
jarfile "chap8/sobject-1.jar" signed successfully

signing: chap8/sobject-2.jar
Generating chap8/sobject-2.arc/META-INF/manifest.mf file..
--> inlineScripts/1
--> inlineScripts/2
--> inlineScripts/3
--> inlineScripts/4
--> inlineScripts/5
--> inlineScripts/6
--> inlineScripts/7
--> inlineScripts/8
Generating zigbert.sf file..
adding chap8/sobject-2.arc/META-INF/manifest.mf to
chap8/sobject-2.jar...(deflated 57%)
adding chap8/sobject-2.arc/META-INF/zigbert.sf to
chap8/sobject-2.jar...(deflated 51%)
adding chap8/sobject-2.arc/META-INF/zigbert.rsa to
chap8/sobject-2.jar...(deflated 40%)
jarfile "chap8/sobject-2.jar" signed successfully
0 errors, 1 warning.
```

Moving or Editing Signed Script Files

After you have generated the `.jar` file, you can move it and your associated
HTML files to the server. Because there is a rigid link between the hash value of a
script element both when it is signed and when the user loads it, you must be
very careful when moving or copying a signed script between servers of different
operating systems. A pure binary transfer of HTML files where every byte is the
same should not interfere with the signature. However, if you change the
representation of an HTML source file when you move it between systems, the
signature no longer works.

By the same token, if you make any editing changes to the source code of a signed
script, you must regenerate the `.jar` file.

Summary of the Object Signing Process

This section provides a brief summary of the object signing process.

Before you can create signed scripts, you need the following items:

- Security Certificate
- JAR Packager

Once you have the tools in place, you prepare a script for signing by including the name of the JAR file as part of the ARCHIVE attribute in the first <SCRIPT> tag of the file and either assigning it a unique value for the ID attribute or specifying the SRC attribute.

In addition you include the ID attribute with a unique label as part of the <SCRIPT> tag and for each individual signed element that you include in the script. These ID attributes are used by the JAR packager to create a hash table that is used to verify the script and ensure that it has not been altered.

You use the `netscape.security.PrivilegeManager.enablePrivilege([target])` method to identify the target for the signed script elements you want users to be able to access.

After the script is complete, you run the JAR packager.

Then, you copy the `.jar` file and HTML file(s) to your server for deployment.

New Event Model

▼ COMPARISON OF OLD AND NEW EVENT MODELS

▼ LIST OF EVENTS

▼ EVENT OBJECT

▼ EVENT OBJECT

▼ EVENT MANAGEMENT EXAMPLE

JavaScript actions in the browser are largely event driven. Events are actions that take place usually because a user does something such as clicking a mouse button, pressing a key, or typing text into a text field or text area. Scripts can also initiate events by using the appropriate method to initiate an action.

Event handlers enable scripts to react to an event that has occurred.

You define an event handler by using the following syntax:

```
<TAG handler="JavaScript code">
```

You can also create an event handler by defining an event handler property with the following syntax:

```
document.onmouseover = eventHandler
```

The JavaScript 1.2 release expands the event model to include several new events and also adds an event object and an Event object. The new functionality enables you to capture and handle events before they reach their intended target.

Comparison of Old and New Event Models

In previous versions of JavaScript, the object on which the event occurs handles the event, and any event handler that you include in a script takes action or reactions after the event occurs. The sequence for the old event model goes like this:

1. A user takes an action on a target UI element such as a click or mouseOver.

2. If present, an event handler executes some JavaScript code or function.

3. The script continues.

The old event model was very simple. The browser itself handled a lot of the transitions for the programmer. Including an event handler as part of the definition of the target UI element is simple and straightforward. This way of handling events is still supported and effective in the JavaScript 1.2 release and beyond.

The new event model introduced in the JavaScript 1.2 release is much more powerful. It also introduces a very different kind of programming. The new event model moves more toward the way events are handled in user interface toolkits such as X window system or Windows.

You can handle events only within the window area. Events related to other portions of the browser window are outside the event management model for JavaScript.

Because the JavaScript 1.2 release provides the capabilities for a window or document to capture certain types of events before it reaches its intended target, the story is much more complicated.

The sequence for the new event model goes like this:

1. A user presses the mouse button.

2. The mouse generates a `mouseDown` event.

3. The interface card receives the event and signals the operating system.

4. The operating system receives the event and passes it to the window manager.

5. The window manager receives the event and sees that it belongs to a Navigator window.

6. Navigator receives the event and checks to see if there is a JavaScript window event handler.

7. If the window has an event handler, then the browser invokes the JavaScript event handler.

If not, the browser passes the event to the related document or layer.

8. If the document has a JavaScript event handler, the event is passed to it.

If not, the event flows to the appropriate object.

9. If the object has an event handler, it gets the event.

If not, the event is ignored and the script continues.

With the advent of the new event model, you can think of events as being divided between "raw" events and "cooked" events. The raw events are:

- `mouseDown`

- `mouseUp`

- `mouseMove`

- `mouseOut`

- `keyDown`

- `keyPress`

- `keyUp`

All other events are derived (cooked) from these events. For example, the `click` event triggers on `mouseDown` and issues on `mouseUp`. The `blur` event is simply a variation of `mouseOut`.

Because you, as Web author, can intercept every user action and provide an event handler at every step of the way, you now can write much more powerful JavaScript applications. For example, if you are writing a graphics application, the user chooses the type of object (square, circle, line, polygon) to draw, and clicks to define the size and shape of the object. You would write event handlers to interpret the click-drag-release of the mouse button to define the object. You would then process the event and display something on the screen resulting from the user's actions.

This type of event programming is very different from JavaScript 1.1 because actions in the application are controlled completely by the user. The user is quite likely to press a button and then do something completely unexpected, such as click on the Stop button in the browser toolbar. You must be able to handle those types of events. If you don't work all the way down through the hierarchy and handle everything, your program can get into weird states.

New Methods for Event Handling

The events in this new event model traverse the object hierarchy from the window object, down through the document, through any existing layers, to reach the final target. To enable you to intercept events at any point in the object hierarchy, the `window` and `document` objects have the following new methods to manipulate events:

- `captureEvents(Event.EVENTNAME)`
- `releaseEvents(Event.EVENTNAME)`
- `routeEvents(Event.EVENTNAME)`
- `handleEvent(Event.EVENTNAME)`

The `layer` object provides the following methods to manipulate events:

- `captureEvents(Event.EVENTNAME)`
- `releaseEvents(Event.EVENTNAME)`
- `routeEvents(Event.EVENTNAME)`

You specify the events for these methods as static properties of the `Event` (with a capital E) object, as shown in the following example.

```
slctBtn.captureEvents(Event.MOUSEDOWN | Event.MOUSEUP)
```

If you want to capture events in pages loaded from different locations from a window with frames, you need to create a signed script and call the `window.enableExternalCapture()` method. For more information about signed scripts, see Chapter 8, "Object Signing."

Because you can intercept events at any level, you can prevent the user actions from affecting your page at all, if you so choose. You could, for example, create a demo page that does not respond at all to any clicks of the mouse button. You would intercept the event and not pass it along to its target. Another possible use would be to enable users to view a page but not to interact with it unless they have the proper password access.

Outline for Event Handling

You capture events on a window, document, or layer by using the following rough outline:

1. If you want to capture events in pages loaded from different locations from a window with frames, create a signed script and call the `window.enableExternalCapture()` method.

2. Use the `captureEvents()` method (from within a signed script to capture external events) to define what event to capture. The argument to the method is a mask of the events.

3. Define a function to handle the event.

4. Within the function, provide options for how to handle the event:

    ```
    return true - Continue normal event processing
    return false - Block normal event processing
    ```

5. Call the `routeEvent()` method to have JavaScript look for other event handlers for the event.

6. Call the `handleEvent()` method to explicitly call the event handler for an event.

7. Register the function as the window's event handler for the event.

8. Use the `releaseEvents()` method to release the events.

9. If using a signed script, call the `window.disableExternalCapture()` method.

Processing Captured Events

Once you declare that you are going to capture an event, you also need to define a function to handle that event and then tell the event handler to use the new function.

The following extract from the `event.html` script shown completely in the section "Event Management Example" on page 307 shows some of the functions defined to handle the routing of events.

```
// The following functions handle the routing of
// events.

function winHandler(ev) {
   evMsg(ev.type, "window")
   routeEvent(ev)
   return true
}

function docHandler(ev) {
   evMsg(ev.type, "document")
   ev.target.handleEvent(ev)
   return true
}

function setWinCapture(evType) {
   var evStr="Event."+evType.toUpperCase()
```

```
    if (setWinCapture.arguments.length>1) {
        for (var i=1; i<setWinCapture.arguments.length; i++) {
            evStr+=" | Event."+setWinCapture.arguments[i].toUpperCase()
        }
    }
    window.captureEvents(eval(evStr))
    return true
}
```

The return code of the event handler function must return a Boolean value. A value of `true` means to continue processing the event. In event processing, the final event handler determines the fate of the event. If it cancels the event by returning `false`, the next level needs to cancel the event. A value of `false` means cancel further processing of the event. If a function or another event handler processes the event, you want to return `false`.

Then, you assign the function to the event handler, as shown in the following code extract.

```
// assign the event handler functions

window.onclick=winHandler
window.onmousedown=winHandler
window.onmouseup=winHandler
document.onclick=docHandler
document.onmousedown=docHandler
document.onmouseup=docHandler
```

Releasing Captured Events

You use the `releaseEvents()` method to turn off event capturing with the following syntax:

```
object.releaseEvents(event)
```

The *event* is the same as for the `CaptureEvents()` method

```
window.releaseEvents(Event.CLICK)
```

You can also define a function to release events, as shown in the following code extract.

```
function relDocCapture(evType) {
    var evStr="Event."+evType.toUpperCase()
    if (relDocCapture.arguments.length>1) {
        for (var i=1; i<relDocCapture.arguments.length; i++) {
            evStr+=" | Eent."+relDocCapture.arguments[i].toUpperCase()
        }
    }
}
```

```
        document.releaseEvents(eval(evStr))
        return true
    }
```

List of Events

Table 9-1 lists all of the events and event handlers that are available in the
JavaScript 1.2 release. New events and event handlers are indicated by an
asterisk.

Table 9-1 Events and Event Handlers

Event	Event Handler	When Event Happens
abort	onAbort	The user aborts the loading of an image (for example, by clicking a link or clicking on the Stop button).
blur	onBlur	A form element loses focus or when a window or frame loses focus.
change	onChange	A select, text, or textarea field loses focus and its value has been modified.
click	onClick	The user or a script clicks on an object in a form.
dblClick*	onDblClick*	The user double-clicks a form element or a link.
dragDrop*	onDragDrop*	The user drops an object onto something else, such as dropping a file on the browser window.
error	onError	An error occurs during the loading of a document or image.
focus	onFocus	A window, frame, or frameset receives focus, or a form element receives input focus.
keyDown*	onKeyDown*	The user presses a key.
keyPress*	onKeyPress*	The user presses or holds down a key.
keyUp*	onKeyUp*	The user releases a key.
load	onLoad	The browser finishes loading a window or all of the frames within a FRAMESET tag.
mouseDown*	onMouseDown*	The user presses a mouse button.
mouseMove*	onMouseMove*	The user moves the pointer.
mouseOut	onMouseOut	The pointer leaves an area (client-side image map) or a link from inside that area or link.
mouseOver	onMouseOver	The pointer moves over an object or area from outside that object or area.
mouseUp*	onMouseUp*	The user releases a mouse button.
move	onMove	The user or script moves a window or frame.

Table 9-1 Events and Event Handlers (Continued)

Event	Event Handler	When Event Happens
reset*	onReset*	The user resets a form (clicks a Reset button).
resize*	onResize*	The user or script resizes a window or frame.
select	onSelect	The user selects some of the text within a text or textarea field.
submit*	onSubmit*	The user submits a form.
unload	onUnload	The user exits a document.

Note – The JavaScript 1.2 release recognizes limited mixed-case and lowercase use of events and event handlers. For example, you can explicitly call an event handler by using either *element*.onclick or *element*.onClick. However, *element*.OnClick or *element*.ONCLICK are not recognized.

When an event occurs, an event object is created and is associated with the event. The event object provides information about the event such as the location of the pointer. The event object contains properties that describe a JavaScript event. The properties of the event object vary, depending on the type of the event. The event object that is created when an event occurs is passed as an argument to an event handler.

event Object

The event object contains a set of properties but has no methods or event handlers. When an event occurs, the event object is passed as an argument to an event handler.

You do not create event objects themselves because they are created automatically by Netscape Communicator when an event occurs. You reference events by using the following syntax:

```
event.propertyname
```

The properties for the event object are listed in alphabetical order in Table 9-2. Each of these properties is gettable but not settable.

Table 9-2 Properties for the event Object

Properties	Description
data	Array of strings containing the URLs of dropped objects.
height	Number specifying the height of the window or frame in pixels.
layerX	Number specifying either the object width when passed with the resize event or the horizontal position of the cursor in pixels relative to the layer in which the event occurred. layerX is synonymous with x.
layerY	Number specifying either the object height when passed with the resize event or the vertical position of the cursor in pixels relative to the layer in which the event occurred. layerY is synonymous with y.
modifiers	String specifying the modifier keys associated with a mouse or key event. Modifier key values are: ALT_MASK, CONTROL_MASK, SHIFT_MASK, and META_MASK.
pageX	Number specifying the horizontal position of the cursor in pixels relative to the page.
pageY	Number specifying the vertical position of the cursor in pixels relative to the page.
screenX	Number specifying the horizontal position of the cursor in pixels relative to the screen.
screenY	Number specifying the vertical position of the cursor in pixels relative to the screen.
target	String representing the object to which the event was originally sent.
type	String representing the event type.
which	Number specifying either the mouse button that was pressed or the ASCII value of a pressed key. For a mouse, 1 is the left button, 2 is the middle button, and 3 is the right button.
width	Number that represents the width of the window or frame in pixels.

The properties that are passed to a specific event handler are specific to each individual event handler. Not all of these properties are relevant to each event type.

Table 9-3 describes the new and revised event handlers, shows which objects they can handle events for, and lists the event object properties used by the event.

Table 9-3 Events and Event Handlers

Event Handler	Objects	event Object Properties
onAbort	image	type, target
onBlur	button, checkbox, fileUpload, Layer, password, radio, reset, select submit, text textarea, window	type, target
onChange	fileUpload, select, text, textarea	type, target
onClick	button, document, checkbox, link, radio, reset, submit	type, target, layerX, layerY, pageX, pageY, screenX, screenY, which, modifiers
onDblClick*	document, link	type, target, layerX, layerY, pageX, pageY, screenX, screenY, which, modifiers
onDragDrop*	window	type, target, data, modifiers, screenX, screenY
onError	image, window	type, target
onFocus	button, checkbox, fileUpload, Layer, password, radio, reset, select, submit, text, textarea, window	type, target
onKeyDown*	document, image, link, textarea	type, target, layerX, layerY, pageX, pageY, screenX, screenY, which, modifiers
onKeyPress*	document, image, link, textarea	type, target, layerX, layerY, pageX, pageY, screenX, screenY, which, modifier

Table 9-3 Events and Event Handlers (Continued)

Event Handler	Objects	event Object Properties
onKeyUp*	document, image, link, textarea	type, target, layerX, layerY, pageX, pageY, screenX, screenY, which, modifiers
onLoad	image, Layer, window	type, target, width, height
onMouseDown*	button, document, link	type, target, layerX, layerY, pageX, pageY, screenX, screenY, which, modifiers
onMouseMove*	Must explicitly set to be associated with a particular object	type, target, layerX, layerY, pageX, pageY, screenX, screenY
onMouseOut	Layer, link	type, target, layerX, layerY, pageX, pageY, screenX, screenY
onMouseOver	Layer, link	type, target, layerX, layerY, pageX, pageY, screenX, screenY
onMouseUp*	button, document, link	type, target, layerX, layerY, pageX, pageY, screenX, screenY, which, modifiers
onMove	window	type, target, screenX, screenY
onReset*	form	type, target
onResize*	window	type, target, width, height
onSelect	text, textarea	type, target
onSubmit*	form	type, target
onUnload	window	type, target

Event Object

The `Event` object provides a series of properties that event handling routines use as constants.

You reference these values by using the following syntax:

```
Event.EVENTNAME
```

You also use these values as arguments to any of the event handling methods to specify which events you want to capture, release, or route. You can specify a list of events to handle by providing a list of `Event` object properties and separating them with the OR operator (|).

Property	Value
ALT_MASK	Integer for Alt key
CONTROL_MASK	Integer for Control key
SHIFT_MASK	Integer for Shift key
META_MASK	Integer for Meta key
MOUSEDOWN	Integer for mouse down event
MOUSEUP	Integer for mouse up event
MOUSEOVER	Integer for mouse over event
MOUSEOUT	Integer for mouse out event
MOUSEMOVE	Integer for mouse move event
CLICK	Integer for click event
KEYDOWN	Integer for key down event
KEYUP	Integer for key up event
KEYDOWN	Integer for key down event
KEYUP	Integer for key up event
KEYPRESS	Integer for key press event
DRAGDROP	Integer for drag and drop event
MOVE	Integer for move event
RESIZE	Integer for resize event

Event Management Example

The following `event-1.html` script illustrates how to use the new event management structure. As you click and type in the text field, the text area displays the hierarchy and sequence of events as they occur.

```
<!--

                event-1.html

This document illustrates the event management structure of Netscape
Navigator 4.0 and above.

-->
<HTML>
    <HEAD>
      <TITLE>Advanced Event Management</TITLE>

<SCRIPT LANGUAGE="JavaScript">
<!--

// The evMsg function displays a message in the
// textarea box.

function evMsg(evType, evTarget) {
    var msgStr=""
    msgStr+="A "+evType+" event"
    msgStr+=" was received for the "+evTarget
    msgStr+=" object.\n"
    document.testFrm.evBox.value+=msgStr
}

// The following functions handle the routing of
// events.

function winHandler(ev) {
    evMsg(ev.type, "window")
    routeEvent(ev)
    return true
}

function docHandler(ev) {
    evMsg(ev.type, "document")
    ev.target.handleEvent(ev)
    return true
}

function setWinCapture(evType) {
```

```
      var evStr="Event."+evType.toUpperCase()
      if (setWinCapture.arguments.length>1) {
         for (var i=1; i<setWinCapture.arguments.length; i++) {
         evStr+=" | Event."+setWinCapture.arguments[i].toUpperCase()
         }
      }
      window.captureEvents(eval(evStr))
      return true
   }

   function relWinCapture(evType) {
      var evStr="Event."+evType.toUpperCase()
      if (relWinCapture.arguments.length>1) {
         for (var i=1; i<relWinCapture.arguments.length; i++) {
         evStr+=" | Event."+relWinCapture.arguments[i].toUpperCase()
         }
      }
      window.releaseEvents(eval(evStr))
      return true
   }

   function setDocCapture(evType) {
      var evStr="Event."+evType.toUpperCase()
      if (setDocCapture.arguments.length>1) {
         for (var i=1; i<setDocCapture.arguments.length; i++) {
         evStr+=" | Event."+setDocCapture.arguments[i].toUpperCase()
         }
      }
      document.captureEvents(eval(evStr))
      return true
   }

   function relDocCapture(evType) {
      var evStr="Event."+evType.toUpperCase()
      if (relDocCapture.arguments.length>1) {
         for (var i=1; i<relDocCapture.arguments.length; i++) {
         evStr+=" | Event."+relDocCapture.arguments[i].toUpperCase()
         }
      }
      document.releaseEvents(eval(evStr))
      return true
   }

   // assign the event handler functions

   window.onclick=winHandler
   window.onmousedown=winHandler
   window.onmouseup=winHandler
```

```
document.onclick=docHandler
document.onmousedown=docHandler
document.onmouseup=docHandler

// The following functions handle the receiving
// of events. Consequently, they are called receivers

var oldValue=""

function logEv(ev) {
   evMsg(ev.type, ev.target.type)
   return true
}

// This is the function that identifes the events to capture

function startDoc(ev) {
   document.testFrm.someText.value=""
   document.testFrm.evBox.value=""
   evMsg(ev.type, ev.target.type)
   setWinCapture("click", "mousedown", "mouseup")
   setDocCapture("click", "mousedown", "mouseup")
   return true
}

function exitDoc(ev) {
   evMsg(ev.type, ev.target.type)
   relWinCapture("click", "mousedown", "mouseup")
   relDocCapture("click", "mousedown", "mouseup")
   return true
}

function saveOld(fieldObj, ev) {
   evMsg(ev.type, ev.target.type)
   oldValue=fieldObj.value
   fieldObj.focus()
   fieldObj.select()
   return true
}

function keepChange(fieldObj, ev) {
   evMsg(ev.type, ev.target.type)
   if (!confirm("Keep the change?")) {
      fieldObj.value=oldValue
      return false
   }
   return true
}
```

```
function checkField(frmObj, ev) {
   evMsg(ev.type, ev.target.type)
   if (frmObj.someText.value=="") {
      alert("The field is empty")
      frmObj.someText.focus()
      return false
   }
   return true
}

//-->
</SCRIPT>
  </HEAD>

  <BODY ONLOAD="return startDoc(event)" ONUNLOAD="return
exitDoc(event)">

   <P>Enter some text in the following box and then click the
&quot;Check Field&quot; button. Delete the text you entered and click
the button again.</P>

   <FORM NAME="testFrm">

   <P>Enter text in this box: <INPUT TYPE="TEXT" NAME="someText"
SIZE="30" ONCHANGE=" return keepChange(this, event)" ONFOCUS="return
saveOld(this, event)" ONBLUR="return logEv(event)" ONSELECT="return
logEv(event)"></P>

   <P><INPUT TYPE="BUTTON" NAME="checkText" VALUE="Check Field"
ONCLICK="return checkField(this.form, event)" ONBLUR="return
logEv(event)" ONDBLCLICK="return logEv(event)" ONFOCUS="return
logEv(event)" ONMOUSEDOWN="return logEv(event)" ONMOUSEUP="return
logEv(event)"></P>

   <P><TEXTAREA NAME="evBox" ROWS="10" COLS="56"
WRAP="Off"></TEXTAREA></P>

   </FORM>
  </BODY>
</HTML>
```

Figure 9–1 shows the result of loading the event-1.html script.

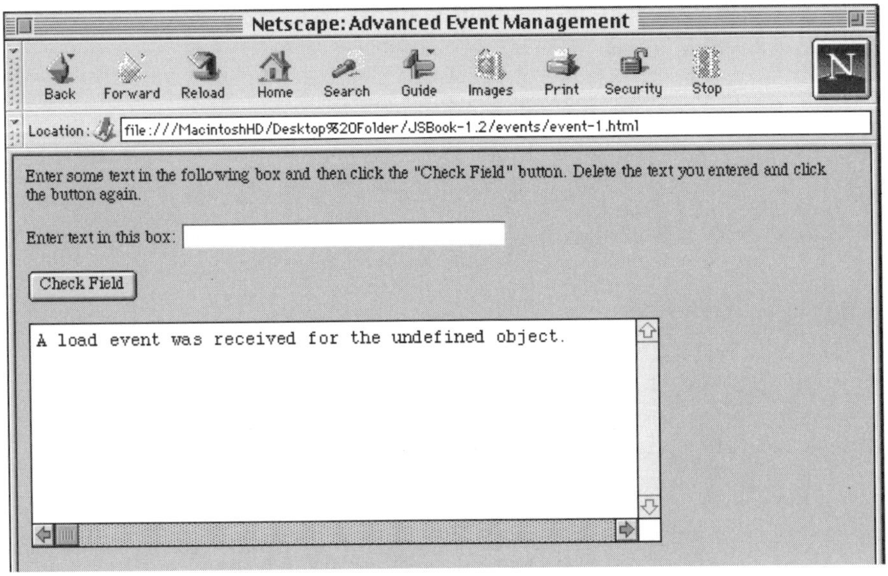

Figure 9–1 Result of loading the `event-1.html` script

When you click in the text field, a focus event is received for the text object and a message is displayed in the text area, as shown in Figure 9–2.

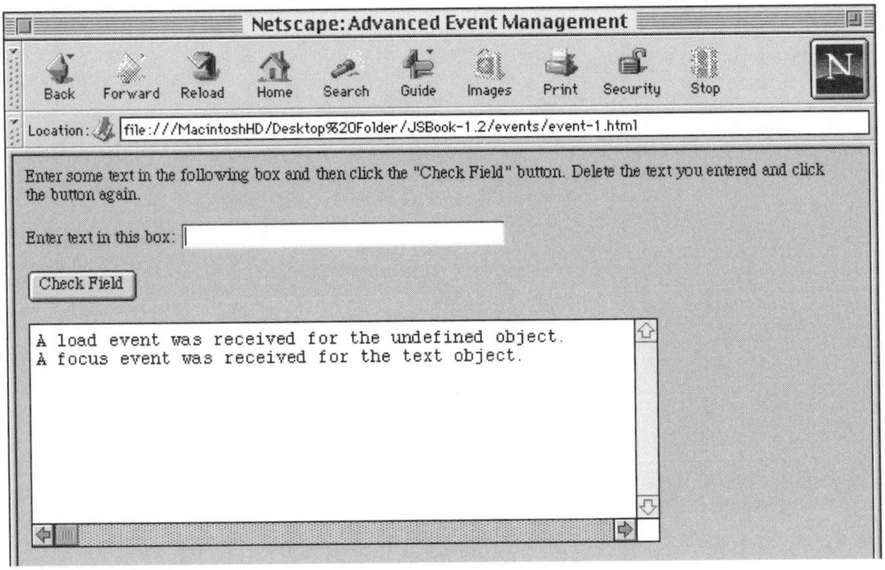

Figure 9–2 Focus event received

When you type text in the text field and click on the Check Field button, an alert is displayed, as shown in Figure 9–3, asking you if you want to save the changes.

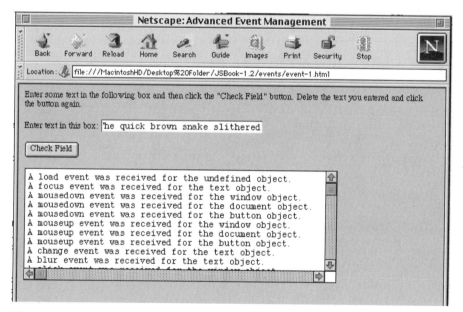

Figure 9–3 Alert generated by the `event-1.html` script

Clicking on the OK button adds a long list of events reflecting the events that were received, as shown in Figure 9–4.

Figure 9–4 List of events received

If you trace closely through the list of events in this example, you'll notice that when the focus switches to the dialog box, it has no exposed event handlers. Because a dialog box is a separate window, even the window event handlers don't see the event. So, you won't see the events that result from user action in the dialog box.

For other examples of event handlers, see "Putting It All Together" on page 199, and "Examples of Signed Scripts" on page 274.

Global Objects

▼ OBJECT OBJECT

▼ NAVIGATOR OBJECT

▼ NUMBER OBJECT

▼ STRING OBJECT

▼ SCREEN OBJECT

Global objects are not created automatically by an HTML tag definition and are not part of the object hierarchy or of the document object model.

The JavaScript 1.2 release changes the following existing global objects.

- `function` object. See "Functions" on page 51 for changes to functions and information about new properties of the `function` object.

- `Object` object

- `Number` object

- `String` object

- `Navigator` object

The JavaScript 1.2 release adds the following new global objects.

- `event` object — Contains properties that describe a JavaScript event. This object is passed as an argument to an event handler when the event occurs.

- `Event` object — Different from the `event` object, contains a set of constants that you use to reference specific events. For information about the `event` and `Event` objects, see Chapter 9, "New Event Model."

- `RegExp` object — Contains properties and methods that you can use to perform pattern matching in strings. For information about the `RegExp` object, see Chapter 7, "Regular Expressions."

- `screen` object — Contains properties that describe the display screen and its colors.

Object Object

The `Object` object is a primitive JavaScript object type. All of the methods for the `Object` object are available to the rest of the JavaScript objects. You use the object constructor new `Object()` to create new objects, but you do not otherwise refer explicitly to the `Object` object by name.

With the JavaScript 1.1 release, the following three methods of the `Object` object were made available to all objects:

- `eval()`

- `toString()`

- `valueOf()`

The JavaScript 1.2 release adds the following additional methods of the `Object` object:

- `handleEvent()`

- `watch()`

- `unwatch()`

eval() Method Change

In Navigator 2.0, `eval()` was a global function. In Navigator 3.0, `eval()` was also a method of every object. However, `eval()` has been changed back to being a global function in Navigator 4.0 to conform with the ECMA-262 standard.

handleEvent() Method

The handleEvent() method is a method of any object that has event handlers: window, document, layer, and all HTML elements. You use it to invoke the handler for a specific event.

> **Method**
>
> *objectReference*.handleEvent(*event*)
>
> **Returns**
>
> The value returned by the event handler that is invoked to handle the event.

For more information see Chapter 9, "New Event Model."

watch() and unwatch() Methods

The watch() method is useful as a debugger. You use it to watch for a property to be assigned a value and run a handler function when that happens.

> **Method**
>
> *objectReference*.watch(*property, handlerFunction*)
>
> *objectReference*.unwatch(*property*)
>
> **Returns**
>
> Old value and new value for the property.

The watch() method watches for assignment to a property and calls handler(property, oldvalue, newvalue) whenever property is set. The return value of handler() becomes the new value of property. Thus, for example, handler() can prevent the value from changing by always returning oldvalue.

If a watchpoint is set for a property and you delete that property, the watchpoint still remains. If the property is later recreated, the watchpoint is still in effect.

To remove a watchpoint, use the unwatch() method.

navigator Object

The `navigator` object contains properties and methods that describe the browsers published by Netscape. Other browsers may not be able to use information returned by the `navigator` object, although Microsoft Internet Explorer does support this object. The `navigator` object is automatically created on the client by the JavaScript runtime engine.

The JavaScript 1.2 release provides two new properties and one new method for the navigator object, as listed in Table 10-1. The `navigator` object has no event handlers.

Table 10-1 New Properties and Methods for the navigator Object

Properties	Methods	Event Handlers
language	preference()	None
platform		

Getting the Name of the Browser Language

The JavaScript 1.2 release provides a `language` property for the `navigator` object that enables you to determine what translation the Navigator client is running. The value returned is usually a two-character code, such as en, but sometimes it is longer. For example, occasionally a language subtype is returned as a five-character code, such as `jp_JP` for Japanese.

Property	Value	Gettable	Settable
language	string	Yes	No

The value returned by the `language` property is related to the internationalization locale concept. A locale string has the following format:

```
language[_territory[.encoding]]
```

- *language* is the two-letter ISO 639 abbreviation for the language name.
- *territory* is the two-uppercase-letter ISO 3166 abbreviation for the territory name.

- *encoding* is the name of the character encoding mapping between numbers and characters. For western languages, encoding is typically the codeset, such as ASCII or 8859-1. For Asian languages, where encoding can involve multiple codesets, the encodings have names such as UJIS or EUC.

Getting the Name of the Platform

The JavaScript 1.2 release provides a platform property for the `navigator` object that enables you to get the machine type for which Navigator was compiled. Note that this may differ from the actual machine type because of version differences, emulators, or other reasons.

Property	Value	Gettable	Settable
platform	string	Yes	No

Platform values are:

- `Win32`
- `Win16`
- `Mac68k`
- `MacPPC`
- Various UNIX platforms

Netscape provides a feature called SmartUpdate that enables software to be automatically and securely installed on a user's computer, triggering installation directly from a Web page. If you use SmartUpdate to download software to a client computer, you can use the `platform` property to ensure that the trigger downloads the appropriate JAR files. The triggering page checks the Navigator version before checking the platform property. For information on using SmartUpdate, see:

```
http:// developer.netscape.com/library/documentation/
communicator/jarman/index.htm.
```

Example of Using navigator Object Properties

The following `navigator.html` script uses the properties of the navigator object to display all of the the properties for a Macintosh PowerPC computer except `mimeTypes` and `plugins`.

```
<!--

            navigator.html

This script displays the properties of the navigator object.

-->

<HTML>
  <HEAD>
    <TITLE>Displaying the navigator Object Properties</TITLE>
  </HEAD>

    <BODY>

    <P>This script displays all of the properties of the navigator
object, except for the mimeTypes and plugins properties.</P>

<SCRIPT LANGUAGE="JavaScript">

<!--

with(document) {
    write("appCodeName: "+navigator.appCodeName+"<BR>")
    write("appName: "+navigator.appName+"<BR>")
    write("appVersion: "+navigator.appVersion+"<BR>")
    write("language: "+navigator.language+"<BR>")
    write("platform: "+navigator.platform+"<BR>")
    write("userAgent: "+navigator.userAgent+"<BR>")
}

//-->

</SCRIPT>
  </BODY>
</HTML>
```

Figure 10–1 shows the result of loading the navigator.html script.

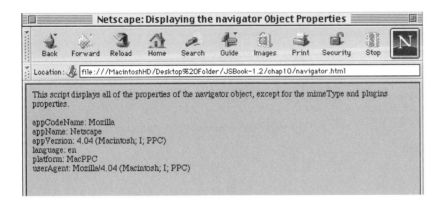

Figure 10–1 Result of loading the `navigator.html` script

Setting Navigator Preferences from a Signed Script

The `preference()` method provided in the JavaScript 1.2 release enables a signed script to get and set certain Navigator preferences.

Method

preference(*preferenceName*)

preference(*preferenceName, setValue*)

Returns

The value of the preference. If you use the method to set the value, it returns the new value.

Reading a preference with the `preference()` method requires the `UniversalPreferencesRead` privilege. To set a preference requires the `UniversalPreferencesWrite` privilege. For more information on setting these privileges, refer to Chapter 8, "Object Signing."

Table 10-2 lists the preferences you can get and set values for by using the `preferences()` method.

Table 10-2 Navigator Preferences

Task	Preference	Values
Automatically load images	`general.always_load_images`	`true ∣ false`
Enable Java	`security.enable_java`	`true ∣ false`
Enable JavaScript	`javascript.enabled`	`true ∣ false`
Enable style sheets	`browser.enable_style_sheets`	`true ∣ false`
Enable SmartUpdate	`autoupdate.enabled`	`true ∣ false`
Accept all cookies	`network.cooke.cookieBehavior`	`0`
Accept only cookies that get sent back to the originating server	`network.cookie.cookieBehavior`	`1`
Disable cookies	`network.cookie.cookieBehavior`	`2`
Warn before accepting cookie	`network.cookie.warnAboutCookies`	`true ∣ false`

Number Object

The `Number` object was implemented in the JavaScript 1.1 release (Navigator 3.0). Because you rarely need to create a `Number` object, we referred to it only obliquely in *Jumping JavaScript, Volume One* in the chapter "Working with Strings and String Objects."

The only change to the `Number` object in the JavaScript 1.2 release is to fix the return value of a number that does not contain a well-formed numeric literal. Instead of returning an error if the value is a string instead of a number, the `Number` object now returns `NaN` (not a number).

For completeness, this section describes all of the properties and methods of the `Number` object.

The primary uses for the Number object are to access its properties and to create numeric objects that you can add properties to. The properties and method for the Number object are listed in Table 10-3.

Table 10-3 Properties and Methods for the Number Object

Properties	Methods	Event Handlers
MAX_VALUE	toString	None
MIN_VALUE		
NaN		
NEGATIVE_INFINITY		
POSITIVE_INFINITY		
prototype		

Testing for Maximum and Minimum Values for a Number

You can use the MAX_VALUE and MIN_VALUE properties of the Number object to determine the maximum numeric value or smallest positive numeric value representable in JavaScript.

Property	Value	Gettable	Settable
MAX_VALUE	1.79E+308	Yes	No
MIN_VALUE	2.22E-308	Yes	No

Because these properties are static properties of the Number object, you reference them as Number.MAX_VALUE and Number.MIN_VALUE.

Using the NaN Property

The NaN (not a number) property of the Number object is returned as an unquoted literal string: NaN. NaN is always unequal to any other number, including NaN itself. You cannot use the NaN property to check for a not-a-number value; use the isNaN() function instead.

You can use the NaN property to show an error condition for a function that should return a valid number.

Property	Value	Gettable	Settable
NaN	NaN	Yes	No

Testing for Negative and Positive Infinity

You can use the NEGATIVE_INFINITY and POSITIVE_INFINITY properties of the Number object to determine whether a number is a positive or negative infinity number.

Property	Value	Gettable	Settable
NEGATIVE_INFINITY	"_Infinity"	Yes	No
POSITIVE_INFINITY	"Infinity"	Yes	No

Because these properties are static properties of the Number object, you reference them as Number.NEGATIVE_INFINITY and Number.POSITIVE_INFINITY.

The values "-Infinity" and "Infinity" behave mathematically like infinity; anything multiplied by infinity is infinity and anything divided by infinity is 0.

The JavaScript language does not have a literal for infinity.

Creating Your Own Properties for a Number Object

The prototype property is an advanced scripting feature. You can use the prototype property to create your own properties or methods that apply to all of the objects you create with the new Number statement.

Property	Value	Gettable	Settable
prototype	string	Yes	No

Converting Numbers to Strings

Every object, including the Number object, has a `toString()` method that you can use to convert a number to a string.

Method
toString()
toString(radix)
Returns
A string representing the specified object.

You can specify the base number, called the radix, to be used in the conversion. If you do not specify a base number, the `toString()` method uses base 10 for decimal numbers. You specify the radix as a value in parentheses following the function. The radix is an integer between 2 and 16.

For example, you can create a new number that is base 10 and convert it to hexadecimal and binary by the following statements:

```
var n = new Number(10)
document.write("Number in hex = "n.toString(16)",
in bin = "n.toString(2)")
```

String Object

The `String` object enables you to perform operations on an object that represents a series of characters in a string. The JavaScript 1.2 release adds the following eight new methods to the `String` object and changes the existing `split()` and `substring()` methods.

- `charCodeAt()` — Returns the ISO-Latin-1 codeset value of the character at the index.

- `concat()` — Combines the text of two strings and returns a new string.

- `fromCharCode()` — Returns a string from the specified sequence of ISO-Latin-1 codeset values.

- `match(pattern)` — Matches a regular expression against a string.

- `replace(pattern,string)` — Matches a regular expression and a string and replaces the matched substring with a new substring.

- `search()` — Searches for a match between a regular expression and a specified string.

- `slice()` — Extracts a section of a string and returns a new string.

- `substr()` — Returns the characters in a string beginning at the specified location through the specified number of characters.

Determining the ISO-Latin-1 Codeset Value of a Character in a String

The ISO-Latin-1 codeset numerically defines a set of characters with a code ranging from 0 to 255. The first 0 to 127 characters in the ISO-Latin-1 codeset are an exact match of the ASCII character set values. The JavaScript 1.2 release provides the `charCodeAt()` method for the `String` object to enable you to determine the ISO-Latin-1 codeset value of individual characters.

Method

string.charCodeAt((*index*))

Returns

Three-digit ISO-Latin-1 codeset value for the character at the specified index.

If you do not specify an *index*, the default value is 0, which is the first position in the string.

Getting a String from a Sequence of ISO-Latin-1 Codeset Values

The JavaScript 1.2 release provides the `fromCharCode()` method for the `String` object to enable you to get characters from a sequence of ISO-Latin-1 codeset values. This method is particularly useful in combination with the `KeyDown`, `KeyPress`, and `KeyUp` events, which return the ASCII value of the key pressed at the time the event occurred. You can use the `fromCharCode()` method to determine the actual letter, number, or symbol of the key that was pressed.

> **Method**
>
> string.fromCharCode(*num1, num2, ..., numn*)
>
> **Returns**
>
> String (not a String object) from the specified sequence of ISO-Latin-1 codeset values.

numn is a sequence of ISO-Latin-1 codeset values.

Combining Strings.

The JavaScript 1.2 release provides the `concat()` method for the `String` object to enable you to combine the text from two strings and return a new string.

> **Method**
>
> *string1*.concat(*string2*)
>
> **Returns**
>
> New string containing the combined text of two specified strings.

Searching, Matching, and Replacing Strings

The search(), match(), and replace() methods of the String object are provided in the JavaScript 1.2 release to work in combination with the new RegExp object to enable you to easily manipulate strings using regular expressions. For more information about regular expressions and examples of how to use these methods, see Chapter 7, "Regular Expressions."

Method

*string.*search(*regexp*)

*string.*match(*regexp*)

*string.*replace(*regexp, newSubstring*)

Returns

search() returns the index of the regular expression inside the string, if successful. Otherwise, returns -1.

match() returns the string matched.

replace() returns a new substring that replaces the matched substring with a new substring.

Extracting Substrings from a String

With the JavaScript 1.2 release, you are provided with a number of alternative ways to extract substrings from a string. In addition to the substring() and split() methods, which has been revised in the JavaScript 1.2 release, you can use the slice() and substr() methods to extract a section of a string and return a new string.

You can use the slice() method to extract a section of a string and return it as a new string.

Method

*string.*slice(*index, (endIndex)*)

Returns

New string containing the extracted elements.

index specifies the index element at which to begin the extraction. *endIndex* specifies the index element at which to end the extraction. The *endIndex* index is not included as part of the new string. Remember that index element numbers begin at 0. You can also specify *endIndex* as a negative number indicating an offset from the end of the string. If you omit the *endIndex* argument, the slice() method extracts to the end of the string.

You can use the substr() method to extract a section of a string starting from a specified index location and through the number of characters that you want to extract.

Method

string.substr(index, (length))

Returns

New string containing the extracted elements.

The index of the first character is always 0, and the index of the last character is string.length-1. The substr() method begins extracting characters at the index and collects the number of characters you specify as the optional length parameter. If you do not specify a length, the substr() method extracts characters to the end of the string.

If you specify a negative index number, the substr() method uses it as a character index from the end of the string.

The substring() method has been modified in the JavaScript 1.2 release so that if you specify LANGUAGE="JavaScript1.2" in the <SCRIPT> tag, substring(x,y) no longer swaps x and y.

Example of Extracting Substrings from a String
The following string-1.html script shows the difference in the substring() method between the JavaScript 1.1 and 1.2 releases.

```
<!--

                    string-1.html

This example shows the difference in the operation of the substring
method between JavaScript 1.1 and JavaScript 1.2. The example also
shows string object methods in JavaScript 1.2.

-->
```

```
<HTML>
  <HEAD>
    <TITLE>Extracting Portions of a String</TITLE>

<SCRIPT LANGUAGE="JavaScript">
<!--
var testStr=new String("A string test")
//-->
</SCRIPT>
  </HEAD>

  <BODY>

    <P>The substring() method with
LANGUAGE=&quot;JavaScript&quot;:</P>

<SCRIPT LANGUAGE="JavaScript">
<!--
with (document) {
   write("All tests use the string: "+testStr+"<BR>")
   write("substring(2, 7) returns: "+testStr.substring(2, 7)+"<BR>")
   write("substring(7, 2) returns: "+testStr.substring(7, 2)+"<BR>")
}
//-->
</SCRIPT>

    <P>The substring() method with
LANGUAGE=&quot;JavaScript1.2&quot;:</P>

<SCRIPT LANGUAGE="JavaScript1.2">
<!--
with (document) {
   write("substring(2, 7) returns: "+testStr.substring(2, 7)+"<BR>")
   write("substring(7, 2) returns: "+testStr.substring(7, 2)+"<BR>")
   write("substring(2) returns: "+testStr.substring(2)+"<BR>")
   write("substring(2, -6) returns: "+testStr.substring(2, -6)+"<BR>")
}

//-->
</SCRIPT>

    <P>The slice() and substr() methods of JavaScript 1.2:</P>

<SCRIPT LANGUAGE="JavaScript1.2">
<!--
```

```
with (document) {
    write("slice(2, 7) returns: "+testStr.slice(2, 7)+"<BR>")
    write("slice(2, -5) returns: "+testStr.slice(2, -5)+"<BR>")
    write("slice(2) returns: "+testStr.slice(2)+"<BR>")
    write("substr(2, 6) returns: "+testStr.substr(2, 6)+"<BR>")
    write("substr(2) returns: "+testStr.substr(2)+"<BR>")
}


//-->
</SCRIPT>
    </BODY>
</HTML>
```

Figure 10–2 shows the result of loading the `string-1.html` script.

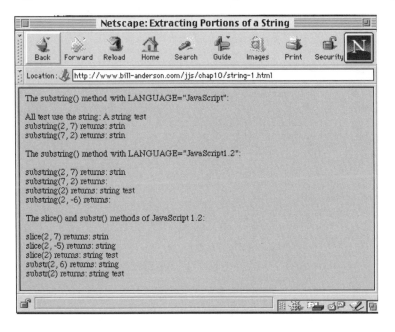

Figure 10–2 Result of loading the `string-1.html` script

Splitting Strings

The `split()` method has been modified in the following ways in the JavaScript 1.2 release:

- You can specify a regular expression argument as well as a fixed string as a way to split the object string.

- You can specify a limit count so that the `split()` method does not include trailing empty elements in the resulting array.

- When you specify LANGUAGE="JavaScript1.2" in the <SCRIPT> tag, string.split(" ") splits on any sequence of one or more whitespace characters including spaces, tabs, line feeds, and carriage returns.

Methods

string.split("*delimiterCharacter*")

Returns

An array of items separated by the *delimiterCharacter*

The following string-2.html script shows the differences in the split() method between the JavaScript 1.1 and 1.2 releases.

```
<!--

                          string-2.html

This document shows the difference between the behavior of the split()
method in JavaScript 1.2 versus previous versions of JavaScript.

-->
<HTML>

  <HEAD>
    <TITLE>Splitting a String into an Array</TITLE>

<SCRIPT LANGUAGE="JavaScript">
<!--

var spaceStr=new String("A  short test    ")
var colonStr=new String("A::short:test:::")
//-->
</SCRIPT>
  </HEAD>

  <BODY>

    <P>This example uses the split command on a string with spaces as
       delimiters and a second string with colons as delimiters. Colons
are used because document.write(array) separates the elements with
commas.Because it is hard to see spaces, the colon-delimited version
of the string is:</P>
```

```
    <P>A::short:test::::</P>

<P>The results of splitting this string with
<CODE>LANGUAGE=&quot;JavaScript&quot;</CODE> are:</P>

<SCRIPT LANGUAGE="JavaScript">
<!--
spaceArray1=spaceStr.split(" ")
document.write("The space-delimited array has "+spaceArray1.length+"
elements: ")
document.write(spaceArray1+"<BR>")
colonArray1=colonStr.split(":")
document.write("The colon delimited array has "+colonArray1.length+"
elements: ")
document.write(colonArray1+"<BR>")
//-->
</SCRIPT>

<P>The results of splitting this string with
<CODE>LANGUAGE=&quot;JavaScript&quot;</CODE> are:</P>

<SCRIPT LANGUAGE="JavaScript1.2">
<!--
spaceArray2=spaceStr.split(" ")
document.write("The space-delimited array has "+spaceArray2.length+"
elements: ")
document.write(spaceArray2+"<BR>")
colonArray2=colonStr.split(":")
document.write("The colon-delimited array has "+colonArray2.length+"
elements: ")
document.write(colonArray2+"<BR>")
//-->
</SCRIPT>
  </BODY>
</HTML>
```

Figure 10–3 shows the result of loading the `string-2.html` script.

```
┌─────────────────────────────────────────────────────────────┐
│ ▦      Netscape: Splitting a String into an Array          ▦ │
├─────────────────────────────────────────────────────────────┤
│   ◀      ◀     ◀     ⌂      ✎      ⬆      ◎     ⬛     🔒    N  │
│  Back  Forward Reload Home  Search Guide  Images Print Security│
├─────────────────────────────────────────────────────────────┤
│ Location : 🔖 http://www.bill-anderson.com/jjs/chap10/string-2.html│
├─────────────────────────────────────────────────────────────┤
│ This example uses the split command on a string with spaces as delimiters and a second string │
│ with colons as delimiters. Colons are used because document.write(array) separates the        │
│ elements with commas. Since it is hard to see spaces, the colon delimited version of the string│
│ is:                                                                                            │
│                                                                                                │
│ A::short:test:::                                                                               │
│                                                                                                │
│ The results of splitting this string with LANGUAGE="JavaScript" is:                            │
│                                                                                                │
│ The space delimited array has 7 elements: A,,short,test,,,                                     │
│ The colon delimited array has 7 elements: A,,short,test,,,                                     │
│                                                                                                │
│ The results of splitting this string with LANGUAGE="JavaScript1.2" is:                         │
│                                                                                                │
│ The space delimited array has 3 elements: ["A", "short", "test"]                               │
│ The colon delimited array has 7 elements: ["A", "", "short", "test", "", "", ""]               │
│                                                                                                │
├─────────────────────────────────────────────────────────────┤
│ 🔒 ▢                                          ▦ ⚙ ▥ ⬒ ⬓ ✓ ▤ │
└─────────────────────────────────────────────────────────────┘
```

Figure 10–3 Result of loading the `string-2.html` script

screen Object

The `screen` object contains properties that describe the screen and colors of the user's display. The JavaScript runtime engine automatically creates the `screen` object. You can access the read-only properties of the `screen` object to find out information about the user's display.

Table 10-4 lists the properties for the `screen` object.

Table 10-4 Properties for the screen Object

Properties	Description
availHeight	Height of the available part of the screen, in pixels. Permanent or semipermanent user interface features such as the Macintosh menu bar or the Windows Taskbar are not included.
availWidth	Width of the available part of the screen, in pixels. User interface features such as the Windows Taskbar are not included.
colorDepth	The bit depth of the color palette if one is used. If no color palette is used, the value is derived from `screen.pixelDepth`.

Table 10-4 Properties for the screen Object (Continued)

Properties	Description
height	Height of the screen in pixels.
pixelDepth	Screen color resolution in bits per pixel.
width	Width of the screen in pixels.

The following `screen.html` script displays the screen properties.

```
<!--

                    screen.html

This example displays the properties of the screen object.

-->

<HTML>
  <HEAD>
    <TITLE>Displaying the Properties of the screen Object</TITLE>
  </HEAD>

  <BODY>

    <P>The properties of the current screen are as follows:</P>

<SCRIPT LANGUAGE="JavaScript1.2">

<!--

with (document) {
    write("Screen Height: "+screen.height+"<BR>")
    write("Screen Width: "+screen.width+"<BR>")
    write("Available Height: "+screen.availHeight+"<BR>")
    write("Available Width: "+screen.availWidth+"<BR>")
    write("Color Depth: "+screen.colorDepth+"<BR>")
    write("Pixel Depth: "+screen.pixelDepth+"<BR>")
}

//-->

</SCRIPT>
  </BODY>
</HTML>
```

Figure 10–4 shows the result of loading the `screen.html` script on a high-resolution monitor.

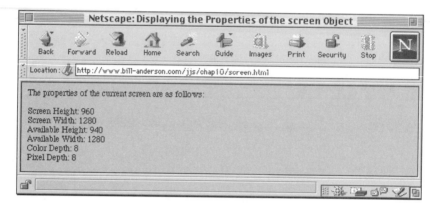

Figure 10–4 Result of loading the `screen.html` script on a high-resolution monitor

Figure 10–5 shows the result of loading the `screen.html` script on a medium-resolution monitor.

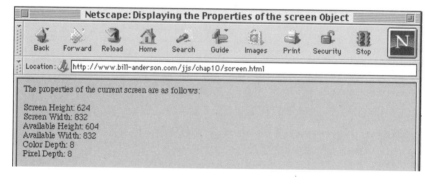

Figure 10–5 Result of loading the `screen.html` script on a medium-resolution monitor

What's New in the Window Object

▼ SHOWING OR HIDING WINDOW USER INTERFACE ELEMENTS

▼ CONTROLLING WINDOW DIMENSIONS

▼ DETERMINING THE CURRENT POSITION OF A VIEWED PAGE

▼ ACCESSING TOOLBAR BUTTONS PROGRAMMATICALLY

▼ FINDING A TEXT STRING WITHIN A WINDOW

▼ OPENING A NEW WEB BROWSER WINDOW

▼ MOVING AND RESIZING WINDOWS

▼ CALLING FUNCTIONS FROM THE SETTIMEOUT() METHOD

▼ SETTING AND CLEARING INTERVALS

▼ CAPTURING EVENTS FROM OTHER WINDOWS

▼ INTERCEPTING A DRAGDROP EVENT

▼ INTERCEPTING A MOVE EVENT

▼ INTERCEPTING A RESIZE EVENT

The JavaScript 1.2 release adds quite a few new properties, methods, and event handlers to the `window` object to enable it to handle layers and style sheets.

This chapter describes what's new in the `window` object.

Table 11-1 lists the new properties, methods, and event handlers for the `window` object. For a complete list of properties, methods, and event handlers for the `window` object, see "window Object" on page 479.

Table 11-1 New Properties, Methods, and Event Handlers for the window Object

Properties	Methods	Event Handlers
innerHeight	back()	onDragDrop
innerWidth	captureEvents()	onMove

Table 11-1 New Properties, Methods, and Event Handlers for the
window Object (Continued)

Properties	Methods	Event Handlers
locationbar	clearInterval()	onResize
menubar	disableExternalCapture()	
outerHeight	enableExternalCapture()	
outerWidth	find()	
pageXOffset	forward()	
pageYOffset	handleEvent()	
personalbar	home()	
scrollbars	moveBy()	
statusbar	moveTo()	
toolbar	open()	
	print()	
	releaseEvents()	
	resizeBy()	
	resizeTo()	
	routeEvent()	
	scrollBy()	
	scrollTo()	
	setInterval()	
	setTimeout()	
	stop()	

Showing or Hiding Window User Interface Elements

The JavaScript 1.2 release adds six properties to the `window` object that you can use to either show or hide the following user interface elements:

- `locationbar` — Represents the location bar of the browser window, which is the region containing the bookmark and URL areas.

- `menubar` — Represents the menu bar of the browser window, which contains drop-down menus such as File, Edit, View, Go, Communicator, Bookmarks.

- `personalbar` — Represents the personal bar (also called the directories bar) of the browser window. This region enables easy access to certain bookmarks.

- `scrollbars` — Represents the vertical and horizontal scrollbars for the document area of the browser window.

- `status bar` — Represents the status bar of the browser window, which is the region containing the security indicator and browser status.

- `toolbar` — Represents the toolbar of the browser window, which contains the navigation buttons such as Back, Forward, Reload, and Home.

Each of these properties has a `visible` property that can be set to `true` to show the user interface element or to `false` to hide the element. For security reasons, you must have `UniversalBrowserWrite` privileges to set the value of the `visible` properties. The following example would hide these user interface elements:

```
self.locationbar.visible=false;
self.menubar.visible=false;
self.personalbar.visible=false;
self.toolbar.visible=false;
self.scrollbars.visible=false;
self.statusbar.visible=false;
```

Property	Value	Gettable	Settable
locationbar.visible	Boolean	Yes	Yes
menubar.visible	Boolean	Yes	Yes
personalbar.visible	Boolean	Yes	Yes
scrollbar.visible	Boolean	Yes	Yes
statusbar	Boolean	Yes	Yes
toolbar.visible	Boolean	Yes	Yes

See "Example of Modifying Window Properties" on page 341 for an example using these properties.

Controlling Window Dimensions

The JavaScript 1.2 release adds four properties to the `window` object that you can use to control window dimensions.

You can use the `innerHeight` and `innerWidth` properties to specify in pixels the vertical and horizontal dimensions of the content area of the window.

To create a window smaller than 100 x 100 pixels, you need to grant the `UniversalBrowserWrite` privilege and set these properties in a signed script.

You can use the `outerHeight` and `outerWidth` properties to specify in pixels the vertical and horizontal dimensions of the outside boundary of the window.

Property	Value	Gettable	Settable
innerHeight	pixels	Yes	Yes
innerWidth	pixels	Yes	Yes
outerHeight	pixels	Yes	Yes
outerWidth	pixels	Yes	Yes

Example of Modifying Window Properties

The following `modify.html` script shows how to use the new window
properties to modify a test window. Even though the script includes the
`UniversalBrowserWrite` privilege, it was not created as a signed script. You
can run it locally, but it displays error messages if you run it from a server. For
more information on creating signed scripts, see Chapter 8, "Object Signing."

```
<!--
                       modify.html

This example modifies the properties of a test window.
-->
<HTML>

  <HEAD>
    <TITLE>Modifying the Properties of a Test Window</TITLE>

<SCRIPT LANGUAGE="JavaScript1.2">
<!--
var errNum="Not an integer."
var intPat=/^\d+$/
function warnError (fieldObj, errMsg) {
   alert(errMsg)
   fieldObj.focus()
   fieldObj.select()
   return false
}
function isEmpty(str) {
   return(str==null || str=="")
}
function isInteger(str) {
   return intPat.test(str)
}
function openTestWin() {
   twin=window.open("", "testWin")
   twin.document.open()
   twin.document.write("This is the test window.")
   twin.document.close()
   return true
}
function closeTestWin() {
   if (!twin.closed) twin.close()
}
function setInner(frmObj) {

netscape.security.PrivilegeManager.enablePrivilege("UniversalBrowser
Write")
```

```
      if (!isEmpty(frmObj.winInnerHeight.value)) {
         if (isInteger(frmObj.winInnerHeight.value)) {
            twin.innerHeight=Number(frmObj.winInnerHeight.value)
         }
         else return warnError(frmObj.winInnerHeight, errNum)
      }
       if (!isEmpty(frmObj.winInnerWidth.value)) {
         if (isInteger(frmObj.winInnerWidth.value)) {
            twin.innerWidth=Number(frmObj.winInnerWidth.value)
         }
         else return warnError(frmObj.winInnerWidth, errNum)
      }
   return true
}
function setOuter(frmObj) {

netscape.security.PrivilegeManager.enablePrivilege("UniversalBrowser
Write")
      if (!isEmpty(frmObj.winOuterHeight.value)) {
         if (isInteger(frmObj.winOuterHeight.value)) {
            twin.outerHeight=Number(frmObj.winOuterHeight.value)
         }
         else return warnError(frmObj.winOuterHeight, errNum)
      }
      if (!isEmpty(frmObj.winOuterWidth.value)) {
         if (isInteger(frmObj.winOuterWidth.value)) {
            twin.outerWidth=Number(frmObj.winOuterWidth.value)
         }
         else return warnError(frmObj.winOuterWidth, errNum)
      }
   return true
}
function setInterface(frmObj) {

netscape.security.PrivilegeManager.enablePrivilege("UniversalBrowser
Write")
   twin.locationbar.visible=frmObj.winLocationbar.checked
   twin.menubar.visible=frmObj.winMenubar.checked
   twin.personalbar.visible=frmObj.winPersonalbar.checked
   twin.scrollbars.visible=frmObj.winScrollbars.checked
   twin.statusbar.visible=frmObj.winStatusbar.checked
   twin.toolbar.visible=frmObj.winToolbar.checked
   return true
}
//-->
</SCRIPT>
  </HEAD>
```

```
<BODY ONLOAD="openTestWin()" ONUNLOAD="closeTestWin()">

    <P>When you set the following properties, you are modifying the
properties of the current screen.</P>
    <FORM NAME="testFrm">
    <TABLE WIDTH="100%" BORDER="2">
      <TR>
        <TD COLSPAN="2" WIDTH="30%">

        <P>innerHeight: <INPUT TYPE="TEXT" NAME="winInnerHeight"
SIZE="4" MAXLENGTH="4"></P></TD>
        <TD WIDTH="30%">

        <P>innerWidth: <INPUT TYPE="TEXT" NAME="winInnerWidth" SIZE="4"
MAXLENGTH="4"></P></TD>
        <TD>

        <P><INPUT TYPE="BUTTON" NAME="innerBtn" VALUE="Set Inner
Dimensions" ONCLICK="setInner(this.form)"></P></TD>
        </TR>
        <TR>
        <TD COLSPAN="2" WIDTH="30%">

        <P>outerHeight: <INPUT TYPE="TEXT" NAME="winOuterHeight"
SIZE="4" MAXLENGTH="4"></P></TD>
        <TD WIDTH="30%">

        <P>outerWidth: <INPUT TYPE="TEXT" NAME="winOuterWidth" SIZE="4"
MAXLENGTH="4"></P></TD>
        <TD>

        <P><INPUT TYPE="BUTTON" NAME="outerBtn" VALUE="Set Outer
Dimensions" ONCLICK="setOuter(this.form)"></P></TD>
        </TR>
        <TR>
        <TD COLSPAN="2" WIDTH="30%">

        <P>locationbar: <INPUT TYPE="CHECKBOX" NAME="winLocationbar"
CHECKED="CHECKED"></P></TD>
        <TD WIDTH="30%">

        <P>menubar: <INPUT TYPE="CHECKBOX" NAME="winMenubar"
CHECKED="CHECKED"></P></TD>
        <TD ROWSPAN="3">

        <P><INPUT TYPE="BUTTON" NAME="userBtn" VALUE="Set User
Interface" ONCLICK="setInterface(this.form)"></P></TD>
        </TR>
```

```
      <TR>
        <TD COLSPAN="2" WIDTH="30%">

          <P>personalbar: <INPUT TYPE="CHECKBOX" NAME="winPersonalbar"
CHECKED="CHECKED"></P></TD>
        <TD WIDTH="30%">

          <P>scrollbars: <INPUT TYPE="CHECKBOX" NAME="winScrollbars"
CHECKED="CHECKED"></P></TD>
      </TR>
      <TR>
        <TD COLSPAN="2" WIDTH="30%">

          <P>statusbar: <INPUT TYPE="CHECKBOX" NAME="winStatusbar"
CHECKED="CHECKED"></P></TD>
        <TD WIDTH="30%">

          <P>toolbar: <INPUT TYPE="CHECKBOX" NAME="winToolbar"
CHECKED="CHECKED"></P></TD>
      </TR>
    </TABLE></FORM>
  </BODY>
</HTML>
```

When you load the `modify.html` script, a security window is displayed asking
if you are willing to permit changes to the browser window. When you click on
the Grant button, the `modify.html` script is loaded, as shown in Figure 11–1. A
test window, not shown, is also opened.

Figure 11–1 Result of loading the `modify.html` script

Determining the Current Position of a Viewed Page

You can use the `pageXOffset` and `pageYOffset` properties of the `window` object to determine the current `x` and `y` position of a viewed page, in pixels.

Property	Value	Gettable	Settable
pageXOffset	pixels	Yes	No
PageYOffset	pixels	Yes	No

These properties are useful only in DHTML scripts where you have multiple documents in the same window or frame. Otherwise, they always return a value of 0,0.

Example of Determining the Current Position of a Viewed Page

The following function extracted from the `resize.html` script uses the `pageXOffset` and `pageYOffset` properties to display the page offset in a test window. See "Example of Moving and Resizing a Window" on page 356 for the complete script.

```
function openTestWin() {
    twin=window.open("", "testWin", featureStr)
    twin.document.open()
    twin.document.write('<H4 ALIGN="CENTER">Test Window</H4>')
    twin.document.write("<P>pageXOffset = " + twin.pageXOffset +
"</P>")
    twin.document.write("<P>pageYOffset = " + twin.pageYOffset +
"</P>")
    twin.document.close()
    return true
}
```

Figure 11–2 shows the page offset displayed in the test window. Because there is only one document, the offset is 0,0.

Netscape:
Test Window
pageXOffset = 0
pageYOffset = 0

Figure 11–2 Page offset

Accessing Toolbar Buttons Programmatically

The JavaScript 1.2 release adds five methods to the `window` object that enable you to programmatically activate the Back, Forward, Stop, Home, and Print buttons in the browser toolbar:

Method
back()
forward()
stop()
home()
print()
Returns
Nothing.

The `back()` method is equivalent to the user clicking on the Back button in the browser toolbar. It undoes the last step anywhere within the top-level window. By contrast, the `back()` method of the `history` object backs up the current window or frame history by one step.

The `forward()` method is equivalent to the user clicking on the Forward button in the browser toolbar. It is the same as `history.go(1)`.

The `stop()` method is equivalent to the user clicking on the Stop button in the browser toolbar. This action stops the current download.

The `home()` method is equivalent to the user clicking on the Home button in the browser toolbar. It points the browser to the URL specified in the user's home page preferences.

The `print()` method is equivalent to the user clicking on the Print button in the browser toolbar. It prints the contents of the window.

Because these methods modify the browser window, you must use them in a signed script.

Example of Accessing Toolbar Buttons Programmatically

The following `wintoolbar-1`, `wintoolbar-2`, and `wintoolbar-3` scripts combine to show an example of accessing the toolbar buttons programmatically to create a custom toolbar. These examples were not created as a signed script, so you can run them locally, but error messages are displayed if you try to run them from a server.

The following `wintoolbar-1.html` script turns off the standard tool bars and then loads the frame for the test. It also contains the code to enable `UniversalBrowserWrite` privileges.

```
<!--
                        wintoolbar-1.html

This script turns off the standard toolbars and then loads the frames
for the test. This script attempts to restore the old settings when
the browser leaves this document by going back to the home page.
--><HTML>
<HEAD>
<META NAME="GENERATOR" Content="NetObjects ScriptBuilder 2.01">
<TITLE>Creating a New Toolbar</TITLE>
<SCRIPT LANGUAGE="JavaScript">
<!--
// save the old settings
oldLocation = window.locationbar.visible
oldMenu = window.menubar.visibile
oldPersonal = window.personalbar.visible
oldTool = window.toolbar.visible
netscape.security.PrivilegeManager.enablePrivilege("UniversalBrowser
Write")
window.locationbar.visible = false
window.menubar.visible = false
window.personalbar.visible = false
window.toolbar.visible = false

function leaveTest() {

netscape.security.PrivilegeManager.enablePrivilege("UniversalBrowser
Write")
    window.locationbar.visible = oldLocation
    window.menubar.visible = oldMenu
    window.personalbar.visible = oldPersonal
    window.toolbar.visible = oldTool
}
//-->
</SCRIPT>
</HEAD>
```

```
<FRAMESET COLS="150,*" ONUNLOAD="leaveTest()">
    <FRAME SCROLLING="auto" NAME="tools" SRC="wintoolbar-2.html">
    <FRAME SCROLLING="auto" NAME="action" SRC="wintoolbar-3.html">
</FRAMESET>
</HTML>
```

The following `wintoolbar-2.html` script contains the new toolbar for the example and uses the `back()`, `forward()`, `stop()`, `home()`, and `print()` methods.

```
<!--

                    wintoolbar-2.html


A simple document that contains the new tools for this test.
--><HTML>
<HEAD>
<META NAME="GENERATOR" Content="NetObjects ScriptBuilder 2.01">
<TITLE>Tool Bar</TITLE>
</HEAD>
<BODY>
<H4 ALIGN="CENTER">Tool Bar</H4>
<FORM NAME="btnForm">
    <P>
    <INPUT TYPE="button" NAME="backBtn" VALUE="Go Back"
ONCLICK="parent.action.back()"><BR>
    <INPUT TYPE="button" NAME="frwdBtn" VALUE="Go Forward"
ONCLICK="parent.action.forward()"><BR>
    <INPUT TYPE="button" NAME="homeBtn" VALUE="Go Home"
ONCLICK="parent.action.home()"><BR>
    <INPUT TYPE="button" NAME="reloadBtn" VALUE="Reload"
ONCLICK="parent.action.location.reload(true)"><BR>
    <INPUT TYPE="submit" NAME="findBtn" VALUE="Find Text"
ONCLICK="parent.action.find()"><BR>
    <INPUT TYPE="button" NAME="printBtn" VALUE="Print"
ONCLICK="parent.action.print()"><BR>
    <INPUT TYPE="button" NAME="stopBtn" VALUE="Stop"
ONCLICK="parent.action.stop()"><BR>
    </P>
</FORM>
</BODY>
</HTML>
```

The following `wintoolbar-3.html` script contains the text that is displayed in the action window of this example.

```
<!--

                        wintoolbar-3.html

The initial document for the action window of the test.
--><HTML>
<HEAD>
<META NAME="GENERATOR" Content="NetObjects ScriptBuilder 2.01">
<TITLE>Document Frame</TITLE>
</HEAD>
<BODY>
<H1 ALIGN="CENTER">Custom Toolbars</H1>
<P>This example demonstrates the use of custom toolbars.
The main window is stripped of the locationbar, personalbar,
and default toolbar. The toolbar on the left replaces the
standard toolbar.</P>
<P>Following are some pages for testing the toolbar:</P>
<P><A HREF="../dhtml/resume-maris.html">Resume for Maris</A></P>
<P><A HREF="../dhtml/resume-janice.html">Resume for Janice</A></P>
</BODY>
</HTML>
```

Figure 11–3 shows the result of loading the `wintoolbar-1.html` script after clicking on the Grant button in the security window.

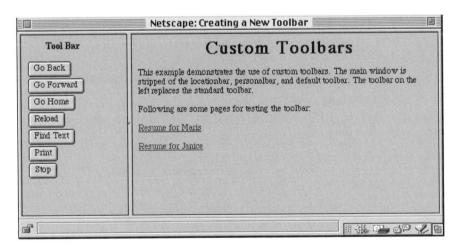

Figure 11–3 Result of loading the `wintoolbar-1.html` script

You can click on either of the links to load text into the frame and experiment with the toolbar controls.

Finding a Text String within a Window

You can use the `find()` method of the window object to find a text string within the contents of the specified window.

Method
find(*string*, casesensitive, backward)

Returns
True if string is found. Otherwise, false.

The `find()` method takes three optional parameters:

- `string` — Optional text string for which to search. When a string is specified with no other parameters, the browser performs a case-insensitive forward search. When a string is not specified, the method displays the Find dialog box, enabling the user to enter a search string.

- `casesensitive` — Optional Boolean value. If specified, performs a case-sensitive search. Must be used in conjunction with the `backward` parameter.

- `backward` — Optional Boolean value. If specified, searches backward. Must be used in conjunction with the `casesensitive` parameter.

Example of Finding a Text String within a Window

The following excerpt from the `wintoolbar-2.html` script, shown completely in "Example of Accessing Toolbar Buttons Programmatically" on page 347, uses the `find()` method to enable you to search for text within a window.

```
ONCLICK="parent.action.location.reload(true)"><BR>
    <INPUT TYPE="submit" NAME="findBtn" VALUE="Find Text"
ONCLICK="parent.action.find()"><BR>
```

When you click on the Find Text button, a popup window is displayed. You can use the checkboxes to specify that the search is case sensitive, to search backwards, or to wrap the search. Type the text in the Find text field, as shown in Figure 11–4, and click on the Find button.

Find On Page

Find: foundry

☐ Case Sensitive   ☐ Find Backwards
☐ Wrap Search

Cancel   Find

Figure 11–4 Result of clicking on the Find button

If the text is found, the first occurrence is highlighted, as shown in Figure 11–5.

Figure 11–5 Result of finding text in a window

If the text is not visible in the window, the page scrolls to display the highlighted match.

Opening a New Web Browser Window

In the JavaScript 1.2 release, the open() method provides a number of new window features that you can use to set additional window features. You use the window.open() method to create a new window and specify its features. Using this method is similar to choosing New Navigator Window from the File menu of the browser.

You specify the parameters for the open() method in the following order. Square brackets ([ ]) indicate items that are optional:

Method

(winVar) = window.open("*URL*","*windowName*",("*windowFeatures*")

Returns

An instance of the window object; null if the method fails.

The new `windowFeatures` available in the JavaScript 1.2 release are listed in Table 11-2:

Table 11-2 Values for New windowFeatures Attributes

Option	Value	Description
alwaysLowered	[=yes|no] | [=1|0]	Creates a new window that floats below other windows whether or not it is active. This secure feature must be set in signed scripts.
alwaysRaised	[=yes|no] | [=1|0]	Creates a new window that floats on top of other windows whether or not it is active. This secure feature must be set in signed scripts.
dependent	[=yes|no] | [=1|0]	Creates a new window as a child of the current window. When its parent window closes, a dependent window also closes. On Windows platforms, a dependent window does not show on the task bar.
hotkeys	[=yes|no] | [=1|0]	Disables all but the security and quit hotkeys in a new window that has no menu bar.
innerHeight	pixels	Specifies the height of the content area of the window, in pixels. You must use a signed script to create a window smaller than 100 x 100 pixels. This feature replaces height, which remains as part of the 1.2 release for backward compatibility.

Table 11-2 Values for New windowFeatures Attributes (Continued)

Option	Value	Description
innerWidth	pixels	Specifies the width of the content area of the window, in pixels. You must use a signed script to create a window smaller than 100 x 100 pixels. This feature replaces width, which remains as part of the 1.2 release for backward compatibility.
outerHeight	pixels	Specifies the vertical height of the outside boundary of the window in pixels. You must use a signed script to create a window smaller than 100 x 100 pixels.
outerWidth	pixels	Specifies the width of the outside boundary of the window, in pixels. You must use a signed script to create a window smaller than 100 x 100 pixels.
screenX	pixels	Specifies the distance the new window is positioned from the left side of the screen, in pixels. You must use a signed script to position a window off screen.
screenY	pixels	Specifies the distance the new window is positioned from the top of the screen, in pixels. You must use a signed script to position a window off screen.
titlebar	[=yes|no] | [=1|0]	Creates a window with a title bar. You must use a signed script to set the titlebar to no.
z-lock	[=yes|no] | [=1|0]	Creates a new window that does not rise above other windows when activated. You must use a signed script to set this secure feature.

Behavior of the alwaysLowered, alwaysRaised, and z-lock features is specific to each windowing platform. For Macintosh platforms, an alwaysLowered browser window is below all other browser windows but is not necessarily below windows in other open applications. For Windows platforms, an alwaysLowered or z-lock browser is below all windows in all open applications.

Features that were available with the open() method in earlier releases are listed in Table 11-3:

Table 11-3 Values for Previous windowFeatures Attributes

Option	Value	Description
toolbar	[=yes|no] | [=1|0]	Back, Forward, and other buttons in the row.
location	[=yes|no] | [=1|0]	Field displaying the current URL.
directories	[=yes|no] | [=1|0]	"What's New" and other buttons in the row.
status	[=yes|no] | [=1|0]	Status bar at the bottom of window.
menubar	[=yes|no] | [=1|0]	Menu bar at top of window (except on Macintosh systems, because the menu bar is not in the browser window).
scrollbars	[=yes|no] | [=1|0]	Scrollbars are displayed if document is larger than the window.
resizable	[=yes|no] | [=1|0]	Elements that enable users to resize the window.
width	pixels	Width of the window, in pixels.
height	pixels	Height of the window, in pixels.

You can have a maximum of 100 Communicator windows open at once. If you set the opener property of child windows to null, JavaScript can garbage collect the parent windows. If you do not set the opener property to null, the parent window object remains even though it is not really needed.

For an example of creating a signed script to open a new browser window, see "Examples of Signed Scripts" on page 274.

Moving and Resizing Windows

In support of layers in the JavaScript 1.2 release, you can use the following methods to move and resize a window by the specified number of pixels and scroll the contents of a window by a specified number of pixels.

Method

moveBy(*horizontal, vertical*)

moveTo(*x-coordinate, y-coordinate*)

resizeBy(*horizontal, vertical*)

resizeTo(*outerWidth, outerHeight*)

scrollBy(*horizontal, vertical*)

scrollTo(*x-coordinate, y-coordinate*)

Returns

Nothing.

The moveBy() and resizeBy() methods move or resize the window by adding or subtracting the number of pixels you specify in the horizontal and vertical direction to the current location.

The scrollBy() method scrolls the contents in the window by adding or subtracting the specified number of pixels to or from the current scrolled location.

The moveTo() method move the top-left corner of the window to the specified x-y screen coordinates.

The resizeTo() method changes the dimensions of the window by setting its outerWidth and outerHeight properties. The upper-left corner remains anchored and the lower right corner moves.

The scrollTo() method scrolls the viewing area of the window so that the specified x-y coordinate becomes the top-left corner.

As with all of the window resizing methods, if you want to exceed any of the boundaries of the screen or change a window's size to be smaller than the enforced minimum size of 100 x 100 pixels, you need the UniversalBrowserWrite privilege. For more information about object signing security, see Chapter 8, "Object Signing."

Example of Moving and Resizing a Window

The following `resize.html` script opens two windows. The first window contains text fields and buttons that you can use to move or resize the second window.

```
<!--

                    resize.html

This example moves and resizes a test window.
-->
<HTML>

  <HEAD>
    <TITLE>Moving and Resizing Windows</TITLE>

<SCRIPT LANGUAGE="JavaScript1.2">
<!--
var featureStr="dependent=yes,resizable=yes,screenX=50,screenY=50"
var errNum="Not a valid integer."
var errX="Missing the horizontal position."
var erry="Missing the vertical position."
var intPat=/^\d+$/
var intSignedPat=/^[+-]*\d+$/
function warnError (fieldObj, errMsg) {
    alert(errMsg)
    fieldObj.focus()
    fieldObj.select()
    return false
}
function isEmpty(str) {
    return(str==null || str=="")
}
function isInteger(str) {
    return intPat.test(str)
}
function isSignedInteger(str) {
    return intSignedPat.test(str)
}
function openTestWin() {
    twin=window.open("", "testWin", featureStr)
    twin.document.open()
    twin.document.write('<H4 ALIGN="CENTER">Test Window</H4>')
    twin.document.write("<P>pageXOffset = " + twin.pageXOffset +
"</P>")
    twin.document.write("<P>pageYOffset = " + twin.pageYOffset +
"</P>")
    twin.document.close()
```

```
        return true
    }
    function checkBy(fieldX, fieldY) {
        if (isEmpty(fieldX.value))
            return warnError(fieldX, errX)
        if (!isSignedInteger(fieldX.value))
            return warnError(fieldX, errNum)
        if (isEmpty(fieldY.value))
            return warnError(fieldY, errY)
        if (!isSignedInteger(fieldY.value))
            return warnError(fieldY, errNum)
        return true
    }
    function checkTo(fieldX, fieldY) {
        if (isEmpty(fieldX.value))
            return warnError(fieldX, errX)
        if (!isInteger(fieldX.value))
            return warnError(fieldX, errNum)
        if (isEmpty(fieldY.value))
            return warnError(fieldY, errY)
        if (!isInteger(fieldY.value))
            return warnError(fieldY, errNum)
        return true
    }
    function doMoveBy(frmObj) {
        if (checkBy(frmObj.winX, frmObj.winY)) {
            twin.moveBy(frmObj.winX.value, frmObj.winY.value)
            return true
        }
        return false
    }
    function doMoveTo(frmObj) {
        if (checkTo(frmObj.winX, frmObj.winY)) {
            twin.moveTo(frmObj.winX.value, frmObj.winY.value)
            return true
        }
        return false
    }
    function doResizeBy(frmObj) {
        if (checkBy(frmObj.winX, frmObj.winY)) {
            twin.resizeBy(frmObj.winX.value, frmObj.winY.value)
            return true
        }
        return false
    }
    function doResizeTo(frmObj) {
        if (checkTo(frmObj.winX, frmObj.winY)) {
            twin.resizeTo(frmObj.winX.value, frmObj.winY.value)
```

```
        return true
    }
    return false
}
//-->
</SCRIPT>
  </HEAD>

  <BODY ONLOAD="openTestWin()">

    <P>You can move and resize a test window by using the form
below.</P>
    <FORM NAME="testForm">
    <TABLE WIDTH="100%">
      <TR>
        <TD>

        <P>horizontal: <INPUT TYPE="TEXT" NAME="winX" SIZE="4"
MAXLENGTH="4"></P></TD>
        <TD>

        <P>vertical: <INPUT TYPE="TEXT" NAME="winY" SIZE="4"
MAXLENGTH="4"></P></TD>
      </TR>
      <TR>
        <TD></TD>
        <TD></TD>
      </TR>
      <TR>
        <TD>

        <P><INPUT TYPE="BUTTON" NAME="winMoveByBtn" VALUE="Move By"
ONCLICK="doMoveBy(this.form)"></P></TD>
        <TD>

        <P><INPUT TYPE="BUTTON" NAME="winResizeBy" VALUE="Resize By"
ONCLICK="doResizeBy(this.form)"></P></TD>
      </TR>
      <TR>
        <TD>

        <P><INPUT TYPE="BUTTON" NAME="winMoveToBtn" VALUE="Move To"
ONCLICK="doMoveTo(this.form)"></P></TD>
        <TD>

        <P><INPUT TYPE="BUTTON" NAME="winResizeToBtn" VALUE="Resize
To" ONCLICK="doResizeTo(this.form)"></P></TD>
      </TR>
```

```
        </TABLE></FORM>
      </BODY>
   </HTML>
```

Figure 11–6 shows the result of loading the `resize.html` script. A test window, not shown, is also opened. Typing horizontal and vertical pixel values into the text fields and clicking on the buttons resizes and moves the test window.

Figure 11–6 Result of loading the `resize.html` script

Calling Functions from the setTimeout() Method

Previous releases provided `setTimeout()` and `clearTimeout()` methods to enable you to evaluate an expression once after a specified period of time. In the JavaScript 1.2 release, the `setTimeout()` method was enhanced to enable you to also call functions. However, this capability does not work, and Netscape has dropped it from the latest documentation.

Method

setTimeout(*expression, msec*)

Returns

timeoutID, where *timeoutID* is an identifier that is used only to cancel the evaluation with the clearTimeout() method

Setting and Clearing Intervals

The JavaScript 1.2 release provides `setInterval()` and `clearInterval()` methods. In contrast to the `setTimeout()` method which is evaluated once, the `setInterval()` method enables you to evaluate an expression every time a specified number of milliseconds elapses. The expression is evaluated or the function is called until you cancel it by calling the `clearInterval()` method.

> **Method**
>
> setInterval(*expression, msec*)
>
> clearInterval(*intervalID*)
>
> **Returns**
>
> Nothing.

Note – The `setInterval()` method was also designed to enable you to call functions. However, this capability does not work, and Netscape has dropped it from the latest documentation

---

Example of setTimeout() Method and Setting and Clearing Intervals

The following `timer.html` script uses the `setTimeout()`, `setInterval()`, and `clearInterval()` methods to display the local date and time.

```
<!--

                    timer.html

This example shows how methods are replaced based on the use of
different values for the LANGUAGE attribute. It also show both
the setTimeout() method for browsers before NN4.0, and the
setInterval() method for NN4.0 and above.

-->

<HTML>

  <HEAD>
    <TITLE>Displaying the Local Date and Time</TITLE>
```

```
<SCRIPT LANGUAGE="JavaScript">
<!--

var timerID=null
var timerOn=false

function dispTime() {
   var curDate=new Date()
   document.clock.clockDisplay.value=curDate.toLocaleString()
   timerID=setTimeout("dispTime()", 1000)
   timerOn=true
}

function stopClock() {
   if (timerOn) clearTimeout(timerID)
   document.clock.clockDisplay.value=""
   timerOn=false
}

function startClock() {
   stopClock()
   dispTime()
}

//-->

</SCRIPT>
<SCRIPT LANGUAGE="JavaScript1.2">
<!--

function dispTime() {
   var curDate=new Date()
   document.clock.clockDisplay.value=curDate.toLocaleString()
}

function stopClock() {
   if (timerOn) clearInterval(timerID)
   document.clock.clockDisplay.value=""
   timerOn=false
}

function startClock() {
   stopClock()
   timerID=setInterval("dispTime()", 1000)
   timerOn=true
}

//-->
```

```
</SCRIPT>
  </HEAD>

<BODY>
  <FORM NAME="clock">
  <TABLE WIDTH="60%">
    <TR>
      <TD COLSPAN="2">
    <P><INPUT TYPE="TEXT" NAME="clockDisplay" SIZE="30"></P></TD>
      </TR>

    <TR>
      <TD>
    <P><INPUT TYPE="BUTTON" NAME="startClockBtn" VALUE="Start
Clock" ONCLICK="startClock()"></P></TD>
      <TD>
    <P><INPUT TYPE="BUTTON" NAME="stopClockBtn" VALUE="Stop Clock"
ONCLICK="stopClock()"></P></TD>
      </TR>

  </TABLE></FORM>
  </BODY>
</HTML>
```

Figure 11–7 shows the result of loading the `timer.html` script and clicking on the Start Clock button.

Figure 11–7 Result of loading the `timer.html` script

Capturing Events from Other Windows

Part of the new event model available with the JavaScript 1.2 release is a set of methods for the `window` and `document` objects that enable you to capture events in pages that are loaded from different locations before the target object gets the event. For security reasons, you must have the `UniversalBrowserWrite` privilege and use the `captureEvents()` method in a signed script.

Method

enableExternalCapture()

captureEvents(*eventType*)

routeEvent(*event*)

handleEvent(*event*)

releaseEvents(*eventType*)

disableExternalCapture()

Returns

Nothing.

For a complete description of the new event model and the `event` object, see Chapter 9, "New Event Model."

Intercepting a DragDrop Event

The `onDragDrop` event handler enables you to intercept a `DragDrop` event and perform scripting actions when a user drops an object onto the browser window.

Event Handler

onDragDrop

Syntax

onDragDrop="*JavaScript code*"

The `onDragDrop` event handler uses the following properties of the `event` object:

- `type` — The type of event.
- `target` — The object to which the event was originally sent.
- `data` — An array of strings containing the URLs of the objects dropped. Getting the `data` property requires the `UniversalBrowserRead` privilege.
- `modifiers` — The list of modifier keys held down when the event occurred.
- `screenX, screenY` — The location of the pointer at the time the event occurred.

Intercepting a Move Event

The `onMove` event handler enables you to intercept a `move` event and perform scripting actions when a user or a script moves a window or a frame.

Event Handler

onMove

Syntax

onMove="*JavaScript code*"

The `onMove` event handler uses the following properties of the `event` object:

- `type` — The type of event.
- `target` — The object to which the event was originally sent.
- `screenX, screenY` — The location of the pointer at the time the event occurred.

Intercepting a Resize Event

The onResize event handler enables you to intercept a resize event and perform scripting actions when a user or a script moves a window or a frame.

Event Handler

onResize

Syntax

onResize="*JavaScript code*"

The onResize event handler uses the following properties of the event object:

- type — The type of event.
- target — The object to which the event was originally sent.
- width, height — The width and height of the window or frame in pixels.

What's New in Documents

▼ ANCHOR OBJECT

▼ ARRAY OBJECT

▼ BUTTON OBJECT

▼ DOCUMENT OBJECT

▼ IMAGE OBJECT

▼ LINK OBJECT

▼ TEXTAREA OBJECT

The JavaScript 1.2 release has added new properties, methods, and event handlers to the following objects that you use in documents.

- `Anchor`

- `Array`

- `button`

- `document`

- `image`

- `link`

- `textarea`

This chapter describes the new elements of these objects.

Anchor Object

An `Anchor` object is created for each anchor created for each pair of `<A></A>` HTML tags that defines a NAME attribute. These objects are stored in an array in the `document.anchors` property. You access an `Anchor` object by indexing this array.

Previous versions of the `Anchor` object had no properties. The JavaScript 1.2 release adds a `text` property to the `Anchor` object.

Property	Value	Gettable	Settable
text	string	Yes	No

The `text` property contains the content of the corresponding `<A>` tag when it has a named anchor or a link. You reference the text property by using the following syntax:

```
anchorName.text
```

where `anchorName` is the name of the anchor defined by the NAME attribute of the `<A>` tag.

Example of Using the text Property

If you create an anchor with a NAME or HREF attribute, you can access the name or the link with the text property. For example, if you create a named anchor, as shown below:

```
<A NAME="foo">This text is in a named anchor.</A>
```

you would access the NAME value in the following way:

```
document.anchors[0].text
```

If you create an anchor with a link, as shown below:

```
<A HREF="http://www.netscape.com">This text is in a link.</A>
```

you would access the HREF value in the following way:

```
document.links[0].text
```

Array Object

The `Array` object represents a collection of individual data items that are organized so that the entire collection can be treated as a single piece of data.

The JavaScript release enables you to create arrays by using literal notation. It also provides a set of new methods that enables you to extract information about matches between regular expressions and strings.

Creating an Array by Using Literal Notation

In previous releases, you created a new `Array` object by using the `new` keyword, as shown in the following example that creates an new, empty array with no elements:

```
anArray = new Array()
```

With the JavaScript 1.2 release, when the `<SCRIPT>` tag specifies `LANGUAGE="JavaScript1.2"` you can create new arrays by using literal notation:

```
anArray = [element0, element1, ..., elementn ]
```

You specify the list of values for the elements in the array as a comma-separated list between square brackets. You do not have to specify all elements in the new array. If you put two commas in a row, the array is created with spaces for the unspecified elements.

When you create an array by using literal notation in a top-level script, JavaScript interprets the object each time it evaluates the expression containing the array literal. In addition, if you use a literal array in a function, it is created each time the function is called.

New Array Object Methods

The JavaScript 1.2 release provides the following new methods for the `Array` object:

- `concat()`
- `pop()`
- `push()`
- `shift()`
- `unshift()`
- `slice()`

- `splice()`
- `sort()`

Combining Elements from Two Arrays

The JavaScript 1.2 release provides a new `concat()` method for the `Array` object. You can use the `concat()` method to create a new array that contains a copy of the elements from the original arrays.

Method

arrayName1.concat(arrayName2)

Returns

A one-level-deep array that contains copies of the elements from the original arrays.

Elements from the original arrays are copied into the new array as follows:

- The `concat()` method copies object references, not the actual object, into the new array. Both the original and the new arrays refer to the same object. If a referenced object changes, the changes are reflected in both the original and the new arrays.

- The `concat()` method copies strings and numbers into the new array. Changes to the string or number in one array do not affect the other arrays.

- When a new element is added to either array, the other array is not affected.

Example of Combining Elements from Two Arrays

The following `arrayConcat.html` script combines the elements from two arrays.

```
<!--

                    arrayConcat.html

Concatenates two arrays.

-->

<HTML>
    <HEAD>

        <TITLE>Concatenate Two Arrays</TITLE>
```

```
<SCRIPT LANGUAGE="JavaScript">

<!--

function dispArray (objArray) {
    for (var i=0; i<objArray.length; i++) {
        document.write(objArray[i]+"<BR>")
    }
}

//-->
</SCRIPT>
  </HEAD>

  <BODY>
    <P>Array 1 contents:</P>

<SCRIPT LANGUAGE="JavaScript">

<!--

exArray1 = new Array("red", "green", "blue")
dispArray(exArray1)

//-->
</SCRIPT>

    <P>Array 2 contents:</P>

<SCRIPT LANGUAGE="JavaScript">

<!--

exArray2 = new Array("orange", "yellow", "purple")
dispArray(exArray2)

//-->
</SCRIPT>

    <P>Concatenated Array</P>

<SCRIPT LANGUAGE="JavaScript1.2">

<!--

exArray3 = exArray1.concat(exArray2)
dispArray(exArray3)
```

```
//-->

</SCRIPT>
  </BODY>
</HTML>
```

Figure 12–1 shows the result of loading the `arrayConcat.html` script.

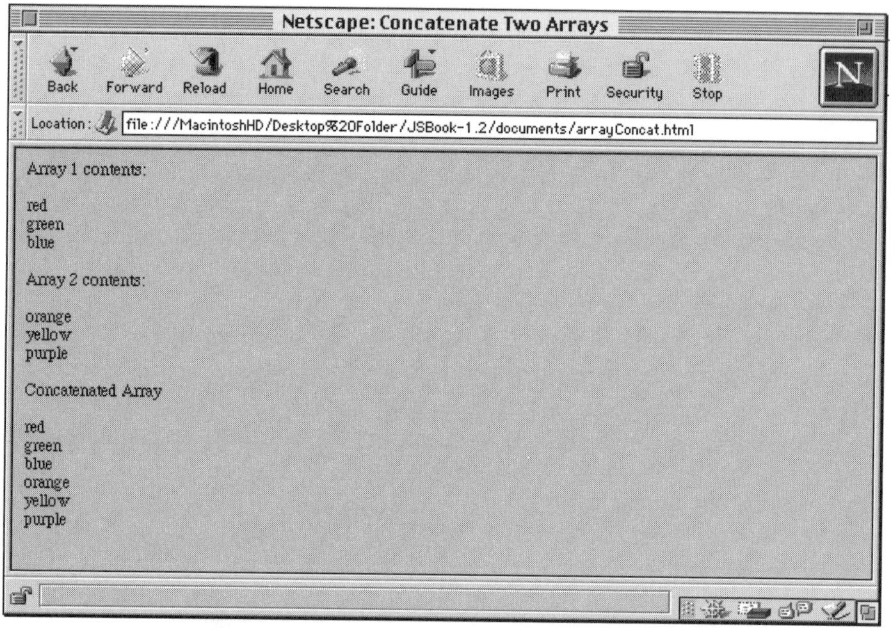

Figure 12–1 Result of loading the `arrayConcat.html` script

Adding and Removing Elements from the End of an Array

The JavaScript 1.2 release provides two new methods to enable you to add or remove elements from the end of an array. You can use the `pop()` method to remove the last element from an array and return that element. You can use the `push()` method to add one or more elements to the end of an array and return the last element added. Both of these methods change the length of the array.

Method

arrayName.pop()

arrayName.push()

Returns

Last element that is removed from the array.

Last element that is removed from the array.

Note – The behavior of the push() method in the JavaScript 1.2 release is analogous to the behavior of push in Perl 4. In the JavaScript 1.3 release, the behavior of the push() method is changed to return the new length of the array, which is analogous to the behavior of push in Perl 5.

Adding and Removing Elements from the Beginning of an Array

The JavaScript 1.2 release provides two new methods to enable you to add or remove elements from the beginning of an array. You can use the shift() method to remove the first element of an array and return that element. You can use the unshift() method to add one or more elements to the beginning of an array and return the length of the new array. Both of these methods change the length of the array.

Method

arrayName.shift()

arrayName.unshift()

Returns

First element that is removed from the array.

Length of the new array.

Note – Unlike the push() method, which returns the last element in the array, the unshift() method returns the length of the new array.

Example of Adding Elements to the Beginning and End of an Array

The following arrayPop.html script uses the pop(), push(), shift(), and unshift() methods to add and remove elements from the beginning and the end of an array.

```
<!--

                            arrayPop.html

This script illustrates the use of the shift() and pop() methods of
the array object.
-->
<HTML>
<HEAD>
<META NAME="GENERATOR" Content="NetObjects ScriptBuilder 2.01">
<TITLE>Shift and Pop for Arrays</TITLE>
<SCRIPT LANGUAGE="JavaScript1.2">
<!--
//
// global variables
var theArray = new Array("Element One", "Element Two",
                    "Element Three", "Element Four")
var msg = ""
function shiftOn() {
    theArray.unshift(document.testArray.testData.value)
    dispArray()
}
function shiftOff() {
    document.testArray.testData.value = theArray.shift()
    dispArray()
}
function pushOn() {
    theArray.push(document.testArray.testData.value)
    dispArray()
}
function popOff() {
    document.testArray.testData.value = theArray.pop()
    dispArray()
}
function dispArray() {
    msg = ""
    for (var i = 0; i < theArray.length; i++) {
        msg = msg + theArray[i] + "\n"
```

```
      }
      document.testArray.arrayBox.value = msg
}
//-->
</SCRIPT>

</HEAD>
<BODY ONLOAD="dispArray()">
<H1 ALIGN="CENTER">Shift and Pop for Arrays</H1>
<P>This example illustrates the shifting of elements on
and off the beginning of an array and popping them on
and off the end of an array.</P>
<FORM NAME="testArray" METHOD="get">
   <P><INPUT TYPE="text" SIZE=30 MAXLENGTH=50 NAME="testData"></P>
   <P><INPUT TYPE="button" NAME="unshiftBtn" VALUE="Add to Beginning"
ONCLICK="shiftOn()">
      <INPUT TYPE="button" NAME="pushBtn" VALUE="Add to End"
ONCLICK="pushOn()"></P>
   <P><INPUT TYPE="button" NAME="shiftBtn" VALUE="Remove First Element"
ONCLICK="shiftOff()">
      <INPUT TYPE="button" NAME="popBtn" VALUE="Remove Last Element"
ONCLICK="popOff()"></P>
   <P><TEXTAREA NAME="arrayBox" ROWS=10 COLS=50 WRAP="physical">
</TEXTAREA></P>
</FORM>
</BODY>
</HTML>
```

Figure 12–2 shows the result of loading the `arrayPop.html` script.

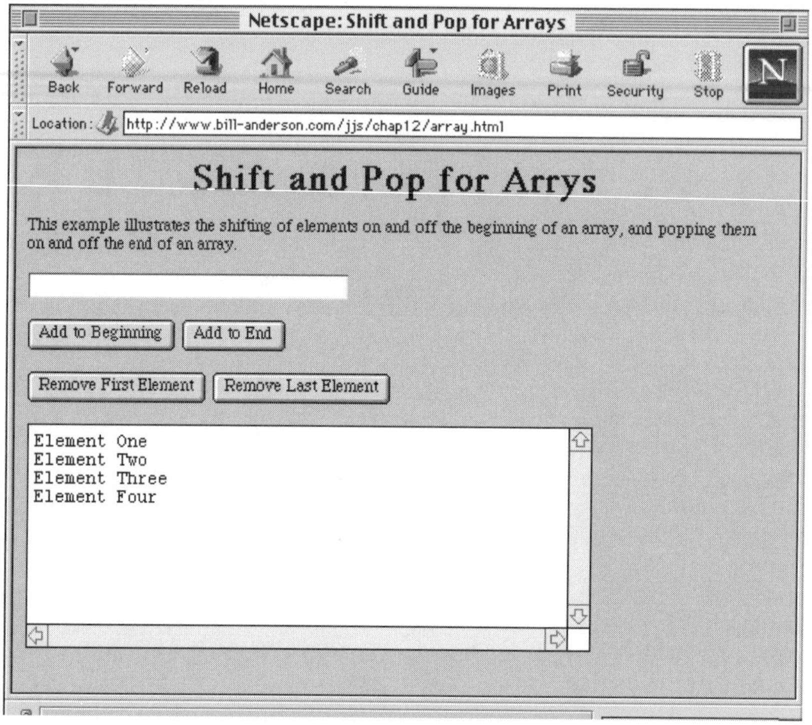

Figure 12–2 Result of loading the `arrayPop.html` script

Type a new element for the array in the text field and click on the appropriate button to add the element to the beginning or to the end of the array displayed in the text area. Figure 12–3 shows that a new element, Element Five, has been added to both the beginning and the end of the array.

```
┌─────────────────────────────────────────────────────────────────┐
│ ▣          Netscape: Shift and Pop for Arrays                 ▣  │
├─────────────────────────────────────────────────────────────────┤
│   🔽      🔖      🔄      🏠      🔍      📖      📷     🖨     🔓    ⏸   │ N │
│  Back  Forward  Reload   Home   Search  Guide  Images  Print Security Stop │
├─────────────────────────────────────────────────────────────────┤
│ Location: 🔖 http://www.bill-anderson.com/jjs/chap12/array.html   │
├─────────────────────────────────────────────────────────────────┤
│                                                                   │
│               Shift and Pop for Arrys                             │
│                                                                   │
│  This example illustrates the shifting of elements on and off the │
│  beginning of an array, and popping them on and off the end of an │
│  array.                                                           │
│                                                                   │
│  ┌────────────────────────────────┐                              │
│  │ Element Five                   │                              │
│  └────────────────────────────────┘                              │
│                                                                   │
│  ┌──────────────────┐  ┌──────────────┐                          │
│  │ Add to Beginning │  │  Add to End  │                          │
│  └──────────────────┘  └──────────────┘                          │
│                                                                   │
│  ┌──────────────────────┐  ┌─────────────────────┐               │
│  │ Remove First Element │  │ Remove Last Element │               │
│  └──────────────────────┘  └─────────────────────┘               │
│                                                                   │
│  ┌────────────────────────────────────────────────────┐  ⇧      │
│  │ Element Five                                        │         │
│  │ Element One                                         │         │
│  │ Element Two                                         │         │
│  │ Element Three                                       │         │
│  │ Element Four                                        │         │
│  │ Element Five                                        │         │
│  │                                                     │         │
│  │                                                     │  ⇩      │
│  │ ⇦ ▓▓▓▓                                          ⇨  │         │
│  └────────────────────────────────────────────────────┘         │
│                                                                   │
└─────────────────────────────────────────────────────────────────┘
```

Figure 12–3 New element added to the array

Clicking on the Remove First Element and Remove Last Element removes elements from the beginning or the end of the array. The element that is removed from the text area is displayed in the text field.

Adding and Removing Elements from Specific Locations within an Array

The JavaScript 1.2 release provides two new methods, `slice()` and `splice()`, to enable you to add or remove elements from specified index locations within an array. You can use the `slice()` method to extract a section of an array and return it as a new array. You can use the `splice()` method to change the contents of an array, adding new elements while removing old elements.

Method

arrayName.slice(*index*, (*endIndex*))

Returns

New array containing the extracted elements.

`index` specifies the index element at which to begin the extraction. `endIndex` specifies the index element at which to end the extraction. The `endIndex` index is not included as part of the new array. Remember that index element numbers begin at zero. You can also specify `endIndex` as a negative number indicating an offset from the end of the array. If you omit the `endIndex` argument, the `slice()` method extracts to the end of the sequence.

Method

arrayName.splice(*index*, number, (*newElement1*, ..., *newElementN*))

Returns

New array.

`index` specifies the index element at which to start the array. *number* is an integer that specifies how many array elements to remove. If *number* is 0, no elements are removed. If you do not remove any elements, specify at least one new element. The `newElement` arguments are a comma-separated list of elements to add to the array. If you do not specify any elements, the `splice()` method removes elements from the array.

Example of Adding and Removing Elements from a Specific Location in an Array
The following `arraySlice.html` script uses the `slice()` method to add and remove elements from a specific location in an array.

```
<!--


                    arraySlice.html


Example for extracting elements from an array.


-->
```

```
<HTML>
  <HEAD>

    <TITLE>Extracting Elements from an Array</TITLE>

<SCRIPT LANGUAGE="JavaScript">

<!--

function dispArray (objArray) {
   for (var i=0; i<objArray.length; i++) {
      document.write(objArray[i]+"<BR>")
   }
}

//-->

</SCRIPT>
  </HEAD>

  <BODY>

    <P>The initial array.</P>

<SCRIPT LANGUAGE="JavaScript">

<!--

exArray1 = new Array(6)
for (var i=0; i<exArray1.length; i++) {
   exArray1[i] = "Element"+i
}

dispArray(exArray1)

//-->

</SCRIPT>

    <P>Extracting from beginSlice = 3 to the end of the array.</P>

<SCRIPT LANGUAGE="JavaScript1.2">

<!--

exArray2 = exArray1.slice(3)
dispArray(exArray2)
```

```
//-->
</SCRIPT>

      <P>Extracting from beginSlice = 0 to endSlice = 3.</P>

<SCRIPT LANGUAGE="JavaScript1.2">

<!--

exArray3 = exArray1.slice(0, 3)
dispArray(exArray3)

//-->
</SCRIPT>

      <P>Extracting from beginSlice = 0 to endSlice = -3</P>

<SCRIPT LANGUAGE="JavaScript">

<!--

exArray4 = exArray1.slice(0, -3)
dispArray(exArray4)

//-->
</SCRIPT>
  </BODY>
</HTML>
```

Figure 12–4 shows the result of loading the `arraySlice.html` script.

Netscape: Extracting Elements from an Array

| Back | Forward | Reload | Home | Search | Guide | Images | Print | Security | Stop | N |

Location: file:///MacintoshHD/Desktop%20Folder/JSBook-1.2/documents/arraySlice.html

```
The initial array.

Element0
Element1
Element2
Element3
Element4
Element5

Extracting from beginSlice = 3 to the end of the array.

Element3
Element4
Element5

Extracting from beginSlice = 0 to endSlice = 3.

Element0
Element1
Element2

Extracting from beginSlice = 0 to endSlice = -3

Element0
Element1
Element2
```

Figure 12–4 Result of loading the `arraySlice.html` script

Sorting Array Elements

The JavaScript 1.2 release has fixed the `sort()` method so that it now works on all platforms. In addition, it no longer converts undefined elements to `null`. Instead, they return as `undefined`. Undefined elements are now sorted to the end of the array.

Method

arrayName.sort((compareFunction))

Returns

Array of entries in the order determined by the *compareFunction* algorithm. If `compareFunction` is not provided, the sort is alphabetical.

button Object

As part of the new event model, the JavaScript 1.2 release provides two new event handlers for the button object:

- The onMouseDown event handler executes JavaScript code when the user presses a mouse button.

- The onMouseUp event handler executes JavaScript code when the user releases a mouse button.

These event handlers are also added to the document and link objects.

Event Handler

onMouseDown

onMouseUp

Syntax

```
<FORM>
<INPUT TYPE = "button"
NAME = "Button Name"
VALUE = "Button Text"
onMouseDown = "JavaScript code"
onMouseUp = "JavaScript code">
</FORM>
```

The onMouseDown event handler enables you to intercept a MouseDown event and perform scripting actions when a user presses the mouse button. The onMouseUp event handler enables you to intercept a MouseUp event and perform scripting actions when a user releases the mouse button.

When onMouseDown or onMouseUp returns false, the default action is canceled.

The onMouseDown and onMouseUp event handlers use the following properties of the event object:

- type — The type of event.

- target — The object to which the event was originally sent.

- `layerX, layerY, pageX, pageY, screenX, screenY` — The pointer location at the time the `MouseDown` event occurred.

- `which` — 1 for a left-mouse-button down and 3 for a right-mouse-button down.

- `modifiers` — The list of modifier keys held down when the event occurred.

Example of Using button Object Event Handlers

The following `buttons.html` script shows how the `button` object responds to various event handlers. The results of the events are displayed in a text area.

```
<!--

                    buttons.html

How the button object responds to various event handlers.

-->

<HTML>
  <HEAD>

    <TITLE>Event Handlers and Buttons</TITLE>

<SCRIPT LANGUAGE="JavaScript">

<!--

function dispMsg(ev) {
    var msg="A "+ev.type+" event"
    msg+=" on mouse button "+ev.which
    msg+=".\n\r"
    document.tstFrm.txtBox.value+=msg
}

//-->
</SCRIPT>
  </HEAD>

  <BODY>

    <P>Try clicking on the following button and check the text area
to see the events generated. Don't forget to try the right mouse
button, the TAB key, and the return key.</P>

    <FORM NAME="tstFrm">
```

```
        <P><INPUT TYPE="BUTTON" NAME="tstBtn" VALUE="Click Me"
ONCLICK="dispMsg(event)" ONMOUSEDOWN="dispMsg(event)"
ONMOUSEUP="dispMsg(event)" ONDBLCLICK="dispMsg(event)"
ONFOCUS="dispMsg(event)" ONBLUR="dispMsg(event)"></P>

        <P><TEXTAREA NAME="txtBox" ROWS="10" COLS="40"
WRAP="Physical"></TEXTAREA></P>

        <P><INPUT TYPE="BUTTON" NAME="clrBtn" VALUE="Clear Message Area"
ONCLICK="document.tstFrm.txtBox.value=''"></P>

        </FORM>
      </BODY>
   </HTML>
```

Figure 12–5 shows the result of loading the `buttons.html` script and clicking on the Click Me button.

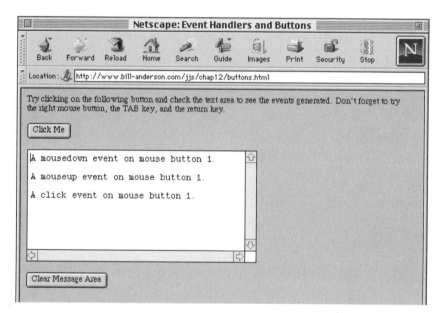

Figure 12–5 Result of loading the `buttons.html` script

document Object

The JavaScript 1.0 and 1.1 document object provides the properties and methods to work with information about anchors, forms, links, the document title, the current location and URL, and the current colors.

The JavaScript 1.2 release provides the new properties and methods listed in Table 12-1 along with new event handlers that are provided as part of the new event model. For a complete list of properties, methods, and event handlers for the document object, see "document Object" on page 452.

Table 12-1 New Properties, Methods, and Event Handlers for the document Object

Properties	Methods	Event Handlers
classes	captureEvents()	onDblClick
ids	getSelection()	onKeyDown
tags	handleEvent()	onKeyPress
	releaseEvents()	onKeyUp
	routeEvent()	onMouseDown
		onMouseUp

Getting Style Classes, ID, and Tags Attributes

The three new properties added to the document object in the JavaScript 1.2 release enable you to reference CLASS, ID, and TAG attributes that you may have defined as part of the <STYLE> tag when you create style sheets. For more information about style sheets, see Chapter 3, "Style Sheets."

Property	Value	Gettable	Settable
classes	string	Yes	No
ids	string	Yes	No
tags	string	Yes	No

Managing Events

As part of the new event model in the JavaScript 1.2 release, the document object provides a set of methods to enable you to capture, handle, route, and release events.

Method

captureEvents(*eventType*)

handleEvent(*event*)

routeEvent(*event*)

releaseEvents(*eventType*)

Returns

Nothing.

For more information on how to use these methods, see Chapter 9, "New Event Model."

Getting the Current Selection

The JavaScript 1.2 release provides a getSelection() method that enables you to get a string containing the text of the current selection from the current document.

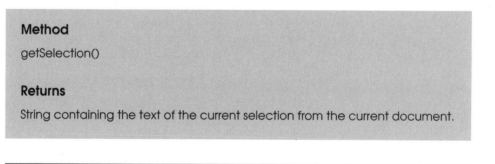

Method

getSelection()

Returns

String containing the text of the current selection from the current document.

Note – You cannot use the getSelection() method to determine selected areas in another window.

Example of Getting the Current Selection

The following `getselection.html` script uses the `captureEvents()` method to trap the clicking of the mouse button to make a selection. It uses the `getSelection()` method to display the selected text in an alert window.

```
<!--

                    getselection.html

Example for using the getSelection() method of the document object.

-->

<HTML>
  <HEAD>

    <TITLE>Using document Object Event Handlers</TITLE>

<SCRIPT LANGUAGE="JavaScript1.2">
<!--

function clickHdlr(ev) {
   if (ev.target.name=="dspSlct") {
      alert('you selected: \n'+document.getSelection())
      return false
   }
return true
}

document.captureEvents(Event.MOUSEDOWN)
document.onmousedown=clickHdlr

//-->

</SCRIPT>
  </HEAD>

  <BODY>

    <P>This test uses the captureEvents() method to trap the clicking
of the mouse button. Select any text on this page and then press the
getSelection button ,using either mouse button to show how the
document object event handler functions.</P>

    <FORM><INPUT TYPE="BUTTON" NAME="dspSlct" VALUE=" Display
Selection">

    </FORM>
```

```
    </BODY>
    </HTML>
```

Figure 12–6 shows the result of loading the `getselection.html` script.

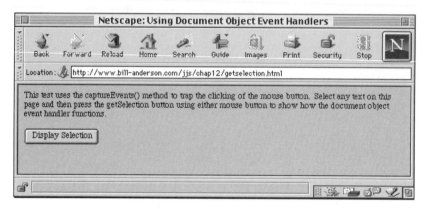

Figure 12–6 Result of loading the `getselection.html` script

Selecting any text in the window and clicking on the Display Selection button displays an alert showing the text that you selected, as shown in Figure 12–7.

Figure 12–7 Alert displaying text that was selected

Controlling Events When Users Press or Release a Mouse Button

As part of the new event model, the JavaScript 1.2 release provides two new event handlers for the `document` object to control events when users press or release a mouse button:

- The `onMouseDown` event handler executes JavaScript code when the user presses a mouse button.

- The onMouseUp event handler executes JavaScript code when the user releases a mouse button.

These event handlers are also added to the button and link objects.

> **Event Handler**
>
> onMouseDown
>
> onMouseUp
>
> **Syntax**
>
> onMouseDown = "*JavaScript code*"
>
> onMouseUp = "*JavaScript code*"

The onMouseDown event handler enables you to intercept a MouseDown event and perform scripting actions when a user presses the mouse button. The onMouseUp event handler enables you to intercept a MouseUp event and perform scripting actions when a user releases the mouse button.

When onMouseDown or onMouseUp returns false, the default action is canceled.

The onMouseDown and onMouseUp event handlers use the following properties of the event object:

- type — The type of event.
- target — The object to which the event was originally sent.
- layerX, layerY, pageX, pageY, screenX, screenY — The pointer location at the time the MouseDown event occurred.
- which — 1 for a left-mouse-button down and 3 for a right-mouse-button down.
- modifiers— The list of modifier keys held down when the event occurred.

Controlling Events When Users Double-click a Mouse Button

As part of the new event model, the JavaScript 1.2 release provides an onDblClick event handler for the document object that executes JavaScript code when the user double-clicks on a form element or a link.

Event Handler

onDblClick

Syntax

onDblClick = "*JavaScript code*"

Note – DblClick is not implemented on the Macintosh platform.

The onDblClick event handler uses the following properties of the event object:

- type — The type of event.

- target — The object to which the event was originally sent.

- layerX, layerY, pageX, pageY, screenX, screenY — The pointer location at the time the MouseDown event occurred.

- which — 1 for a left-mouse-button double-click and 3 for a right-mouse-button double-click.

- modifiers— The list of modifier keys held down when the event occurred.

Controlling Events When Users Press or Release a Key

As part of the new event model, the JavaScript 1.2 release provides three new event handlers for the document object to control events when users press or release a key on the keyboard:

- The onKeyDown event handler executes JavaScript code when the user presses a key on the keyboard. A KeyDown event always occurs before a KeyPress event. If onKeyDown returns false, no KeyPress events occur.

- The onKeyUp event handler executes JavaScript code when the user releases a key on the keyboard.

- The onKeyPress event handler executes JavaScript code when the user presses or holds down a key on the keyboard. A KeyPress event occurs immediately after a KeyDown event only if onKeyDown returns a value other than false. A KeyPress event occurs repeatedly until the user releases the key.

These event handlers are also added to the image, link, and textarea objects.

Event Handler

onKeyDown

onKeyUp

onKeyPress

Syntax

onKeyDown = "*JavaScript code*"

onKeyUp = "*JavaScript code*"

onKeyPress = "*JavaScript code*"

The onKeyDown, onKeyUp, and onKeyPress event handlers use the following properties of the event object:

- type — The type of event.
- target — The object to which the event was originally sent.
- layerX, layerY, pageX, pageY, screenX, screenY — The pointer location at the time the MouseDown event occurred.
- which — 1 for a left-mouse-button down and 3 for a right-mouse-button down.
- modifiers— The list of modifier keys held down when the event occurred.

image Object

As part of the new event model, the JavaScript 1.2 release provides three new event handlers for the link object to control events when users press or release a key on the keyboard:

- The onKeyDown event handler executes JavaScript code when the user presses a key on the keyboard. A KeyDown event always occurs before a KeyPress event. If onKeyDown returns false, no KeyPress events occur.

- The onKeyUp event handler executes JavaScript code when the user releases a key on the keyboard.

- The onKeyPress event handler executes JavaScript code when the user presses or holds down a key on the keyboard. A KeyPress event occurs immediately after a KeyDown event only if onKeyDown returns a value other than false. A KeyPress event occurs repeatedly until the user releases the key.

These event handlers are also added to the document, link, and textarea objects.

Event Handler

onKeyDown

onKeyUp

onKeyPress

Syntax

onKeyDown = "*JavaScript code*"

onKeyUp = "*JavaScript code*"

onKeyPress = "*JavaScript code*"

The onKeyDown, onKeyUp, and onKeyPress event handlers use the following properties of the event object:

- type — The type of event.

- target — The object to which the event was originally sent.

- layerX, layerY, pageX, pageY, screenX, screenY — The pointer location at the time the MouseDown event occurred.

- which — 1 for a left-mouse-button down and 3 for a right-mouse-button down.

- modifiers— The list of modifier keys held down when the event occurred.

link Object

A link object is created for each anchor created for each pair of <A></A> HTML tags that defines an HREF attribute. These objects are stored in an array in the document.links property. You access an Anchor object by indexing this array.

The JavaScript 1.2 release adds a text property to the `link` object.

Property	Value	Gettable	Settable
text	string	Yes	No

The `text` property contains the content of the corresponding `<A>` tag when it has a named anchor or a link. You reference the text property by using the following syntax:

```
links.text
```

Example of Using the text Property

If you create an anchor with a NAME or HREF attribute, you can access the name or the link with the text property. For example, if you create a named anchor, as shown below:

```
<A NAME="foo">This text is in a named anchor.</A>
```

you would access the NAME value in the following way:

```
document.anchors[0].text
```

If you create an anchor with a link, as shown below:

```
<A HREF="http://www.netscape.com">This text is in a link.</A>
```

you would access the HREF value in the following way:

```
document.links[0].text
```

Controlling Events When Users Press or Release a Mouse Button

As part of the new event model, the JavaScript 1.2 release provides two new event handlers for the `link` object:

- The `onMouseDown` event handler executes JavaScript code when the user presses a mouse button.

- The `onMouseUp` event handler executes JavaScript code when the user releases a mouse button.

These event handlers are also added to the `button` and `document` objects.

Event Handler

onMouseDown

onMouseUp

Syntax

<A HREF="*URL*" ;

  onMouseDown="*JavaScript code*"

  onMouseUp="*JavaScript code*">

  anchorName

</A>

The `onMouseDown` event handler enables you to intercept a `MouseDown` event and perform scripting actions when a user presses the mouse button. The `onMouseUp` event handler enables you to intercept a `MouseUp` event and perform scripting actions when a user releases the mouse button.

When `onMouseDown` or `onMouseUp` returns `false`, the default action is canceled.

The `onMouseDown` and `onMouseUp` event handlers use the following properties of the `event` object:

- `type` — The type of event.
- `target` — The object to which the event was originally sent.
- `layerX`, `layerY`, `pageX`, `pageY`, `screenX`, `screenY` — The pointer location at the time the `MouseDown` event occurred.
- `which` — 1 for a left-mouse-button down and 3 for a right-mouse-button down.
- `modifiers`— The list of modifier keys held down when the event occurred.

Controlling Events When Users Double-click a Mouse Button

As part of the new event model, the JavaScript 1.2 release provides an `onDblClick` event handler for the `link` object that executes JavaScript code when the user double-clicks on a form element or a link.

Event Handler

onDblClick

Syntax

onDblClick = "*JavaScript code*"

Note – DblClick is not implemented on the Macintosh platform.

The onDblClick event handler uses the following properties of the event object:

- type — The type of event.

- target — The object to which the event was originally sent.

- layerX, layerY, pageX, pageY, screenX, screenY — The pointer location at the time the MouseDown event occurred.

- which — 1 for a left-mouse-button double-click and 3 for a right-mouse-button double-click.

- modifiers— The list of modifier keys held down when the event occurred.

Controlling Events When Users Press or Release a Key

As part of the new event model, the JavaScript 1.2 release provides three new event handlers for the link object to control events when users press or release a key on the keyboard:

- The onKeyDown event handler executes JavaScript code when the user presses a key on the keyboard. A KeyDown event always occurs before a KeyPress event. If onKeyDown returns false, no KeyPress events occur.

- The onKeyUp event handler executes JavaScript code when the user releases a key on the keyboard.

- The onKeyPress event handler executes JavaScript code when the user presses or holds down a key on the keyboard. A KeyPress event occurs immediately after a KeyDown event only if onKeyDown returns a value other than false. A KeyPress event occurs repeatedly until the user releases the key.

These event handlers are also added to the document, image, and textarea objects.

Event Handler

onKeyDown

onKeyUp

onKeyPress

Syntax

onKeyDown = "*JavaScript code*"

onKeyUp = "*JavaScript code*"

onKeyPress = "*JavaScript code*"

The onKeyDown, onKeyUp, and onKeyPress event handlers use the following properties of the event object:

- type — The type of event.

- target — The object to which the event was originally sent.

- layerX, layerY, pageX, pageY, screenX, screenY — The pointer location at the time the MouseDown event occurred.

- which — 1 for a left-mouse-button down and 3 for a right-mouse-button down.

- modifiers— The list of modifier keys held down when the event occurred.

Controlling Events When Users Press or Release a Mouse Button

As part of the new event model, the JavaScript 1.2 release provides two new event handlers for the link object:

- The onMouseDown event handler executes JavaScript code when the user presses a mouse button.

- The onMouseUp event handler executes JavaScript code when the user releases a mouse button.

These event handlers are also added to the `button` and `document` objects.

Event Handler

onMouseDown

onMouseUp

Syntax

<A HREF="*URL*" ;

 onMouseDown="*JavaScript code*"

 onMouseUp="*JavaScript code*">

 anchorName

 </A>

The `onMouseDown` event handler enables you to intercept a `MouseDown` event and perform scripting actions when a user presses the mouse button. The `onMouseUp` event handler enables you to intercept a `MouseUp` event and perform scripting actions when a user releases the mouse button.

When `onMouseDown` or `onMouseUp` returns `false`, the default action is canceled.

The `onMouseDown` and `onMouseUp` event handlers use the following properties of the `event` object:

- `type` — The type of event.

- `target` — The object to which the event was originally sent.

- `layerX`, `layerY`, `pageX`, `pageY`, `screenX`, `screenY` — The pointer location at the time the `MouseDown` event occurred.

- `which` — 1 for a left-mouse-button down and 3 for a right-mouse-button down.

- `modifiers` — The list of modifier keys held down when the event occurred.

textarea Object

As part of the new event model, the JavaScript 1.2 release provides three new event handlers for the `textarea` object to control events when users press or release a key on the keyboard:

- The onKeyDown event handler executes JavaScript code when the user presses a key on the keyboard. A KeyDown event always occurs before a KeyPress event. If onKeyDown returns false, no KeyPress events occur.

- The onKeyUp event handler executes JavaScript code when the user releases a key on the keyboard.

- The onKeyPress event handler executes JavaScript code when the user presses or holds down a key on the keyboard. A KeyPress event occurs immediately after a KeyDown event only if onKeyDown returns a value other than false. A KeyPress event occurs repeatedly until the user releases the key.

These event handlers are also added to the document, image, and link objects.

Event Handler

onKeyDown

onKeyUp

onKeyPress

Syntax

onKeyDown = "*JavaScript code*"

onKeyUp = "*JavaScript code*"

onKeyPress = "*JavaScript code*"

The onKeyDown, onKeyUp, and onKeyPress event handlers use the following properties of the event object:

- type — The type of event.

- target — The object to which the event was originally sent.

- layerX, layerY, pageX, pageY, screenX, screenY — The pointer location at the time the MouseDown event occurred.

- which — 1 for a left-mouse-button down and 3 for a right-mouse-button down.

- modifiers— The list of modifier keys held down when the event occurred.

Appendix A

What's New in JavaScript 1.3

This appendix describes the new features and changes in JavaScript 1.3. The most significant change to JavaScript 1.3 is that it now complies with the following two specifications:

- The European Computer Manufacturers Association (ECMA) ECMA-262 specification

- The International Organization for Standards specification, ISO-16262

This document also describes the following new features and changes to JavaScript 1.3.

New Features

The JavaScript 1.3 release offers the following new features:

- Unicode compliance

- New top-level properties: `NaN`, `Infinity`, and `undefined`
- Global function `isFinite()`
- `toSource()` method
- New and changed features of the `Date` object
- New `call()` and `apply()` methods of the `function` object
- Strict equality operators
- JavaScript console that records JavaScript error messages

Changes

The JavaScript 1.3 release made changes to the following areas:

- Specification of the version of JavaScript
- Equality operator
- `Array` object
- `replace()` method of `String` object
- `Boolean` object
- `toString()` function

JavaScript and ECMA

JavaScript is Netscape's cross-platform, object-based scripting language for client and server applications. It contains the elements common to both client- and server-side JavaScript. The ECMA specification is based on the core language subset of client-side JavaScript 1.1.

ECMA is the international standards association for information and communication systems. Standardization means that when you write JavaScript code, it should behave the same way in all applications that support the standard.

ECMA completed the first version of the ECMAScript specification, ECMA-262, in June 1997. ECMAScript, as defined by the ECMA, is an object-oriented programming language for performing computations and manipulating objects within a host environment. More recently, the ECMA-262 standard was also approved by ISO. Note that ECMA does not specify the Document Object Model (DOM), being standardized by W3C, which defines the way in which the HTML document objects are exposed to scripts.

Non-ECMA-262 Features of JavaScript 1.2 and 1.3

The following features in the JavaScript 1.3 core language are not in the current ECMA specification. These value-added extensions to the language are expected in the next version of ECMA specification.

Keywords and Operators

- Strict equality operators
- Vertical tab (\v or \u000B) as an escape sequence.

Statements

- `label` (JavaScript 1.2)
- `switch` (JavaScript 1.2)
- `do...while` (JavaScript 1.2)
- `export` (JavaScript 1.2)
- `import` (JavaScript 1.2)

Built-in Objects

- `RegExp` (JavaScript 1.2)

Methods of the Built-in Objects

- `toSource()`

Object object

- `watch()` method (JavaScript 1.2)
- `unwatch()` method (JavaScript 1.2)

function object

- `arity` property (JavaScript 1.2)
- `apply()` method
- `call()` method call

Array object

- `index` property
- `input` property (JavaScript 1.2)
- `concat()` method (JavaScript 1.2)
- `pop()` method (JavaScript 1.2)
- `push()` method (JavaScript 1.2)
- `shift()` method (JavaScript 1.2)

- `unshift()` method (JavaScript 1.2)

- `slice()` method (JavaScript 1.2)

- `splice()` method (JavaScript 1.2)

String object

- `concat()` method (JavaScript 1.2)

- `match()` method (JavaScript 1.2)

- `search()` method (JavaScript 1.2)

- `slice()` method (JavaScript 1.2)

- `substr()` method (JavaScript 1.2)

Specifying the Version of JavaScript

You can use the LANGUAGE attribute with the `<SCRIPT>` tag to specify the version of JavaScript with which the script complies. If you do not specify a LANGUAGE attribute, the default is to use the latest version of JavaScript supported by the browser. Table A-1 shows the LANGUAGE attributes supported by each version of Navigator/Communicator.

Table A-1 LANGUAGE Attributes Supported by Navigator/Communicator Versions

Version	Supported LANGUAGE Attributes
Navigator 1.x	No JavaScript support
Navigator 2.0	`<SCRIPT LANGUAGE="JavaScript">`
Navigator 3.0	`<SCRIPT LANGUAGE="JavaScript">` `<SCRIPT LANGUAGE="JavaScript1.1">`

Communicator and Navigator 4.0-4.05	`<SCRIPT LANGUAGE="JavaScript">`
	 `<SCRIPT LANGUAGE="JavaScript1.1">`
	 `<SCRIPT LANGUAGE="JavaScript1.2">`

Communicator and Navigator 4.06-4.5	`<SCRIPT LANGUAGE="JavaScript">`
	 `<SCRIPT LANGUAGE="JavaScript1.1">`
	 `<SCRIPT LANGUAGE="JavaScript1.2">`
	 `<SCRIPT LANGUAGE="JavaScript1.3">`

Unicode

Unicode provides a standard way to encode multilingual text and common technical and mathematical symbols. It is a universal, fixed-width, character-coding standard for the interchange and display of the principal written languages. Unicode includes the languages of Americas, Europe, Middle East, Africa, India, Asia, and Pacifica, as well as historic scripts and technical symbols.

Note – Unicode does not currently support all modern or archaic scripts.

Support for Unicode means you can use non-Latin, international and localized characters, and special technical symbols in JavaScript programs. Because Unicode is compatible with ASCII, programs can use ASCII characters. You can use non-ASCII Unicode characters in the comments and string literals of JavaScript.

In string literals, you can also use the Unicode escape sequence, which consists of six ASCII characters. The escape sequence comprises \u and a four-digit hexadecimal number. For example, \u0041 represents the Unicode character A. Each Unicode escape sequence in JavaScript adds one character to the string value.

Unicode is modeled after the ASCII (American Standard Code for Information Interchange) character set. Unicode uses a numerical value and name for each character. The character encoding specifies the identity of the character and its numeric value (code position), as well as the bit representation of its value. The 16-bit numeric value (code value) is defined by a hexadecimal number and the U prefix.

Unicode is compatible with ASCII characters and is supported by many programs. The first 128 Unicode characters have the same byte values as the corresponding ASCII characters. The Unicode characters U+0020 through U+007E are equivalent to the ASCII characters 0x20 through 0x7E. Unicode uses a 16-bit value for each character and allows for more than 65,000 unique characters. Unicode version 2.0 contains 38,885 characters and supports an extension mechanism.

The JavaScript use of the Unicode escape sequence is different from that of Java. In JavaScript, the escape sequence is never interpreted as a special character first. In other words, a line terminator escape sequence inside a string does not terminate the string before it is interpreted by the function.

JavaScript ignores any escape sequence if it is used in comments. The escape sequence works the same way as the \n.

The following code generates an information dialog box with the copyright symbol and the string "Netscape Communication".

```
alert("\u00A9 Netscape Communication");
```

Table A-2 lists frequently used special characters and their Unicode values.

Table A-2 Unicode Special Characters

Unicode Value	Name	Format Name	Description
\u0009	Tab	<TAB>	White space
\u000B	Vertical Tab	<VT>	White space
\u000C	Form Feed	<FF>	White space
\u0020	Space	<SP>	White space
\u000A	Line Feed	<LF>	Line terminator
\u000D	Carriage Return	<CR>	Line terminator
\u000b	Backspace	<BS>	Escape sequence
\u0009	Horizontal Tab	<HT>	Escape sequence
\u0022	Double Quote	"	Escape sequence
\u0027	Single Quote	'	Escape sequence
\u005C	Backslash	\	Escape sequence

For characters to be displayed properly, a client such as Netscape Navigator 4.x must support Unicode. The client platform must also support Unicode and have an appropriate Unicode font available. Unicode fonts frequently do not display all the Unicode characters. Some platforms, such as Windows 95, provide a partial support for Unicode.

To receive non-ASCII character input, the client must send the input as Unicode. Standard enhanced keyboards do not support additional Unicode characters. Often, the only way to input Unicode characters is by using Unicode escape sequences. Although Unicode enables users to create composite characters by typing the base character followed by one or more nonspacing marks, JavaScript does not support this option.

For more information on Unicode, see the Unicode Consortium Web site and *The Unicode Standard*, Version 2.0, published by Addison-Wesley, 1996.

New Top-level Properties

The following three properties are defined as properties of the Object object. They are also primitive values.

- NaN

- Infinity

- undefined

NaN Property

NaN represents Not-a-Number. In JavaScript 1.2, NaN was defined only as a property of the Number object. In JavaScript 1.3, NaN is also available as a top-level property. When the JavaScript engine is initialized, the initial value of NaN is NaN.

Property	ValueGettable	Settable
NaN	NaN Yes	No

NaN is always unequal to any other number, including NaN itself. Use the isNaN() method to check for a NaN value. The Number constructor, parseFloat(), and parseInt() return NaN if the value specified in the parameter is not a number.

The following code extract from the globalMath.html script shows that (0/0.) is NaN and that NaN does not equal NaN. For the complete script, see "Example Using the isFinite() Global Function" on page 407.

```
document.write("isNaN(0/0.) -> " + (isNaN(0 / 0.)) + "<BR>")
document.write("(0/0.) == NaN -> " + ((0 / 0.) == NaN) + "<BR>")

// However, a variable set to NaN returns true when tested by isNaN.

document.write("isNaN(intTst = NaN) -> " + (isNaN(intTst = NaN)))
document.write("</P")
```

Infinity Property

Infinity represents a positive infinite number value. In JavaScript 1.2, infinity was defined only as the static POSITIVE_INFINITY and NEGATIVE_INFINITY properties of the Number object.

Property	Value	Gettable	Settable
Infinity	Number.POSITIVE_INFINITYYes	No	

In JavaScript 1.3, `Infinity` is defined as a property of the `Object` object and is available when the JavaScript engine is initialized. The value `Infinity` (positive infinity) is greater than any other number including itself. This value behaves mathematically like infinity; for example, anything multiplied by `Infinity` is `Infinity`, and anything divided by `Infinity` is 0.

The following code extract from the `globalMath.html` script uses the `Infinity` property with the new `isFinite()` global method. For the complete script, see "Example Using the isFinite() Global Function" on page 407.

```
document.write("isFinite(Infinity) -> " + (isFinite(Infinity)) +
"<BR>")
```

undefined Property

JavaScript 1.2 does not provide an undefined value. In the JavaScript 1.3 release, a variable that has not been assigned a value is of type `undefined`. You can use the `undefined` property to determine whether a variable has a value. JavaScript methods or statements that do not have an assigned value also now return `undefined`.

Property	ValueGettable	Settable
undefined	undefinedYes	No

In JavaScript 1.3, `undefined` is also a property of the `Object` object, although ECMA-262 specifies that `undefined` is a primitive value only and is not a property of the `Object` object.

The following extract from the `globalMath.html` script uses the `undefined` property to show that the `Array` constructor now produces an array of a specific size with undefined elements. For the complete script, see "Example Using the isFinite() Global Function" on page 407.

```
tstArray = new Array(1)

document.write("<P>tstArray[0] == undefined -> " + (tstArray[0] ==
undefined) + "</P>")
```

isFinite() Global Function

You can use the new `isFinite()` global function to determine if a number is a finite number.

Function

isFinite(*number*)

Returns

false if the argument is NaN, positive infinity, or negative infinity; otherwise, returns true.

Example Using the isFinite() Global Function

The following `globalMath.html` script uses the `isFinite()` global function in combination with the new `NaN` and `Infinity` properties. It also uses the new global `undefined` property with the `Array` constructor.

```
<!--


                 globalMath.html

This script demonstrates the use of the new global math properties
and functions.

-->
<HTML>
<HEAD>
 <TITLE>Global Math Properties and Functions</TITLE>
 </HEAD>

<BODY>

<H1 ALIGN="CENTER">Global Math Properties and Functions</H1>

<P>The following test shows that the Array constructor now
produces  an array of a specific size with undefined elements.
The test uses the global <KBD>undefined</KBD> property
for this test.</P>

<SCRIPT LANGUAGE="JavaScript1.3">

<!--
```

```
tstArray = new Array(1)

document.write("<P>tstArray[0] == undefined -> " + (tstArray[0] ==
undefined) + "</P>")

//-->
</SCRIPT>

<HR>

<P>The following tests illustrate the use of the new <KBD>NaN</KBD> and
<KBD>infinity</KBD> properties, in combination with the
<KBD>isFinite()</KBD> global function.</P>

<SCRIPT LANGUAGE="JavaScript1.3">

<!--

document.write("<P>")

document.write("isFinite(10/2) -> " + (isFinite(10 / 2)) + "<BR>")

document.write("isFinite(Infinity) -> " + (isFinite(Infinity)) + "<BR>")

document.write("isFinite(1/0.) -> " + (isFinite(1 / 0.)) + "<BR>")

document.write("(1/0.) == Infinity -> " + ((1 / 0.) == Infinity) + "<BR>")

// The following test show tshat (0/0.) is a NaN as required
// by the IEEE specifications. The second test shows that NaN does
// not equal NaN, also according to the IEEE specifications.

document.write("isNaN(0/0.) -> " + (isNaN(0 / 0.)) + "<BR>")
document.write("(0/0.) == NaN -> " + ((0 / 0.) == NaN) + "<BR>")

// However, a variable set to NaN returns true when tested by isNaN.

document.write("isNaN(intTst = NaN) -> " + (isNaN(intTst = NaN)))
document.write("</P>")

//-->
</SCRIPT>
</BODY>
</HTML>
```

Figure A-1 shows the result of loading the `globalMath.html` script.

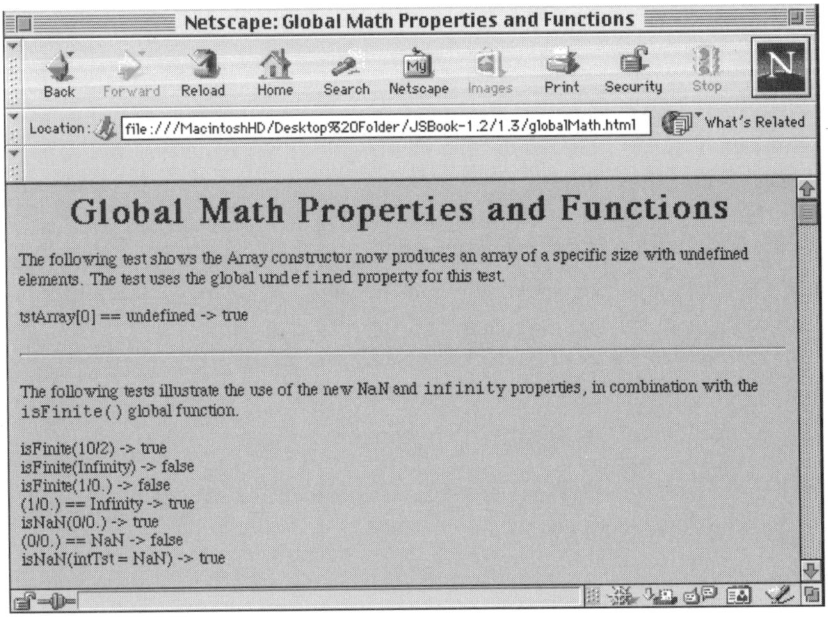

Figure A-1 Result of loading the `globalMath.html` script

toSource() Method

The `toSource()` method of the `Object` object is available to all built-in core JavaScript objects. The `toSource()` method is based on the `toString()` method from the `Object` and `Array` objects. You can use `toSource()` to create a copy of an object.

Method

toSource()

Returns

A string representation of the object.

Note – The `toSource()` method is not currently in ECMA-262. It has been proposed for the next release of ECMA specification.

`toSource()` returns a string representation of the object, which you can use to create a new object. You can pass the returned string to other functions and use it to perform other scripting actions.

Example of Using the toSource() Method

The following `toSource.html` script shows how the `toSource()` method behaves with the built-in `Array`, `Boolean`, and `String` objects.

```
<!--


                        toSource.html


The toSource() method provides a means for creating new objects from
other objects by generating a constructor for the object.

--><HTML>
<HEAD>
<TITLE>The toSource() Method</TITLE>
</HEAD>

<BODY>

<H1 ALIGN="CENTER">The toSource() Method</H1>

<P>The <KBD>toSource()</KBD> method returns the literal value for
an object. This enables you to create a new object from the old
object. The following example shows how the <KBD>toSource()</KBD>
method behaves with some of the built-in objects.</P>

<H3>Test with Array Object</H3>

<SCRIPT LANGUAGE="JavaScript1.3">

<!--
tstArray = new Array("test", 4, "foo", 10)
document.write("<P>tstArray.toSource() -> " + tstArray.toSource() +
"</P>")
newArray = eval(tstArray.toSource())
document.write("<P>newArray = eval(tstArray.toSource()) -> " +
newArray.toSource() + "</P>")
```

```
//-->
</SCRIPT>

<H3>Test with Boolean Object</H3>

<SCRIPT LANGUAGE="JavaScript1.3">
<!--

tstBool = new Boolean(true)
document.write("<P>tstBool.toSource() -> " + tstBool.toSource() +
"</P>")
newBool = eval(tstBool.toSource())
document.write("<P>newBool = eval(tstBool.toSource()) -> " +
newBool.toSource() + "</P>")

//-->
</SCRIPT>

<H3>Test with String Object</H3>
<SCRIPT LANGUAGE="JavaScript1.3">
<!--

tstStr = "test string"
document.write("<P>tstStr.toSource() -> " + tstStr.toSource() +
"</P>")
newStr = eval(tstStr.toSource())
document.write("<P>newStr = eval(tstStr.toSource()) -> " +
newStr.toSource() + "</P>")

//-->
</SCRIPT>
</BODY>
</HTML>
```

Figure A-2 shows the result of loading the `toSource.html` script.

Netscape: The toSource() Method

Back | Forward | Reload | Home | Search | Netscape | Images | Print | Security | Stop

Location: file:///MacintoshHD/Desktop%20Folder/JSBook-1.2/1.3/toSource.html — What's Related

The toSource() Method

The toSource() method returns the literal value for an object. This enables you to create a new object from the old object. The following example shows how the toSource() method behaves with some of the built-in objects.

Test with Array Object

tstArray.toSource() -> ["test", 4, "foo", 10]

newArray = eval(tstArray.toSource()) -> ["test", 4, "foo", 10]

Test with Boolean Object

tstBool.toSource() -> (new Boolean(true))

newBool = eval(tstBool.toSource()) -> (new Boolean(true))

Test with String Object

tstStr.toSource() -> (new String("test string"))

newStr = eval(tstStr.toSource()) -> (new String("test string"))

Figure A-2 Result of loading the `toSource.html` script

Date Object

The JavaScript 1.3 release changes the Date object significantly to conform to the ECMA specification. Previous versions of the Date object depended on platform-specific date information and behavior. The changes in the JavaScript 1.3 release provide a uniform behavior across platforms and remove all previous platform dependencies.

The Date object now supports a number of new Universal Coordinated Time methods (UTC methods), as well as local time methods. UTC refers to the time as set by the World Time Standard. The local time is the time known to the computer where the JavaScript code is executed.

The date is measured in milliseconds since midnight 01 January, 1970 UTC. A day holds 86,400,000 milliseconds. The Date object range is –100,000,000 days to 100,000,000 days relative to 01 January, 1970 UTC. With the compound constructor of the JavaScript 1.3 Date object, you can now specify an instance of time in milliseconds.

Table A-3 lists the properties and methods for the Date object. The properties and methods that have been added in the JavaScript 1.3 release are marked with an asterisk.

Table A-3 Properties and Methods for the Date Object

Properties	Methods	Event Handlers
prototype	eval()	None
	get/setDate()	
	getDay()	
	get/setFullYear*	
	get/setFullUTCYear*	
	get/setHours()	
	get/setMilliseconds*	
	get/setMinutes()	
	get/setMonth()	
	get/setSeconds()	
	get/setTime()	
	get/setUTCDate*	
	get/setUTCDay*	
	get/setUTCFullYear*	
	get/setUTCHours*	
	get/setUTCMilliseconds*	
	get/setUTCMinutes*	
	get/setUTCMonth*	
	get/setUTCSeconds*	
	get/setYear()	

Table A-3 Properties and Methods for the Date Object (Continued)

Properties	Methods	Event Handlers
	getTimezoneOffset()	
	parse()	
	toGMTString()	
	toLocaleString()*	
	toString()	
	toUTCString*	
	UTC()*	
	valueOf()	

New Date Constructor

The compound constructor for the Date object now supports milliseconds specified as *ms_num*. To specify the milliseconds, use the following syntax.

```
Date(yr_num, mo_num, day_num, [hr_num[, , min_num[, [sec_num[,
ms_num]]]])
```

The following parameters are optional:

- *hr_num* — Integer value for hours
- *min_num* — Integer value for minutes
- *sec_num* — Integer value for seconds
- *ms_num* — Integer value for milliseconds.

Getting the UTC in Milliseconds

The `Date.UTC()` method is a static method of the `Date` object. You do not create a new `Date` object to use it. You can use it directly. You use this method as `Date.UTC()`. It takes a comma-separated list of values as parameters and displays the date in the following format:

```
Sat Feb 01 20:45:12 1997
```

Method

Date.UTC(*year,month,date,(,hours(,min(,sec(,ms))))*)

Returns

The number of milliseconds since 1/1/70 UTC

The `Date.UTC()` method now supports a milliseconds parameter.

You provide the parameters in the sequence yy, mm, dd [hh, mm, ss, ms].

```
yy = year after 1900 or
yyyy = full year
mm = 0-11
dd = 1-31
hh = 0-23
mm = 0-59
ss = 0-59
ms = 0-999
```

The `Date.UTC()` method uses Universal Coordinated Time (UTC) instead of the local time. `Date.UTC()` returns a time value as a number instead of creating a `Date` object.

If a parameter you specify is outside of the expected range, the UTC method updates the other parameters to allow for your number. For example, if you use 15 for the month, the year is updated by one (year + 1) and 3 is used for the month.

Getting and Setting the Year

The Date object provides two new sets of methods for getting and setting the year.

Method
getFullYear()
setFulYear(*year*(,*month*(,*date*)))
getFullUTCYear()
setFullUTCYear()

Returns/Uses

A four-digit number with the specified year of the specified date according to local time.

A four-digit number with the specified year according to Universal Coordinated Time.

You provide the parameters in the sequence *year*[, *month*[, *date*]].

```
year = full year, for example, 1999
month = 0-11
date = 1-31
```

If you specify a date, you must also specify a month.

If you do not specify the month and date parameters, the values are returned from the getMonth() and getDate() methods. If a parameter you specify is outside of the expected range, these methods update the other parameters to allow for your number. For example, if you use 15 for the month, the year is updated by one (year + 1) and 3 is used for the month.

JavaScript Dates and the Year 2000

The behavior of the getYear() method for the Date object changed as JavaScript evolved.

JavaScript 1.0. In the JavaScript 1.0 release, the getYear() method starts numbering years by subtracting 1900 from the four-digit year, which results in two-digit values, such as 86 and 98, for the twentieth century. For the twenty-first century, the getYear() method starts with the number 100. You need only add 1900 to the value returned by the getYear() method to obtain the four-digit year. The JavaScript 1.0 release does not correctly handle years before 1970.

JavaScript 1.1 and 1.2. Starting with the JavaScript 1.1 release and continuing through JavaScript 1.2, the `getYear()` method returns the year according to the following rules:

- Years before 1900 are returned as a four-digit year.

- Years for the twentieth century are returned as two-digit years.

- Years from 2000 and beyond are returned as four-digit years.

JavaScript 1.3. As browsers begin to comply with ECMAScript standards, the `getYear()` method changes yet again. The ECMAScript standard specifies that the `getYear()` method returns years before 1900 as negative values. Any year after 1900 is a positive integer. Thus, the year 2000 is 100, which is the result returned in the JavaScript 1.0 release.

Starting with the JavaScript 1.3 release, Netscape recommends that you always specify the complete four-digit year. To assist you in specifying the complete year, JavaScript 1.3 includes new `setFullYear()`, `getFullYear()`, `setFullUTCYear()`, and `getFullUTCYear()` methods. The `getFullYear()` method returns the absolute year number according to local time, for example, 1998. The `getFullUTCYear()` method returns the absolute year number according to Universal Coordinated Time, for example, 1998. The `setFullYear()` method sets the full (absolute) year for a specified date. The `setFullUTCYear()` method sets the full (absolute) year for a specified date according to Universal Coordinated Time. Use these new methods instead of the `getYear()` and `setYear()` methods, which are supported for backward compatibility only.

See "Example of the toLocaleString() Method" on page 426 for an example of using the `getFullYear()` and `setFullYear()` methods.

Getting and Setting Milliseconds

The JavaScript 1.3 release enables you to specify milliseconds as the parameter for many of its methods and also provides the following new methods to enable you to get and set the millisecond value for the time.

Method

geMilliseconds()

setMilliseconds(*0-999*)

Returns/Uses

An integer between 0 and 999

If you specify a number outside the 0–999 range, the other stored variables in the Date object are updated to accommodate the number you specify. For example, if you specify 1005, the number of milliseconds is 5 and the number of seconds in the Date object is incremented by 1.

See "Example of the toLocaleString() Method" on page 426 for an example of using the getMilliseconds() and setMilliseconds() methods.

Getting and Setting the Month, Date, and Day as a UTC Value

The following six new methods have been added to the Date object in the
JavaScript 1.3 release to enable you to get and set the month, date, and day of the
week as UTC values.

Method

getUTCMonth()

setUTCMonth(*0-11*(,*1-31*))

getUTCDate()

setUTCDate(1-31)

getUTCDay()

setUTCDay(0-6)

Returns/Uses

A number representing the month (0-11) and/or date (1-31) according to
Universal Coordinated Time

For the get/setUTCDay() methods, a number from 0-6 representing the day of
the week, with 0 for Sunday, 1 for Monday, and so on.

getUTCMonth() returns an integer between 0 and 11, where 0 corresponds to
January, 1 to February, 3 to March, and so on. If the date is specified,
getUTCMonth() returns the date as an integer between 1 and 31.

When you use the setUTCMonth() method, the month is required and the date
is optional.

getUTCDate() returns an integer between 1 and 31 corresponding to the date of
the month.

For local time, úse the getMonth() getDate(), and getDay() methods.

Getting and Setting the Time as a UTC Value

The following new methods have been added to the `Date` object in the JavaScript 1.3 release to enable you to get and set hours, minutes, and seconds as UTC values.

Method

getUTCHour()

setUTCHour(*0-23(,0-59(,0-59(, ms))*)

getUTCMinutes()

setUTCMinutes(*,0-59(,0-59(, ms))*)

getUTCSeconds()

setUTCSeconds(*0-59(, ms)*)

getUTCMilliseconds()

setUTCMilliseconds(0-999)

Returns/Uses

A number representing the hours (0-23), minutes (0-59), seconds (0-59), and milliseconds (0-999) according to Universal Coordinated Time.

The `setUTCHours()` method enables you to set optional parameters specifying minutes, seconds, and milliseconds. If you plan to specify milliseconds, you must also specify minutes and seconds.

The `setUTCminutes()` method enables you to set optional parameters specifying seconds and milliseconds. If you plan to specify milliseconds, you must also specify seconds.

The `setUTCseconds()` method enables you to set an optional parameter specifying milliseconds.

The `setUTCmilliseconds()` method enables you to set milliseconds.

Example of Using UTC Methods

The following `dateUTC.html` script uses the `toUTCString()` method described in the next section to display the current UTC date. Clicking on the get buttons displays the value of the current date returned for each component. Typing a different value in the text field and clicking on the set buttons changes the date in the text field to use the new values.

```
<!--

                          dateUTC.html

This example illustrates the new methods for manipulating
the UTC time for a Date object.

-->

<HTML>
<HEAD>
<TITLE>Date Object UTC Methods</TITLE>
<SCRIPT LANGUAGE="JavaScript">
<!--

workDate = new Date()

function showDate() {
   document.tstForm.tstDate.value = workDate.toUTCString()
}

function initDate() {
   showDate()
   dispYear = document.tstForm.UTCyear
   dispMonth = document.tstForm.UTCmonth
   dispDate = document.tstForm.UTCdate
   dispDay = document.tstForm.UTCday
   dispHours = document.tstForm.UTChours
   dispMinutes = document.tstForm.UTCminutes
   dispSeconds = document.tstForm.UTCseconds
   dispMilliseconds = document.tstForm.UTCmilliseconds
}

//-->
</SCRIPT>
</HEAD>

<BODY ONLOAD="initDate()">

<H1 ALIGN="CENTER">Date Object UTC Methods</H1>

<P></P>

<FORM NAME="tstForm">
   <CENTER>
   <P>UTC Date: <INPUT TYPE="text" NAME="tstDate" SIZE="40"></P>
   </CENTER>
```

```
<P><INPUT TYPE="text" SIZE=10 NAME="UTCyear">
   <INPUT TYPE="button" NAME="getYearBtn"
    VALUE="getUTCYear"
    ONCLICK="dispYear.value = workDate.getUTCFullYear()">
   <INPUT TYPE="button" NAME="setYearBtn"
    VALUE="setUTCYear"
   ONCLICK="workDate.setUTCFullYear(dispYear.value); showDate()">
  <BR>
   <INPUT TYPE="text" SIZE=10 NAME="UTCmonth">
   <INPUT TYPE="button" NAME="getMonthBtn"
    VALUE="getUTCMonth"
    ONCLICK="dispMonth.value = workDate.getUTCMonth()">
   <INPUT TYPE="button" NAME="setMonthBtn"
    VALUE="setUTCMonth"
    ONCLICK="workDate.setUTCMonth(dispMonth.value); showDate()">
  <BR>
   <INPUT TYPE="text" SIZE=10 NAME="UTCdate">
   <INPUT TYPE="button" NAME="getDateBtn"
    VALUE="getUTCDate"
    ONCLICK="dispDate.value = workDate.getUTCDate()">
   <INPUT TYPE="button" NAME="setDateBtn"
    VALUE="setUTCDate"
    ONCLICK="workDate.setUTCDate(dispDate.value); showDate()">
  <BR>
   <INPUT TYPE="text" SIZE=10 NAME="UTCday">
   <INPUT TYPE="button" NAME="getDayBtn"
    VALUE="getUTCDay"
    ONCLICK="dispDay.value = workDate.getUTCDay()">
  <BR>
   <INPUT TYPE="text" SIZE=10 NAME="UTChours">
   <INPUT TYPE="button" NAME="getHoursBtn"
    VALUE="getUTCHours"
    ONCLICK="dispHours.value = workDate.getUTCHours()">
   <INPUT TYPE="button" NAME="setHoursBtn"
    VALUE="setUTCHours"
    ONCLICK="workDate.setUTCHours(dispHours.value); showDate()">
  <BR>
   <INPUT TYPE="text" SIZE=10 NAME="UTCminutes">
   <INPUT TYPE="button" NAME="getMinutesBtn"
    VALUE="getUTCMinutes"
    ONCLICK="dispMinutes.value = workDate.getUTCMinutes()">
   <INPUT TYPE="button" NAME="setMinutesBtn"
    VALUE="setUTCMinutes"
    ONCLICK="workDate.setUTCMinutes(dispMinutes.value);
showDate()">
  <BR>
   <INPUT TYPE="text" SIZE=10 NAME="UTCseconds">
   <INPUT TYPE="button" NAME="getSecondsBtn"
```

```
        VALUE="getUTCSeconds"
        ONCLICK="dispSeconds.value = workDate.getUTCSeconds()">
      <INPUT TYPE="button" NAME="setSecondsBtn"
       VALUE="setUTCSeconds"
        ONCLICK="workDate.setUTCSeconds(dispSeconds.value);
  showDate()">
    <BR>
        <INPUT TYPE="text" SIZE=10 NAME="UTCmilliseconds">
        <INPUT TYPE="button" NAME="getMillisecondsBtn"
       VALUE="getUTCMilliseconds"
        ONCLICK="dispMilliseconds.value =
  workDate.getUTCMilliseconds()">
        <INPUT TYPE="button" NAME="setMillisecondsBtn"
         VALUE="setUTCMilliseconds"
      ONCLICK="workDate.setUTCMilliseconds(dispMilliseconds.value);
  showDate()">
    </P>
  </FORM>
  </BODY>
  </HTML>
```

Figure A-3 shows the result of loading the `dateUTC.html` script and clicking on each of the get buttons.

Netscape: Date Object UTC Methods

| Back | Forward | Reload | Home | Search | Netscape | Images | Print | Security | Stop | N |

Location: file:///MacintoshHD/Desktop%20Folder/JSBook-1.2/1.3/dateUTC.html What's Related

Date Object UTC Methods

UTC Date: Fri, 06 Nov 1998 01:43:36 GMT

1998	getUTCYear	setUTCYear
10	getUTCMonth	setUTCMonth
6	getUTCDate	setUTCDate
5	getUTCDay	
1	getUTCHours	setUTCHours
43	getUTCMinutes	setUTCMinutes
36	getUTCSeconds	setUTCSeconds
555	getUTCMilliseconds	setUTCMilliseconds

Figure A-3 Result of loading the `dateUTC.html` script

Obtaining a UTC Date String

You can use the `toUTCString()` method to convert a date to a string in Universal Coordinated Time. The format of the string that is returned depends on the user's computer platform, but it usually has a format similar to the IETF standard date format:

```
Wed, 27 Oct 1998 13:58:02 GMT
```

Method

toUTCString()

Returns

Date string in Universal Coordinated Time.

The `toUTCString()` method behaves in the same way as the `toGMTString()` method provided in earlier releases. Use the `toUTCString()` method instead of `toGMTString()`, which is provided for backward compatibility. For local time, use the `toString()` method.

The following extract from the `dateUTC.html` script uses the `toUTCString()` method to format the current date in Universal Coordinated Time. For the complete script, see "Example of Using UTC Methods" on page 420.

```
function showDate() {
    document.tstForm.tstDate.value = workDate.toUTCString()
}
```

Changes to the Date Methods

The following methods for the `Date` object that were supported in the JavaScript 1.2 release now take extra optional parameters in the JavaScript 1.3 release:

```
setMonth(month[, date])

setHours(hours[, min[, sec[, ms]]])

setMinutes(min[, sec[, ms]])

setSeconds(sec[, ms])
```

These methods are similar to equivalent `setUTC*` methods, except that they set the date information according to local time. If you do not specify these optional parameters, the appropriate `get*` methods are used. If the number specified for any of the parameter is outside of the range expected, the `Date` method updates the `Date` object according. For example, if you use 100 for seconds, the minutes stored in the `Date` object are updated by 1 and 40 is used for the seconds.

toLocaleString() Method

The `toLocaleString()` method uses the operating system for formatting dates. It converts the date to a string, using the formatting convention of the operating system where the script is running. For example, in the United States, the month appears before the date (10/31/98), whereas in Europe the date appears before the month (31.10.98). If the operating system is not year-2000 compliant and does not use the full year for years before 1900 or over 2000, then `toLocaleString()` also returns a string that is not year-2000 compliant.

Example of the toLocaleString() Method

The following `dateLocal.html` script uses the `toLocaleString()` method to display the local date and provides buttons with the `getYear()`, `setYear()`, `getFullYear()`, `setFullYear,()`, `getMilliseconds()`, and `setMilliseconds()` methods to enable you to modify the local date.

```
<!--
                        dateLocal.html

This example illustrates the new methods for manipulating
the local time for a Date object.
-->
<HTML>
<HEAD>
<TITLE>Date Object Local Methods</TITLE>
<SCRIPT LANGUAGE="JavaScript">
<!--
workDate = new Date()
function showDate() {
   document.tstForm.tstDate.value = workDate.toLocaleString()
}
function initDate() {
   showDate()
   dispYear = document.tstForm.year
   dispFullYear = document.tstForm.fullYear
   dispMilliseconds = document.tstForm.milliseconds
}
//-->
</SCRIPT>

</HEAD>
<BODY ONLOAD="initDate()">
<H1 ALIGN="CENTER">Date Object Local Methods</H1>
<P></P>
<FORM NAME="tstForm">
  <CENTER>
  <P>Local Date: <INPUT TYPE="text" NAME="tstDate" SIZE="40"></P>
  </CENTER>
  <P><INPUT TYPE="text" SIZE=10 NAME="year">
     <INPUT TYPE="button" NAME="getYearBtn"
      VALUE="getYear"
      ONCLICK="dispYear.value = workDate.getYear()">
     <INPUT TYPE="button" NAME="setYearBtn"
      VALUE="setYear"
      ONCLICK="workDate.setYear(dispYear.value); showDate()">
  <BR>
     <INPUT TYPE="text" SIZE=10 NAME="fullYear">
```

```
    <INPUT TYPE="button" NAME="getFullYearBtn"
     VALUE="getFullYear"
     ONCLICK="dispFullYear.value = workDate.getFullYear()">
    <INPUT TYPE="button" NAME="setFullYearBtn"
     VALUE="setFullYear"
     ONCLICK="workDate.setFullYear(dispFullYear.value); showDate()">
  <BR>
    <INPUT TYPE="text" SIZE=10 NAME="milliseconds">
    <INPUT TYPE="button" NAME="getMillisecondsBtn"
     VALUE="getMilliseconds"
     ONCLICK="dispMilliseconds.value = workDate.getMilliseconds()">
    <INPUT TYPE="button" NAME="setMillisecondsBtn"
     VALUE="setMilliseconds"
     ONCLICK="workDate.setMilliseconds(dispMilliseconds.value);
showDate()">
  </P>
</FORM>
</BODY>
</HTML>
```

Figure A-4 shows the result of loading the `dateLocal.html` script on a Macintosh computer with the MacOS™ 8.1 operating system.

Figure A-4 Result of loading the `dateLocal.html` script

On the Macintosh, when you type the year 2000 in the first text field and click on the setYear button, the full year is displayed.

However, if you load the dateLocal.html script on a PC running Windows 3.1, the local date is displayed as 11/09/98. Typing the year 2000 in the first text field and clicking on the setYear button displays the date in the Local Date field as 11/09/00.

New Methods of function Object

JavaScript includes two new methods for the function object, which are proposed for the future ECMA specification:

- call()

- apply()

call() Method

The call() method replaces the caller() method, which is included for backward compatibility. The call() method enables you to execute a method of another object in a different object context.

> **Method**
>
> call(this.*Arg*, *arg1*, *arg2*, ...)
>
> **Returns**
>
> Nothing.

this.*Arg* is the parameter for the calling object, and *arg1*, *arg2*, ... are optional parameters of arguments for the object.

By using the call() method, you can write a method once and then inherit it in another object without having to rewrite the method for the new object. When calling an existing function, you can assign a different this object that refers to the calling object.

apply() Method

The `apply ()` method enables you to apply a method of another object in the context of the calling object. You can assign a different `this` object, which refers to the calling object, when calling an existing function.

Method

call(this.*Arg*, *argArray*)

Returns

Nothing.

The `apply()` method is similar to the `call()` method except for the type of arguments it supports. Instead of a named set of parameters, you can use an arguments array. You can use an array literal or an array object.

`this.Arg` is the parameter for the calling object, and `argArray` is an optional parameter of an argument array for the object. For example,

```
apply(this,[name, value]
```

for an array literal, or

```
apply(this,newArray(name,value))
```

for an array object.

You can also use `arguments` for the `argArray`. `arguments` is a special property of the activation object. You can use it for all unspecified arguments of the called object. You do not have to know the arguments of the called object when you use the `apply` method. You can use `arguments` to pass all the arguments to the called object. The called object is then responsible for handling the arguments.

Strict Comparison Operators

In the JavaScript 1.2 release, the == and != comparison operators were changed in the following ways:

If the <SCRIPT> tag uses LANGAGE="JavaScript1.2", then the equals (==) and not equal to (!=) comparison operators work differently than in the 1.0 and 1.1 releases. In JavaScript 1.2, these comparison operators behave in the following ways:

- The == and ! = operators never attempt to convert operands from one type to another.

- The == and ! = operators always compare identity of like-typed operands. If the operands do not have like type, they are not equal.

In the JavaScript 1.3 release, the == and ! = comparison operators revert back to their JavaScript 1.0 and 1.1 behavior, converting the types of operands before making the comparison. Two strict comparison operators are also added:

- === equals

- ! == not equal to

These new operators are not part of the current ECMA specification but will be included in the next version.

These new operators perform equality comparisons on operands of the same type. The operators never convert operands from one type to another. Use the strict comparison operators if you want to make sure the two operands are of both a specific type and value. If the type of operand does not matter but the value should be the same, use the standard == comparison operator.

Comparisons are made in the following ways:

- Strings are compared by using Unicode values. Two strings are equal when they have exactly the same sequence of characters, the same length, and the same characters in corresponding positions.

- Two numbers are equal when they have the same number value.

- NaN is not equal to anything, including NaN.

- Positive and negative zeros are equal.

- Two objects are equal if they refer to the same object.

- Boolean operands are the same if they are both true or false.

The strict comparison operators return a Boolean value. If the two operands are the same, === returns true. If the two operands are not equal, ! == returns true. Otherwise, they return false. For example, 9 === "9" returns false, whereas 9 == "9" returns true.

Example of Comparison Operators

The following equalityComp.html script shows the behavior of the comparison operators in different versions of JavaScript when comparing an integer to a string.

```
<!--

                   equalityComp.html

This script shows the difference in the behavior of the comparison
operators between the different versions of JavaScript. The JavaScript
1.3 section also illustrates the strict comparison operators.

-->

<HTML>
<HEAD>
<TITLE>The Strict Comparison Operator</TITLE>
<SCRIPT LANGUAGE="JavaScript">
<!--

testInt = 5
testStr = "5"

//-->
</SCRIPT>
</HEAD>

<BODY>

<H1 ALIGN="CENTER">The Strict Comparison Operator</H1>

<P>The following tests show the behavior of different versions of
JavaScript when comparing an integer to a string. For the purpose of
these tests, <KBD>testInt = 4</KBD> and <KBD>testStr =
"4"</KBD>.</P>

<H3>JavaScript 1.1</H3>

<SCRIPT LANGUAGE="JavaScript1.1">
<!--

document.write("<P>int == str -> " + (testInt == testStr) + "<BR>")
document.write("int != str -> " + (testInt != testStr) + "</P>")

//-->
</SCRIPT>

<H3>JavaScript 1.2</H3>

<SCRIPT LANGUAGE="JavaScript1.2">
<!--
```

```
document.write("<P>int == str -> " + (testInt == testStr) + "<BR>")
document.write("int != str -> " + (testInt != testStr) + "</P>")

// The last test returns true because the objects are different.
//-->
</SCRIPT>

<H3>JavaScript 1.3</H3>

<SCRIPT LANGUAGE="JavaScript1.3">
<!--

document.write("<P>int == str -> " + (testInt == testStr) + "<BR>")
document.write("int != str -> " + (testInt != testStr) + "</P>")
document.write("<P>int === str -> " + (testInt === testStr) + "<BR>")
document.write("int !== str -> " + (testInt !== testStr) + "</P>")

//-->
</SCRIPT>
</BODY>
</HTML>
```

Figure A-5 shows the result of loading the `equalityComp.html` script.

Netscape: The Strict Comparison Operator

Back | Forward | Reload | Home | Search | Netscape | Images | Print | Security | Stop | N

Location: file:///MacintoshHD/Desktop%20Folder/JSBook-1.2/1.3/equalityComp.htm What's Related

The Strict Comparison Operator

The following tests show the behavior of different versions of JavaScript when comparing an integer to a string. For the purpose of these tests, `testInt = 4` and `testStr = "4"`.

JavaScript 1.1

```
int == str -> true
int != str -> false
```

JavaScript 1.2

```
int == str -> false
int != str -> true
```

JavaScript 1.3

```
int == str -> true
int != str -> false

int === str -> false
int !== str -> true
```

Figure A-5 Result of loading the `equalityComp.html` script

JavaScript Console

Netscape Navigator and Communicator 4.06 and 4.5 now support a JavaScript console window similar to the Java console. The JavaScript console window displays all JavaScript error messages. In the future, the console may also support non-JavaScript messages and warnings.

The text of JavaScript error messages looks the same whether they are displayed in the JavaScript console or in the traditional error dialogs.

Currently, JavaScript error descriptions are not internationalization-friendly. They are always displayed in English regardless of the locale.

In Communicator 4.5, on the Macintosh platform, the default behavior when a JavaScript error is encountered is to display a message in the message area at the bottom of the window, as shown in Figure A-6.

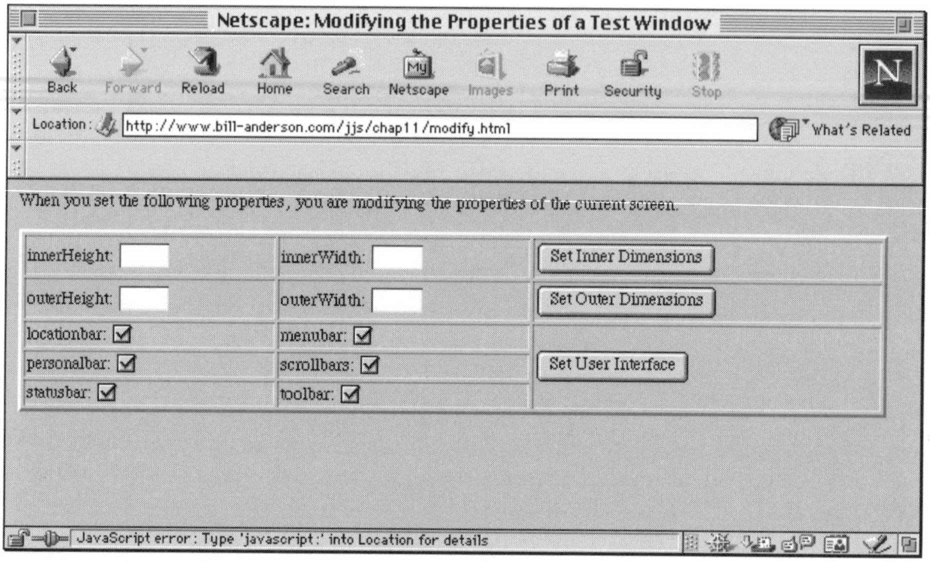

Netscape: Modifying the Properties of a Test Window

| Back | Forward | Reload | Home | Search | Netscape | Images | Print | Security | Stop |

Location: http://www.bill-anderson.com/jjs/chap11/modify.html   What's Related

When you set the following properties, you are modifying the properties of the current screen.

innerHeight: [ ]	innerWidth: [ ]	Set Inner Dimensions
outerHeight: [ ]	outerWidth: [ ]	Set Outer Dimensions
locationbar: ☑	menubar: ☑	
personalbar: ☑	scrollbars: ☑	Set User Interface
statusbar: ☑	toolbar: ☑	

JavaScript error: Type 'javascript:' into Location for details

Figure A-6 Message about a JavaScript error

To display the console window, type `javascript:` into the Location text field and press Return. Be sure to include the colon. The console window is displayed showing the error message, as shown in Figure A-7.

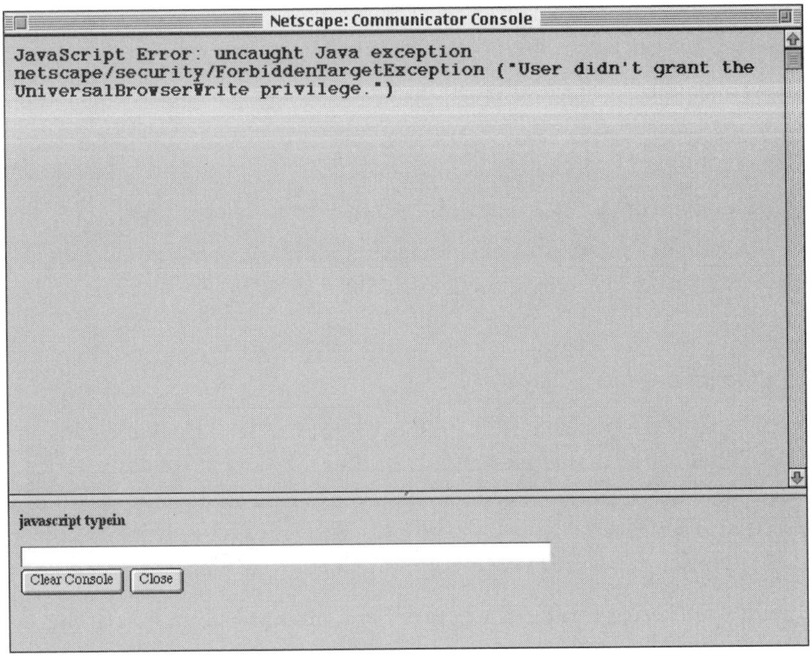

Figure A-7 JavaScript console window

Setting the JavaScript Console Preferences

You can edit the Navigator preference file to set preferences for the JavaScript console. The preference file is in the specific user's directory. For example, under NT, you may find the preference file, `prefs.js`, under *Netscape path*\Users*username*. Make sure Navigator is not running when you edit your preferences or it may overwrite your customization.

To have the JavaScript console automatically open when a JavaScript error occurs, add the following line to your preferences file.

```
user_pref("javascript.console.open_on_error", true);
```

When a JavaScript error occurs, the console window opens automatically and scrolls down to the new error message.

If you prefer to have the error dialog box open when an error occurs, add the following line to your preference file.

```
user_pref("javascript.classic.error_alerts", true);
```

Changes in JavaScript 1.3

The following section describes changes to JavaScript 1.2 that have been made in JavaScript 1.3. These features do not perform as they did in JavaScript 1.2. You must make the appropriate changes to your code for it to be JavaScript 1.3 compliant.

Comparison Operators

The == and != comparison operators in JavaScript 1.3 revert to the JavaScript 1.1 implementation. If the types of the operands are different, JavaScript converts them before making the comparison. A Boolean value is returned as the result of the comparison. For example, 9 == "9" returns true. You do not have to know if an operand is a string or a number before making a comparison.

When operands are of the same type, the comparison operators function in the same way as a strict comparison operator:

- Null and Undefined types are equal.

- NaN is not equal to NaN or any other operand.

- Positive and negative zeros are equal.

- If the two operands are of type String, Number, Boolean, or Object but they are not of the same type, JavaScript tries to convert the operands to an appropriate type for the comparison.

- When a number and a string are compared, the string is converted to a number value.

- JavaScript tries to convert the string numeric literal to a Number type value. First, a mathematical value is derived from the string numeric literal. Next, this value is rounded to nearest Number type value.

- If one of the operands is a Boolean, the Boolean operand is converted to 1 if it is true and +0 if it is false.

- If an object is compared with a number or string, JavaScript tries to return the default value for the object.

- Operators try to convert the object to a primitive value, a String or Number value, using the valueOf() and toString() methods of the objects. If the attempt to convert the object fails, a runtime error is generated.

Use the strict comparison operators if the operands must be of a specific type and value or if the exact type of the operands is important.

Changes to the Array Object

This section describes the changes to the Array object in the JavaScript 1.3 release.

Length property

The length property of an array is now an unsigned, 32-bit integer. The value of the length property is an integer with a positive sign and a value less than 2 to the 32 power.

Constructor

In the JavaScript 1.2 release, when you specified a single parameter, the Array constructor returned a single-element array. Although ArrayLength was documented as a unique parameter for a single parameter (argument) constructor in JavaScript 1.2, it acted in the same way as a multiple parameter constructor.

In JavaScript 1.3, when you use a single-parameter constructor, the constructor verifies if the argument is a number. If it is a number, the constructor converts the number to an unsigned, 32-bit integer and generates an array with the length property (size of the array) set to the integer. The initial value of the elements of Array is undefined.

The following arrayComp.html script shows the differences in the Array constructor between the JavaScript 1.2 and 1.3 releases.

```
<!--


                    arrayComp.html


Compares the behavior of the Array constructor in JavaScript 1.3 as
compared to JavaScript 1.2.


-->
<HTML>
<HEAD>
<TITLE>Array Constructor Comparison</TITLE>
```

```
</HEAD>

<BODY>

<H1 ALIGN="CENTER">Array Constructor Comparison</H1>

<P>In JavaScript 1.2, the Array constructor created an array with a
single element. The following tests show the difference between
JavaScript 1.2 and JavaScript 1.3, when creating an array with
<KBD>tstArray = new Array(4)</KBD>:</P>

<H3>JavaScript 1.2</H3>

<SCRIPT LANGUAGE="JavaScript1.2">
<!--

var tstArray1 = new Array(4)
document.write("<P>Array length = " + tstArray1.length + "<BR>")
document.write("Array values = " + tstArray1.toString() + "</P>")

//-->
</SCRIPT>

<H3>JavaScript 1.3</H3>

<SCRIPT LANGUAGE="JavaScript1.3">
<!--

var tstArray2 = new Array(4)
document.write("<P>Array length = " + tstArray2.length + "<BR>")
document.write("Array values = " + tstArray2.toString() + "</P>")

//-->
</SCRIPT>
</BODY>
</HTML>
```

Figure A-8 shows the result of loading the `arrayComp.html` script.

Array Constructor Comparison

Netscape: Array Constructor Comparison

Location: file:///MacintoshHD/Desktop%20Folder/JSBook-1.2/1.3/arrayComp.html — What's Related

Array Constructor Comparison

In JavaScript 1.2, the Array constructor created an array with a single element. The following tests shows the difference between JavaScript 1.2 and JavaScript 1.3, when creating an array with `tstArray = new Array(4)`:

JavaScript 1.2

Array length = 1
Array values = [4]

JavaScript 1.3

Array length = 4
Array values = ,,,

Figure A-8 Result of loading the `arrayComp.html` script

push() Method

In JavaScript 1.2, the `push()` method returned the last element added to an array, which is analogous to the behavior of `push()` in Perl 4. In JavaScript 1.3, `push()` returns the new length of the array, which is analogous to the behavior of `push()` in Perl 5.

splice() Method

In JavaScript 1.2, if only one element was removed, the `splice()` method returned the element removed. In JavaScript 1.3, `splice()` always returns an array containing the removed elements. If one element is removed, an array of one element is returned.

replace() Method of String Object

In JavaScript 1.3, the `replace()` method of the `String` object supports the nesting of a function in place of the second argument. A function used in this way is often called a lambda expression.

Method

replace(*regexp, newSubString*)

replace(*regexp, function*)

Returns

Nothing.

If you specify a function as the second parameter, it is invoked after the match has been performed. You can dynamically generate the string that will replace the matched substring in your function. The result of the function call is used as the replacement value.

Example of Using the New replace() Method of the String Object

The following `replace1-3.html` script uses functions as a way to define the replacement string.

```
<!--


                        replace1-3.html


Example of how to use a function with the replace() method in
regular expressions.

-->
<HTML>
  <HEAD>
    <TITLE>Replacing a Substring with Another String</TITLE>

<SCRIPT LANGUAGE="JavaScript1.3">
<!--

testStr1="There is nothing like a holiday."
testStr2="A rose is a rose."
testStr3="John Smith"

re2=/rose/g
re3=/(\w+)\s(\w+)/
```

```
//-->
</SCRIPT>
  </HEAD>
  <BODY>

    <P>Replacing matches:</P>

<SCRIPT LANGUAGE="JavaScript1.3">
<!--

document.write("Old String: "+testStr1+"<BR>")
testRes1=testStr1.replace(/holiday/,

    function tstSingle(Str){
        return prompt("Replace holiday with:", Str)
    })

document.write("New String:: "+testRes1+"<BR>")
document.write("<HR>")
document.write("Old String: "+testStr2+"<BR>")

//
// Notice that the function is called for each occurrence
// of the search string.

testRes2=testStr2.replace(re2,

    function tstMulti(Str) {
        return prompt("Replace rose with", Str)
    })

document.write("New String:: "+testRes2+"<BR>")
document.write("<HR>")

//-->
</SCRIPT>

    <P>Replacing remembered substrings:</P>

<SCRIPT LANGUAGE="JavaScript1.3">
<!--

document.write("Old String: "+testStr3+"<BR>")
document.write("Swap the order.<BR>")
testRes3=testStr3.replace(re3,

    function testParm(Str, P1, P2) {
```

```
        return (P1 + ", " + P2)
    })

document.write("New String: "+testRes3+"<BR>")

//-->
</SCRIPT>
  </BODY>
</HTML>
```

When you load the `replace1-3.html` script, the first function displays a prompt window, shown in Figure A-9, that you can use to type a replacement string.

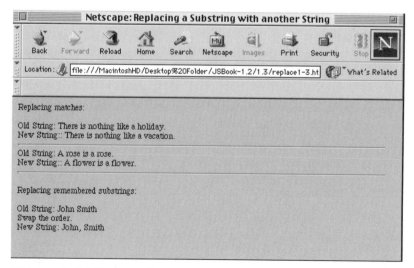

Figure A-9 Result of loading the `replace1-3.html` script

When you click on the OK button, another prompt window is displayed for the next string, followed by a third. Figure A-10 shows the page after the replacements have been made.

Figure A-10 Replaced text in the `replace1-3.html` example

Boolean Object

In JavaScript 1.2 conditional tests, a Boolean `false` object was treated as false. When a `Boolean` object was used as the condition in an `if` statement, JavaScript 1.2 returned the value of the `Boolean` object. If the value for the `Boolean` object was `false`, the statement was evaluated to false. In JavaScript 1.3, the `if` statement only verifies if the condition is really a `Boolean` object and returns `true` if it is true. All objects are considered true in a conditional test, including the Boolean `false` object.

toString() Method

In JavaScript 1.2, the `toString()` method of the `Object` and `Array` objects returned an object or array literal string.

In JavaScript 1.3, the `toString()` method of an object returns `[object type]`, where *type* is the name of the object type or the name of the constructor function that created the object.

JavaScript Quick Reference

▼ JavaScript Objects

▼ Control Structures

▼ Operators

▼ Reserved JavaScript Keywords

▼ Escape Characters for String Formatting

▼ HTTP MIME Types

JavaScript Objects

This section provides an alphabetical list of JavaScript objects with HTML (where appropriate) and summary information about each object's properties, methods, and event handlers. Table B-1 lists the symbols used to identify each element by release.

Table B-1 Symbols Used to Identify Elements by Release

Symbol	JavaScript Release	Navigator/Communicator Release
None	1.0	2.0
* (Asterisk)	1.1	3.0
† (Dagger)	1.2	4.0
‡ (Double dagger)	1.3	4.06-4.5

Anchor Object

The Anchor object requires the NAME attribute of the <A> tag. When it has a URL, it also has a reference in the links array.

HTML

```
<A
HREF = "URL" | NAME = "destination"
[TARGET = "WindowName"]
>
Text of anchor
</A>
```

Properties

Property	Value	Gettable	Settable
text[†]	string	Yes	No

Methods

None

Event Handlers

None

applet Object

HTML

```
<APPLET
CODE = "filename.class"
WIDTH = number
HEIGHT = number
MAYSCRIPT
[CODEBASE = "base directory for the applet"]
[ALT = "alternative character data that is displayed if the
browser cannot run the applet"]
[NAME = "name for the applet instance"]
[ALIGN =
left|right|top|texttop|middle|absmiddle|baseline|bottom|
absbottom]
[VSPACE = number]
[HSPACE = number]>
[ARCHIVE =JavaClass.zip]
<PARAM NAME = "NameOfParameter"  VALUE = "Value">
</APPLET>
```

Properties

All public properties of the Java applet.

Methods

```
init()
start()
stop()
destroy()
```

and all public methods of the Java applet.

Event Handlers

```
None
```

Area Object

HTML

```
<MAP NAME="areaMapName"
    <AREA
        COORDS="x1,y1,x2,y2,..."  |  "x-center,y-center,radius"
        HREF = "URL"
        [NOHREF]
        [SHAPE = "rect"  |  "poly"  |  "circle"  |  "default"]
        [TARGET = "WindowName"]
        [onMouseOver = "JavaScript code"]
        [onMouseOut = "JavaScript code"]
    >
</MAP>
```

Properties

You reference properties of the Area object by using the document.links array and location properties. The area object does not have any properties of its own.

Property	Value	Gettable	Settable
links.length	number	Yes	No
links(index).target	string	Yes	Yes
(location object properties)			

Methods

```
eval()*
handleEvent()†
```

```
toString()*
valueOf()*
```

Event Handlers

```
onMouseOut
onMouseOver
```

Array Object*

Properties

Property	Value	Gettable	Settable
length	number	Yes	Yes
prototype*	string	Yes	Yes

Methods

```
concat()†
eval()*
handleEvent()†
join()
pop()†
push()†
reverse()
shift()†
slice()†
sort()
splice()†
toString()*
unshift()†
valueOf()*
```

Event Handlers

None

Boolean Object*
Properties

Property	Value	Gettable	Settable
prototype*	string	Yes	Yes

button Object
HTML

```
<FORM>
<INPUT TYPE = "button"
[NAME = "Button Name"]
VALUE = "Button Text"
onBlur = "JavaScript code"
onClick = "JavaScript code"
onFocus = "JavaScript code">
</FORM>
```

Properties

Property	Value	Gettable	Settable
form*	containing form object	Yes	No
name	string	Yes	No
type*	string	Yes	No
value	string	Yes	No

Methods

```
blur()
click()
eval()*
focus()
handleEvent()†
toString()*
valueOf()*
```

Event Handlers

```
onBlur
onClick
onFocus
onMouseDown†
onMouseUp†
```

checkbox Object

HTML

```
<FORM>
<INPUT TYPE = "checkbox"
NAME = "Box Name"
VALUE = "checkboxValue"
[checked]
onBlur = "JavaScript code"
onClick = "JavaScript code"
onFocus = "JavaScript code"
checkboxLabel>
</FORM>
```

Properties

Property	Value	Gettable	Settable
checked	Boolean	Yes	Yes
defaultChecked	Boolean	Yes	No
form*	containing form object	Yes	No
name	string	Yes	No
type*	string	Yes	No
value	string	Yes	No

Methods

```
blur()
click()
eval()*
focus()
handleEvent()†
toString()*
valueOf()*
```

Event Handlers
```
onBlur
onClick
onFocus
```

Date Object

Properties

Property	Value	Gettable	Settable
prototype*	string	Yes	Yes

Methods
```
eval()*
get/setDate()
getDay()
```
get/setFullYear[‡]

get/setFullUTCYear[‡]
```
get/setHours()
```
get/setMilliseconds[‡]
```
get/setMinutes()
get/setMonth()
get/setSeconds()
get/setTime()
```
get/setUTCDate[‡]

get/setUTCDay[‡]

get/setUTCHours[‡]

get/setUTCMilliseconds[‡]

get/setUTCMinutes[‡]

get/setUTCMonths[‡]

get/setUTCSeconds[‡]
```
get/setYear()
getTimezoneOffset()
```
handleEvent()[†]
```
parse("dateString")
toGMTString()
toLocaleString()*
toString()*
```
toUTCString()[‡]
```
UTC(date vals)
valueOf()*
```

Event Handlers

None

document Object

HTML

```
<BODY
[BACKGROUND = "backgroundImage"]
[BGCOLOR = "backgroundColor"]
[FGCOLOR = "foregroundColor"]
text
[LINK = "linkColor"]
[ALINK = "activatedLinkColor"]
[VLINK= "visitedLinkColor"]>
</BODY>
```

Properties

Property	Value	Gettable	Settable
alinkColor	hexadecimal string or predefined JavaScript Color	Yes	No
anchors()	array	Yes	No
applets()*	array	Yes	No
bgColor	hexadecimal string or predefined JavaScript color	Yes	No
classes[†]	array	Yes	No
cookie	string	Yes	Yes
domain*	string	Yes	Yes
embeds()*	array	Yes	No
fgColor	hexadecimal string or predefined JavaScript Color	Yes	No
forms	array	Yes	No
ids[†]	array	Yes	No
images()*	array	Yes	No
lastModified	date string	Yes	No
linkColor	hexadecimal string or predefined JavaScript color	Yes	No
links()	array	Yes	No
location	string	Yes	No
plugins()*	array	Yes	No
referrer	string	Yes	No

Property	Value	Gettable	Settable
title	string	Yes	No
URL*	string	Yes	No
vlinkColor	hexadecimal string or predefined JavaScript color	Yes	No

Methods

```
captureEvents()†
clear()
close()
eval()*
getSelection()†
handleEvent()†
open()
releaseEvents()†
routeEvent()†
toString()*
valueOf()*
write()
writeln()
```

Event Handlers

```
onDblClick†
onKeyDown†
onKeyPress†
onKeyUp†
onMouseDown†
onMouseUp†
```

event Object†

An `event` object is created whenever an event occurs. The object can be queried to determine information about the event. Added in JavaScript 1.2 (Navigator 4). This object is different from the built-in `Event` object.

Properties

Property	Value	Gettable	Settable
data()	array	Yes	No
height	number	Yes	No
layerX	number	Yes	No
layerY	number	Yes	No
modifiers	string	Yes	No
pageX	number	Yes	No
pageY	number	Yes	No
screenX	number	Yes	No
screenY	number	Yes	No
target	string	Yes	No
type	string	Yes	No
which	number	Yes	No
width	number	Yes	No

Methods

```
eval()*
toString()*
valueOf()*
```

Event Handlers

```
None
```

Event Object[t]

The Event object is a built-in object that holds mask values used by event handlers and the captureEvent() method. This object is different from the event object. Added in JavaScript 1.2 (Navigator 4).

Properties

Property	Value
ALT_MASK	Integer for Alt key
CLICK	Integer for click event
CONTROL_MASK	Integer for Control key
DRAGDROP	Integer for drag and drop event
KEYDOWN	Integer for key down event
KEYUP	Integer for key up event
KEYPRESS	Integer for key press event
META_MASK	Integer for Meta key
MOUSEDOWN	Integer for mouse down event
MOUSEUP	Integer for mouse up event
MOUSEOVER	Integer for mouse over event
MOUSEOUT	Integer for mouse out event
MOUSEMOVE	Integer for mouse move event
MOVE	Integer for move event
RESIZE	Integer for resize event
SHIFT_MASK	Integer for Shift key

Methods

```
eval()*
toString()*
valueOf()*
```

Event Handlers

```
None
```

fileUpload Object*

HTML

```
<FORM
<INPUT
    NAME = "name"
    type = "file"
    [onBlur = "JavaScript code"]
```

```
        [onChange = "JavaScript code"]
        [onFocus = "JavaScript code"]>
    </FORM>
```

Properties

Property	Value	Gettable	Settable
form*	containing form object	Yes	No
name	string	Yes	No
type*	string	Yes	No
value	string	Yes	No

Methods

```
blur()
eval()*
focus()
handleEvent()†
toString()*
valueOf()*
```

Event Handlers

```
onBlur
onChange*
onFocus
```

form Object

HTML

```
<FORM
NAME = "formName"
TARGET = "windowName"
ACTION = "serverURL"
METHOD= "GET | POST"
enctype = "MIMEType"
[onReset = "JavaScript code"]
[onSubmit = "JavaScript code"] >
</FORM>
```

Properties

Property	Value	Gettable	Settable
action	URL	Yes	Yes
elements()	array	Yes	No
encoding	MIMETypeString	Yes	Yes
length	number	Yes	No
method	GET or POST	Yes	Yes
name	string	Yes	No
target	windowNameString	Yes	Yes

Methods

```
eval()*
handleEvent()†
reset()*
submit()
toString()*
valueOf()*
```

Event Handlers

```
onReset*
onSubmit
```

function Object*

Properties

Property	Value	Gettable	Settable
arguments()	array	Yes	No
arity†	number	Yes	No
caller	string	Yes	No
prototype	string	Yes	Yes

Methods

```
apply()‡
call()‡
```

```
toString()*
```

Event Handlers

None

hidden Object

HTML

```
<FORM>
<INPUT TYPE = "hidden"
NAME = "fieldNane"
[VALUE = "contents"]>
</FORM>
```

Properties

Property	Value	Gettable	Settable
form*	containing form object	Yes	No
name	string	Yes	No
type*	string	Yes	No
value	string	Yes	No

Methods

None

Event Handlers

None

history Object

Properties

Property	Value	Gettable	Settable
current*	URL	Yes	No
length	number	Yes	No
next*	URL	Yes	No
previous*	URL	Yes	No

Methods

```
back()
eval()*
forward()
go()
toString()*
valueOf()*
```

Event Handlers

None

image Object

HTML

```
<IMG
SRC = "ImageURL"
[LOWSRC = "LowResImageURL"]
[NAME = "ImageName"]
[WIDTH = "Pixels" | "PercentValue"]
[HEIGHT = "Pixels" | "PercentValue"]
[HSPACE = "Pixels"]
[VSPACE = "Pixels"]
[BORDER = "Pixels"]
[ALIGN = "left" | "right" | "top" | "absmiddle" | "absbottom" |
"texttop" | "middle" | "baseline" | "bottom" ]
[ISMAP]
[USEMAP = "#AreaMapName"]
[onLoad = "JavaScript code"]
[onAbort = "JavaScript code"]
[onError = "JavaScript code"]
>
```

Properties

Property	Value	Gettable	Settable
border	pixels	Yes	No
complete	Boolean	Yes	No
height	pixels	Yes	No
hspace	pixels	Yes	No
lowsrc	URL	Yes	No
name	string	Yes	No
prototype*	string	Yes	Yes
src	URL	Yes	Yes
vspace	pixels	Yes	No
width	pixels	Yes	No

Methods

```
eval()*
handleEvent()†
toString()*
valueOf()*
```

Event Handlers

```
onAbort
onError
onKeyDown†
onKeyPress†
onKeyUp†
onLoad
```

layer Object[†]

HTML

```
<LAYER
ABOVE=name
BACKGROUND=URL
BELOW=name
BGCOLOR=color
CLASS=name
CLIP=edge
```

```
LEFT=n
NAME=name
SRC=URL
STYLE=style
TOP=n
VISIBILITY=value
WIDTH=n
Z-INDEX=n >
body_content
</LAYER>
```

Properties

Property	Value	Gettable	Settable
above	string	Yes	No
background	URL	Yes	Yes
below	string	Yes	No
bgColor	hexadecimal string or predefined JavaScript color	Yes	Yes
clip.bottom	number (pixels)	Yes	Yes
clip.height	number (pixels)	Yes	Yes
clip.left	number (pixels)	Yes	Yes
clip.right	number (pixels)	Yes	Yes
clip.top	number (pixels)	Yes	Yes
clip.width	number (pixels)	Yes	Yes
document	string	Yes	No
id/name	string	Yes	No
left	number	Yes	No
pageX	number (pixels)	Yes	Yes
pageY	number (pixels)	Yes	Yes
parentLayer	string	Yes	No

Property	Value	Gettable	Settable
siblingAbove	string	Yes	No
siblingBelow	string	Yes	No
src	URL	Yes	Yes
top	number	Yes	No
visibility	show | hide | inherit	Yes	Yes
zindex	number	Yes	Yes

Methods

```
captureEvents()eval()
handleEvent()
load(url,width)
moveAbove()
moveBelow()
moveBy(x,y)
moveTo(x,y)
moveToAbsolute(x,y)
releaseEvents()
ResizeBy(width,height)
ResizeTo(width,height)
routeEvents()
toString()
valueOf()
```

Event Handlers

```
onMouseOut
onMouseOver
```

link Object

HTML

```
<A
HREF = "URL" | [NAME = "destinationTag"]
[TARGET = "WindowName"]
{REL =stylesheet | fontdef | alternate | start| next| prev| contents|
index| glossary | copyright| section| subsection | appendix | help |
bookmark]
TYPE = "text/css" | "text/JavaScript"
TITLE = "title"
[onClick = "JavaScript code"]
[onMouseOut = "JavaScript code"]
```

```
[onMouseOver = "JavaScript code"]
>
Text of anchor
</A>
```

Properties

Property	Value	Gettable	Settable
hash	string	Yes	Yes
host	string	Yes	Yes
hostname	string	Yes	Yes
href	URL	Yes	Yes
pathname	string	Yes	Yes
port	string	Yes	Yes
protocol	string	Yes	Yes
search	string	Yes	Yes
target	string	Yes	No

Methods

```
eval()*
handleEvent()†
toString()*
valueOf()*
```

Event Handlers

```
onClick
onDblClick†
onKeyDown†
onKeyPress†
onKeyUp†
onMouseDown†
onMouseOut*
onMouseOver
```

location Object

Properties

Property	Value	Gettable	Settable
hash	string	Yes	Yes
host	string	Yes	Yes
hostname	string	Yes	Yes
href	URL	Yes	Yes
pathname	string	Yes	Yes
port	string	Yes	Yes
protocol	string	Yes	Yes
search	string	Yes	Yes

Methods

```
eval()*
reload()*
replace()*
toString()*
valueOf()*
```

Event Handlers

None

Math Object

Properties

Property	Value	Description
E	2.718281828459045091	Euler's constant
LN2	0.6931471805599452862	Natural log of 2
LN10	2.302585092994045901	Natural log of 10
LOG2E	1.442695040888963387	Log base-2 of E
LOG10E	0.4342944819032518167	Log base-10 of E
PI	3.14592653589793116	π
SQRT1_2	0.7071067811865475727	Square root of 0.5
SQRT2	1.414213562373095145	Square root of 2

Methods

```
abs()
acos()
asin()
atan()
atan2()*
ceil()
cos()
eval()*
exp()
floor()
log()
max()
min()
pow()
random()
round()
sin()
sqrt()
tan()
toString()*
valueOf()*
```

Event Handlers

None

mimeType Object*

Properties

Property	Value	Gettable	Settable
description	string	Yes	No
enabledPlugin	string	Yes	No
type	string	Yes	No
suffixes	string	Yes	No

Methods

```
eval()*
toString()*
valueOf()*
```

Event Handlers

None

navigator Object

Properties

Property	Value	Gettable	Settable
appCodeName	string	Yes	No
appName	string	Yes	No
appVersion	string	Yes	No
language[†]	string	Yes	No
mimeTypes()*	array	Yes	No
platform[†]	string	Yes	No
plugins()*	array	Yes	No

Property	Value	Gettable	Settable
userAgent	string	Yes	No

Methods

```
eval()*
javaEnabled()*
plugins.refresh()
preferences()
taintEnabled()*
toString()*
valueOf()*
```

Event Handlers

```
None
```

Object Object

Properties

Property	Value	Gettable	Settable
Infinity[‡]	Number.POSITIVE_INFINITY	Yes	No
NaN[‡]	NaN	Yes	No
undefined[‡]	undefined	Yes	No

Methods

```
escape()
eval(expression)
isFinite(number)‡
isNaN(expression)*
Number(object)†
object.toString()*
object.valueOf()*
parseFloat("string")
parseInt("string")
String(object)†
toSource()‡
unescape()
```

Event Handlers

None

password Object

HTML

```
<FORM>
<INPUT TYPE = "password"
NAME = "Field Name"
VALUE = "Contents"
SIZE = "Character Count"
[onBlur = "JavaScript code"]
[onFocus = "JavaScript code"]
[onSelect = "JavaScript code"]>
</FORM>
```

Properties

Property	Value	Gettable	Settable
defaultValue	string	Yes	No
form*	containing form object	Yes	No
name	string	Yes	No
type*	string	Yes	No
value	string	Yes	No

Methods

```
blur()
eval()*
handleEvent()†
focus()
select()
toString()*
valueOf()*
```

Event Handlers

```
onBlur
onFocus
onSelect
```

plugin Object*

HTML

```
<EMBED
SRC = "Source URL"
WIDTH = number in pixels for the embedded object
HEIGHT = number in pixels for the embedded object
ATTRIBUTE_1="..."
ATTRIBUTE_2="..."
ATTRIBUTE_3="...">
CHARACTERS
</EMBED>
```

Properties

Property	Value	Gettable	Settable
description	string	Yes	No
filename	string	Yes	No
length	integer	Yes	No
name	string	Yes	No

Methods

```
eval()*
refresh()
toString()*
valueOf()*
```

Event Handlers

None

radio Object

HTML

```
<FORM>
<INPUT TYPE = "radio"
NAME = "radioGroupName"
VALUE = "radioValue"
[CHECKED]
[onBlur = "JavaScript code"]
[onClick = "JavaScript code"]
[onFocus = "JavaScript code"]
radioButtonLabel
</FORM>
```

Properties

Property	Value	Gettable	Settable
checked	Boolean	Yes	No
defaultChecked	Boolean	Yes	No
form*	containing form object	Yes	No
length	integer	Yes	No
name	string	Yes	No
type*	string	Yes	No
value	string	Yes	No

Methods

```
blur()
click()
eval()*
handleEvent()†
focus()
toString()*
valueOf()*
```

Event Handlers

```
onBlur*
onClick
onFocus*
```

RegExp Object[†]

The RegExp object is a built-in object used for creating patterns and working with regular expressions. A regular expression is a pattern that is used to match combinations of characters in strings. Use the expression new RegExp(s,m) to create a pattern based on the pattern string s and modifier string m.

Properties

Property	Value	Gettable	Settable
$0, $1, $2m … $9	string	Yes	No
global	Boolean	Yes	No
IgnoreCase	Boolean	Yes	No
input	string	Yes	No
$_	string	Yes	No
lastIndex	integer	Yes	Yes
lastMatch	string	Yes	No
$&	string	Yes	No
lastParen	string	Yes	No
$+	string	Yes	No
leftContent	string	Yes	No
$`	string	Yes	No
multiline	Boolean	Yes	No
$*	Boolean	Yes	No
rightContent	string	Yes	No
$'	string	Yes	No
source	string	Yes	No

Methods

```
compile(s,m)
eval()
exec()
test()
toString()
valueOf()
```

Event Handlers

None

reset Object

HTML

```
<FORM>
<INPUT TYPE = "reset"
NAME = "Button Name"
VALUE = "Button Text"
[onBlur = "JavaScript code"]
[onClick = "JavaScript code"]
[onFocus = "JavaScript code"]>
</FORM>
```

Properties

Property	Value	Gettable	Settable
form*	containing form object	Yes	No
name	string	Yes	No
type*	string	Yes	No
value	string	Yes	No

Methods

```
blur()
click()
eval()*
handleEvent()†
toString()*
valueOf()*
```

Event Handlers

```
onBlur
onClick
onFocus
```

screen Object†

The screen object is a built-in object that contains information about the screen in which the browser is running.

Properties

Property	Value	Gettable	Settable
availHeight	number (pixels)	Yes	No
availWidth	number (pixels)	Yes	No
colorDepth	number	Yes	No
height	number (pixels)	Yes	No
pixelDepth	number (pixels)	Yes	No
width	number (pixels)	Yes	No

Methods

```
eval()
toString()
valueOf()
```

Event Handlers

None

select Object

HTML

```
<FORM>
<SELECT
    NAME = "listName"
    [SIZE = "number"]
    [MULTIPLE]
    [onBlur = "JavaScript code"]
    [onChange = "JavaScript code"]
    [onFocus = "JavaScript code"]>
        <OPTION
        [SELECTED]
        [VALUE="string"]>
        listItem
</SELECT>
</FORM>
```

Properties

Property	Value	Gettable	Settable
form*	containing form object	Yes	No
length	integer	Yes	No
name	string	Yes	No
options(n)	array	Yes	No
options(*n*).defaultSelected	Boolean	Yes	No
options(*n*).index	integer	Yes	No
options(*n*).selected	Boolean	Yes	Yes
options(*n*).text	string	Yes	Yes
options(*n*).value	string	Yes	Yes
selectedIndex	Integer	Yes	Yes
type*	string	Yes	No

Methods

```
blur()
eval()*
handleEvent()†
focus()
toString()*
valueOf()*
```

Event Handlers

```
onBlur
onChange
onFocus
```

String Object

Properties

Property	Value	Gettable	Settable
length	integer	Yes	No
prototype*	string	Yes	Yes

Methods

anchor()
big()
blink()
bold()
charAt()
charCodeAt()[†]
concat()[†]
eval()*
fixed()
fontcolor()
fontsize()
fromCharCode()[†]
indexOf()
italics()
lastIndexOf()
link()
match(p)[†]
replace(p,s)[†]
search()[†]
slice()[†]
small()
split(char)[†]
strike()
sub()
substr()[†]
substring()[†]
sup()
toLowerCase()
toString()*
toUpperCase()
valueOf()*

Event Handlers
None

submit Object

HTML

```
<FORM>
<INPUT TYPE = "submit"
[NAME = "Button Name"]
VALUE = "Button Text"
[onBlur = "JavaScript code"]
[onClick = "JavaScript code"]
[onFocus = "JavaScript code"]>
</FORM>
```

Properties

Property	Value	Gettable	Settable
form*	containing form object	Yes	No
name	string	Yes	No
type*	string	Yes	No
value	string	Yes	No

Methods

```
blur()
click()
eval()*
handleEvent()†
focus()
toString()*
valueOf()*
```

Event Handlers

```
onBlur
onClick
onFocus
```

text Object

HTML

```
<FORM>
<INPUT TYPE = "text"
```

```
NAME = "Field Name"
VALUE = "Contents"
SIZE = "Character Count"
[onBlur = "JavaScript code"]
[onChange = "JavaScript code"]
[onFocus = "JavaScript code"]
[onSelect = "JavaScript code"]>
</FORM>
```

Properties

Property	Value	Gettable	Settable
defaultValue	string	Yes	No
form*	containing form object	Yes	No
name	string	Yes	No
type*	string	Yes	No
value	string	Yes	Yes

Methods

```
blur()
eval()*
handleEvent()†
focus()
select()
toString()*
valueOf()*
```

Event Handlers

```
onBlur
onChange
onFocus
onSelect
```

textarea Object

HTML

```
<FORM>
<TEXTAREA
NAME = "Field Name"
ROWS = "NumberOfRows"
COLS = "NumberOfColumns"
[WRAP = "off" | "virtual" | "physical"]
```

```
[onBlur = "JavaScript code"]
[onChange = "JavaScript code"]
[onFocus = "JavaScript code"]
[onSelect = "JavaScript code"]>
defaultText
</TEXTAREA>
</FORM>
```

Properties

Property	Value	Gettable	Settable
defaultValue	string	Yes	No
form*	containing form object	Yes	No
name	string	Yes	No
type*	string	Yes	No
value	string	Yes	No

Methods

```
blur()
eval()*
handleEvent()†
focus()
select()
toString()*
valueOf()*
```

Event Handlers

```
onBlur
onChange
onFocus
onKeyDown†
onKeyPress†
onKeyUp†
onSelect
```

window Object

HTML

```
<FRAMESET>
    COLS = "NumberOfColumns"
    ROWS = "NumberOfRows"
```

```
[FRAMEBORDER = YES | NO]
[BORDER = pixelSize]
[BORDERCOLOR = colorSpecification]
[onLoad = "JavaScript code"]
[onUnload = "JavaScript code"]
[onFocus = "JavaScript code"]
[onBlur = "JavaScript code"]
      <FRAME
          SRC = "URL"
          NAME = "NameOfFirstFrame"
          [BORDER = pixelSize]
          [BORDERCOLOR = colorSpecification]>
</FRAMESET>
<BODY
...
[onBlur = "JavaScript code"]
[onFocus = "JavaScript code"]
[onLoad = "JavaScript code"]
[onUnload = "JavaScript code"]
[onDragDrop = "JavaScript code"]
[onReSIZE = "JavaScript code"]
[onMove = "JavaScript code"]>
</BODY>
```

Properties

Property	Value	Gettable	Settable
closed	Boolean	Yes	No
defaultStatus	string	Yes	Yes
document	document object	Yes	No
frames()	array of window objects	Yes	No
history	history object	Yes	No
innerHeight[†]	pixels	Yes	Yes
innerWidth[†]	pixels	Yes	Yes
length	integer	Yes	No
location	location object	Yes	Yes

Property	Value	Gettable	Settable
locationbar[†]	Boolean	Yes	Yes
menubar[†]	Boolean	Yes	Yes
name	windowName	Yes	No
opener*	window object or null	Yes	No
outerHeight[†]	pixels	Yes	Yes
outerWidth[†]	pixels	Yes	Yes
pageXOffset	pixels	Yes	No
pageYOffset	pixels	Yes	No
parent	windowName	Yes	No
personalbar[†]	Boolean	Yes	Yes
self	windowName	Yes	No
scrollbars[†]	Boolean	Yes	Yes
status	string	Yes	Yes
statusbar[†]	Boolean	Yes	Yes
toolbar[†]	Boolean	Yes	Yes
top	windowName	Yes	No
window	windowName	Yes	No

Methods

```
alert()
back()†
blur()*
captureEvents()†
clearInterval()†
clearTimeout()
close()
```

```
confirm()
disableExternalCapture()†
enableExternalCapture()†
find()†
eval()
focus()*
forward()†
handleEvent()†
home()†
moveBy()†
moveTo()†
open()†
print()†
prompt()
releaseEvents()†
resizeBy()†
resizeTo()†
routeEvent()†
scroll()*
scrollBy()†
scrollTo()†
setInterval()†
setTimeout()†
stop()†
toString()*
valueOf()*
```

Event Handlers

```
onBlur*
onDragDrop†
onerror*
onFocus*
onLoad
onMove†
onResize†
onUnload
```

Control Structures

```
if (condition) {
    statementsIfTrue
}


if (condition) {
    statementsIfTrue
} else {
    statementsIfFalse
}


variable = condition ? value1 : value2


for ([initial expression]; [condition]; [new expression]) {
    statements
}


for (var in object) {
    statements
}


while (condition) {
    statements
}


with (object) {
    statements

}
```

The following control structures are new with the JavaScript 1.2 release:

```
label:statement

break
break:label

continue
continue:label

switch(expression) {
  case label :
    statement
    break
  case label :
```

```
      statement
      break
    ...
  default :
      statement
}

do
  statement
while ( condition )

export
import
```

Operators

The JavaScript 1.2 release adds a `delete` operator.

The syntax for the delete operator is:

```
delete objectName.property
delete objectname[index]
delete property (only valid within a with statement)
```

Table B-2 lists the mathematical operators.

Table B-2 Mathematical Operators

Operator	Operation
+	Addition
−	Subtraction
*	Multiplication
/	Division
%	Modulus (return the remainder of a division)

Table B-3 lists the assignment operators.

Table B-3 Assignment Operators

Operator	Operation
=	Equals
+=	Add by value
-=	Subtract by value
*=	Multiply by value
/=	Divide by value
%=	Modulo by value
<<=	Left shift by value
>>=	Right shift by value
>>>=	Zero fill by value
&=	Bitwise AND by value
^=	Bitwise OR by value
|=	Bitwise XOR by value

Table B-4 lists the comparison operators.

Table B-4 Comparison Operators

Operator	Operation
==	Equals
===	Strict equals comparison of both type and content
!=	Not equal to
!==	Strict not equal to comparison of both type and content
>	Greater than

Table B-4 Comparison Operators (Continued)

Operator	Operation
>=	Greater than or equal to
<	Less than
<=	Less than or equal to

Table B-5 lists the unary operators.

Table B-5 Unary Operators

Operator	Operation
–	Unary negation
~	Bitwise complement
++	Increment
––	Decrement

Table B-6 lists the binary operators.

Table B-6 Binary Operators

Operator	Operation
&	Bitwise AND
|	Bitwise OR
^	Bitwise XOR
<<	Left shift
>>	Right shift
>>>	Zero fill right shift

Table B-7 lists the Boolean operators.

Table B-7 Boolean Operators

Operator	Operation
&&	AND
||	OR
!	NOT

Table B-8 lists JavaScript operator precedence where 1 is the highest precedence and operators with precedence closest to 1 are evaluated before operators with lower precedence.

Table B-8 JavaScript Operator Precedence

Precedence Level	Description	Operator
1	Nested parentheses are evaluated from innermost to outermost.	( )
	Array index value	[ ]
2	Negation and increment	!
		~
		–
		++
		– –
3	Multiplication, division, modulo	*
		/
		%
4	Addition and subtraction	+
		–
5	Bitwise shifts	<<
		>>
		>>>

Table B-8 JavaScript Operator Precedence (Continued)

Precedence Level	Description	Operator
6	Comparison operators	< <= > >=
7	Equality	==, === !=, !==
8	Bitwise XOR	^
9	Bitwise OR	|
10	Logical AND	&&
11	Logical OR	||
12	Conditional expression	?:
13	Assignment operators	= += -+ *= /= %= <<= >>= >>>= &= ^= |=
14	comma	,

Reserved JavaScript Keywords

Table B-9 lists JavaScript reserved keywords.

Table B-9 Reserved JavaScript Keywords

abstract	else	int	synchronized
boolean	enum[‡]	interface	this
break	extends	long	throw
byte	false	native	throws
case	final	new	transient
catch	finally	null	true
char	float	package	try
class	for	private	typeof
const	function	protected	var
continue	goto	public	void
debugger[‡]	if	return	volatile
default	implements	short	while
delete	import	static	with
do	in	super	
double	instanceof	switch	

Escape Characters for String Formatting

Table B-10 lists the escape characters for string formatting.

Table B-10 Escape Characters for String Formatting

Escape Sequence	Description	Character/ Abbreviation
\b	Backspace	BS
\t	Horizontal tab	HT
\n	Line feed	LF

Table B-10 Escape Characters for String Formatting (Continued)

Escape Sequence	Description	Character/ Abbreviation
\f	Form feed	FF
\r	Carriage return	CR
\"	Double quote	"
\'	Single quote	'
\\	Backslash	\
\ *OctalDigit*	Octal escape	One of 0 1 2 3 4 5 6 7
\ *OctalDigit OctalDigit*	Octal escape	One of 0 1 2 3 4 5 6 7
\ *ZeroToThree OctalDigit OctalDigit*	ZeroToThree escape	One of 0 1 2 3
\ *xHexDigit HexDigit*	Hexadecimal escape	One of 0 1 2 3 4 5 6 7 8 9 a b c d e f A B C D E F

HTTP MIME Types

Table B-11 lists commonly used MIME types and the file name suffix that is recognized by most servers.

Table B-11 Commonly Used MIME Types

Type/Subtype	Extension
application/activemessage	
application/andrew-inset	
application/applefile	
application/atomicmail	
application/cals-1840	
application/commonground	
application/cybercash	
application/dca-rft	
application/dec-dx	
application/eshop	
application/font-tdpfr	pfr
application/iges	
application/mac-binhex40	
application/macwriteii	
application/mathematica	

Table B-11 Commonly Used MIME Types (Continued)

Type/Subtype	Extension
application/msword	
application/news-message-id	
application/news-transmission	
application/octet-stream	bin
application/oda	oda
application/pdf	pdf
application/postscript	ai, eps, ps
application/remote-printing	
application/riscos	
application/rtf	rtf
application/sgml	
application/slate	
application/vnd.framemaker	
application/vnd.koan	
application/vnd.mif	
application/vnd.ms-artgalry	
application/vnd.ms-excel	
application/vnd.ms-powerpoint	
application/vnd.ms-project	
application/vnd.ms-tnef	
application/vnd.ms-works	
application/vnd.music-niff	
application/vnd.svd	
application/vnd.truedoc	
application/wuta	
application/wordperfect5.1	
application/x-bcpio	bcpio
application/x-cpio	cpio
application/x-csh	csh
application/x-dvi	dvi
application/x-gtar	gtar
application/x-hdf	hdf
application/x-latex	latex

Table B-11 Commonly Used MIME Types (Continued)

Type/Subtype	Extension
application/x-mif	mif
application/x-netcdf	nc, cdf
application/x-sh	sh
application/x-shar	shar
application/x-sv4cpio	sv4cpio
application/x-sv4crc	sv4crc
application/x-tar	tar
application/x-tcl	tcl
application/x-tex	tex
application/x-texinfo	texinfo, texi
application/x-troff	t, tr, roff
application/x-troff-man	man
application/x-troff-me	me
application/x-troff-ms	ms
application/x-ustar	ustar
application/x-wais-source	src
application/x400-bp	
application/zip	zip
audio/32kadpcm	
audio/basic	au, snd
audio/x-aiff	aif, aiff, aifc
audio/x-wav	wav
image/cgm	
image/g3fax	
image/gif	gif
image/ief	ief
image/jpeg	jpeg, jpg, jpe
image/naplps	
image/tiff	tiff, tif
image/vnd.dwg	
image/vnd.dxf	
image/vnd.svf	
image/x-cmu-raster	ras

Table B-11 Commonly Used MIME Types (Continued)

Type/Subtype	Extension
image/x-portable-anymap	rpnm
image/x-portable-bitmap	pbm
image/x-portable-graymap	pgm
image/x-portable-pixmap	ppm
image/x-rgb	rgb
image/x-xbitmap	xbm
image/x-xpixmap	xpm
image/x-xwindowdump	xwd
message/external-body	
message/http	
message/news	
message/partial	
message/rfc8222	
multipart/alternative	
multipart/appledouble	
multipart/digest	
multipart/form-data	
multipart/header-set	
multipart/mixed	
multipart/parallel	
multipart/related	
multipart/report	
multipart/voice-message	
text/enriched	
text/html	html, htm
text/plain	txt
text/richtext	rtx
text/sgml	
text/tab-separated-values	tsv
text/x-settext	etx
video/mpeg	mpeg, mpg, mpe
video/quicktime	qt, mov

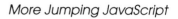

Table B-11 Commonly Used MIME Types (Continued)

Type/Subtype	Extension
video/vdn.vivo	
video/x-msvideo	qvi
video/x-sgi-movie	movie

Glossary

cascading style sheets (CSS)   A W3C standard for defining style sheets that control the look of Web page content.

child   For CSS and JavaScript styles, an HTML element that is contained by another HTML element.

contextual selection criteria   For CSS and JavaScript styles, a style definition that is applied only to an HTML element that is used in a specific context.

CSS1   A W3C standard that provides a way to define style sheets that control the look of Web page content.

CSS2   A W3C standard that combines CSS1 and CSS-P standards both for style sheets and for positioning of HTML content.

CSS-P   A W3C standard that defines positioning of blocks of HTML content.

cursive font   A font, such as Zapf-Chancery, that imitates handwriting.

declaration   The bracketed part of a CSS rule that identifies the property and assigns it a value.

digital certificate   A small software package that gets downloaded and bound to an individual copy of the Navigator 4 browser on a specific computer. Web authors use the digital certificate to create signed scripts.

document object model (DOM)   A standards specification that defines what scriptable entities are maintained in a browser's memory when a document is loaded. Scripts can dynamically access the objects that are an inherent part of that document without referring back to the server for more data.

dynamic fonts   The term that Bitstream Inc. uses to describe the technology behind its TrueDoc fonts, which are designed and stored in a compact data structure called a portable font resource.

dynamic HTML   An aggregation of standards specifications that come from a variety of standards bodies and proprietary development. These standards are combined to enable script writers to write HTML code that can be modified programmatically without the need to reload a document before changes are displayed.

ECMAScript   The European Computer Manufacturers Association standardization of Netscape's implementation of the client-side JavaScript 1.1 language.

fantasy font   A font, such as Blippo Bold, that is used for artistic effect.

font family   One of the following generic families that you can use in designating fonts in HTML documents: serif, sans-serif, monospace, cursive, fantasy. It can also mean the specific typeface implementation such as Times Roman or Palatino.

Greenwich mean time (GMT)   The mean solar time determined by the 0 degree prime meridian that runs through Greenwich, England. GMT,also called universal time (UT), is based on astronomical observations.

HTML   Hypertext markup language standards provide the basic structural elements of a Web page.

hotkeys   A keyboard or key combination that initiates a specified action regardless of what else the computer is currently doing.

JAR packager   A stand-alone command-line tool that Web authors use to create digital signatures. The JAR packager uses the Java Archive (JAR) format to create a JAR file containing the digital signatures and a hash table used to verify the validity and integrity of a signed script.

Java Archive (JAR) format   A set of conventions for associating digital signatures, installer scripts, and other information with files in a directory.

layer A positioned block of HTML content created by using either the CSS positioning syntax or the Netscape Navigator 3.0 <LAYER> tag.

monospace font A font that imitates old-fashioned typewriters or computer display fonts such as Courier. Each letter takes up the same space, regardless of its width. An i takes up the same space as an m.

object signing A set of tools and technologies that Netscape provides in the Navigator 4 release to enable Java applets and JavaScript objects to selectively access system resources that would otherwise have to remain off limits for security reasons.

parent For CSS and JavaScript styles, an HTML element that contains one or more additional HTML elements.

portable font resource (PFR) The compact data structure used to store dynamic fonts so that they are available for downloading along with a Web page.

pseudoclass For CSS styles, a class that enables Web authors to apply a style to an element that does not exist in HTML source.

pseudoelements For CSS styles, a list of elements defined by W3C that enables Web authors to apply a style. The only pseudoelement currently supported by Netscape is Anchor.

regular expression A pattern used to match character combinations in strings. In JavaScript, regular expressions are also objects.

rule A statement about one stylistic aspect of one or more elements in a CSS style sheet.

sansserif A type style that lacks the embellishment of a small line used to finish off a main stroke of a letter, as at the top and bottom of M.

scope The section of program or script where a particular item such as a variable or function can be accessed.

selector The name of an HTML tag, without its <> brackets, that is used to specify the tag that uses a CSS style definition.

serif A fine line used to finish off a main stroke of a letter, as at the top and bottom of M.

signed script A script, stored in a JAR file, that contains a digital signature. This signature enables users to identify and verify the provider of scripts that allow access to system resources with security implications.

style sheet   One or more rules about stylistic elements that apply to an HTML document.

Signing Tool   Netscape's version of a JAR packager used to create signed scripts.

type face   A specific implementation of a font family such as Times Roman or Palatino.

universal coordinated time   UTC is the specified date represented as an integer that is the number of milliseconds since midnight Greenwich mean time (GMT) on January 1, 1970, and the specified date. UTC is based on the atomic clock rather than on astronomical observations.

x-height   The height of the lowercase letter x in a font that is used to determine the point size for a font.

XML   Extensible Markup Language. The "next solution" to Web programming, XML is a subset of the standard generalized markup language (SGML).

zigbert   A Perl script used to create signed scripts before the capability was added to the Netscape Signing Tool Version 1.1. If you have Signing Tool Version 1.1, you no longer need to use `zigbert.exe` to create signed scripts.

Index

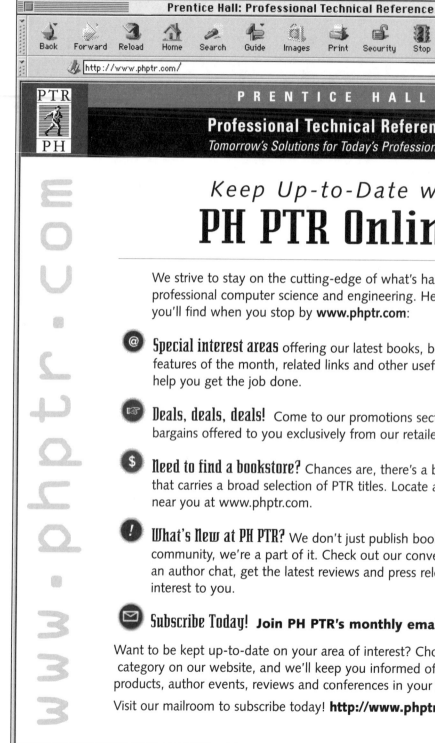

IMPORTANT—READ CAREFULLY BEFORE OPENING SEALED CD-ROM

This CD-ROM contains sample code from More Jumping JavaScript.

SUN MICROSYSTEMS LICENSE AGREEMENT

This is a legal agreement between the purchaser of this book/CD-ROM package ("You") and Sun Microsystems, Inc. By opening the sealed CD-ROM you are agreeing to be bound by the terms of this agreement. If you do not agree to the terms of this agreement, promptly return the unopened book/CD-ROM package to the place you obtained it for a full refund.

SOFTWARE LICENSE FOR SAMPLE CODE

1. Grant of License. Sun Microsystems grants to you ("Licensee") a non-exclusive, non-transferable license to use the software programs (sample code) included on the CD-ROM without fee. The software is in "use" on a computer when it is loaded into the temporary memory (i.e. RAM) or installed into the permanent memory (e.g. hard disk, CD-ROM, or other storage device). You may network the software or otherwise use it on more than one computer or computer terminal at the same time.

2. Copyright. The CD-ROM is copyrighted by Sun Microsystems, Inc. and is protected by United States copyright laws and international treaty provisions. Therefore, you must treat the CD-ROM like any other copyrighted material. Individual software programs on the CD-ROM are copyrighted by their respective owners and may require separate licensing.

3. More Jumping JavaScript Sample Code. Sun Microsystems, Inc. grants you a royalty-free right to reproduce and distribute the sample code or scripts provided that you: (a) distribute the sample code or scripts only in conjunction with and as a part of your software application; (b) do not use Sun Microsystems, Inc. or its authors' names, logos, or trademarks to market your software product; and (c) agree to indemnify, hold harmless and defend Sun Microsystems, Inc. and its authors and suppliers from and against any claims or lawsuits, including attorneys fees, that arise or result from the use or distribution of your software product.

DISCLAIMER OF WARRANTY

The SOFTWARE (including instructions for its use) is provided "AS IS" WITHOUT WARRANTY OF ANY KIND. SUN MICROSYSTEMS and any distributor of the SOFTWARE FURTHER DISCLAIM ALL IMPLIED WARRANTIES INCLUDING WITHOUT LIMITATION ANY IMPLIED WARRANTIES OF MERCHANTABILITY OR OF FITNESS FOR A PARTICULAR PURPOSE. THE ENTIRE RISK ARISING OUT OF THE USE OR PERFORMANCE OF THE SOFT-WARE OR DOCUMENTATION REMAINS WITH YOU.

IN NO EVENT SHALL SUN MICROSYSTEMS, ITS AUTHORS, OR ANY ONE ELSE INVOLVED IN THE CREATION, PRODUCTION, OR DELIVERY OF THE SOFTWARE BE LIABLE FOR ANY DAMAGES WHATSOEVER (INCLUD-ING, WITHOUT LIMITATION, DAMAGES FOR LOSS OF BUSINESS PROFITS, BUSINESS INTERRUPTION, LOSS OF BUSINESS INFORMATION, OR OTHER PECUNIARY LOSS) ARISING OUT OF THE USE OF OR INABILITY TO USE THE SOFTWARE OR DOCUMENTATION, EVEN IF SUN MICROSYSTEMS HAS BEEN ADVISED OF THE POS-SIBILITY OF SUCH DAMAGES, BECAUSE SOME STATES/COUNTRIES DO NOT ALLOW THE EXCLUSION OF LIMITATION OF LIABILITY FOR CONSEQUENTIAL OR INCIDENTAL DAMAGES, THE ABOVE LIMITATION MAY NOT APPLY TO YOU.

U.S. GOVERNMENT RESTRICTED RIGHTS

The SOFTWARE and documentation are provided with RESTRICTED RIGHTS. Use, duplication, or disclosure is subject to restrictions as set forth in subparagraph (c)(1)(ii) of The Rights in Technical Data and Computer Software clause at DFARS 252.227-7013 or subparagraphs (c)(1) and (2) of the Commercial Computer Software—Restricted Rights 48 CFR 52.227-19.

Should you have any questiosn concerning this Agreement, or if you desire to contact Sun Microsystems for any reason, please write: Sun Microsystems, Inc., 901 San Antonio Rd., Palo Alto, California, 94303.

Copyright ©1998 Sun Microsystems, Inc.

About the CD

This CD contains all of the script examples referred to in the book. These examples illustrate the new features of JavaScript 1.2 and JavaScript 1.3 that are available in the Navigator 4.0 and 4.5 versions of the JavaScript language. The scripts on this CD have not been tested on Internet Explorer.

The script examples for this book are also available from the following URL: http://www.bill-anderson.com/jjs

The CD was created with Creative Digital Research's CDR Publisher HyCD, which integrates PC, Macintosh, and UNIX formats onto a single CD. HyCD is compliant with the ISO 9660 CD-ROM format, as well as the Macintosh HFS CD-ROM format, and supports RockRidge and Joliet extensions.

Use your Web browser to load the index.html file on the CD. Links are provided to all of the scripts from the book, which are organized in the following directory structure.

```
1.3/
core/
dhtml/
documents/
events/
global/
images/
objectsigning/
positioning/
regExp/
style/
windows/
```

Technical Support

Prentice Hall does not offer technical support for this software. If there is a problem with the media, however, you may obtain a replacement CD by emailing a description of the problem. Send your email to:

disc_exchange@prenhall.com